King Vidor in Focus

ALSO OF INTEREST
AND FROM MCFARLAND

John Ford in Focus: Essays on the Filmmaker's Life and Work
(*Edited by* Kevin L. Stoehr *and* Michael C. Connolly, 2008)

Nihilism in Film and Television: A Critical Overview from Citizen Kane *to* The Sopranos (Kevin L. Stoehr, 2006)

Film and Knowledge: Essays on the Integration of Images and Ideas
(*Edited by* Kevin L. Stoehr, 2002)

King Vidor in Focus
On the Filmmaker's Artistry and Vision

KEVIN L. STOEHR *and* CULLEN GALLAGHER

McFarland & Company, Inc., Publishers
Jefferson, North Carolina

LIBRARY OF CONGRESS CATALOGUING-IN-PUBLICATION DATA

Names: Stoehr, Kevin L., 1967– author. | Gallagher, Cullen, 1985– author.
Title: King Vidor in focus : on the filmmaker's artistry and vision / Kevin L. Stoehr and Cullen Gallagher.
Description: Jefferson, North Carolina : McFarland & Company, Inc., Publishers, 2024 | Includes bibliographical references, filmography, and index.
Identifiers: LCCN 2024009547 | ISBN 9781476670096 (paperback : acid free paper) ♾
ISBN 9781476652498 (ebook)
Subjects: LCSH: Vidor, King, 1894–1982—Criticism and interpretation. | Motion picture producers and directors—United States—Biography. | Motion pictures—United States—History—20th century.
Classification: LCC PN1998.3.V54 S76 2024 | DDC 791.4302/33092 [B]—dc23/eng/20240528
LC record available at https://lccn.loc.gov/2024009547

BRITISH LIBRARY CATALOGUING DATA ARE AVAILABLE

ISBN (print) 978-1-4766-7009-6
ISBN (ebook) 978-1-4766-5249-8

© 2024 Kevin L. Stoehr and Cullen Gallagher. All rights reserved

No part of this book may be reproduced or transmitted in any form or by any means, electronic or mechanical, including photocopying or recording, or by any information storage and retrieval system, without permission in writing from the publisher.

Front cover: King Vidor on the set of the 1931 film *Street Scene*
(United Artists/Photofest)

Printed in the United States of America

McFarland & Company, Inc., Publishers
Box 611, Jefferson, North Carolina 28640
www.mcfarlandpub.com

The authors dedicate this book to their respective parents—Brian and Suzanne Gallagher and Robert and Loretta Stoehr—and to their late friend Charles Silver. Charles was an esteemed film historian and served for decades as a long-time curator and Film Study Center director in the Department of Film at the Museum of Modern Art. Charles was also the author of *An Auteurist History of Film*, *The Western Film*, and *Marlene Dietrich*, among other publications. Charles helped to organize the first comprehensive King Vidor film retrospective at the Museum of Modern Art in the fall of 1972. Over the decades, he assisted countless film scholars with their research and work and his contributions to cinema history, sometimes credited and sometimes not, are immeasurable.

Acknowledgments

The authors would like to thank Alice Persons and Paul Thur for their valuable assistance in the editorial work during the completion of this book. We also thank Luke Bonzani for his helpful research that was sponsored by the Center for Interdisciplinary Teaching and Learning at Boston University. We especially thank Professor Natalie McKnight, Dean of the College of General Studies at Boston University, for her support of our project and for providing funds to cover the photo fees. We offer our gratitude to Whitney Wallace, David Alff, Lisa Camp, and the rest of the staff at McFarland for their patience and assistance throughout the process as well as to the folks at Photofest in New York City for their help with the film photos that appear in the book. We are indebted to our late friend Charles Silver, Curator and Film Study Center director in the Department of Film at the Museum of Modern Art. And very special thanks to Erick Daniel Rostro Martinez for his kind support during the finishing stage of this project.

Table of Contents

Acknowledgments — vi

Preface — 1

Introduction: A Boy's Love of Moving Images — 5

ONE. 1913–1917: Missing Reels and First Films — 11

TWO. 1918–1919: The Turning Point — 15
    Bud's Recruit (1918)   15
    The Turn in the Road, Better Times, The Other Half, Poor Relations
        (All 1919)   18

THREE. 1920–1921: The Humanist Emerges — 24
    The Family Honor, The Jack-Knife Man, Mothercraft,
        The Sky Pilot, and *Love Never Dies*   24

FOUR. 1922–1923: Rising and Falling Stars — 37
    The Woman of Bronze, Three Wise Fools, The Real Adventure,
        Dusk to Dawn, Conquering the Woman, and *Peg O' My Heart*   37

FIVE. 1924: Personality Crisis — 46
    Wild Oranges   46
    Gulliver's Travels, Happiness, Wine of Youth, His Hour,
        The Wife of the Centaur   51

SIX. 1925: *Proud Flesh* and *The Big Parade* — 59
    Proud Flesh   59
    The Big Parade   61

SEVEN. 1926: *La Bohème* and *Bardelys the Magnificent* — 71
    La Bohème   71
    Bardelys the Magnificent   76

EIGHT. 1927–1928: *The Crowd, The Patsy,* and *Show People* — 81
    The Crowd (1928)   81
    The Patsy (1928)   93
    Show People (1928)   97

NINE. 1929: *Hallelujah* — 102

TEN. 1930: *Not So Dumb* and *Billy the Kid* — 110
    Not So Dumb   110
    Billy the Kid   113

Eleven. 1931: *Street Scene* and *The Champ* 119
    Street Scene   119
    The Champ   122

Twelve. 1932: *Bird of Paradise* and *Cynara* 128
    Bird of Paradise   128
    Cynara   132

Thirteen. 1933: *The Stranger's Return* 136

Fourteen. 1934–1936: *Our Daily Bread, So Red the Rose, The Wedding Night,* and *The Texas Rangers* 147
    Our Daily Bread (1934)   147
    So Red the Rose (1935)   152
    The Wedding Night (1935)   157
    The Texas Rangers (1936)   160

Fifteen. 1937: *Stella Dallas* 165

Sixteen. 1938–1939: *The Citadel* and *The Wizard of Oz* 173
    The Citadel (1938)   173
    The Wizard of Oz (1939)   182

Seventeen. 1940: *Comrade X* and *Northwest Passage* 185
    Comrade X   185
    Northwest Passage   190

Eighteen. 1941–1944: *H.M. Pulham, Esq.* and *An American Romance* 204
    H.M. Pulham, Esq. (1941)   204
    An American Romance (1944)   208

Nineteen. 1946: *Duel in the Sun* 213

Twenty. 1948–1949: *On Our Merry Way, The Fountainhead,* and *Beyond the Forest* 227
    On Our Merry Way (1948)   227
    The Fountainhead (1949)   230
    Beyond the Forest (1949)   242

Twenty-One. 1951–1955: *Lightning Strikes Twice, Japanese War Bride, Ruby Gentry,* and *Man Without a Star* 248
    Lightning Strikes Twice (1951)   248
    Japanese War Bride (1952)   250
    Ruby Gentry (1952)   253
    Man Without a Star (1955)   259

Twenty-Two. 1956–1959: *War and Peace* and *Solomon and Sheba* 264
    War and Peace (1956)   264
    Solomon and Sheba (1959)   272

Twenty-Three. 1964 and 1980: *Truth and Illusion* and *The Metaphor* 277
    Truth and Illusion (1964)   277

The Metaphor (1980)   285
Author's Transcript of *Truth and Illusion*   289

Filmography: King Vidor as Director   295
Chapter Notes   303
Bibliography   317
Index   325

Preface

"I think the definition of an artist is to express your own individuality."[1]—King Vidor, 1968

"I do feel films are the top medium of expression."[2]—King Vidor, 1971

The career of King Wallis Vidor (1894–1982), one of Hollywood's most prolific filmmakers, spans the history of American cinema from the peak of the silent era to the decline of Hollywood's Golden Age. Vidor was once listed in the *Guinness Book of World Records* for having achieved "the Longest Career as a Film Director." His first film was the short silent documentary "Hurricane in Galveston," and while the start of his career is almost universally dated as 1913, Vidor later mentioned that his actual recording of this major storm in the director's hometown took place in 1909, the year of the famous Velasco hurricane along the eastern Texas coast. According to records, there was no major hurricane in that region in 1913. The storm of 1909 recalled the devastating "Great Galveston hurricane" of 1900 that killed more than 8,000 residents, a natural disaster that Vidor had witnessed as a boy.[3] The vulnerability of the human individual in the face of the overwhelming power of Mother Nature, along with the importance of community for one's survival and well-being, had certainly left an imprint on Vidor's memory.

Vidor's first feature-length movie, *The Turn in the Road* (1919), which he also wrote, was rooted in his Christian Science upbringing and it was this spiritual philosophy, combined with his other philosophical musings over the decades, that helped to shape the overall moral vision and worldview underlying much of his work throughout the rest of his career. Later in his life, after more or less retiring from Hollywood as a feature film director, he made his experimental short documentary *Truth and Illusion* (1964). While seldom seen at the time, it was really the first of its kind, a film that explored Vidor's own personal philosophy of reality while also trying to demonstrate that philosophical thoughts could be expressed in cinematic images. The director's speculations and ruminations that are articulated in this documentary are clearly rooted in Christian Science. His final film, also a short documentary, was completed in 1980 and titled *The Metaphor*. It centers on a dialogue between Vidor and one of his most ardent fans, the painter Andrew Wyeth. They discuss the enormous influence of the director's silent classic *The Big Parade* (1925) on Wyeth's artistry (the painter tells Vidor that he has seen the film "180 times") as well as the importance of symbolism, landscape, and the subconscious in the life of the artist.

Vidor's total body of work is one of the most diverse and complex in the history of Hollywood filmmaking. Vidor's most notable movies include, among others, his three silent era masterworks—*The Big Parade* (1925), *The Crowd* (1928), and *Show People* (1928)—and, in the sound era, such films as *Hallelujah* (1929), *Street Scene* (1931), *The Champ* (1931), *The Stranger's Return* (1933), *Our Daily Bread* (1934), *Stella Dallas* (1937), *The Citadel* (1938), *Northwest Passage* (1940), *H.M. Pulham, Esq.* (1941), *An American Romance* (1944), *Duel in the Sun* (1946), *Beyond the Forest* (1949), *The Fountainhead* (1949), *Ruby Gentry* (1952), and *War and Peace* (1956). Toward the end of the silent era, many regarded Vidor as the greatest of all Hollywood directors—even greater than Griffith and Chaplin and Keaton—especially after the astonishing commercial and critical success of *The Big Parade* and after the bold personal vision for *The Crowd*. In the sound era, in addition to helming a long series of impressive and fascinating films, Vidor served as the uncredited director of most of the early black-and-white Kansas scenes in *The Wizard of Oz* (1939), including the famous cyclone sequence and the legendary scene in which Dorothy sings "Somewhere Over the Rainbow." And so, with his contributions to that film classic alone, he had created some of the most popular and iconic movie scenes in the history of American cinema, even though almost no one at the time knew that Vidor had directed them. Victor Fleming had left the making of *The Wizard of Oz* toward the end of production so that he could take over *Gone with the Wind*. In fact, Vidor had been offered the job of directing *Gone with the Wind* after George Cukor had left the project due to disagreements with producer David Selznick. Vidor passed on the job and instead agreed to finish *The Wizard of Oz* as a favor to his friend Fleming.

The director had also been a pioneering leader in the creation of the Screen Directors Guild (later known as the Directors Guild of America) and he served as its first president (1936–1938). He was also a member of the controversial Motion Picture Alliance for the Preservation of American Ideals (MPAPAI), first formed in 1944 to help "protect" the movie industry from the influence of communism and fascism. Upon "retiring" from feature filmmaking after the release of his Biblical epic *Solomon and Sheba* in 1959, Vidor continued to think and write about film, philosophy, and his own long career. Indeed, he is one of the few major Hollywood directors who has dedicated himself to the task of explaining his work and his chosen art form to the public—not only in many interviews but also in his own writings. His illuminating autobiography, *A Tree Is a Tree*, was published in 1953 and two decades later he completed a comprehensive book about his profession and art, *King Vidor on Film Making* (1973). Vidor was presented with the Screen Directors Guild's Lifetime Achievement Award in 1957 and, after having been nominated five times for the Academy Award for Best Director (*The Crowd*, *Hallelujah*, *The Champ*, *The Citadel*, *War and Peace*), he received an honorary lifetime achievement Oscar in 1979.

After the two epic films that he made in the second half of the 1950s (*War and Peace* and *Solomon and Sheba*), Vidor tried to realize several projects that he had in mind, even though they failed to come to fruition. These projects included updated sound era re-makes of his silent movies *The Crowd* and *The Turn in the Road*, a film biography of Christian Science founder Mary Baker Eddy, an adaptation of Nathaniel Hawthorne's novel *The Marble Faun*, a film biography of the troubled actor James Murray (lead actor of *The Crowd*), an adaptation of Bruce Catton's Civil War book *A Stillness at Appomattox*, and a movie about the Spanish writer Miguel de Cervantes as a young man. None of these projects were actualized, though Vidor came close in a few instances: he had gained the interest of Francis Ford Coppola in producing the James Murray story and the interest of producer Arthur Jacobs in a re-make of *The Crowd*.[4] And in an effort to complete a screenplay based on the unsolved 1922 murder of early Hollywood actor-director William Desmond Taylor, Vidor did such detailed research on the murder that author Sidney D. Kirkpatrick, in his best-selling book *A Cast of Killers* (published in 1986), re-traces Vidor's research and concludes that the director was in fact the first to solve the case. As with his affinity for planning and supervising large-scale epic films as well as intricate psychological dramas, Vidor had always been something of a natural-born strategist and "detective" who enjoyed fitting pieces together into a greater whole.

In addition to trying to realize the above-mentioned projects after he "retired" from feature filmmaking, Vidor traveled around the world to attend many tributes and retrospectives. It was around this time, especially after the rise of auteur theory in cinema circles, that many film scholars and historians began to revive an interest in his career and to give him the full appreciation that he deserved. The first comprehensive Vidor retrospective was held at the Museum of Modern Art in 1972, which the director attended. More recently, in February and March of 2020, the 70th Berlin International Film Festival (the Berlinale) featured a 35-film King Vidor retrospective. And in August of 2022, Film at Lincoln Center in New York City organized a ten-day retrospective that included many of Vidor's most notable movies.

Up until now, the only comprehensive book on Vidor that provides a detailed survey of his entire oeuvre has been Raymond Durgnat and Scott Simmon's *King Vidor, American*, first published in 1988. That book is a serious, multifaceted exploration of Vidor and it includes many illuminating observations about Vidor's vision and films. One weakness is a frequently abstruse approach that jumps back and forth at times between a few too many interpretive frameworks, along with more than a few sentences that border on the arcane. The book in your hands is one that is designed to be comprehensive but also to appeal as much to the general film-loving reader as to the dedicated scholar of cinema.

The co-authors have attempted here to provide a survey of Vidor's total body of work, starting with his boyhood fascination with motion pictures and ending with 1980's *The Metaphor*, his final film. Along the way, we have also attempted to chart the evolution of the director's artistry and to connect that artistry with his overall moral worldview and spiritual philosophy. Of course, considering that we are dealing with one of the most productive filmmakers who had the longest directing career in the Hollywood movie business, there were countless challenges in trying to cover everything. Our primary goal here is to provide a bird's eye view of his work as a totality so that readers can consider individual films within their greater artistic context. Another goal is to draw the general reader's attention to lesser-known and under-appreciated works by Vidor (e.g., most of his silent films as well as such sound era movies as *Street Scene*, *The Stranger's Return*, *The Citadel*, *Northwest Passage*, *Comrade X*, *Japanese War Bride*, and *Truth and Illusion*, to name but several). And yet another goal here is to put into proper perspective some of his films that have tended to be quickly stereotyped by later critics (e.g., *Duel in the Sun*, *Beyond the Forest*, and *War and Peace*).

But at the end of the day, given the vastness of Vidor's career in cinema, decisions had to made about what should be elaborated upon in more detail and what should not. For example, we touch only cursorily on *The Wizard of Oz*—for which Vidor contributed most of the black-and-white Kansas scenes along with the Technicolor "We're Off to See the Wizard" scene—given its popularity and reference in so many other books. And more could have certainly been said about *The Fountainhead*, which is a lesser Vidor film that has nonetheless drawn a great deal of attention because it is based on the best-selling, controversial novel by Ayn Rand (and because Rand herself wrote the screenplay). Ultimately, we have tried to put such films into the greater context of King Vidor's overall artistry and vision while reserving room for discussions of the director's lesser known, least discussed, and less appreciated works.

Introduction:
A Boy's Love of Moving Images

"A Creed and a Pledge: I believe in the motion picture that carries a message to humanity. I believe in the picture that will help humanity to free itself from the shackles of fear and suffering that have so long bound it with iron chains.... So long as I direct pictures, I will make only those founded upon the principle of right and I will endeavor to draw upon the inexhaustible source of Good for my stories, my guidance, and my inspiration."—King Vidor, circa 1920[1]

King Wallis Vidor (his given birth name) was born in Galveston, Texas, on February 8, 1894 (incidentally, one week after the birth of director John Ford and seven months before that of Jean Renoir). In an interview with Nancy Dowd for the Directors Guild of America Oral History project, he discussed his family history and their beginnings in Texas. His paternal grandfather, he recalled, had been born in Budapest, Hungary, and traveled to the United States "as the press representative and general manager of a prominent Hungarian violinist named Rimini." Once Rimini's year-long stay in America had ended, Vidor's grandfather stayed on and traveled from New York to Galveston by ship, eventually entering the cotton industry and starting a family. His paternal grandmother, "of Scotch and English parentage," hailed from Key West, Florida. Vidor confesses a lack of detailed knowledge about his maternal family other than that they were from Texas and had been involved in Galveston politics.[2]

In this interview Vidor reminisces fondly about his hometown; one gets an instant glimpse of his keen and nostalgic sense of place, one that reverberates through his many films. Vidor, like Ford and Renoir, is a master of using a story's setting to generate mood and atmosphere. This emphasis on the nuances and resonances of the immediate environment is apparent, for example, in the picturesque rural backdrops of *The Stranger's Return* (1933), *Our Daily Bread* (1934), *The Wedding Night* (1935), parts of *An American Romance* (1944), and *Ruby Gentry* (1952). The same emphasis is expressed clearly in the frontier terrains of Vidor's Westerns and quasi–Westerns: *Billy the Kid* (1930), *The Texas Rangers* (1936), *Northwest Passage* (1940), *Duel in the Sun* (1946), and *Man Without a Star* (1955). It is also evident in the bustling cityscapes of *The Crowd* (1928) and *The Fountainhead* (1949). Vidor recalls the atmosphere and diversity of his hometown:

> Galveston was a very cosmopolitan type of place, strange for Texas and strange for the United States. On the block where I lived there was a French speaking family, and across the street lived a German speaking family. Galveston was an island, and it was a tremendous port, so it attracted people of all nationalities. The houses were very close together, and I grew up in this atmosphere of many languages and cultures. To a boy, the town had tremendous atmosphere. Because of all this activity and since it was an island, it was sort of a resort town and almost considered beyond the law. The gambling and prostitution went on long after it was outlawed in other Texas towns. I have very graphic memories of activities around the town such as the drayage of cotton, a street called The Strand, the mule teams and the cotton wagons, the noise—and it was all tremendous.[3]

Given this warm remembrance of his childhood hometown, it is easy to see where Vidor gained his intimate feeling for place, not to mention his deep appreciation for cultural diversity, an appreciation that is expressed in the diversity and complexity of a film oeuvre that ranges from his tale of African American life in the South in *Hallelujah* (1929) to his under-appreciated *Japanese War Bride* (1952), the story of an American veteran of the Korean War who, because of his wife and their newly-born son, must contend with various forms of racism after his return home.

Vidor had an innate eye and feeling for the art of the moving image even, to some degree, before he knew about movie cameras. This is clear from the very first paragraph of his 1953 autobiography *A Tree Is a Tree*, where he provides a clear example of the type of aesthetic sensitivity he possessed from an early age. His later reflection on this early incident and the way that he describes it, even if shaped by his accumulated experience as a film director, gives a clear illustration of his youthful fascination with certain visual elements that were emphasized in a consistent fashion throughout his many films. Above all, Vidor pays special attention to those elements or aspects of his art that are often difficult to define or analyze conceptually: visual composition, a sense of motion and rhythm (tempo/pacing), and mood (or what Vidor sometimes also calls "atmosphere"). This was a boyhood image that really stuck in his mind throughout most of his life, and he emphasizes that scene in the very first paragraph of his memoir:

> I stood at the end of the pier, waiting for my first swimming lesson. I was ten, and this was in my native town of Galveston, Texas. A short distance off in the bay a diving platform floated on the calm water. Boys of all ages were crawling aboard, testing their courage by jumping or diving from three levels. The larger boys, diving in graceful form from the top, seemed to float down. The smaller boys scrambled out of the water and immediately hurled themselves from the lowest raft feet first, headfirst, frontward, backward, sideways—suggesting a pizzicato movement in contrast to the waltzlike grace of the highest divers. Those in between on the five-foot board created a broken tempo or syncopation which blended with the other two: one boy would raise his hands in preparation for a dive, change his mind, grab his nose instead, and finish with a jump; another would mount the platform, take a look, decide it was too high, and return with a grotesque crawl to the dock below. I saw in the scene music reduced to movement; I felt its rhythm, tempo, beauty, humor; I was aware of form and composition, of line and action. I wanted to record it, to show others what had been shown to me; there must be some way of capturing and preserving what I saw and felt. I would think about it. I had not yet seen, or even heard of, the motion-picture camera.[4]

The description evokes the title of one of Vidor's now-lost short films, *Tad's Swimming Hole* (1918), made as part of a series of youth morality tales (see Chapter One). While no images of the film survive, a brief synopsis was reported in *The Moving Picture World*: "A number of boys are shown enjoying themselves at the old swimming hole in the bend of the creek, and they are shown disporting themselves on the bank and in the water minus bathing suits, clad only in nature's garb."[5] The nudity, however naturalistic, was a problem for the Chicago board of censors who cut "all close-ups of naked boys facing the camera."[6] What is more significant than the foreshadowing is that the characteristics of Vidor's swimming reverie—its subject, setting, and style—suggest that his signature cinematic sensibility was already being formed at a very young age and was grounded in his own life. His understanding of movement, his penchant toward naturalistic action, and his glorification of the simple pleasures of life presage the sorts of shots and scenes that would soon become staples of Vidor's movies.

At the start of his memoir, Vidor remembers that the first movie he ever saw was George Méliès' 1902 pioneering fantasy short *A Trip to the Moon*, screened at Galveston's Grand Opera House when he was about fifteen. He states that, at the time, he did not know that this remarkable film had been made about eight years earlier. Vidor relates that he saw it with two boyhood friends and they tried to figure out how the moving images were made. The future director maintained that they were created by photography, while the others argued that the images had been painted, frame by frame. Vidor reported that he soon found an answer when he discovered a diagram of a movie camera in an issue of *Popular Mechanics* magazine.[7] While Vidor shied away from the science fiction/fantasy genre throughout his career, a genre that was initiated with *A Trip to the Moon*, he was obviously captured by the film's magic in a way that planted the seeds of a lifelong obsession and profession.

As an adolescent Vidor obtained a job at Galveston's first "movie theater," taking tickets during his summer vacation and working morning till night. The theater was actually one half of a music store and separated from the rest of the store by a thin wall.[8] Vidor recalls substituting for the projectionist during the man's lunch and dinner breaks, which entailed climbing up a "small ladder through the sixteen-inch-square-hole in the hot galvanized box."[9] The task of changing the reels was dangerous, as he later described, given the tight confines of the booth and the fact that the loose reels were stored temporarily in a hamper and could easily catch fire at any time due to the possibility of "sparks from the sputtering arc."[10] This job gave Vidor the opportunity to study, through many repeated viewings, countless film shorts from the early days of cinema: "I soon became familiar with every frame of every film."[11] Some of these split-reel film shorts (usually running, in total, five to seven minutes) were French comedies featuring Max Linder, a master of the art of pantomime. Vidor credits Linder's films as having taught him much about this art of silent physical expression; this no doubt had a tremendous influence on Vidor's later direction of performers in the silent era.[12] Young Vidor was quickly learning the art of film and its capacity for depicting thoughts and emotions through the actors' facial expressions and body movements as well as mise en scène, camera angles, and camera movement.

In his memoir, Vidor also discusses his repeated viewings of the 1907 two-reel *Ben Hur*, which featured the later Western star William S. Hart. He made a close study of the actors' uses of pantomime, switching from a focus on facial expressions during one viewing to bodily gesture and movement during another viewing. Ironically, about fifteen years later, Vidor was asked, while working for Goldwyn Studios and about to undertake *Wild Oranges* (1924), to direct the multimillion-dollar production of *Ben-Hur: A Tale of the Christ* (1925) featuring film star Ramon Novarro. He declined the "biggest directorial plum of that day" because of his concerns with the authenticity of certain plot elements, a concern that was sparked by the memory of his own youthful criticism of the earlier version.[13] Interestingly, he was also asked to direct the later, more famous 1959 version with Charlton Heston, but he again declined the offer and that assignment went to William Wyler (with the film later winning eleven Oscars in total, including Best Picture, Best Director, and Best Actor).[14] His reasons for having turned down the 1959 version included a lack of preparation time and his desire to remain in California at the time rather than undertaking a long shoot in Italy. Ironically, he would soon embark on his lengthy production of the Biblical epic *Solomon and Sheba* (1959) in Spain, though that production would allow for more script preparation time while he was still at home in California.[15] Vidor later said: "Many times I've thought what a fool I was to turn down [the 1959] *Ben Hur* for a less important picture."[16]

He also recalled that his father, who was in the lumber business and had purchased a large area of hardwood forest in the Dominican Republic, hoped that King would grow up to build the railroad that was needed there to haul the lumber to make it marketable. But Vidor credits his friend Roy Clough with having put him definitively on the path to a career in filmmaking when Vidor visited his pal one day and discovered that Roy was trying to invent his own movie camera.[17] In 1909, the two teenagers would then use their primitive camera and their "precious one-hundred-foot roll of negative" to document a major hurricane that hit Galveston.[18] They rushed to the shoreline with their homemade machine once they realized that a major storm had started, one that echoed the devastating hurricane that had pounded Galveston on September 8, 1900, killing approximately a third of its population of 29,000. Vidor experienced that hurricane as a six-year-old young boy.[19] Their recording of the 1909 hurricane, titled "Hurricane in Galveston" and later credited as Vidor's filmmaking "debut," was shipped to Chicago to be developed and printed. Vidor dates this hurricane as taking place in 1909 in his interview with Dowd, so it was shot in 1909 and evidently not shown publicly in theaters until 1913. This would date the start of Vidor's filmmaking as four years earlier than generally recorded. Histories of Galveston hurricanes include the great storm of 1900 and the

Velasco hurricane of 1909 and one in 1915, but they do not include any similar event in 1913. As Vidor recalls: "In spite of a hazy and blurred image, it had successful runs throughout our part of the state. I had been a witness and participant in recording an actual dramatic event on motion-picture film. It made an indelible mark on my psyche. School classes became progressively less interesting, and I was impatient to get started in this new profession."[20]

ONE

1913–1917

Missing Reels and First Films

"I want to make pictures that will give people at least one little idea that's worthwhile."[1]—King Vidor, 1920

The nascent works of King Vidor, like so many films from cinema's first three decades which have disappeared due to neglect and decay, are nothing more than titles on paper. His earliest movies, in fact, possess no titles to identify them: footage sent to newsreel companies, and then spliced together and distributed around the country with the work of other uncredited filmmakers. The loss is especially devastating for someone like Vidor, because without these films we are missing the foundations of an aesthete whose career spanned seven decades. Vidor, like John Ford, whose earliest works date back to 1916, was one of the few directors whose careers included masterworks in both the silent and sound eras. Vidor began directing a mere five years after D.W. Griffith, whose first directorial efforts were in 1908. More importantly, Vidor's body of work parallels the development of narrative cinema. And like a silent feature whose first reel is missing save for its intertitles, the absence of Vidor's earliest works means that not only are the structural foundations for his filmmaking narrative incomplete, but the visuals (the most crucial element) are missing and must be inferred from reports that can only hint at the missing images.

Vidor was invigorated after making *Hurricane in Galveston* when he was still a teenager. He contacted Mutual Weekly in New York and was hired as a newsreel cameraman. The problem was that he owned no camera. Fifty miles away in Houston, a chauffeur named John Boggs did own a camera, and a partnership was born: Hotex Motion Picture Company.[2] As preparation for their first subject, *Military Parade in Houston* (1914), Vidor returned to the cinema where years before he had studied the screen as an usher: "I sat with a stopwatch and notebook and tried to estimate the number of cuts or scenes in a thousand-foot reel, the length of individual scenes, the distance of the subject from the camera, and various other technical details of which one is not usually conscious while watching the unrolling of a film."[3] For an amateur, Vidor was already a budding professional, with an eye for images and a feel for tempo. The latter is a factor that would become a preeminent concern for Vidor, from the synchronized marching in *The Big Parade* and his musical numbers in *Hallelujah* and *The Wizard of Oz* to the use of cutting and camera movement to create mobility in the static tenement setting of *Street Scene*.

Boggs' and Vidor's next production was *In Tow* (1914), about car races on Galveston Beach. A two-reeler, it was also Vidor's first narrative venture, which he wrote and in which he acted as the lead. (The female lead was to be played by Florence Arto, who caught Vidor's eye when she passed by in the back seat of a car. However, due to her family's disapproval she could not accept the role. Months later, she and Vidor would marry, and Florence Vidor would become the star of many of his films over the next several years.)[4] The success of *In Tow* brought them to the attention of a young local stage comedian from Galveston who was looking to break into movies: Edward Sedgwick, the future director of Buster Keaton in such films as *The Cameraman* (1928), *Spite Marriage* (1929), *Free and Easy* (1930), *Doughboys* (1930), *The Passionate Plumber* (1932), *Speak Easily* (1932), and *What! No Beer?* (1933). Under the Hotex banner, Vidor co-wrote and Sedgwick co-wrote and directed several short films. Raymond Durgnat and Scott Simmon's critical study *King Vidor, American* cites two titles from 1914, *Beautiful Love* and *The Heroes*, but notes: "Other Hotex films, the titles of which are lost, were made by the same production team."[5]

After failing to sell the Hotex films in New York, Vidor and Florence—now married—decided to move to California to try their luck in the film industry. In order to finance their journey, they devised a scheme based upon the blossoming filmmaker's previous experience as a newsreel photographer. As Vidor reported in his memoir *A Tree Is a Tree*: "As exploitation, the Ford Motor Company was making a weekly news feature and travelogue, giving it free to the theaters. Now and then a Ford car would go through a scene, and each subtitle carried the word 'Ford,' but the film had no other advertising. My plan was to shoot interesting scenes en route and sell them to the Ford Motor Company."[6] The content of these films, which suggest some fusion of early cinematic *actualities* and corporate commercials, is yet another question mark in Vidor's early career. What, if any, Vidorian touches these films possessed is unknown. However, some of the touchstones of Vidor's mature style—an eye for the diversity and natural beauty of American landscapes, as well as a penchant for shooting on location—are perhaps rooted in these now-lost Ford Motor Company shorts.

One Vidorian aspect of the Ford shorts that we can be sure of is the use of cinema to convey an ethical and social message. From his early Judge Brown shorts through his final feature, *Solomon and Sheba*, Vidor's films are filled with moral lessons and questions. One of the only Ford shorts that Vidor describes in his autobiography is a public safety message about car safety: the risk of having one's car stolen when one leaves keys in the ignition of an unoccupied vehicle.[7]

After arriving in San Francisco, the Vidors sold their Ford for ferry tickets to Los Angeles. There they contacted an acquaintance from Texas, Corrine Griffith, who had found success with Vitagraph. Corrine arranged for Florence to join Vitagraph's stable of actors while Vidor focused on writing stories in hopes of breaking into the industry. Vidor's first sale was *When It Rains, It Pours!* (1916).[8] It was a film that, according to the director, was written in order to take advantage of a "month-long California rainstorm" that was halting Vitagraph's production schedule of films meant for sunnier weather.[9] That same year, Vidor also appeared as a chauffeur in a Paramount production for director Frank Lloyd, *The Intrigue*.

Vidor finally landed a position at Universal as a script clerk, which involved "keep[ing] the accounts of the individual to which I was attached."[10] Unfortunately, a contract clause prevented Vidor from also selling scripts to the studio while in his current position. To circumvent this restriction, Vidor adopted the pen name "Charles K. Wallis," a combination of his father's first name and his own middle name. The director later described the consequences: "I managed to peddle half a dozen film stories and I did it with a perfectly clear conscience, since the choice of competitive material was so appallingly bad. ... After six months of deceptive practice, I went to the production department, confessed my sins, and got fired. Then I went to the head of the scenario department, pointed out what favorable reviews the stories of Charles K. Wallis had received ... and I was employed as a writer in the comedy department. I was to write three short comedy scenarios a week."[11]

Just how many films Vidor wrote during this period is unknown save for a few titles, such as *What'll We Do with Uncle?* (1917)[12] and *A Bad Little Good Man* (1917),[13] Vidor's first western (albeit a farce), a genre to which he would return frequently throughout his career. "I was writing comedies for Universal," Vidor remembered, "and I'd take 'em in and they'd say 'You'll have to put some pep into this' and then I'd go home and put in some slapstick stuff and take out the human interest."[14] Durgnat and Simmon also cite two additional shorts from this period: *Dan's Daring Drama; or, Harem-Scare Em* and *Just My Sister*.[15]

Another script written during this period would provide Vidor with a pivotal contact who would change his life and career. The film was *The Fifth Boy* (1917), based on a story by Judge Willis Brown, a celebrated juvenile court judge who was interested in turning his courtroom experiences into family-friendly films that could help to motivate and reform youths.[16] Brown had come to Universal at the invitation of producer and studio owner Carl Laemmle. Vidor had previously worked with Brown during his time as a free-lance newsreel cameraman.[17] Curiously, the first story Judge Brown contributed was not one of Brown's famed boy narratives, but one initially called *Nancy's Baby* starring Violet MacMillan (who had previously appeared as Dorothy under L. Frank Baum's direction in *His Majesty, the Scarecrow of Oz* in 1914).[18] *The Fifth Boy* concerns a group of misfit boys who steal chickens and have to earn money on their own to pay back for the stolen property. One of the boys, however, steals more chickens and the Judge is ready to send all of the boys to jail until the guilty party steps forward and takes responsibility.[19] Upon its release, the short film was praised as "human and real, with smiles and tears and will delight them all, old and young."[20]

An article in *Motion Picture News* indicates that *The Fifth Boy* was to be the first in "a series of human interest comedy dramas depicting boy life in one-reel subjects to be made at Universal City" and that Raymond B. Wells, previously associated with the Universal as feature director, was in charge of the producing.[21] *The Fifth Boy*, however, was both the first and the last Judge Brown production for Universal under the direction of Raymond B. Wells. The rest of the series would be produced independently by Brown for Boy City Film, and the director of the remaining films would be King Vidor.[22]

Two

1918–1919

The Turning Point

"'King is never daunted.... He is always optimistic and keeps saying that everything will turn out all right and it does."[1]—Florence Vidor (his first wife and frequent lead actress), 1919

"The motion pictures offer the greatest avenue for the molding of human thought that the world has ever known."[2]—King Vidor, 1919

Bud's Recruit (1918)

Bud's Recruit (1918) is a comedic propaganda short about two brothers, each representing a political stance on America's involvement in World War I: the interventionist (Bud) and the isolationist (Reggie). Bud leads a ragtag group of kids (the titular recruits) in make-believe war maneuvers in the woods, while his brother lounges in the backyard doing his best to look like a Jazz Age sophisticate. Too young to enlist, Bud impersonates the older Reggie and signs up. His plan is foiled when word gets around town that Reggie will be going to war. With the whole town proud of something he did not do, Reggie decides to leave town. After seeing a Selective Service poster, Reggie has a change of heart and arrives for duty just as Bud arrives. Reggie goes off to war, while his family watches, proud of his decision.

Bud's Recruit is significant not only for being the earliest—and only—surviving example of King Vidor's silent short films as a director, but also because it appears to be the work of a mature artist, despite being so early in Vidor's filmography. Stylistically and thematically, it anticipates many of Vidor's films to come, suggesting that despite being hired to work for Judge Willis Brown, Vidor was already conceiving of his film work in terms of a personal vision, finding ways to inject himself into projects, and leaving traces of his own artistry.

As the film begins, we are introduced to young Bud in front of a tattered bivouac, blowing a bugle. He wears a rope for a belt, a crumpled hat, military rags meant for a larger body, and keeps his sleeves rolled up—a boyish Teddy Roosevelt type. Bud is the first of Vidor's "everyman" protagonists—in this case, "everyboy" might be more appropriate, considering his age. When he blows the horn, boys come from all directions—collapsing from handstands, sliding down trees, emerging from foliage, running over the hills, biking down the lane, and one even runs from the wash bucket with soap still on his face. It is a cast of ragamuffins that presages the Little Rascals and the Dead End Kids: young, spirited, slightly disheveled, slightly mischievous, all-American youngsters. There is an optimism and boundless energy from the moment they appear on screen, even though they cannot line up properly and look rather ragged in their torn clothing. Visual gags—remnants of Vidor's early gigs as a slapstick writer—abound, such as when a little boy, deemed too small for the gang because he is not tall enough to reach the mark on a tree trunk, stands on a rock to increase his height. Bud snickers at the gimmick but allows the boy to join up, giving him a drum.

Armed with wooden sticks for rifles, Bud's recruits line up and march. The scene is the earliest indication of Vidor's fondness for synchronized movement on screen and his attention to visual rhythm within the frame. Despite its brevity, the scene does seem significant in that it foreshadows a later more famous display of militaristic marching and synchronous steps in *The Big Parade* when the soldiers are walking through the forest.

In contrast with the outdoors, rough-and-tumble episode that announced Bud and his gang, Vidor now introduces Bud's brother, Reggie Oscar Gilbert, in a strikingly parodic manner. He is lounging in a garden chair in the backyard, sipping from a straw and smoking a cigarette—his manicured version of "the outdoors." Unlike Bud's clothing, Reggie wears circular glasses and a spotless all-white outfit. A closeup of the mother smiling in approval is contrasted with a closeup of the family's servant shaking his head in disapproval. Scott Simmon makes note of another link between *Bud's Recruit* and *The Big Parade*, which also "opens with a similar doting mother and her initially slacker son. But seven years had given Vidor, and America, time to come to a darker understanding of the price exacted for patriotism."[3]

What's most striking about *Bud's Recruit* is the number of connections it has to Vidor's later films. One or two could be written off as mere coincidence, but the sheer number of them suggests that this short film was really the first step for Vidor in terms of exploring certain geographic and narrative concerns. Its rural American setting sets the tone for many of Vidor's films to come, such as *Jack-Knife Man* and *The Stranger's Return*. The social satire of Reggie is echoed in such Jazz Age comedies as *Wine of Youth*, *Proud Flesh*, and *The Patsy*. The way that war could divide a family would form the foundation of both *Japanese War Bride* and *War and Peace*. And significantly, the militaristic milieu would be explored further (and with greater depth and drama) in *The Big Parade*, *So Red the Rose*, and especially *Northwest Passage*, where a major commands his own group of soldiers (albeit professional ones).

As the first of Judge Brown's independent films (after one previous short at Universal in 1917, *The Fifth Boy*), *Bud's Recruit* is an anomaly in the series, as it is the only one not to feature Judge Brown himself as a character, and not to be based on one of his own cases. Early publicity for the series reads: "With the exception of the first release, the Judge Brown stories are founded on real incidents noted by Judge Brown in his long fight on behalf of his great army of juvenile friends."[4] It raises the question, why begin a brand with something so atypical? The most likely answer is that it was an opportunistic show of patriotism at a time when the government was openly asking for the film industry to assist with the war effort. "Some weeks ago moving picture companies were urged to assist the Government in its publicity campaign for recruits for the Army and Navy by making use of attractively designed Government posters and advertising matter in their own posters and pictures," reported *The Dramatic Mirror*. "One of the first companies to respond to this request was General Film Company."[5] *Motion Picture News* corroborates this theory: "General Film Company has responded to the request of the Government for posters which will aid in the recruiting campaign. ... Many other posters and cards issued by the Government were introduced during the filming of 'Bud's Recruit' ... Appeals issued to the public by the Navy and Army recruiting departments and the food administration were used liberally in the various sets and locations used by the producers and add greatly to the charm and interest of the story."[6] Not only were promotional ads for *Bud's Recruit* made to resemble recruitment posters, but Vidor used them as recurring visual motifs throughout the film: Bud's half of the bedroom has recruitment posters that he gazes upon and imitates (whereas Reggie's half has tennis rackets above his bed), and Reggie's change of heart comes after seeing a poster.

As a publicity stunt, the maneuver worked, clinching headlines for the short film and helping to establish the series as commercially and critically successful. "A hit over the country," reported *Moving Picture World*. "Extra prints of this subject have been made to cope with the demand."[7] *Picture-Play Magazine*'s "The Picture Oracle" also praised the film: "They are indeed very human little pictures, and I have enjoyed every one of them. 'Bud's Recruit' I thought especially good. King Vidor is the name of the director of these pictures, and he deserves a world of praise for the pleasant films he has made of the Judge's stories."[8]

In all, twenty Judge Brown shorts were produced. In addition to *Bud's Recruit*, Vidor is believed to have directed fifteen others: *The Chocolate of the Gant*, *Marrying Off Dad*, *The Lost Lie*, *Tad's Swimming Hole*, *Thief or Angel*, *The Rebellion*, *The Preacher's Son*, *A Boy Built City*, *The Accusing Toe*, *I'm a Man*, *Love of Bob*, *Dog vs. Dog*, *The Three Fives*, *The Case of Bennie*, and *Kid Politics*, all from 1918. Four other shorts were made: *The Demand of Dugan*, *Shift the Gear*, *Freck*, *Gum Drops and Overalls*, and *Danny Asks Why*, all from 1919.[9] It is unlikely that Vidor directed those last four, since by 1919 he was already engaged in his first four feature films that year: *The Turn in the Road*, *Better Times*, *The Other Half*, and *Poor Relations*. The director of those last four is still unknown; however, *Motion Picture News* mentions another director who was involved in the project: "Director King W. Vidor and Director McQuarrie are engaged in preparing Judge Brown's stories at the studios of the Boy City Film Company at Culver City, Cal."[10] While the rest of the series remains lost, synopses of the films (included in an appendix) suggests that the content was similar to *Bud's Recruit*: wholesome, moral-driven, rugged, and optimistic Americana. Such characteristics would be hallmarks of Vidor's films for years to come; however, it would take only a couple of years and a couple of movies in order for darkness and doubt to begin to creep into Vidor's sensibility.

* * * *

The Turn in the Road, Better Times, The Other Half, Poor Relations (All 1919)

Even when he was directing the Judge Brown shorts, King Vidor had his eye on feature film production. He even went so far as to cut together several of the shorts in an attempt to pass them off as one cohesive feature-length movie to potential financiers. "I didn't get away with it," Vidor conceded. "I couldn't convince them. Today they would have been accepted very readily just by the quality of their directing, but the goal was to be able to maintain interest throughout, and to be able to handle the money involved in a full-length film."[11] Vidor ultimately found the necessary support from the people who enabled him to become a director: "I went to the doctors who put up the money for the [Judge Brown] boys' films and I sold them the idea of making the feature film. We formed the Brentwood Film Company. They belonged to the Brentwood Country Club and we played some golf there."[12]

For his first long-form movie, Vidor could not have chosen a more apt title than *The Turn in the Road*. The film proved to be just that for Vidor, and its success ensured that he would have a career as a feature film director. It is devastating that such a significant film is lost. Without it, we are not only missing Vidor's advancement from short to feature, but also his debut as a writer-director, as *The Turn in the Road* was a

Director King Vidor (at approximately age 25), around the time that his first feature film *The Turn in the Road* (1919) was made (Photofest).

project very close to Vidor's heart. From interviews and articles that have survived, it is apparent that not only did Vidor inject much of his own faith and philosophy into the story, but that it was also the first step towards a star-less story of the common people that would culminate with *The Crowd* (1928): "This picture demanded the extreme of realism and naturalness in its treatment, for it deals with life of today as it is known by the average American," explained Vidor. "Its humor, pathos, suspense, and climax are drawn from everyday life. Over action or over characterization would ruin the picture."[13] Much like James Murray, the lead actor in *The Crowd*, the lead in *The Turn in the Road*, Lloyd Hughes, was also a relative newcomer to cinema, having appeared in only a handful of movies; this was his first starring role. Such parallels make the loss of *The Turn in the Road* movie even greater, as it seems likely that Vidor already had sown the seeds of his future masterpiece in his very first feature.

Exhibitors Herald described *The Turn in the Road* as "a religious play asking and answering the question 'What is God?'"

> Paul Perry, son of a money-mad father, marries the daughter of an orthodox minister. His wife's sister is deeply in love with him. When his wife dies in childbirth, Paul loses faith in the "God to Whom the will of man should meekly bow" and running from the house, wanders for six years. In the meantime, his sister-in-law raises the son whom Paul has never seen. Little Bob is the means of softening the heart of Perry's father and incidentally saving him from death at the hands of his employees, who demand better living conditions and higher wages. Perry, returning, is taught by his son that "God is love," and finds happiness in the love of his son and his sister-in-law.[14]

In terms of pure narrative, *The Turn in the Road* appears to be a departure from the rough-and-tumble, slapstick morality tales that Vidor was writing and producing for Judge Brown. While clearly just as message driven as the short films, Vidor has left behind youthful antics for a decidedly mature, soul-searching story. With only a synopsis to go on, it is hard to know how subtly (or not) the material was handled; however, it seems to be a didactic and bold declaration of principles. This did not go unnoticed by the press at the time.

Wid's Daily observed, "There is an underlying thought which leans decidedly towards Christian Science, this though being that the man who seeks God will only find Him where he finds love, there being no God where love does not exist. ... In the last reel we find the hero home, with his boy speaking many titles which get over the Christian Science thoughts."[15] This aspect of the film drew special attention: "Engraved invitations ... were sent to the leading Christian Scientists of Seattle by John Hamrick, of the Rex [Theater]," was reported in *Wid's Daily*. "Hamrick selected the people of this sect as his guests because the theme of the photoplay, 'God is Love,' is the basis of the Christian Science doctrines."[16]

At the time, Vidor was evasive when it came to the issue of faith and his movie. "Motion pictures with a principle and not founded upon a specific form of religion has been my endeavor," the director said. However, he proceeded to completely contradict himself with his next statement. "I am not trading on the name of any religion although in *The Turn in the Road*.... I have incorporated a scientific principle, a principle I might add which has brought peace, contentment and prosperity to many millions of people."[17] As wily as it might appear, Vidor's explanation confirms that, to him, it is not a matter of faith so much as fact: Christian Science is, in his eyes, science and not religion.

In his book-length interview with Nancy Dowd and David Shepard, Vidor explained the "answers" his characters were seeking in *The Turn in the Road*:

> I was a Christian Scientist, and [the answers] were basically metaphysical. It was a simple thing of truth, or God, good predominates, and the shadows. I remember I illustrated a scene with a little boy who got up and opened a window in the barn loft and said, "The darkness is only the absence of light." It was in suffering and tragedy that we try to make the unreal real, that reality was this: Just to be conscious is a miracle in itself, just as life and the awareness of consciousness of living is itself harmonious and good. It's only what we impinge upon that, add on to our fears and ignorance, that makes it otherwise. All the fear and suffering could be dissolved just like the darkness by opening the windows of our minds.[18]

In that same interview, Vidor also went more in depth regarding his roots as a Christian Scientist, which revealed his beliefs in "miracles" such as the child-savior at the end of *The Turn in the Road*, as well as other farfetched *deus ex machinas* in *The Other Half, Better Times*, and other early films:

> My mother was [a Christian Scientist.] ... I got interested in it when I was fifteen or sixteen years old, after going to many doctors and discovering that they didn't seem to know what they were talking about. I was disillusioned with doctors and medicine because I had a nervous problem and they couldn't agree on what the problem was. I wanted to grab hold of something more general, more basic, something that affected the whole man rather than just pieces of the anatomy.[19]

Unfortunately, most of the discussion that survives around *The Turn in the Road* is thematic rather than visual. Vidor's expression, "The darkness is only the absence of light," suggests a visual correlation with his philosophy, and there are certainly compositions in *The Sky Pilot, Love Never Dies*, and *Jack-Knife Man* that focus on sunlight and how it illuminates both environment and character; however, without the film, we can only speculate what sort of images Vidor created. *Motion Picture News* vaguely noted, "The story has a rural touch."[20] What we do know for certain is that the film was booked at Quinn's Superba in Los Angeles, where it "completed a run of eight weeks ... surpassing all records at this house, [and] was purchased last week by the Robertson-Cole Company, from the Brentwood Film Corporation, which produced the picture. This production will be published through Exhibitors Mutual."[21] With national distribution secured, Vidor and *The Turn in the Road* were officially a hit.[22]

Vidor wasted no time getting back behind the camera. His next production for Brentwood was *Better Times*, another lost film whose legacy can only be gleaned from textual accounts. The American Film Institute Catalog of Feature Films provides the most coherent synopsis of what is Vidor's most audacious and most nonsensical plot yet:

> Inspired by a motto she reads on a calendar, Nancy Scroggs, the daughter of the owner of a rundown hotel in a once famous health resort, decides to round up some customers. She drives her dilapidated 1902 Ford to the train station and picks up vacationing Peter Van Alstyne and, using Christian Science reasoning, she convinces him to ignore his doctor's orders and eat all he wants. Peter boasts of the food, and soon he and Nancy fall in love while they run a thriving hotel. Peter receives a telegram that Nancy assumes is from another love interest, and leaves town. Nancy's father loses the hotel gambling and drowns himself, then with the life insurance left to her, Nancy goes to finishing school. Envious of the other girls' love letters, she pretends to get letters from a famous baseball player. To humiliate her, they take her to a ballgame, but when she sees that the player is actually Peter, she leaps over a rail into his arms.[23]

From this jumble, the only discernable Vidorian elements are his increased interest in melodramatic excess and his unflinching faith in Christian Science as a plot device. Reviews at the time were positive, albeit brief and largely uninformative as to his visual style: "It is Director Vidor's handling of the type that makes them so real," *Wid's Daily* reported. "Through small, but nevertheless important touches in his character drawing, he registers those points most essential in this sort of work. He also carries the small-town atmosphere at all times, and shows a knowledge of the lives and customs of village folk."[24] *Photoplay* offered more imaginative praise, drawing a literary comparison that unfortunately lacked any significant explanation: "He shows an almost Dickensesque facility for the little lights and shadows of existence."[25] *Motion Picture News* suggested that exhibitors talk up the film's faith-based story: "The Christian Science 'business' injected will absorb and interest more people than some exhibitors generally imagine. ... Try and secure a list of the members of the Christian Science churches and mail them a special invitation to see their beliefs demonstrated in a photoplay."[26]

Following *Better Times* was *The Other Half*—which, thankfully, exists in a nearly complete version available online courtesy of EYE Film Institute Netherlands. It is the story of two friends who return from World War I with their class boundaries erased. Jimmy works at the factory run by Donald's father. Donald is offered an executive position, but he turns it down in favor of working his way up from the bottom. After his father's sudden death, Donald is forced to take over the company, and his sympathies for the lower class vanish. Cutting corners on safety leads to an accident causing Jimmy to lose his sight. Meanwhile, Jimmy's girlfriend, Jeannie, was also injured on the job. While caring for her, Donald's fiancé, Katherine, takes an interest in the workers and revives their newsletter. With the workers ready to revolt against Donald, she publishes an editorial and is able to convince Donald to reform, and the two lovers are reunited. Jimmy miraculously regains his vision, Jeannie recovers, and the two of them are married.

With its post–World War I setting, *The Other Half* seems like a spiritual sequel to *Bud's Recruit*, with Jimmy and Donald taking the place of the two politically opposed brothers in the Judge Brown short whose differences are overcome by a common interest in the war. More prescient, however, is how Vidor structures the narrative around the concept of "the return," a motif that sets into motion *The*

Stranger's Return, *Japanese War Bride*, and *Ruby Gentry*, and that also provides the resolution to *The Jack-Knife Man*, *Love Never Dies*, *The Big Parade*, *Hallelujah*, and *So Red the Rose*.

To visually represent the class conflict of the protagonists, Vidor uses dichotomous compositions. Like *Bud's Recruit*, the characters' ideals are manifested in their costumes: Jimmy often seen in uniform and Donald in his suit. More cinematic is Vidor's use of editing in the concurrent proposal scenes: the more wholesome, Americana proposal from Jimmy to Jeannie on the front porch contrasts with the more formal, class-conscious proposal from Donald to Katherine in Donald's elegant living room. (This, too, echoes the indoor/outdoor split associations with characters from *Bud's Recruit*, with Bud often visualized outdoors and Reggie indoors.)

Once again, Vidor's religious didacticism provided the spectacularly unrealistic finale of Jimmy regaining his sight. *Motion Picture News* went so far as to suggest that exhibitors call attention to this contrivance, and stir up controversy among audience members of different ideologies:

> When you book this picture it would be wise to call attention to the last two pictures written and produced by the same director … [and their] theme of Christian Science recognized by a fast growing creed. Even those opposed to it like doctors, etc., will be curious to know to what lengths this director will go. … Provoke a controversy with any leading member or group of the medical profession by asking him if he believes it is not just a wee bit overdrawn to see a blind man regain his sight through "science." This is your big bet and worth many columns of publicity to you if you handle it right.… Get busy on this and cash in.[27]

Exhibitors Herald, on the other hand, was far less the provocateur. They praised the film by writing, "[It] demands the attention of every exhibitor in that it represents the work of King W. Vidor and ZaSu Pitts, a director and an actress that are bound to find a big future in the industry. It is in every sense a good picture, the sort of play that everybody will enjoy and remember."[28]

Next for Vidor was *Poor Relations*, another lost film. The American Film Institute's Catalog of Feature Films describes the basic plot:

> Dorothy Perkins, the eldest daughter of a simple, wholesome country family, leaves for the big city to study architecture after winning a competition. She is a success, and meets Monty Rhodes, the son of aristocratic parents. Despite his parents' objections, Monty and Dorothy marry, but Mrs. Rhodes continually humiliates Dorothy for her lack of breeding. When she finally succeeds in driving the heartbroken Dorothy back to her own family, Monty realizes his mistake, and follows her to the country where he finds happiness with his wife and his poor relations.[29]

Issues of class division recall *Bud's Recruit* and *The Other Half*, and anticipate more in-depth explorations in *Proud Flesh*, *Wine of Youth*, *The Patsy*, and especially *Stella Dallas* and *Ruby Gentry*. Admiration for rural customs and folksy values has been a traditional Vidorian quality since his earliest shorts—visually, he never strayed too far from the initial landscapes he documented for newsreels and on the road to California (and when he did stray, it was never for more than a film or two, as he would always find a way to return to the small towns he knew well).

Laurence Reid's review in *Motion Picture News* is curious in that it highlights certain qualities that also are reminiscent of *The Crowd*. However, without the film it is only a speculated connection: "the story offers an unusually simple theme which does not contain a single dramatic situation or climax. It exudes sentiment and heart interest, and naturally, a wealth of local color. Of action and suspense it has none; but it does have considerable character drawing. And a lesson; don't forget that. … This picture will not offer you any moving moments. It is exceedingly quiet."[30] *Wid's Daily* was likewise unenthusiastic: "It is not a great picture by any manner of means but good average program stuff with nothing about it that is in the least offensive. … Director Vidor has made a sincere attempt to fill the picture with human interest and has succeeded most admirably."[31]

Even with only one surviving (and incomplete at that), Vidor's first four films suggest rapid development as an artist thematically and philosophically. Locations, character types, narrative structures, politics, and faith were already recurring from film to film. He may have been finding his way, but in a sense he already knew where he was going (if not exactly how to get there, either artistically or professionally).

Poor Relations was released on November 1, 1919, Vidor's fourth feature that year for Brentwood. It would be his last. Less than one month earlier, on October 4, 1919, *Motion Picture News* reported, "King Vidor … has severed ties with the Brentwood Company and has left for New York to complete arrangements for making pictures with his own producing company."[32]

Three

1920–1921

The Humanist Emerges

> "It was perhaps a slight exaggeration, but one could certainly say that his sensibility was unique. There was more idealism in him than one found in most American directors of his time. And more individuality. And more romanticism, too."[1]—Richard Schickel, "King Vidor: Romantic Idealist" (1993)

The Family Honor, The Jack-Knife Man, Mothercraft, The Sky Pilot, and *Love Never Dies*

It is fitting that so many of Vidor's films involve roads, either literally or metaphorically, for he was—and remained—a journeyman director. The term is ironic and seemingly contradictory considering his status as an auteur and how, even from his earliest films, Vidor embedded his authorial imprint. Nevertheless, Vidor was a journeyman in three ways: first, he was a consummate man of nature who liked to take his camera and crew on the road in order to film on-location; second, he frequently incorporated geographical and spiritual "journeys" into his narratives; and third, he knew when an opportunity was too good to pass up, and when no opportunity presented itself, he created one. From the homemade camera of his youth to his newsreel endeavors with the chauffeur, from his road trip to California filming for the Ford Motor Company to the gag work in Hollywood, and from Judge Brown to Brentwood, Vidor was a self-made man ... with a little help from those with money. This set into a pattern to which Vidor would stick for the duration of his career—moving from one studio to another, in and out of independent and small productions, mixing popular with personal projects, adapting to the times and shifting currents in the industry and technological advances, and yet always finding a way to keep working and to keep making films that were recognizably Vidorian.

Vidor did not sit still for long after making his entry into the world of feature film directing. After completing four features in 1919—*The Turn in the Road, Better Times, The Other Half,* and *Poor Relations*—Vidor announced he was already moving on to a bigger and better contract:

At the end of the first year with the Brentwood Film Company I had gone to New York and had written offers from every film company, but I selected The First National Exhibitors, which financed theatre chains. I felt that I would have more freedom ... and I made a contract with them for four or six pictures with an option that they could take up after two. I came back to Los Angeles having no studio to work in, I didn't even own a home, and I had seventy-five thousand dollars to make a film.[2]

The first thing Vidor did was invest a portion of his newly acquired capital in the creation of a private studio called "Vidor Village." Vidor's father sold the family insurance business and moved to Hollywood to help manage the project. "For fifteen thousand dollars we bought a square block on Santa Monica Boulevard in Hollywood," Vidor recalled in his memoir. "We then constructed one enclosed stage and a few smaller buildings designed to be used as small-town locations in the films I planned to make."[3] With a new contract and a new studio, 1920 was poised to be a pivotal year in Vidor's fast-developing career. In conjunction with these advancements, Vidor published his "Creed and Pledge" in *Variety*. This statement enunciated clearly his approach to filmmaking:

1. I believe in the motion picture that carries a message to humanity.

2. I believe in the picture that will help humanity to free itself from the shackles of fear and suffering that have so long bound it with iron chains.

3. I will not knowingly produce a picture that contains anything I do not believe to be absolutely true to human nature, anything that could injure anyone or anything unclean in thought or action.

4. Nor will I deliberately portray anything to cause fright, suggest fear, glorify mischief, condone cruelty or extenuate malice.

5. I will never picture evil or wrong, except to prove the fallacy of its line.

6. So long as I direct pictures, I will make only those founded upon principles of right, and I will endeavor to draw upon the inexhaustible source of good for my stories, my guidance and my inspiration.[4]

Decades before Andrew Sarris in New York and the *Cahiers du Cinema* critics in France helped usher in the cult of the director, Vidor was already cultivating a public image of the director-as-artist and film-as-philosophy. The "Creed and Pledge" was more than an extension (and watering-down) of his Christian Science ideology. It was a proclamation of a distinctly personal cinema that was moral, spiritual, and fully committed to a humanist worldview distinct from mass entertainment. Various qualities outlined in his six precepts were evident in his earliest surviving films and implicit in the textual accounts of those films not available for viewing, and this list of principles distilled aspects from each of his movies into a cohesive mission statement.

Vidor's premier film for First National, and the first post–"Pledge," was the now-lost production *The Family Honor* (1920). The starring role of Beverly Tucke was played by Vidor's wife Florence; this was their third film together following her starring roles in *The Other Half* and *Poor Relations*. In *Picture-Play Magazine*, Herbert

Howe wrote an extended, rhapsodic review of the film that is insightful for its attention to Vidor's visual style—particularly his use of light, which recalls Vidor's own evocation of light and dark in relation to Christian Science mentioned in the previous chapter—as well as comparing the film to music:

> *The Family Honor* is a family picture. It is for the family, of the family, by the family. It is as difficult to analyze the charm of Vidor plays as it is the charm of personalities. They have a humanizing influence. I would call it "style." Daudet once said, "It is style that perfumes a book." *The Family Honor* is flooded with the fragrance and beauty of the old South. With Vidoric simplicity the story unfolds in an atmosphere perfumed with traditions. In a crumbling manse of Dixie a girl strives to hold the family honor above degrading poverty. Her brother is a slacker in the fight. He is brought to trial for a murder committed in a gambling joint which he frequents. With his sister at his side he faces judgment. The courtroom is filled with a miasma of lies. From without it is darkened by lowering clouds. Into this atmosphere comes a bright-faced youngster, the little brother of the family. As he enters the room and moves down the aisle, the sun smiles through the clouds and casts a halo over him. The false witnesses turn to gaze into the face of the child—index of purity and right thinking. ... Perjury melts in its radiance. One by one the evildoers confess. The elder brother is acquitted, and, with chastened mind, sets forth on the right way. ... *The Family Honor* is a simple melody of life, the expression of a fine composer who will produce yet greater symphony.[5]

The courtroom sequence, for all its zealous melodrama, seems characteristic of the Christian Science–inspired *deus ex machina* of which Vidor was so fond in this era. The specifics of the lighting, however obvious and heavy-handed, sound like the most interesting aspect of the movie, inasmuch as they appear to be an attempt to fuse faith and aesthetics.

Vidor's next film, *The Jack-Knife Man* (1920), was his biggest hit to date. The film survives and can justifiably be called a masterpiece. However humble and modest in scope, the film is thoroughly Vidor, hitting each of the notes of his "Pledge" but without the excesses that reportedly marred *The Family Honor*, *The Other Half*, and even *The Turn in the Road*. Peter Lane lives in a river shanty where he idles away the day building alarm clocks. Widow Potter admonishes him for his reclusive, antisocial ways, but she is secretly in love with him, unable to show her true feelings because of social differences. Late one rainy night, a woman rushes into Peter's cabin with her child, Buddy, collapses, and dies. Peter decides to care for the boy and uses his jack-knife to carve toy animals for him to play with. Peter sells his boat and agrees to float it down river with Buddy to the boat's new owner. Along the way, a tramp, Booge, tries to steal the boat. Because Buddy is amused by Booge's songs, Peter lets Booge stay. When the Child's Rescue Society arrives to take the boy away, they arrest Booge, mistaking him for Peter. Peter and Buddy flee. Stopping in a roadside café, Buddy recognizes a young indentured servant as his sister, Susie. Justice of the Peace Briggles eventually catches Peter and takes away Buddy. Unbeknownst to Peter, Widow Potter adopts Buddy and Susie. Impressed by Peter's woodcarving, Mrs. Montgomery hires him to make new toys. Newly wealthy, Peter cleans up and proposes to Widow Potter. Still homeless, Booge—who is Buddy's real father—sees his son with a new family and decides to let him remain in his new happy home.

Based on a novel by Ellis Parker Butler with a scenario by William Parker (who had also scripted *The Family Honor*), *The Jack-Knife Man* was another of Vidor's proto–*Crowd* everyman stories that could be set in Everytown, USA. Like *The Turn in the Road* before it and *The Crowd* to come, Vidor assembled a star-less cast. For Peter Lane, Vidor cast Fred Turner, a bit player who had parts in *The Miracle Man* (1919) starring Lon Chaney, D.W. Griffith's *The Mother and the Law* (1919) starring Mae Marsh, Marshal Neilan's *Rebecca of Sunnybrook Farm* starring Mary Pickford, Griffith's *Intolerance* (1916), and Christy Cabanne's *The Outlaw's Revenge* (1915) starring pre-directorial Raoul Walsh. For Buddy, Vidor cast the three-year-old Bobby Kelso, a boy who had never appeared in movies before (and never would again) but whose mother met Florence in a hair salon.[6] The only "star" of the film—other than King himself behind the camera—was Vidor's wife, Florence, who has the small role of Mrs. Montgomery.

While the pathos-laden narrative was nothing new for Vidor, where *The Jack-Knife Man* most impresses is in Vidor's direction, which is markedly more sophisticated in composition and more substantial in impact than in any surviving example of Vidor's prior filmmaking. The opening shot of a river has the intimate immediacy and deceptive simplicity of early cinema *actualities*: like a Rothko painting (decades before Rothko touched paint to canvas), the screen is split horizontally into three stripes alternating light-dark-light: an open sky, a tree line, and the river. In the foreground, the deck of a shanty emerges from the frame right, interrupting the symmetry of the frame. In the background are more shanties, and in the middle of the river a man rows a boat, the only motion in an otherwise static shot. It is a very a basic, albeit effective, establishing shot—the river will become the predominant setting of the narrative and provide the path the characters take, and the shanty will be used for the interiors. The placement of the camera on the deck of the foreground shanty is pragmatic but also comfortable—the perspective is that of someone already on the boat, someone familiar with the environment. Metaphorically speaking, the man in the rowboat is dwarfed by the river, and there is a poetic grace to the way he moves with the flow of the river and does not fight against it. It is an introduction to the philosophy of Peter Lane, who accepts all that befalls him. When the Widow Potter admonishes him for his lifestyle, he bows his head; when the doctor mistakenly assumes that Peter's neglect killed the woman, he does not betray her secrets; when Booge tries to steal the boat, Peter lets him stay; when Buddy is amused by Booge's songs, Peter does not express jealousy or resentment; and when Mrs. Montgomery offers the chance to make a living, something that Peter had clearly avoided his whole life, he goes along with it. Peter is true to himself, and that is what matters most to him—not how others view him with their prejudices and misconceptions. It is a subtler invocation of the right way of living advocated by Vidor's Christian Science, and absent is the heavy-handed indoctrination that characterized his earlier efforts to interweave his faith into his films.

Vidor's compositions in *The Jack-Knife Man*, more so than in his previous movies, resemble paintings. After Peter says farewell to a guest, he leans in the open doorway. The camera remains inside the cabin, and the open doorway becomes like a picture frame, with the river in the background. Smoke drifts from a shanty's smokestack on the other bank of the river. Peter's eyes hold off camera, as though he is watching his guest depart. After a moment, Peter's gaze turns away from the camera and he looks out across the river. It is a quiet moment, and Vidor allows it to remain on camera for a few beats before fading out. It is a musical moment—of no narrative importance but significant only for its tempo and the beauty of the shot.

Later, as Peter and Buddy are taking the shanty downriver, Vidor places the static camera on the moving barge, and the contrast between stasis and movement recalls so many Lumière actualities shot on boats in canals, rudimentary examples of a dolly shot, but beautiful in their own simplicity. In the background, sunlight cuts through the clouds in a manner that evokes the Hudson River school of paintings, with an almost violent explosive quality of light and sky. Vidor also begins to experiment with photographic effects in *The Jack-Knife Man*, such as the first shot of Widow Potter in her living room, using an empty chair to help her roll yarn. While she is sitting still in her chair, Vidor cross-fades an exact shot except with Peter Lane in the chair holding the fabric. She smiles and says, "Peter Lane, you never will amount to anything!" After the intertitle, Peter's image fades and Vidor returns to the original composition of Potter with the empty chair. It is a purely visual way of indicating a daydream that would not have been nearly as expressive as a basic cut, nor would it have the same poetic effect if Vidor had resorted to an explanatory intertitle.

Vidor experiments with cross-fading later in the film as well, when Peter is holding a piece of wood and imagining what the final carved toy will look like. It is a clever way of manifesting visually what would otherwise be an internal thought process invisible to the audience. A variation on this application occurs late in the film when Peter is talking with Mrs. Montgomery. Vidor frames Peter in a medium closeup against a dark wall; he is seated holding a piece of wood he intends to carve, and is looking away from the camera at the wall. Peter remains on screen while the wall cross-fades to show a sea of children seated, looking up at Peter and smiling, entranced and delighted by his woodcarving skills. The camera pulls back on both Peter and the children, revealing more and more children as it pulls further back. The shot captures the interior moment when Peter's heart changes, when he has the Christian Science conversion and decides to give back to society, even though the authorities have taken Buddy away from him. The downward angle with which the camera films the children is notable for two reasons: one, it places Peter in a God-like position floating above the children; and two, it foreshadows the final shot of *The Crowd*, with the high-angle reverse tracking shot of the laughing movie theater audience.

The Jack-Knife Man was not only an artistic accomplishment for Vidor, but a critical hit. "King Vidor has proved himself again," wrote Frederick James Smith in *Motion Picture Classic*. "Mr. Vidor it was who startled the celluloid world over a year ago with his *The Turn in the Road*, which, despite certain weaknesses, revealed its producer as possessing a singularly human touch. Being sure of his ability, we have waited for Mr. Vidor to do something bigger. The bigger thing has occurred.... Here is a gently drawn little genre study, finely conceived and done with admirable workmanship and an excellently restrained sympathy. ... it belongs to the photoplay school of tomorrow. No pasteboard melodramatic characters, no machine-made plot development, no trite methods of screen telling are here. For Mr. Vidor—we are sure of this now—is just finding himself and before long he is going to turn out a big and human celluloid document. ... There are photographic moments in the visualization that are veritable camera lyrics."[7]

Wid's Daily also praised the movie, and apparently was convinced that the Sacramento River used in the movie was actually the Mississippi: "Vidor has given the story a delightful production. The Mississippi river scenes are wonderfully true. The long shots of the houseboat floating down the river are beautifully lighted and photographed. The detail of the interiors is such as to make them the most realistic ever filmed."[8] *Photoplay* also appreciated the location photography; however, they were not as easily fooled. "It presents King Vidor at his atmospheric best ... the scenes are effective, the landscapes beautiful, the rain a little thick but very real and the river shots true enough to suggest that they were taken along the shores of the old Father of the Water itself."[9] And *Exhibitors Herald* commented that the film "deserves the critical attention of every American exhibitor. It is King Vidor's best picture to date, and that is sufficient guarantee for those familiar with his past work. An everyday story of everyday people, produced in the realistic manner of the producer's past creations, it is an event of great importance to the screen world and a commercial-artistic triumph."[10]

Fifty-two years after it first premiered, the film screened as part of The Museum of Modern Art's King Vidor retrospective. "One way to view Vidor's career flowing from this ... is to see the clear and parallel influences of Griffith and Chaplin," wrote Charles Silver. "*The Jack-Knife Man* is almost an explicit homage to both of these titans of the American silent era, and the very last image [of Booge watching his children over a fence], virtually an amalgam of *True Heart Susie* and *The Tramp*, is both a visually eloquent tribute to his mentors and an announcement to everyone that a major new talent, King Vidor, had arrived."[11]

After *The Jack-Knife Man*, it did not take long before Vidor was already off on his next journey. "[First National] told me the reason they would not pick up my option was because I had sent the money [unused for *Jack-Knife Man* and *The Family Honor*] back, rather than spending it. ... Florence Vidor was becoming a big star, and after *Family Honor* we signed a contract with Associated Producers."[12] In 1920, Vidor had channeled his vision and philosophy into an identifiable and singular style—now, it was time for him to expand his cinematic canvas.

As 1920 ended and 1921 began, King Vidor's name was mentioned in the press as being attached to two films, both for-hire works for women producers. One was called *Mothercraft*, a project spearheaded by May Bliss Dickinson, national founder of the mother-craft movement which represented the child welfare department of the General Federation of Women's Clubs of America. The film was slated to star Vidor's younger sister, Catherine, as well as Laura La Plante, future star of such silent classics as *The Cat and the Canary* (1927), *The Last Warning* (1929), and *Show Boat* (1929), and who at the time was new to Hollywood and transitioning from a "bathing beauty" into a career as an actress. Dickinson herself wrote the script, and Max Dupont was engaged as the cinematographer.[13] Two weeks later, it was announced that the production "had begun at the King Vidor studios, under the … supervision of King Vidor."[14] Two months later, in March, more contradictory information regarding the actual director was published in *Picture-Play Magazine*: "King Vidor is going to direct a picture of *Mothercraft*."[15] And then, the production seemingly disappears from the headlines. No further information could be found confirming whether the production was actually finished. Judging by how engaged Vidor was in 1921 with two other feature film productions, it seems likely that *Mothercraft* was never made.

Director King Vidor in the 1920s, the decade of his silent era masterworks *The Big Parade* (1925), *The Crowd* (1928), and *Show People* (1928) (Photofest).

The other film Vidor was working on at the end of 1920, however, was made and still exists. *The Sky Pilot* (1921) was a project initiated by Cathrine Curtis and her company, aptly named the Cathrine Curtis Company. At the time, she was hailed as a "pioneer of women producers … one of the few women in the industry's history who has actively directed a motion picture producing company. Stars and other women own their companies, but their connection with executive affairs is seldom as intimate as that of Miss Curtis."[16] A "New York society girl"[17] educated at New York University, Curtis' career in film began when she met author Harold Bell Wright in Arizona, and he cast her in his 1919 movie adaptation of his novel *The Shepherd of the Hills*.[18] Despite being "heavily backed by New York capitalists"[19] and announcing "three Ralph Connor pictures to come from the company in quick succession,"[20] *The Sky Pilot* would be the only film project completed by the Cathrine Curtis Company. Lawsuits regarding rights to adapt of Sir Arthur Conan Doyle's *The Lost World*[21] and a B.P. Schulberg production called *The First Year*[22] preceded an announcement of Curtis declaring bankruptcy in 1924.[23] After a couple of unsuccessful attempts to re-enter the film world, Curtis found fame and notoriety as a reactionary political voice in the 1930s with her short-lived radio program, "Women and Money," and her activist group, the Women Investors Research Institute, "a unique blend of anti–New Deal conservatism and advocacy for women's rights."[24] Glen Jeansonne summed up Curtis as "an isolationist who fused fascist propaganda with maternalism, feminism, and rabid nationalism."[25] In hindsight, Curtis' financial problems should have come as no surprise. Despite all of her New York connections, "halfway through [*The Sky Pilot*], the money ran out." Vidor's autobiography describes having to use all of his own available money to continue the production, and eventually "we had to beg the cast and the crew to finish the film without salary."[26]

The Sky Pilot was based on a novel of the same name by Ralph Connor, and adapted for the screen by Faith Green (who penned several subsequent Connor adaptations, though not for Curtis or Vidor). The titular character is Arthur Moore, a preacher who arrives in the Canadian frontier town of Swan's Creek looking to start his own church. His first sermon is in the local saloon, which ends with a fist-fight between Moore and Ashley Ranch foreman Bill Hendricks. The two men reconcile, and Moore is hired at the Ashley Ranch. After being ambushed by rustlers, Moore falls into the river and is rescued by Gwen, Hendricks' love interest. Gwen's father is secretly involved with the rustlers. Later, she is injured in a cattle stampede and paralyzed. Moore stops the rustlers' plot, and in retaliation they burn his newly constructed church. Gwen's mobility is restored in time to save Moore from the burning building before it collapses and the two are wed.

In the role of Arthur Moore was John Bowers, a silent-era star who did not successfully transition to sound and committed suicide in 1936 at age 50, in the Pacific Ocean (a possible inspiration for Norman Maine in 1937's *A Star Is Born*). As Bill Hendricks, Vidor cast David Butler; this was his third film with Vidor following *The Other Half* and *Better Times*. The most interesting casting was 22-year-old Colleen Moore as Gwen. Moore is better remembered today for her slapstick charm and her expressive face in films such as *Ella Cinders* (1926), where her facial contortions as she reads an acting manual still stand as one of the pinnacles of silent-era comedy. Here, Moore delivers a strikingly different and unexpected performance. Her entrance is unforgettable—standing upright in a wagon hitched to a pack of galloping horses, the reins gripped tight in her hands, she exudes an untamed, pure spirit and wild exuberance. She is a frontier-toughened woman, and through the film Moore delivers a very physical performance, whether it is riding horses, saving Arthur from the river, or crawling through the snow combating her paralysis.

The Sky Pilot exemplifies the best and worst of Vidor's early style: Vidor's compositions and his use of non-studio locations are astonishingly beautiful, and there is a sense of epic grandeur absent from previous films. (While set in Canada, most of the film was shot in Truckee, California, with interiors filmed in Los Angeles at Vidor Village. Vidor's autobiography details the frustrations of filming in Truckee, when premature snowfall interrupted their shooting schedule, forcing them to shovel clear the sets; later, when snow was needed, they were forced to resort to using table salt to create the illusion of winter.)[27] The narrative, on the other hand, still exhibits an excess of melodrama at odds with the naturalistic tendencies of many scenes, and Vidor's reliance on Christian Science for plot resolution once again compromises the realism and believability of the story in the name of didacticism.

The opening sequence is an eloquent example of poetic montage that illustrates Eisenstein's theory of dialectical montage (several years before Eisenstein first published his essay, "A Dialectic Approach to Film Form").[28] In musical terms, the introduction is broken down into three separate movements, each with its own tone, tempo, and melody. True to montage theory, it is the combination of all of the shots through editing that provides a meaning greater than the individual shots. The first movement begins with several shots of nature; beginning with an extreme long shot of a mountain, the camera remains still; it is the editing that moves, with each successive shot bringing us deeper into the valley until we reach the stream—the pathway to civilization, the essence of life (much like the opening metaphor of *The Jack-Knife Man*). And like *The Jack-Knife Man*, it is moving water that is the first sign of movement—of life—in Vidor's film. In Eisensteinian terms, this would be the "thesis."

In the second movement, Vidor presents the "antithesis": a montage of shots outside and inside of Swan Creek's saloon, "The Stopping Place," or, as an intertitle describes it, "the cut-bank of destruction." Instead of a sequence edited for continuity, Vidor offers a fragmented succession of scenes that present the overall environment and take us on a journey deep into "civilization," just as the opening images took us deeper into "nature": cowboys on horseback shooting up the ground (so much for respecting nature); a wide shot of the dimly-lit interior; a close shot with the camera looking straight down the bar, disembodied hands reaching through the crowded frames for their drinks; a close shot of a group of eager men around a dice table reaching to handle their bets; a high-angle shot of a faro game in progress.

Finally, the third movement begins with this intertitle: "Into this little frontier settlement, primitive, godless—came a stranger—from beyond the waving skyline of the foothills." This is the "synthesis" Eisenstein described. There is a low-angle, canted shot with dark clouds on top and dark ground on the bottom, with a slanted tree trunk obscuring the left-hand side of the frame and its branches covering the top. The darkness is in stark contrast to the bright, wide-open shots of this landscape in the first movement. The shadowy tone seemingly has more in common with the interior of the Stopping Place—a sign that the "destruction" of that enclave is spreading into, and corrupting, the purity of nature. The only light is a burst of sunshine in the middle of the frame. Into this spot rides a man on a mule, backlit against the sky. It is as though he is riding on light sent down from the heavens.

Though these are only the establishing shots used to inform the audience of the primary locations and to introduce the protagonist, Vidor already exhibits his sophisticated cinematic palette, one that is equally adept at exterior location shooting as well as interior studio-bound sets. Furthermore, he uses elements within the frame, as well as montage methods, to convey themes and ideas. The lessons learned from his previous films are on full display in this opening sequence.

The centerpiece of *The Sky Pilot* is the stampede. This spectacle is a result of two tendencies of cinema—one, the montage method, as described above—and realism, the actual experience captured on celluloid. The sequence alternates fragmented bits of action contrasting long shots and closeups of frantic cattle, dogs running loose, cowboys and their horses circling the steers. Much of this is real, and there is a thrill that much of the footage is, indeed, authentic. Parts of it, of course, are faked—montage masks some of the artifice, such as the dummy used for Gwen, and sped-up frame rates create an artificially frenetic pace. What is most surprising about this scene is not the technical mastery, but its sheer dynamism. To think that only a year earlier Vidor had made *The Jack-Knife Man* and published his "Pledge"; while he had stayed true to his moral convictions, his cinematic worldview had grown from modest, character-driven stories to a larger-than-life adventure epic. This would become a key tension in Vidor's artistry: the intimate vs. the epic. Vidor never reconciled these two tendencies and, as with David Lean, these two qualities would characterize his films for the rest of his career.

Critics responded positively to *The Sky Pilot*. "A great box office picture. It is delightfully human, has a clever comedy relief and an unusual stampede thrill," wrote *Exhibitors Herald*. "In *The Sky Pilot*, First National has about the best outdoor picture that has been released in many a day."[29] The stampede was singled out in many a review: "The best thrill of the year, being free of trickery so far as the layman can tell," wrote Burns Mantle in *Photoplay*.[30] "Some fine thrills, particularly the stampede scene which is the best thing in *The Sky Pilot*. ... The photography in this spot is certainly excellent, closeups of the girl showing the shadows of the stampeding animals, upon her prostrate form. This scene recalls the stampede sequence in Universal's *Lasca* but Vidor's is equally well done and perhaps a trifle more thrilling," wrote *Wid's Daily*.[31] *Variety* was critical of the Christian Science message: "The story contains little new or exceptional, but the direction, photography and detail are more than satisfactory. The story runs consistently with plenty of action interspersed with comedy and leads to a satisfactory conclusion. However, the uplift lesson—that sufficient faith will nearly cure all physical ills—is rather far-fetched."[32]

Vidor's other feature of 1921, *Love Never Dies*, was his first under his new deal with Associated Producers. "They are affording me perfect freedom in the selection of vehicles and casts, and I am not to be limited in expenditures; in this latter respect, I will be enabled to secure casts that are all-star in the truest sense," Vidor said in *Motion Picture News*. "This is in accordance with the Associated Producer policy of allowing each man his own individual art expression."[33] In only two years, Vidor had risen from a nobody struggling to get his first film financed to a top Hollywood director, and nothing signaled this more than his colleagues at Associated, a veritable who's-who of great directors, including Marshall Neilan, Maurice Tourneur, Allan Dwan, and Thomas Ince, who had this to say about Associated's newest talent: "King Vidor has proven conclusively that he is a director of power, scope and humanness. Those of his pictures which I have seen have always impressed me by their poesy, artistry and purity of sentiment."[34]

Love Never Dies was scripted by Vidor himself and based on William Nathaniel Harben's 1919 novel *The Cottage of Delight*. The story concerns John Trott, an aspiring architect whose mother was a prostitute. While working on a project in another town, he falls in love with Tilly Whaley, and they are wed. When Tilly's father learns about John's mother, he forces his daughter to leave her husband. Unaware that Tilly still loves him, John and his sister leave town on a train. When the train crashes, John falsely claims that the two of them died; they assume new identities and start new lives. Years later, John returns to find Tilly married to Joel. Realizing the two are still in love, Joel throws himself in the river. John is unable to save Joel's life. John and Tilly are remarried, and it is revealed that John's mother is not really his mother after all.

Reuniting with Vidor for the first (and last) time was Lloyd Hughes, who had played Paul Perry in *The Turn in the Road*, and who here plays John Trott; Hughes would go on to co-star in *Ella Cinders* (coincidentally, with the star of Vidor's previous film, Colleen Moore) and *The Lost World* (1925) (also coincidentally, the adaptation Cathrine Curtis failed to produce), ending his career in the 1930s appearing in low-budget action-adventure B movies. In the role of Tilly is Madge Bellamy, one of her earliest starring roles, and her highest profile film to date. Bellamy would go on to work with some of the most prestigious directors in Hollywood in the 1920s, acting in Maurice Tourneur's *Lorna Doone* (1922), John Ford's *The Iron Horse* (1924) and *Lightnin'* (1925), and Frank Borzage's *Lazybones* (1925); however, her career did not transition to sound, save for the cult horror favorite *White Zombie* (1932) with Bela Lugosi. Also returning to work for Vidor was Lillian Leighton, who had played Widow Potter in *The Jack-Knife Man* and who here plays Mrs. Cavanaugh, the town busybody. The film's cinematographer was Max Dupont, whose name had previously been attached to the *Mothercraft* project.

After the Canadian wilderness setting (filmed in California) of *The Sky Pilot*, Vidor returned to familiar territory in *Love Never Dies*, setting the story in the quaint, small town American milieu that was the backdrop for so many of his films up to this point. The story drops the genre-specific thrills that were exhibited in his previous movie in favor of something more intimate. Charles Silver sees this not only as a continuation of Vidor's previous films, but also as an homage to the man Vidor watched at work during his earliest days in Hollywood. "*Love Never Dies*, like *The Jack-Knife Man* ... shows D.W. Griffith exerting a marked influence over the young King Vidor. This is a film very much in the tradition of Griffith's rural southern melodramas such as *True Heart Susie* and *A Romance of Happy Valley*," observes Silver. "It remains a very personal film dealing with one of Vidor's favorite themes, social ostracism."[35]

Griffith's influence on *Love Never Dies* is evident both in its visuals and its characterizations. In the opening sequence, Liz Trott's roommate, Jane Holder, threatens to reveal the secret of her motherhood to John if she does not give her money. Liz complies and Jane tucks the cash into her bosom. The latter is the sort of lusty, demonized gesture that had been absent from Vidor's previous films—he was never one to pass judgment so quickly on his characters, nor to view them with such hardline morality—but could easily have been in a Griffith film. In the film's second sequence, Tilly is introduced with a closeup, leafy branches surrounding her head, and light beaming off her curly hair like a halo, very reminiscent of the way that Griffith and his cinematographer, Billy Bitzer, would frequently photograph Lillian Gish. *Love Never Dies*' climactic river rescue finish also owes a great debt to Griffith's *Way Down East* (1920), released the previous year, and which concluded with a similar, much grander stunt.

Love Never Dies is at its best when Vidor slows the tempo down—such as when Tilly is outside her new home, kneeling in the dirt planting seeds, and she is interrupted by John's tomboyish sister Dora, leaning over the fence and sticking out her tongue. Vidor lovingly films both characters, reveling in homespun delight as Dora introduces Tilly to her headless doll, Sally. The rural locations—front porches, white picket fences, dirt roads, and community picnics—are as evocatively rendered as anything in Vidor's early films. What drags the film down, however, is the script—another example of Vidor's over-reliance on Christian Science's theme of "love conquers all" to conclude the plot quickly and conveniently. It is interesting to see that as Vidor grew more grandiose visually—exerting more precision and eliciting more poetry with his compositions and editing—his narratives suffered. Out of all of his early features, *The Jack-Knife Man* was still the most subtle and successful, neither lapsing into melodrama nor contrivance. It is as though Vidor was searching for any story that could match the images he wanted to create, and between the rustic Americana locations and the train crash and river rescue spectacles, in *Love Never Dies* Vidor was able to convey both the intimate and the epic experiences that are at the core of his style.

The film had a mixed reception. As was becoming typical, critics responded well to Vidor's direction, but less so to the scenarios. "Cannot be said to represent Mr. Vidor at his best because the realities striven for are marred occasionally by a faulty continuity," commented Laurence Reid in *Motion Picture News*: "The director is strong for the simple virtues of love and faith and he manages to express them even when the plot carries illogical treatment. ... King Vidor has gotten away from simple standards to add a couple of melodramatic touches."[36] *Exhibitors Trade Review* reacted similarly: "While the element of human interest is not altogether lacking in this picture, its melodramatic phases are stressed to the extent of absurdity and turn into sheer burlesque. The result is that frequently where the well-meaning director intended to create pathos, a humor angle is developed instead, which raises havoc with the serious trend of the plot."[37] And *Moving Picture World* commented: "As full of inconsistencies as it is of melodrama.... It is almost inconceivable that King Vidor, director of the wonderful 'Sky Pilot,' handled the megaphone for this picture."[38]

Vidor completely neglects *Love Never Dies* in his autobiography. Perhaps it was an oversight, he had nothing interesting to say about it, or perhaps he just wanted the film to be forgotten. In any event, Vidor offered no insight into his own interest in the film or his intentions. It was his eighth feature film in three years. Vidor was a busy man—and he was showing no signs of slowing down, as the next year would show.

FOUR

1922–1923
Rising and Falling Stars

The Woman of Bronze, Three Wise Fools, The Real Adventure, Dusk to Dawn, Conquering the Woman, and *Peg O' My Heart*

In 1922 Vidor completed three more films under the agreement with Associated (following *Love Never Dies*): *The Real Adventure, Dusk to Dawn,* and *Conquering the Woman,* as well as *Peg O' My Heart* as part of a new arrangement for Metro. Unfortunately, not all these films are accessible. *Dusk to Dawn* is considered lost. While *The Real Adventure* is in the Cinémathèque de Toulouse and *Conquering the Woman* at the Cinematheque Royale de Belgique, neither has been widely circulated or made available on home video; *Peg O' My Heart,* while not commercially distributed, has appeared on TCM. These four films are particularly interesting because they are drastically divergent from the works Vidor had been producing. Nineteen twenty-two showcased the other side of Vidor—the journeyman who, occasionally, had to turn out commercial products. Instead of the wholesome, moral parables set in rural America, these films were set in worlds that the characters of *The Jack-Knife Man* could never dream of seeing—New York City, India, Ireland, England, and the South Seas. These new surroundings also allowed Vidor the opportunity to explore new types of stories—metaphysical dramas, cosmopolitan adventures, and high society satires. They also showcased yet another Vidor, Florence, whose stardom by this point had matched—if not eclipsed—King's own.

Florence had been working steadily as an actress since the couple's arrival in Hollywood in 1915 and had even co-starred in Cecil B. DeMille's *Old Wives for New* and *Till I Come Back for You* in 1918. From 1919 to 1920, Florence appeared exclusively in her husband's movies—*The Other Half, Poor Relations, The Family Honor,* and *The Jack-Knife Man*. In 1921 she began a contract with Associated Producers that would elevate her status and change her image. Unlike the roles given to her by her husband, Associated changed Florence's image by casting her in more contemporary stories and emphasizing her characters' strength, independence, and modern mores. In the first of these films, *Lying Lips* (1921), Florence played a high society woman caught between her engagement to a man of her class and her love of a Canadian rancher. While the film received mediocre notices, Florence was singled out: "She is attractive in appearance, but more than that her personality is not easily forgotten."[1] In *Beau Revel* (1921), she played "the hostess of a smart dancing club" who is trapped by a father who disapproves of her relationship with his son. Next, in *Hail the Woman* (1921), she played a young woman whose defiance results in her being kicked out of her home by her "grim and bigoted New England father."[2] This proved to be her breakthrough role: "Florence Vidor Reaches Stardom: Featured Player of *Hail the Woman* Has First Stellar Role in Associated Exhibitors Production."[3] In her next film, *Woman, Wake Up!* (1922), she played a wife whose husband has been spending too much time at "the cabarets," so she "takes a dancing course, acquires a lot of new gowns and proceeds to give him a taste of his own medicine."[4]

The ascendency of Florence Vidor as a star—and the character and story types associated with her image—helps explain the sudden shift in her husband's film style over his next three productions, which would feature Florence in leading roles and continue the trajectory of her previous films, highlighting her acting talents and image as a modern, liberated woman. Florence and King's first film together for Associated was *The Real Adventure* (1922). Scripted by Mildred Considine and based on a novel of the same name by Henry Kitchell Webster, the narrative seems tailor made to Florence's star persona and, judging from the synopsis, appears to be a rehashing of *Woman, Wake Up!*, being another story of a dissatisfied wife, Rose Aldrich, who leaves her husband, Rodney, and heads to the big city to start her own life and make him jealous. Arriving in New York City, she gets a job as a chorus girl and works her way up to being a celebrated costume designer. Ziegfeld offers her a job, but she turns it down to reunite with Rodney after he admits his mistake and the two are reconciled.[5]

The premise of the story is decidedly un–Vidorian, and absent are his invested interests in community, spiritual strength, natural wonder, and love-conquers-all optimism. Instead, the synopsis sounds petty and bland, and merely an excuse to revel in the glamour of the theatrical world. According to reviews, Vidor's direction is likewise vapid and superficial: "The picture abounds in gorgeous scenic effects—strikingly impressive exteriors, such as the snow scenes on Bear Mountain, California, and wonderfully attractive interior sets, as the predominant atmosphere throughout is one of wealth and beauty. There is a display of chic and beautiful gowns which is certain to delight the heart of every woman."[6] *Moving Picture World* praises the movie for its "elements of popular appeal, such as incidents behind the scenes of a musical comedy rehearsal and a wide variety of stunning gowns worn by the chief player."[7]

Like *The Real Adventure*, *Dusk to Dawn* (1922) was not scripted by Vidor, and it is another atypical exercise lacking his characteristic concerns. Adapted from Katherine Hill's novel, *The Shuttle Soul*, and scripted by Frank Howard Clark (a prolific B-western scribe in the late 1920s and early 1930s), the story is about a woman who believes she is two different people with the same soul: Marjorie Lathrop, an American girl whose brother is accused of forgery; and Aziza, a beggar in India. Marjorie is unable to marry the man she loves because, in her alternate life, Aziza has married the Rajah. Marjorie's brother goes missing, but as Aziza she discovers him hiding in India. In the end, the Rajah is killed by a lion, and Aziza sacrifices herself, freeing Marjorie to marry the man she loves after she has proved her brother's innocence.[8] The plot is wild and audacious enough to make the miracle recovery at the conclusion of *The Sky Pilot* seem plausible. Reviews confirm that the film is nothing more than a star vehicle for Florence, who plays both Marjorie and Aziza ("In each case, she is worthy of praise") and an excuse for exotic scenery ("Replete with lavish settings…").[9]

Their third collaboration of 1922 was *Conquering the Woman*, another piece of hokum from screenwriter Frank Howard Clark, this time based on "Kidnapping Coline" by Henry C. Rowland, a serialized novel from the pages *Everybody's Magazine* from 1913 to 1914. On a trip to France, Judith became engaged to a count. Back in New York, her father disapproves and arranges to have her kidnapped and abandoned on a South Seas island with his choice of a suitor. When the count arrives on the island to rescue her, she realizes she is in love with the suitor her father selected.[10] The character of Judith seems like a step backward for Florence, whose previous characters extolled female independence and embraced their partaking of the pleasures of contemporary life. Here, the female protagonist is reduced to a sex object for men to barter and smuggle like contraband. Likewise, the film is a regressive move for King Vidor. His authorial voice has been stifled, and his eye for natural compositions and their spiritual splendor has been reduced to picturesque background shots. "A nice variety of locale," reported *The Film Daily*. "Vidor's scenes of a seaside resort in France give the picture an interesting start with Miss Vidor aquaplaning and swimming. The island life is nicely pictured, showing hero and heroine enjoying the comforts arranged for their enforced isolation. There are numerous attractive marine shots…."[11] The island footage appears to anticipate yet another atypical Vidor film, *Bird of Paradise* (1932), especially the mention of a swimming sequence, which would be repeated in the later film with Dolores Del Rio.

Having completed *The Real Adventure*, *Dusk to Dawn*, and *Conquering the Woman*, King Vidor's career was seemingly at an all-time low. He could not afford to keep Vidor Village open. Furthermore, the high ideals he espoused in "A Creed and Pledge" had all but disappeared from his past three movies. So much for his belief "in the motion picture that carries a message to humanity," and his promise to "not knowingly produce a picture that contains anything I do not believe to be absolutely true to human nature."[12] While his early films may have been clouded at times by his belief in Christian Science, at least there was conviction in his faith and sincerity in the films' shared hope for a better, kinder, and more loving world. Vidor appears to have phoned in all three productions, investing none of himself in any of them. Perhaps the answer to his neglect lies in the strained relationship of husband

and wife, who were now competing as director and star. Vidor remarked on the end of their collaboration in his autobiography: "Florence Vidor's career had gone forward so steadily that she was beginning to be known as 'the first lady of the screen.' ... Somewhere along the roads of our divergent professional interests could be found the cause of our estranged personal relationship and subsequent divorce. With the benefit of such a warm and human beginning, it seemed as if our marriage could stand the severest test. Perhaps it was the toll exacted by the professions we had chosen."[13]

Eight years earlier, King and Florence's relationship began when he wanted her for a role and her family refused. Now, in 1923, after traveling cross-country and embarking on simultaneous film careers, the couple had made their last movie together. Two years later, on July 8, 1925, a notice would appear in the pages of *Variety*, declaring their divorce official: "Florence Vidor has been granted a divorce from King Vidor, picture director, and also awarded the custody of their daughter, Suzanne. Mrs. Vidor asked for no alimony, declaring she is capable of supporting herself. In her testimony she stated that her husband told her that 'the bonds of matrimony interfered with his business and artistic career.'"[14]

Vidor's last project of 1922 was the beginning of a new stage in his career. According to his memoir, he was broke and needed money to keep Vidor Village in operation. In light of how his marriage to Florence was dissolving and how his Associated productions had turned into support for her career instead of furthering his own, perhaps he was also seeking his own independence, or at least new opportunities. Vidor was selected to direct the first film adaptation of J. Hartley Manners' play *Peg O' My Heart*. The production was highly anticipated, as its famed star, Laurette Taylor—husband of Manners—was to make her big screen debut reprising the stage role that originally was written for her. Peg's mother was banished from her high society English family when she married an Irishman. Peg's mother dies and her father raises her on a small farm. Later, she learns that her estranged uncle has died and arranged for her to be educated back in England at the family estate. Unbeknownst to her, the uncle also left money to the family—money they badly need now that they are bankrupt—on the condition that they reform Peg. The family is resentful of Peg, and she refuses to curb her wild, rambunctious ways. She falls in love with her neighbor, Gerald, under the impression that he is a farmer; when he reveals that he is actually royalty, she leaves England for Ireland. Gerald follows, and the two lovers are reconciled.

Vidor accepted the assignment but was dismayed at first: "When I was given a copy of the play, I was shocked to find that all the action took place in a single set. I wondered how so much stage talk could be transformed into motion-picture action." His mood worsened when he was also handed an already completed script, which he considered "terribly static and non-filmic." Conferences with Manners and Taylor, who were keenly involved with the conversion from stage to screen, allowed Vidor to help shape the visual element of the production. "Whenever they talked about 'outside' action, I planned to transpose this into a photographic scene."[15] He would face a similar struggle when adapting *Street Scene* in 1931; however, the lessons learned from *Peg* would allow Vidor to produce a much more cinematic, fluid and mobile film from the theatrical work.

Despite Vidor's efforts, the final cut of *Peg O' My Heart* bears evidence of his frustration. Certain moments are very dynamic, such as the opening and closing sequences in rural Ireland, rendered with all the warmth and intimacy as any of Vidor's American small towns (Peg even hangs off the picket fence, recalling the little sister in *Love Never Dies*). Even the confines of the one-room shack where Peg and her family live manage to inspire Vidor to overcome the spatial limitations through editing: a wide shot of family harmony, Peg playing, mother in bed, and father by her side; closeups of each of their faces, the visual isolation revealing a hidden sorrow beneath their faces; a return to the same wide shot as before, that now seems more desperate and forlorn than earlier; and finally a medium closeup of mother and father who, without the presence of Peg, seem more like husband and wife, and their tender glances and caresses epitomize Vidor's human touch. The most Vidorian moment during Peg's time in England is, not coincidentally, the scene where Peg escapes the confines of the family estate and sneaks into Gerald's apple orchard next door: Peg gets caught stealing and is chased into the bushes by Gerald, culminating with the two of them eating apples, a euphemistic gesture at once naïve yet highly erotic. The moment is also notable for being the earliest sexual moment between two characters in a Vidor film. There was plenty of love in previous movies (and many that ended in marriage), but always of the purest and most sexless kind. There is no trace of sexuality between Peter Lane and Widow Turner in *The Jack-Knife Man*, and despite the title of *Love Never Dies*, John and Tilly seem neutered—these films show a spiritual kind of love, nothing physical or pleasurable. But when Peg and Gerald bite into the apple and look into each other's eyes, it is a Biblical moment whose subtext is undeniable.

The bulk of the film, unfortunately, occurs indoors, and Vidor clearly feels stifled. The shots inside the English mansion are frequently framed to emphasize the enormity of the set, including two flights of stairs, or to squeeze both the floor and chandelier in the same image. It is as though Vidor was instructed to show off the budget in every shot. The sort of intimate yet dynamic interplay with Peg and her family achieved through editing in the opening sequence is never equaled in the English sequences. Too often, it is the just the same static frame, organized and choreographed like a stage play, interrupted by intertitles. Try as he might, Vidor was never able to fully divorce *Peg O' My Heart* from its theatrical origins, and the film is still very text-based.

While Taylor's acting debut was almost universally praised in the press, Vidor's direction was often criticized for the reasons he feared. A critical roundup in *The Film Daily* included the following excerpts: "Laurette Taylor's screen Peg is one of the most vivid and amusing light comedy performances we can remember ... but somewhere in the making of the picture, King Vidor, or someone, did something, or failed to do something, which reduced the pretty stage play to uneven, just pretty fair picture stuff" (*Morning World*). "Vidor's direction on the whole is pleasing, although here and there it smacks of a little screen hokum" (*Daily News*). "So it is not a distinctly cinematographic piece that has come out of the adaptation. The screen version is rather a transliteration of the play" (*Times*).[16]

Whatever shortcomings the film had, both Manners and Taylor were pleased enough with the results to select Vidor to make a film of another of their stage successes, *Happiness*, in 1924. In November 1922, Vidor was announced to be the director of an adaptation of Booth Tarkington's Penrod stories. The film was to be produced by Vidor's old partners, the Brentwood Corporation.[17] Ultimately released as *Penrod and Sam* (1923), the film wound up being directed by William Beaudine (*Sparrows* [1926]), an absurdly prolific director of 372 credits whose career (1915–1976) almost rivals Vidor's own, and produced by J.K. McDonald Productions with distribution from Associated First National Pictures.

As a result of the success of *Peg O' My Heart*, both in terms of its translation from stage to screen and in preserving the star status of its lead actress, Laurette Taylor, 1923 found King Vidor involved with two productions with similar motivations. The first was *The Woman of Bronze* (1923), an independently produced movie intended to resurrect the fading popularity of its star, Clara Kimball Young. The play, written by Henry Kistemaekers, was adapted by husband and wife team Louis D. Lighton and Hope Loring (together, they later scripted *Fig Leaves* [1926] for Howard Hawks; Clara Bow's most iconic film, *It* [1927]; and William Wellman's aviation masterpiece, *Wings* [1927]). Young was to recreate the leading role, in "which the noted stage actress, Margaret Anglin, appeared with marked success on Broadway."[18]

As the saying goes, Young was "born in a trunk" on September 6, 1890, to parents who were traveling actors. Young made her own debut at age three. In 1909, she switched to the big screen and began appearing in films by Vitagraph. She became one of the most popular actresses of the 1910s, appearing in roughly 100 movies that decade, including Maurice Tourneur's *Trilby* (1915). She was also the subject of a highly publicized scandal, an affair with Lewis J. Selznick that ended in divorce from actor James Young. Selznick created a company especially for Young; however, their relationship soon soured, the films did increasingly poorly at the box office, and the company disbanded. In 1922, Samuel Zierler—president of the Commonwealth Film Corporation, a film distributor for the New York and New Jersey area—created his own film company, the Samuel Zierler Photoplay Corporation, whose intent was to profit from the remnants of Young's popularity. It was announced that Zierler's company would produce eight movies per year—five with Clara, and three other "all-star subjects."[19] Just which stars and subjects is unknown, as the business venture folded after the completion of the first five Young films: *The Hands of Nara* (1922), *Enter Madame* (1922), *The Woman of Bronze* (1923), *Cordelia the Magnificent* (1923) and *A Wife's Romance* (1923). Zierler returned to distribution, while Young made two more silent features before retreating to vaudeville and the stage where she had started. She returned to feature films in the 1930s as a lead in B-pictures.

Young plays Vivian, the devoted wife of a sculptor, Leonard. Competing for a million-dollar prize, Leonard begins a new work with a model, Sylvia Morton. An affair develops between artist and model. Vivian takes Leonard on a second honeymoon but cannot get him to lose his desire for Sylvia. Back home, Leonard destroys the statue and runs away. After being missing for months, Leonard returns to find the statue complete, having been reassembled by his mentor at Vivian's request. He begs forgiveness, but Vivian refuses and leaves for Italy. Leonard follows her there, and the couple is reunited.[20] Another script that Vidor did not write, its story lacks his characteristic motifs, and without a surviving print to view, it is hard to know what visual touches he brought to a melodrama whose action seems decidedly stage-bound. Contemporaneous reviews reveal very little. Mary Kelly found the film "effectively screened" except for Young's "tendency to overact."[21] *Exhibitors Trade Review* seemed to agree with Kelly: "King Vidor has directed the feature skillfully, it is handsomely photographed and serves as an excellent vehicle for demonstrating the emotional ability of the star, Clara Kimball Young."[22] On the other hand, *Exhibitors Herald* thought it was "quite a disappointment.... Neither the star nor the director seems to have grasped the spirit of the stage play from which it was adapted. It fails utterly to stir you to the emotional heights expected and lacks the dramatic punch or conviction necessary to put it over." The anonymous reviewer then proceeds to single out nearly every single cast member as being particularly unworthy.[23] Vidor himself completely neglects the film in his memoir, which suggests that it was either inconsequential or embarrassing enough to exclude.

Vidor's second production of that year, however, was anything but inconsequential. It introduced him to the woman who would become the second Mrs. Vidor, Eleanor Boardman. However, the union would not be made official until 1926. *Three Wise Fools* (1923) was Vidor's first project under his new contract to Goldwyn. "King Vidor has been placed under a long-term contract at Goldwyn to direct specials," announced *The Film Daily*. While this gave Vidor a renewed sense of stability in his career, it also marked the end of his own era of independence: "In view of the Goldwyn contract Vidor has given Sol Lesser an option on his studio."[24] Rumored to have cost "a quarter of a million dollars,"[25] the sale was finalized in March 1923 as Lesser's Principal Pictures Corporation took control of the Vidor Village.[26] The loss of his private studio signaled a change in Vidor's career—as he became more famous and more desirable to studios, he was able to climb the industry ladder and ascend to productions with bigger budgets and bigger stars; however, this alienated him from the more personal, modest, star-less films that he aspired to make. This tension between commercialism and Vidor's own film philosophy is present throughout his career. In a way, that is how he was able to afford such longevity—nearly seven decades—in an industry that is notorious for chewing up and spitting out those with ambition, as well as to navigate so many changes in technology and the economy.

Based on the play by Austin Strong, *Three Wise Fools* gave Vidor the opportunity to work with celebrated screenwriter June Mathis. Mathis began on the stage but found her success as one of the silent screen's most respected and influential writers. Among her most famous films are *The Four Horseman of the Apocalypse* (1921) and *The Conquering Power* (1921), both directed by Rex Ingram and starring Rudolph Valentino; *Blood and Sand* (1922), another Valentino vehicle directed by Fred Niblo; and Erich von Stroheim's mammoth *Greed* (1924). Mathis' career was unfortunately cut short by a fatal heart attack in 1927; she was only 40.

While *Three Wise Fools* was intended to recreate its original stage success—incorporating several of the original cast members, including Claude Gillingwater as one of the titular "wise fools"[27]—the film was also intended to make a star out of one of Goldwyn's newest actresses, Eleanor Boardman, who was just finishing work on Rupert Hughes' *Souls for Sale* when Vidor caught sight of her on set. It was love at first sight—almost, as he has already seen "her picture above a soda fountain—a girl in a striped summer dress standing on top of a hill, her legs surrounded almost to the knees by a stand of wheat, her long hair blown by the wind, and the contours of her body following the undulations of the wheatfield. The picture was a large advertisement for the Eastman Kodak Company."[28] Modeling for Kodak was just the start for Boardman, who was working her way up from featured supporting roles in *The Strangers' Banquet* (1922), *Gimme* (1923), and *Vanity Fair* (1923).

A scene from *Three Wise Fools* (1923, directed by King Vidor for Goldwyn Pictures). From left: Claude Gillingwater (as Theodore Findley), William H. Crane (as the Honorable James Trumbull), Eleanor Boardman (as Rena Fairchild/Sydney Fairfield), and Alec B. Francis (as Dr. Richard Gaunt) (Goldwyn Distributing Corporation/Photofest).

The *Three Wise Fools* of the title are a trio of older bachelors who share the unrequited love of the same woman. Her dying wish is for all three to care for her baby. Assuming that it is a little boy, they are surprised to discover it is a blossoming young woman (Boardman). When her father escapes from prison, she is wrongfully accused as an accessory. Ultimately, she and her father are proven innocent of the crimes, and Sydney marries the nephew of one of her guardians.[29] Mathis' script reportedly remained faithful to the stage play, while allowing Vidor to give it a more cinematic flourish. "King Vidor has reproduced the atmosphere, comedy and romance with great success, and elaborated considerably on the suspense angle." As with the train wreck in *Love Never Dies*, Vidor seems to have added spectacle to an otherwise sedentary melodrama. "The prisoners' escape is a big thrill, an aeroplane giving chase to a speed car, in effective scenes that have been added to the original play."[30]

Three Wise Fools is also notable for Vidor's musical direction. While it was common for productions to have either phonographs or live musicians on set to provide atmosphere to the actors, Vidor heard—and saw—in music a cinematic tempo, a visual movement within the frame and between the cuts. It is a technique that he famously perfected in *The Big Parade*; here is one of its earliest iterations. As Vidor stated in his autobiography, "I had been greatly impressed by some of D.W. Griffith's chase sequences and I decided to plan this one on a definite musical crescendo to increase the excitement with each cut of the pursued and pursuers. I selected suitable bits and pieces of symphonic recordings whose tempo seemed to fit the particular action I had in mind. Then, sitting by a phonograph with a metronome, I established the selected beat and noted it opposite the scene on a margin of the script. I gradually advanced the metronomic setting until the action increased in speed, building to a climax."[31]

After two years of struggling with alien material that he did not write and that did not reflect his own ethos, and that was overly indebted to theater, *Three Wise Fools* found Vidor back on track, contributing to the writing and expressing himself cinematically. The following year would be a big one for him, including five feature-length movies, beginning with one that might be considered his second masterwork after *The Jack-Knife Man*: *Wild Oranges* (1924).

Five

1924

Personality Crisis

> "I read Hergesheimer's novel [*Wild Oranges*] three times to acquaint myself thoroughly with the characters before ever attempting a screen adaptation of the story.... The plot is extremely important, but it should not be so distorted that it appears ridiculous on the screen. Next to the plot comes the importance of the characters. The people must be interesting and human."[1]—King Vidor, 1923

Wild Oranges

After *The Turn of the Road* and *The Jack-Knife Man*, Vidor seemed to be on a contradictory trajectory: the more established he became, the budgets became bigger and the projects more high-profile; however, these came at the expense of his own vision. It was a personality crisis: the very qualities which made him celebrated were not often exercised. Through both choice and professional circumstance, Vidor had wanted to be a commercial director, albeit one with distinctly personal morals and visuals, and as a result had taken projects intended to advance his industry standpoint, presumably with the end result of more creative freedom. Up until this point, however, this had resulted mostly in compromised productions that, while popular, did not fully allow the director to explore his own artistic impulses. Vidor's career might have been on the rise, but the quality of the pictures—at least in terms of authorship—had been declining since 1920.

Nineteen twenty-four was a crucial year for Vidor, his busiest by far, with five completed features and one that was planned but never filmed; it also was the year that re-established his own personal artistic imprint with one film, and cemented his commercial status with the others.

Wild Oranges (1924) is unquestionably Vidor's second masterpiece, following *The Jack-Knife Man*. A chamber drama with limited locations (the boat, the house, and the surrounding swamp) and only five characters, it is a tightly knit gothic thriller. It is also a leap forward in terms of characterization, as it is arguably the first psychological narrative in Vidor's filmography, focusing on characters who exist beyond didactic philosophy and moral principle. It is also notable for its sexuality, a disturbed perversion of repression, desire, and violence, that far exceeds the naive flirtations and Biblical fruit metaphors of *Peg O' My Heart*. Furthermore, the film allowed Vidor to return to his beloved outdoors, shooting on location in the Georgia swamplands outside of Savannah.

Based on a novel by Joseph Hergesheimer, Vidor adapted the story with editorial direction from the great June Mathis (who had previously worked with Vidor on *Three Wise Fools*). *Wild Oranges* tells the story of widower John Woolfolk (Frank Mayo), who takes to the seas for three years after the death of his wife in a carriage accident. John's cook and sailing companion is Paul Halvard (Ford Sterling). The two stop at an isolated island in search of fresh water and come across a house inhabited by a reclusive Civil War veteran, Litchfield Stope (Nigel de Brulier), so traumatized by memories of the war that he has withdrawn from civilization, and his granddaughter, Millie Stope (Virginia Valli). The caretaker of the house is the brutish Iscah Nicholas (Charles A. Post), a Neanderthal-ish fugitive wanted for the murder of an elderly woman. Iscah is in love with Millie, but she is frightened of him (he places her in a swamp filled with alligators until she agrees to kiss him). When John arrives, Millie falls in love with him and hopes that he will take her away. Iscah threatens John and destroys Paul's water cask when he comes to fill it up. When John plans a nighttime rescue, Iscah kills Litchfield and ties Millie to a bed. While John struggles with Iscah, Millie is able to free herself. During the fight, a lamp is knocked over which sets the house on fire. As John, Millie, and Paul try to sail away during a treacherous storm, Iscah pursues and shoots at them from shore. Iscah's chained dog behind the house breaks loose and attacks his owner, ripping out his throat. After the trio has escaped, the dog is alone on the pier, looking into the water where bubbles are rising, presumably the result of Iscah's body sinking. The dog returns to the burning ruins of the house, and the trio sail safely away.

Visually, *Wild Oranges* was Vidor's most sophisticated film to date. In a radical departure from cinematic convention, Vidor opens not with a wide shot, but with a closeup of a crumpled bit of paper blowing along the ground. Vidor cuts to a long-shot of a horse-drawn carriage coming towards the camera, with the paper in the foreground. Next is a medium closeup of a young couple sitting at the reins (John Woolfolk and his bride), followed by a return to the long shot as the wind blows the paper in front of the horses, who panic and speed down the road uncontrollably. A succession of long shots of the carriage and medium closeups of the couple climax with a panning long shot that follows as the carriage takes a turn, spilling the woman out of the carriage onto the ground. Unable to find help, John embraces his dead bride on the ground, covering her in kisses. Vidor concludes the sequence by cutting to a closeup of the crumpled piece of paper still blowing along the ground. Two minutes long, it is an extraordinary sequence not only for its dynamic, rhythmic montage, but also for its unconventional entry into the narrative, which begins *in media res* without introduction of the characters, where they are coming from, or where they are going. The unsettling final shot of the paper imbues it with menace, an aura that never leaves the film. It also introduces an important philosophical element to *Wild Oranges*: tragedy exists within nature and so does evil. Whereas *The Sky Pilot* and *Love Never Dies* were built around melodramatic constructs of villainy, here in *Wild Oranges* it is a mere piece of paper and a bit of wind that brings death and devastation to the Woolforts. Is the paper inherently bad? It is just a piece of paper blowing in the wind, a completely natural occurrence; its consequences can also be seen as natural. In this light, *Wild Oranges* is a film of natural human circumstance, just as *The Jack-Knife Man* was, with both films being built upon human interaction rather than generic conventions. Even Iscah, despite his threatening demeanor, is presented more as a psychologically tormented character than an outright villain, driven by psychosexual urges which manifest through violent means (he frequently fingers his phallic-shaped knife and shakes it as a build-up to violence). Furthermore, Iscah is positioned as a mirror image to John: both men carry knives, are in love with Millie, and have retreated from society. This tension between good and evil is crucial to Vidor's vision; his most personal films frequently return to this moral ambivalence, where characters are not passive pawns but investigators whose choices determine the outcome of events. The soldiers of *The Big Parade*, the everypeople of *The Crowd*, the down-and-out father and son of *The Champ*, the morally distraught doctor of *The Citadel*, the dissatisfied middle-class persons of *H.M. Pulham, Esq.*, the loveless marriages of *Ruby Gentry*, the politically-charged xenophobic neighbors of *Japanese War Bride*—these are a few examples of the circumstantial morality that would become the cornerstone of Vidorian drama.

Wild Oranges also marks Vidor's return to the theme of water. The river was the narrative and metaphoric cornerstone of *The Jack-Knife Man*, and here, too, water shapes the geographic and metaphoric boundaries of the film. Cut off from civilization by water, Litchfield, Millie, and Iscah live in a world that protects and entraps them. Nature is both beautiful and frightening, and Vidor's camera lingers on the moss hanging from trees and other flora and fauna such as spiders, loons, raccoons and owls. Voyeuristic motifs recur through *Wild Oranges*, imbuing the film with a fetishistic perversity that seems a world away from the Christian Science puritanism of Vidor's early works (but also anticipates his later noir-ish and sexually driven films, such as *Lightning Strikes Twice*, *Beyond the Forest*, and *Ruby Gentry*). Upon first arriving at the island, John takes a pair of binoculars and surveys his surroundings, the camera adopting his first-person perspective. This is how we are introduced to Millie, whom John sees swimming (Vidor's fixed gaze on Millie as she swims anticipates similar shots in his 1932 film, *Bird of Paradise*, starring Dolores del Rio). Vidor cross-cuts between John's gaze and those of Litchfield and Iscah, who are spying on him unbeknownst to him. Later, when John is exploring the island, Millie spies on him from her house, watching as he takes an orange, cuts into it with a knife, sucks on it and spits it out with a sour expression on his face, only to take a second orange moments later when the taste has turned to sweetness in his mouth. "Wild oranges," reads the title card, "at first surprisingly bitter, but after a moment pungent

Five. Personality Crisis

A violent scene from *Wild Oranges* (1924, directed by King Vidor for Goldwyn Pictures). Charles A. Post (as Iscah Nicholas) is at left with fist raised and an unidentified actor cowers before him. This fascinating, surreal early Vidor film was a precursor of sorts to the director's later expressionistic and highly melodramatic films (Goldwyn Pictures/ Photofest).

and zestful with a never-to-be-forgotten flavor." Here, the fruit takes on a sexual connotation, much like in *Peg O' My Heart*, especially with Millie's covert surveillance. Millie's sexuality is among the most fascinating aspects of *Wild Oranges*, particularly in light of how chaste Vidor's characters in previous movies were. Here, she is as outwardly sexual and forward with John as Iscah was with her. As John eats the fruit, Millie comes over to speak with him and touches his chest all over, her exploratory hand seeing how far she can go. When he leaves without responding to her advances, she calls him back, pulling fruit off the trees and stuffing them into his pockets (a metaphoric reversal in which she "penetrates" him). She then fingers the embroidered initials on John's breast pocket, while Iscah furtively watches on from afar, fingers inside his own gaping mouth. Later in the film, as John and Iscah have their first confrontation, Vidor cuts between their altercation and both Litchfield (who watches from a very noir-ish set of venetian blinds) and a chained-up dog (who seems to embody the barely restrained animalism of the film's protagonists).

Despite the silent medium, sound was frequently a key component of Vidor's direction, particularly in his use of rhythm within the mise en scène as well as in editing. Here, he engages sound in a different manner. When John is entering the house to rescue Millie, he pauses at the bottom of the stairs and looks up. Vidor cuts to a close-up of Iscah's feet as they walk across the floor. Vidor then cuts back to John, who has heard the footsteps and now knows where to proceed. The use of the close-up to indicate sound anticipates a similar shot in Alfred Hitchcock's *Blackmail* (1929), in which a character looks up at the ceiling, which cross-fades to a see-through floor as the upstairs neighbor walks back and forth. While Hitchcock's shot is technically more sophisticated in that it involves more complicated post-production techniques (and also comes five years later), Vidor's shot nonetheless is a noteworthy example of how sound functioned within silent cinema and affected formal construction and narrative comprehension, even without the audible component of an actual soundtrack.

Vidor's direction is spirited and nuanced in ways that were lacking in his previous movies, in which his camera work was often reduced to static, literal records of narrative action. Vidor reuses one double exposure technique from *The Jack-Knife Man* that allows a character onscreen to interact with the apparition of another character, such as when John is alone on the boat and reaches for Millie, who disappears in front of his eyes, only later to reappear leaning on his back while he is behind the wheel. In the midst of all of the film's tension, Vidor seamlessly integrates moments of comedy, many of them involving Paul, a nod to actor Ford Sterling's comedic background. A familiar slapstick face often pictured with a long black goatee, Sterling is most famous as the first chief of the Keystone Cops and appeared in several of Chaplin's earliest movies in 1914 alongside Fatty Arbuckle. In *Wild Oranges*, Sterling may be missing his characteristic facial hair, but his gestural grace (or lack thereof) is unmistakable, such as how he manages to get sprayed with water as he fills the cask. Nor is the slapstick humor solely given to Paul—after John wins his first fight with Iscah over Millie, he gives a swift kick in the pants to Iscah, the most iconic of all slapstick actions.

The production was troubled. James Kirkwood, the original actor for John Woolfolk, received a fractured skull in a horse riding accident after location shooting was finished,[2] forcing Vidor to cast a new actor (Mayo) and shoot studio-bound inserts to mix with long shots from Georgia featuring Kirkwood.[3] Post broke his wrist during one of his on-screen fights with Mayo.[4] But the film was a critical success, receiving Vidor's best reviews in years. "Suggestive of the works of Edgar Allen Poe in the weirdness of its story.... So finely has the weird and uncanny element been handled that you are kept in continual excited suspense," wrote Charles S. Sewall in *Moving Picture World*. "Notwithstanding the really excellent work of the five players, the greatest credit belongs to the author and to King Vidor for the really masterly manner in which he has directed the production. There are evidences of genius in his handling of some of the scenes: for instance, the opening shot, with simply a piece of paper fluttering across a road. Prosaic in itself, but it focuses the attention and leads directly into the story. He has backed up the excellent atmosphere and characterization with no dearth of thrilling incident and action."[5] Frank Elliott wrote in

Motion Picture News, "One can usually depend on 'something different' in a Joseph Hergesheimer story and intelligent adaptation in a King Vidor production. Well, no one will be disappointed in these expectations in *Wild Oranges*, which approaches *Tol'able David* in dramatic intensity, gripping suspense and heart appeal. ... The locale being in Georgia, the picture boasts some of the most artistic exteriors seen in a long time, some of the maritime shots along the shore being comparable to master paintings."[6] George Pardy in *Exhibitors Trade Review*: "King Vidor has performed his directorial task with unerring intelligence and skill. He had unique and really interesting material to weave into picture form and made the most of the opportunity, with truly gratifying results. ... From the beginning a sort of uncanny atmosphere envelops the tale. ... A veritable spirit of terror appears to brood over the darkening glades. There is no escaping the impression that most anything ghastly is liable to happen amid such surroundings and this is borne out by a series of episodes linked into a genuine scaring thriller."[7] Perhaps *Motion Picture News* summed it up best: "[*Wild Oranges*] shows what King Vidor can do when he wants to."[8]

* * * *

Gulliver's Travels, Happiness, Wine of Youth, His Hour, The Wife of the Centaur

As far back as July 1923, both *The Film Daily* and *Camera's Weekly Wake-em-up* announced that Vidor's next project for Goldwyn after *Wild Oranges* would be an adaptation of Jonathan Swift's 1726 novel *Gulliver's Travels*.[9] In September 1923, both *The Story World and Photodramatist* and *Scenario Bulletin Digest* corroborated this rumor.[10] However, the film seems to have never moved beyond the pre-production process, and it remains another tantalizing "what if?" in the career of King Vidor. Just what would Vidor's adaptation have looked like? It's impossible to say. And while the fantastic aspect of Swift's fable would have been far from Vidor's realist aesthetic, something in the element of nature might have resonated with Vidor. For this reason, *Camera's Weekly Wake-em-up* article is of particular interest, since it includes quotes from Vidor on the pre-production process:

> *Gulliver's Travels* is to be filmed on a magnificent scale by King Vidor, Goldwyn director, according to announcement last night by Vice-President Abraham Lehr. ... It was learned that Mr. Vidor and Goldwyn have been making secret preparations for the production for the last month. Elaborate and detailed photographic experiments have been completed. The ingenuity of director and cameraman will be tested in showing Gulliver's visit to Lilliput, where he is a giant in comparison to the natives, and to Brobdingnag, where the size of the inhabitants makes him the smallest dwarf.
>
> "Camera tests at the Goldwyn laboratories have proved that these things can be shown on the screen with absolute fidelity," said Mr. Vidor last night. "The motion picture is the ideal medium for the telling of *Gulliver's Travels*, much better than the printed word, although I am not saying that we shall do a better job than Swift did. I have long wanted to film this classic,

which appeals to the young by its fantasy and to the adult by its satire. It has been in the back of my head for a long time and I have just been waiting for the opportune time to do it. My association with Goldwyn gives me the facilities for such a production. I believe there is a crying need for more imaginative and fanciful productions on the screen. Our growth has been retarded by our worship of realism. Most people get their fill of realism in their own lives and they seek escape into the realm of imagination for their entertainment. The cinema is ideally suited to portray fantasy and myth." Mr. Vidor will not direct *Gulliver's Travels* until after he has finished *Wild Oranges*....[11]

As late as July 1926, *Motion Picture News* still reported the film as being a "coming attraction."[12] Vidor's film, however, never materialized, and no adaptation of Swift's classic novel would result until Dave Fleischer's 1939 animated version. Instead of *Gulliver's Travels*, Vidor found himself retreating to *Peg O' My Heart* territory, this time at the helm of *Happiness*, another adaptation of a play by J. Hartley Manners written for his wife Laurette Taylor. For this production, Vidor was lent by Goldwyn to Metro, and the film was shot in New York City.[13] Laurette plays Jenny Wray, who works in a dress shop to provide for her mother. Jenny makes a delivery to Mrs. Chrystal Pole (played by future gossip columnist extraordinaire Hedda Hopper), who takes an interest in Laurette's future and invites her to live in her mansion. Jenny eventually returns to her Brooklyn home, falls in love with an electrician, Fermony MacDonough (Pat O'Malley), they marry, and Jenny opens her own gown shop.[14]

Critics evidently felt that Vidor was retreading old ground with this film. "[S]lightly disappointing to those who saw and liked *Peg O' My Heart*," reported *Screen Opinions*. "The director has made her overact."[15] *The Film Daily* felt it was "[a] keen disappointment after her success in *Peg O' My Heart*. Neither star nor story capable of getting the picture over. ... King Vidor has missed badly on this one, especially in the handling of the star and her supporting company. ... she has no variation to her playing. It's either a pucker of her lip, a wink of her eye, or a kick; and she fits them in as often as possible."[16] *Exhibitors Trade Review* felt similarly: "The picture does not approach the standard of *Peg O' My Heart*, but Miss Taylor radiates her personality to such an extent that one is willing to overlook a few shortcomings in the way of plot and exaggeration. ... In several scenes the star becomes too exuberant and lets her pep get the best of her with a result that it is obviously overdone."[17]

After the depth of feeling and formal elegance of *Wild Oranges*, *Happiness* seems to be a minor work. *Happiness* was released in March of 1924. One month later one of the most important mergers in film history occurred. Metro, Goldwyn, and Mayer consolidated into the now-famous MGM. Since Vidor had recently been making films for Metro and Goldwyn, this placed him in a potentially advantageous position: a director for the biggest studio in Hollywood. Vidor, understandably, wanted to impress the twenty-four-year-old Irving Thalberg, then the vice president of production (he would be made president of production the following year). As Vidor later reported in his autobiography: "It took perhaps a year for Thalberg to hit his stride, during which time I directed a couple of films unworthy of comment."[18]

Five. Personality Crisis

Though Vidor does not mention it by name, *Wine of Youth* is one of those movies. *Wine of Youth* is another minor work lacking in personality and vision; however, it was a commercially popular film, the sort of work Vidor was doing in order to gain secure footing with his new bosses at MGM. It was based on Mary Crowther's play *Mary the Third*, which was the original working title for the film, until it was changed first to *Don't Deceive Your Children*, and ultimately *Wine of Youth*, a fittingly lurid title that captures the salacious atmosphere of the film. The film begins with the intertitle, "When our grandmothers were young, nice girls pretended to know nothing at all. When our mothers were young, they admitted they knew a thing or two. The girls of today pretend to know all there is to know." This sets up the foundation of the film: a generational conflict between grandmother (Mary the first), mother (Mary the second), and granddaughter (Mary the third).

The first prologue is set in 1870: "Parents say terrible things about jazz, but in 1870 they were just as shocked by the pernicious polka." A scene unfolds that depicts a party for young people in a parlor, featuring a succession of shots of youngsters dancing and the band playing, interspersed with closeups of dancing feet and sheet music. Meanwhile, off in a side room, two men vie for Mary the First's hand. The second prologue begins, "From that polka-romance a daughter was born, and she in her turn shocked her mother by loving the wicked waltz of 1897." The next sequence is, shot for shot, almost the same as the first, but updated for Mary the Second at the turn of the century: "But suddenly the younger generation has burst its bonds!" Mary the Third's introductory party is structured with similar shots as the first two sequences; however, this time the dancing is faster, the partners closer, and the drummer more frantic: "And the daughter of that waltz-wedding wants to think for herself, marry—or not marry—for herself." Mary the Third (Eleanor Boardman) is caught between proposals from forceful lover Hal Martin (William Haines) and the more reserved Lynn Talbot (Ben Lyon). Mary the Third's innovation is to take both beaus to a camp at Lake Roma for a trial honeymoon. Suddenly dismayed with modern ways, Mary fakes illness to end the honeymoon. Returning home, she discovers her parents quarreling, and her fantasy of their perfect marriage is broken. After her mother's collapse is mistaken for a suicide attempt, she and her husband are reconciled. Mary the Third is inspired to call Lynn, whom she has decided to choose over Hal.

Vidor's direction is mostly uninspired and utilitarian, showing the flapper party with women lounging on furniture, smoking, and even sliding down bannisters. Other shots include drinking booze from a ginger ale bottle; a girl fully clothed in the shower; a close-up of a girl's legs as her dress falls to the floor; a gentleman driving girls at 60 m.p.h. and "almost" causing an accident in order to seduce; and someone holding a piece of yarn as an inebriated girl walks away, with each step her sweater unraveling until we see her bare back (a sexy twist on a classic slapstick gag). These were clearly meant to amuse audiences with Jazz Age antics. In this respect, Vidor succeeds; *Wine of Youth* is a lighthearted comedy that indulges in scenes of salacious immorality but ends with traditional morality reasserted. Vidor managed to have his cake and eat it too.

Most of the film, however, is merely filler images meant to illustrate cleverly worded intertitles: "We're all in danger! I'm being swamped by the emptiness of my life. You're in danger of becoming a fussy old woman!" "Granny, you have an evil mind. We aren't going away so we can be indecent! We could stay right at home and do that!" "If nobody ever did anything that hadn't been done before—we'd be a sweet set of dubs." "If I've got to act like a dead man for two weeks, you might kiss me once." "When you were a girl, a man had to look under the table to see if you had any clothes on." "Life's not all skittles and beer, young lady—nor being happy every minute." And the ultimate: "Leave me alone! I'm looking for a piece of cheese—not a husband."

Critics gave the film generally good reviews. "A picture that forcefully presents a vivid cross-section of modern family life and its problems in an absorbing way," wrote Charles S. Sewell in *Moving Picture World*. "It has the snap and lure of well-done jazz scenes, the appeal of intense vital drama, romance, heart-interest and comedy combined in a such a way as to make a picture that should prove highly satisfactory entertainment for the majority."[19] "It's Metro's treat," wrote Herbert K. Cruikshank in *Exhibitors Trade Review*. "We don't remember having seen such quantities of good-looking youths and fascinating flappers for a long time. And parties! Cocktail shakers and what goes in them; speeding roadsters; syncopated music; dancing till dawn; convention tossed about like paper confetti in a Kansas cyclone. And through the haze of cigarette smoke and the feverish fog of jazz atmosphere one at all times sees the idealism of youth groping for the pearls of truth in a muck of modernism."[20]

British writer Elinor Glyn is now best remembered for penning one of the most iconic Jazz Age films, *It* (1927), in which Clara Bow stars as a salesgirl with lots of "it." Before arriving in Hollywood, Glyn was renowned for her risqué romance novels. Though several of her novels and stories had been adapted to the screen, it was Famous Players' Lasky who first invited her to write directly for the movies.[21] Her first screen story, *The Great Moment* (1921, directed by Sam Wood), was written especially for star Gloria Swanson, who was just finishing the six-film run with director Cecil B. DeMille that rocketed her to stardom: *Don't Change Your Husband* (1919), *For Better, For Worse* (1919), *Male and Female* (1919), *Why Change Your Wife?* (1920), *Something to Think About* (1920), and *The Affairs of Anatol* (1921). Wood and Swanson had also teamed up for another Glyn adaptation the following year, *Beyond the Rocks* (1922), in which Swanson plays a wife trapped between her marriage to an older man and her love for a young playboy (Rudolph Valentino). That same year, another Glyn novel was adapted into *Six Days* (1923), in which Corrine Griffith is caught in a proposal dilemma between a wealthy man and an artist whom she loves. In 1924, Glyn herself adapted her popular 1907 novel *Three Weeks*, about a young man's twenty-one day affair with an older woman.

Five. Personality Crisis

As part of his new contract at MGM, King Vidor found himself caught up in the Elinor Glyn wave. Irving Thalberg selected Vidor to direct Glyn's adaptation of her own novel, *His Hour*.[22] The story is about Russian prince Gritzko (John Gilbert), who meets an Englishwoman, Tamara Loraine (Aileen Pringle), while visiting Egypt. The two meet again in Russia, and Tamara is caught between the advances of Gritzko and his rival, Baron Boris Varishkine (Bertram Grassby). The two men duel to decide who will escort her to a ball. Gritzko wins, but Boris survives. Tamara wishes to return to England. Gritzko escorts her through a snowstorm, and the two are waylaid in a cabin overnight. Gritzko tries to seduce her, but Tamara resists, eventually collapsing from exhaustion. Gritzko loosens her clothing while she is asleep. When she wakes up, she believes he has raped her, so she consents to marry him to save face. After they are married, Tamara admits that she loved Gritzko from their first meeting in Egypt.

Among the rarest of Vidor's surviving films, a print of *His Hour* exists at the Museum of Modern Art with Czech intertitles (which have been translated back into English by Lenka Pichlikova Burke). Like *Wine of Youth*, this film was an uncharacteristic assignment, both in terms of content (a debauched look at the sex and party life of Russian royalty) and geography (this would be Vidor's first, but not last, film set in Russia, as he would return in 1940 with *Comrade X* and again in 1956 with *War and Peace*). Further straining Vidor's creativity was a clause in the contract that allowed for Glyn to inject her own influence, which Vidor felt was a sign that he was not hired for his artistic contributions.[23] Ultimately, her interference amounted to minor instances, such as changing seating arrangements of extras, and insisting that John Gilbert stroke Aileen Pringle's cheek with his eyelashes (a scene that was eventually cut).[24]

Aesthetically, *His Hour* is perhaps Vidor's most uncharacteristic film. With the camera mainly focused on documenting decadence, it seems as though Vidor were trying to outdo Cecil B. DeMille in terms of excess. The result is a strangely fetishistic movie with a severe oral fixation: Vidor lingers on shots of lips inhaling and exhaling cigarette smoke during party sequences, and twice Gritzko kisses the unconscious body of Tamara (the first time she is actually awake and only pretending to be asleep, which only magnifies the perversion). Further, Gritzko's seductions are tantamount to rape—during the snowstorm, Tamara puts a gun to her head and threatens suicide if he does not stop chasing her around the room, and Gritzko responds by calmly lighting a cigarette and watching, waiting like a predator for his prey to fall asleep. When she eventually passes out, he not only loosens her clothing but kisses her chest and feet. Whether these gestures are to be interpreted as euphemisms is open to debate; however, there is clear visual evidence that he violated her wishes and touched her body without consent. Furthermore, their marriage can be seen as blackmail, as he refuses to quell rumors that the two of them consensually spent the night together. This relationship is a far cry from the chaste romances of Vidor's earlier films and the high morals of his "Creed and Pledge."

Whereas most of the visuals in *His Hour* are prosaic, the duel is a rare moment of screen artistry. The composition is a long shot, squarely composed with Gritzko and Boris at either side of the screen in front of a door. When both doors shut, the screen goes completely black. The room briefly illuminates when the shots are fired, and smoke fills the darkened room. Both doors then open, with triangles of light dissecting the black frame. With the sharp contrast of light and dark and the geometric configuration of light, the composition almost resembles an Abstract Expressionist artwork, and it shows Vidor at his most formalistic (another uncommon characteristic of Vidor, who was more interested in naturalism).

Despite how different it was from Vidor's earlier films, critics were impressed. "An extremely artistic production ... vibrates with colorful action and tempestuous love-making to a degree that stamps it as a picture with general audience appeal and a good investment for any exhibitor," wrote George T. Pardy in *Exhibitors Trade Review*. "There are plenty of sensational situations but, thanks to the masterly direction of King Vidor and delicately shaded work of a thoroughly competent cast nothing unpleasantly suggestive materializes."[25] *Moving Picture World*: "Unlike *Three Weeks*, the best known of Miss Glyn's novels, this picture does not involve any transgression of the moral code; nevertheless it is in reality a rather daring treatment of a sex theme, one which at times skates on exceedingly thin ice, for it is sex appeal and not love that is dominant. ... It is a colorful, exotic romance that has been cleverly directed by King Vidor. It moves along smoothly, there is good comedy and plenty of snap and fire and is undoubtedly fascinating...."[26] *Screen Opinions* declared it "one of the best pictures of the season." Among the most fascinating responses to the film was from a fan from Bristol, England named Stanley Wallis: "Outrageous in its lack of good taste; it seemed to me inconceivable that such a disgusting exhibit of trashy sex nonsense should have been produced by King Vidor. I considered John Gilbert undeniably artificial; his overemphasized, impassioned glances, his exaggerated smile, the theatrical way in which he seized a candle from the table to light a cigarette, and his crude, hectic love scenes. I have always regarded Mr. Gilbert as being a sincere, earnest, and unassuming young actor, but *His Hour* has altered my mind considerably."[27] What is so interesting about Wallis' reaction is how it diverges from the professional critics in terms of the film's moral and artistic values, and that it was atypical of Vidor's style and quality.

A minor work at best, *His Hour* is notable mainly for being the first large-scale costume picture in Vidor's filmography, as well as his first film with a large-scale cast that included scenes in which he was directing and choreographing action on a mass scale. Moving forward, Vidor's films would more and more involve elements of epic proportion, intermixed with the smaller moments of intimacy that were Vidor's early trademarks. In this light, *His Hour* was important because it most directly allowed Vidor to develop his style and expand his palette, as well as impress the bosses at MGM with the visually grander and bigger productions that he was capable of handling, which would put Vidor on the path to his next masterpiece, *The*

Five. Personality Crisis

A tense and dramatic scene from *His Hour* (1924, directed by King Vidor for Metro-Goldwyn-Mayer) showing John Gilbert (as Gritzko) and Aileen Pringle (as Tamara Loraine) (MGM/Photofest).

Big Parade. Even if he did not have that particular film in mind at this moment, the importance of *His Hour* as a career move was foremost in his mind: "I had not made *The Big Parade*, and was not so confident of myself. I was glad to go along with the new administration and become acquainted with the next executives, but I was not in any position to dictate what I would or would not do. I was glad to continue on with the new management and sell myself to them. ... It was also a big enough picture so that an aspiring director like myself would not turn down the assignment."[28]

John Gilbert and Aileen Pringle were reunited for Vidor's final film of 1924. *The Wife of the Centaur* was Vidor's third successive film about a troublesome romantic triangle. Gilbert plays Jeffrey Dwyer, a writer who is having an affair with wild girl Inez Martin (Pringle), who breaks off the affair to marry Harry Todd (Philo McCullough). When that sours, she tries to return to Jeffrey, who has since married Joan Converse (Eleanor Boardman, her third film with Vidor). Inez follows the couple to a lodge in the mountain. Jeffrey writes a letter to Joan that he intends to go with Inez, but Jeffrey eventually chooses to stay with Joan. Another of Vidor's lost films, this one sounds like another exercise in extended and salacious party scenes, like *The Wine of Youth* and *His Hour*. "His jazzy episodes, including a lively cabaret and swimming party, are brilliantly handled, and, what is still better, not overdone," described *Exhibitors Trade Review*.[29] "It is sex stuff, but King Vidor has handled it intelligently, with good taste and with a fine sense of drama," wrote Agnes Smith in *Picture-Play Magazine*. "What is most important, it is a delightful picture of one of those attractive men that no sane woman would dream of marrying."[30]

Six

1925

Proud Flesh and *The Big Parade*

"I believe in realism, not the sordid kind, but the realism that shows characters in their relation to each other rather than their environment."[1]—King Vidor, 1925

Proud Flesh

"*Proud Flesh* is King Vidor's gentle farewell to his passing youth," wrote Charles Silver in his program notes for the Museum of Modern Art's 1972 Vidor retrospective.[2] Indeed, the film marks the end of an era: Vidor's final film before making *The Big Parade*, which would catapult him to the top of the industry. In this sense, *Proud Flesh* is a fittingly inauspicious closure to Vidor's first decade in Hollywood, a banal assignment nearly devoid of Vidor's personality.

Following in the footsteps of *The Wine of Youth*, *His Hour*, and *The Wife of the Centaur*, *Proud Flesh* was Vidor's fourth film in a row to deal with love triangles (a theme that would recur not only in his own life, but in many of his later films including *Duel in the Sun* and *Ruby Gentry*). This time around, Eleanor Boardman (who would become Vidor's second wife) plays Fernanda, who was born during the San Francisco earthquake and raised in Spain as an orphan. Now a blossoming young lady, Fernanda's foremost suitor is Don Diego Jaime (Harrison Ford). When she informs Don Diego that she plans to visit an uncle who lives in San Francisco and who owns "a house with seventeen bathtubs on a hill," he does not protest. She is upset that he did not protest, but unbeknownst to her, he makes plans to follow her to California. After being ejected by a disagreeable taxi driver in San Francisco, Fernanda accepts a ride to her uncle and aunt's house from Pat O'Malley (played by an actor with the same name) and she laughs when she finds out he is a plumber. Both Pat and Don Diego vie for Fernanda's hand. On a date to Cypress Point, Fernanda initially accepts Pat's marriage proposal, but she later changes her mind. Pat abducts Fernanda from a party at her aunt and uncle's house and takes her to his hunting cabin and refuses to let her go until she marries him. Don Diego arrives and takes Fernanda away. Fernanda again changes her mind and returns to Pat while Don Diego drives off to meet another woman.

While *Proud Flesh* satirizes the romantic dramatics that Vidor had filmed so seriously in *His Hour* (the ball, the competing lovers, and even the cabin abduction), it lacks the spark and wit of Vidor's later parodies such as *The Patsy* and *Show People* (largely because Eleanor Boardman, despite her talents as a dramatic actress, does not have the same comic brilliance of Marion Davies). In terms of pacing, the film drags and its images are mostly static, prosaic shots. Only when Vidor leaves the confines of the indoors and goes on-location in Del Monte, California (part of Monterey) do his compositions come alive.[3] Just like in *The Jack-Knife Man* and *Wild Oranges*, the natural settings inspire Vidor and he has a natural eye for dramatic and scenic framing. The rocky coast, hilly landscapes, and barren trees provide an unusual, almost uncanny counterpoint to what is supposed to be a romantic outing. As Fernanda stands amidst three trees, their naked arms twisting upwards to the sky, the wind blows her dress around her, and in the background waves crash and water explodes: all the movement within the frame suggests a surreal, almost nightmarish landscape more reminiscent of Van Gogh than of the Hudson-River-School-like settings of Vidor's earlier films.

At the end of the sequence, Vidor films the two lovers embraced in close-up, their heads filling the frame. Pat says, "No matter how far apart our worlds are … you love me, and you're going to marry me, Fernanda." She replies, "Yes, Pat." As Fernanda closes her eyes and leans her head back, as though to receive a kiss, Vidor cuts to an upward-angle close-up of the top of a tree, its trunk forking into two leafless, jagged branches. It is a strange cut whose meaning is both clear and ambiguous. Such an edit typically suggests a moment of passion, but cutting to the tree raises many questions. What is the meaning of the fork, as well as the spiked branches? There is an implied sense of unease rather than harmony, as would be expected. And while ocean waves might have suggested a metaphoric orgasm, the skeletal tree, lacking in fruit, is more suggestive of death. While the full intent of Vidor's cut is not known, it is certainly a formally striking moment that stands out in an otherwise vapid film.

In his interview with Nancy Dowd later in his life, Vidor had very little to say about *Proud Flesh* except for one item that he remembered. The recollection relates to the director's consistent emphasis on place and atmosphere, a recurring emphasis that echoes his life-long memories of his boyhood days in Galveston (see Introduction). The movie is set in San Francisco and some on-location shooting was done in the city to make the atmosphere more "convincing." Vidor recalls that he and the cameramen and crew traveled to Carmel and Pebble Beach for some shots and that, at the time they were there, a thick fog had settled along the coast. Vidor asked the cameraman to shoot anyway, including some shots of flying seagulls as an experiment. He later remembered that this fog-shrouded, expressionistic imagery was mentioned in reviews of the film and he concluded: "There was a symbolism working in the fog, creating a better atmosphere than shooting in sunshine.… I did that many times. If there was fog, use it! The same thing applies to rain."[4]

As Sally Benson wrote in her review of *Proud Flesh* in *Picture-Play Magazine*: "Ten years from now I don't expect to wake up in the middle of a storm and remember what a great, big, vital thing it [the movie] was, but the hour and fifteen minutes that it lasted were as nice as could be."[5] Vidor's next film would not be nearly as forgettable.

* * * *

The Big Parade

> "The motion picture play must have a rhythmic flow, a steady movement, a genuine musical beat."[6]—King Vidor, 1926

Vidor's classic silent film about the life of an "Everyman" in World War I, *The Big Parade* (1925) was a box office smash and, due to audience demand, it was kept running in big city theaters for well over a year. This is the film that put Vidor on the Hollywood map and, due to the great financial success for Metro-Goldwyn-Mayer, producer Irving Thalberg instantly approved the director's more personal though far less marketable choice for his next project: *The Crowd*. *The Big Parade* cost MGM $382,000 to make and, during its original release run, it went on to earn gross rentals of nearly $5 million in the United States and well over $1 million overseas, giving MGM its biggest profit-maker of the silent era and its biggest domestic earner until *Gone with the Wind* in 1939.[7] The film eventually grossed around $20 million in worldwide rentals and rivaled D.W. Griffith's *The Birth of a Nation* (1915) as the most successful film of the silent era.[8] In the decade before the first Academy Awards ceremony took place in 1929, the successful movie fan magazine *Photoplay* bestowed an annual "Medal of Honor" on the best film of the year. *The Big Parade* won that special prize as the best motion picture of 1925.[9]

The Big Parade would also quickly turn leading actor John Gilbert and leading actress Renée Adorée into stars, though both were "cursed by fate" to some degree not long after achieving this fame. Gilbert had already starred in Vidor's earlier film *His Hour* (1924) as well as Erich von Stroheim's *The Merry Widow* (1925), which was released only several months before *The Big Parade*. Gilbert would star for Vidor twice more, in *La Bohème* and *Bardeys the Magnificent*, both released in 1926 (see Chapter Seven). Unfortunately, Gilbert's career would decline in the early sound era, chiefly due to studio politics as well as the actor's self-destructive alcoholism (and not, as was later rumored, because his voice was unsuitable for the talkies). Gilbert died at age thirty-eight in January 1936, after a fatal heart attack, a little more than a decade after his star-making role in *The Big Parade*. Adorée, who went on to play Musette in Vidor's *La Bohème* along with Gilbert, contracted tuberculosis in 1930 and spent two years in a sanatorium in an effort to restore her health; but she sadly died at the age of thirty-five in 1933. Both Gilbert and Adorée had also performed cameos as themselves in Vidor's *Show People* (1928).

Vidor came up with the idea for *The Big Parade* in conversation with producer Irving Thalberg when Vidor suggested his idea of making a film about "steel, wheat, or war." The director reflects upon that decision in his autobiography *A Tree Is a Tree*, saying that he told Thalberg that he "was weary of making ephemeral films," ones that "came to town, played a week or so, and then went their way to comparative obscurity or complete oblivion." Vidor reports that Thalberg agreed with him immediately and that they chose war as the theme.[10] One can infer that it was the one of the three themes that would generate the best drama and that was especially suited for the American cinema market not long after World War I had ended. Of course, Vidor would go on to make his "wheat movie" (*Our Daily Bread*) as well as his "steel movie" (*An American Romance*).

Thalberg ordered MGM's "reading department" to send Vidor all of the World War I stories and plays that they could find and Vidor commenced his research. Dissatisfied with what he had read, Vidor was then put in touch with Laurence Stallings, a young writer who had served in World War I and whose play *What Price Glory?*, co-written with Maxwell Anderson, had recently opened in 1924 to great fanfare.[11] (That play would be adapted to film in 1926 by director Raoul Walsh and again in 1952 by director John Ford.) Stallings had also published his very successful

A dramatic scene from the wildly popular silent war classic *The Big Parade* (1925, directed by King Vidor for Metro-Goldwyn-Mayer). Jim Apperson (played by John Gilbert) lies terrified on the battlefield during World War I (MGM/Photofest).

autobiographical novel *Plumes* in 1924, about a military veteran who had lost his leg in battle. Stalling's own leg was severely injured in the war and he would eventually have his leg amputated. He used this story as the basis for the scenario of *The Big Parade*. And Vidor's movie would include a famous re-creation of the Battle at Belleau Wood, the very battle in which Stallings had been wounded.

The movie opens with a title card: "In the Spring of 1917, America was a nation occupied in peaceful progression. Mills were humming with activity—." The first quick images of the film are those of factories, showing the bustling industry of America at the time, a nation busy in preparing for war. These shots are precursors, as it were, of Vidor's focus on factories and industry in his later *An American Romance*. Then we read another title card that might make the student of Vidor's career think of the director's later adaptation of Ayn Rand's *The Fountainhead*: "Buildings climbed skyward, monuments to commerce and profession." Slim (Karl Dane) is introduced first, as a worker on a skyscraper, and then the viewer is introduced to Bull (Tom O'Brien), who is a bartender. We next meet Jim Apperson (Gilbert), the idle son of a wealthy businessman. The daily work is broken by a bell, which is the call to war. After leaving his mother (Claire McDowell), Jim sees Justyn (Claire Adams), his girlfriend. He talks to her about the war and she expresses her fondness for the men who have enlisted (which looks forward to the character of Valette in Vidor's *So Red the Rose* in 1935). This conversation becomes a catalyst for Jim enlisting in the army.

Vidor opens the next scene with a title card about patriotism and we witness a parade in town. Jim is taken by the ecstatic, communal fervor of the event and joins in. The scene shows Jim's sudden change of heart about going to war. We see a close-up shot of his feet tapping in time to the parade band just before he decides to enlist. As Vidor later observed: "The rhythm of the band is how he happened to go to war and leave the automobile standing right in the middle of the street."[12] Then, after he returns home, Jim's parents confront him. His father (Hobart Bosworth) calls him out for his idleness and for his prior refusal to enlist. He tells Jim that every man must be utilized during war. Justyn then enters and tells the family that Jim has indeed enlisted. His father is proud but his mother is heartbroken and the scene closes on a shot of Jim and his mother expressing their deep mutual affection.

The following scene features the enlisted men—Jim, Bull, Slim, and others—in their civilian uniforms marching with guns. The song "You're in the Army Now" helps to define the scene's tempo. We watch as Jim and his fellow soldiers prepare for war. The scene begins with Jim and the soldiers wearing their civilian clothes and then this image dissolves into one of the soldiers marching in their fatigues. We witness symbolically the important transition that all soldiers are forced to undergo. To succeed in war, the citizen must become transformed into a soldier, a killing machine, a process which is shown in many war films but perhaps most graphically in Stanley Kubrick's *Full Metal Jacket* (1987).

The next scene opens with the soldiers marching into the village of Champillon in the French countryside. The soldiers are shown their living quarters—a barn. Jim sees Melisande (Adorée) for the first time since the barn belongs to her family. The men get ready to sleep after quickly preparing the barn for their temporary lodging. Jim opens a package and reads a note from Justyn. There is a cake in the package, one that proves difficult to slice, but Jim manages to divide it and shares the cake with Slim and Bull. He clearly reminisces about Justyn and, no doubt, her seeming love as well as her role in having spurred him to join the Army.

The subsequent scene opens with the soldiers washing their clothes in a river. Vidor shows the lighthearted nature of life at this moment. Jim walks around town in Chaplin-esque comic fashion with a wooden barrel over his head; here he meets up with Melisande and they flirt. We then see a group of soldiers gathering to get their mail and Jim receives his letter from home. We also watch as a soldier gets a shave. The viewer gains a glimpse of the mundane everyday routine that these soldiers experience as they wait to be sent into battle. We also witness the charming romantic scenes between Jim and Melisande, including the memorable one in which they sit on a bench in a courtyard and he attempts to communicate with her, despite the fact that they do not speak each other's language. After trying to consult a small dictionary, Jim pops a piece of chewing gum into his mouth, begins chewing, notices that Melisande is fascinated because she has never seen anyone chewing gum, and he then offers her a piece so that she can give it a try. The pantomime in the scene, necessary for a silent movie of course, is also occasioned within the narrative by the language barrier between the characters. Vidor later reported that he had dreamt up the scene on the spur of the moment after seeing an MGM writer (Donald Ogden Stewart) on the set chewing gum just before the scene was to be filmed. The director called it "one of the best love scenes I have ever directed."[13]

One reason that *The Big Parade* succeeds so well in making us feel that we are immersed in the soldiers' lives and the wartime experience is because of the pacing of the movie and the strategic alternation between peaceful scenes like the ones mentioned above and the tense later action-filled moments, a type of rhythm that we will see in many war films (*The Sands of Iwo Jima, They Were Expendable, Paths of Glory, Apocalypse Now, The Big Red One, Full Metal Jacket, Glory, Gettysburg, 1917,* and the different versions of *All Quiet on the Western Front,* to name but several). All in all, the earlier scenes highlight the stasis of the soldiers' lives in France at the time, just before the violence and terror of battle erupts. The film works especially well because of these emotional contrasts and the tempo resulting from them.

Jim is soon introduced to Melisande's family. While Jim is at dinner with them, Slim and Bull break into the cellar of Melisande's house to steal some wine and they wind up inebriated. Jim and Melisande catch Slim and Bull in the cellar and the three men cause a ruckus. The military police intervene and there is chaos outside the house. Slim and Bull save Jim from the crowd and the MPs and then Jim and Melisande run off to kiss by the river. The following scene opens peacefully and

Six. *Proud Flesh* and *The Big Parade*

A battlefield scene from King Vidor's silent war classic *The Big Parade* (1925, Metro-Goldwyn-Mayer), the box office smash that put him on the map as one of the greatest Hollywood filmmakers. From left: Tom O'Brien (as "Bull"), John Gilbert (as Jim Apperson), and Karl Dane (as "Slim") (MGM/Photofest).

the mail arrives again. Bull sits around commenting on how the war is a "flop"; he is obviously bored. Jim reads another letter from Justyn but he is interrupted by Melisande and the two talk about Justyn. They quarrel and go their separate ways but, not long thereafter, the quiet scene is broken by the bugle that calls the men to action. The regiment will be moving to the front immediately.

In his autobiography, Vidor discusses the way in which he used the method of "musical counterpoint" to parallel the two events in this sequence that take place simultaneously. Jim and Melisande have gone their separate ways after the quarrel but they then frantically search for one another when the bugle sounds and Jim's sergeant orders them to gather their forces and to begin their march. Shots of the two lovers trying to find each other are alternated with shots of the soldiers gathering into unison. Vidor's careful attention to pacing, knowing that this scene will be shaped by parallel editing, is echoed throughout the film and especially in its later battle scene. According to Vidor: "The assembling of the various parts of the forward-moving army in its hurried surge toward battle would constitute a mass of vehicles and men. Each part—the specific movement of trucks, motorcycles, horse-drawn artillery, and men—could be given an individual tempo of its own. The lumbering motor trucks, the rapidly scurrying men on foot, the gliding airplane protection overhead—these were distinctive rhythms which could be blended into a total symphonic effect. When the scenes were staged in Griffith Park ... we engaged several orchestra conductors as assistant directors."[14]

The American troops march out and Melisande clings to Jim, even as he climbs into an army truck of soldiers. But the "parade" soon leaves her behind in the dusty road. Jim looks for objects to throw to Melisande as a sign of his heartfelt farewell and, humorously yet poignantly, he throws one of his shoes in desperation. She grabs the shoe and holds it closely to herself. Amidst this hurried, almost celebratory march, we sense the heartbreak that Jim and Melisande feel due to their parting. But they knew that the moment would come when they would be separated. Following this scene of the men riding and marching off to war, we witness various shots of battle: planes flying, trucks driving toward the front, soldiers fighting. Vidor uses a title card to introduce this: "An endless column surging forward over roads which were never retraced." We are reminded of how permanent the losses of war are. Vidor thus begins the second half of the film with shots of a column of American troops driving towards the front. The scene ends with a point of contrast, with the image of a solitary Melisande crouching as if in prayer on the desolate road.

We then see the soldiers marching to the front and preparing for battle. Officers talk about storming the woods which are filled with snipers. We watch a battle scene unfold in the forest, a scene that is crafted with cinematic techniques that would later be emulated in many a war movie. This is Jim's first exposure to actual battle. Here, we are shown the real destruction of war and it becomes more dramatic in that so many tranquil and lighthearted scenes have led up to it. Vidor begins the scene with a slow march of the soldiers into the woods and he films this initially with a wide camera angle that places the camera behind the march, at a diagonal angle. This is a technique that would be repeated by Kubrick in *Full Metal Jacket* and one that Vidor would use later when depicting the first battle scene of *War and Peace*. The pacing of this scene is also crucial in establishing itself as a role model for later war movies. The march into the Belleau Wood (though filmed in Griffith Park in Los Angeles) is slow and the soldiers move tentatively, which gives the scene its haunting, suspenseful feeling of doom. Once the fighting kicks in, Vidor shows both sides of the battle: he transitions from the German machine guns and artillery to shots of American soldiers being wounded or killed by these weapons. It is in this scene where we really experience the expendability of the foot soldier in war. As in Kubrick's *Paths of Glory* (1957), the soldier on the front lines is little more than a pawn to be sacrificed easily as the result of the decision-making of military superiors.

To assist with the realism of the action scenes, the Army's Signal Corps helped Vidor to acquire almost a hundred reels of World War I documentary combat footage that he studied in planning the battle scenes. As Vidor recalled in his autobiography: "One day, in viewing a section of film, I was struck by the fact that a company of men were passing the camera at a cadence decidedly different from the usual ones. It was a rhythm of suspended animation and their movement suggested an ominous event. There was no sound track, but the whole pattern spelled death.... I was in the realm of my favorite obsession, experimenting with the possibilities of 'silent music.'"[15]

Vidor experimented with a metronome in his projection room and then used the same metronome for filming the scene of the march through the Belleau Wood. He assigned a drummer to match "the metronomic ticks" so that his cast and crew could hear the tempo clearly (within "a range of several hundred yards"). He commanded the actors playing the soldiers to march so that "each step must be taken on a drumbeat, each turn of the head, lift of a rifle, pull of a trigger, in short, every physical move must occur on the beat of the drum." Many of the extras in the scene who were military veterans scoffed at Vidor's idea, asking him if they were performing "some bloody ballet," but Vidor later said that this was indeed "a bloody ballet, a ballet of death."[16] Vidor goes on in his autobiography to say that the initial viewing audiences were mesmerized by this scene of the march through the forest, chiefly due to the metronome-driven pacing. He wrote that at Grauman's Egyptian Theater in Hollywood, when the film was shown, he had given instructions for the live orchestra to cease their playing at the very start of the scene and to resume the music at its end: "With the orchestra suddenly arrested, the slow measured cadences of the film became discernible, and the observer could almost hear the muffled beat of the bass drum heralding impinging danger."[17]

For this scene, Vidor commanded the nearby drummer to beat in the required slow tempo while the men marched deeper into the woods. Vidor recalled: "So when the march was filmed, and it was the first episode we had made, I had a drummer beat the slow time. Involuntarily, the men moved through the woods with the slow shambling, yet steady march that stands out so strongly as picturing the destruction, terror, and mental drunkenness of war.... The motion picture play must have a rhythmic flow, a steady movement, a genuine musical beat.... It isn't possible to achieve complete realism on the screen."[18] The men march into the woods towards what seems to be definite death. The rhythm of this scene is similar to the final battle scene in *War and Peace*, where the tension of the battle is shaped by the slow beat of Napoleon's drummer. In *The Big Parade*, the slow death march helps to build the scene to its climax. It creates a sense of anticipation within the audience that echoes the fear that is in the hearts of the soldiers marching towards their probable destruction. All other aspects of the scene work in tandem with the rhythmic movement of the characters. The use of the metronome gives the scene a feeling of dread while determining the sense of motion. Overall, this idea of "musical" movement is the type of tempo that Vidor employed throughout the whole of the film. Whether a scene is paced to the song "You're in the Army Now," or to a funeral march, the whole film flows according to a musical structure that conditions the slow or fast movements of the characters on the screen.

Dusk then arrives during the battle and the three men hide in a shell hole in the middle of the battlefield. A messenger crawls to their location and tells them that the commanding officer wants one of them to venture out of the hole to attack the German artillery that is bombarding them. The three soldiers engage in a spitting contest to see who the unlucky one will be. Slim loses the contest and, eager for battle up to this point, he now gets his chance. Slim leaves the confines of the shell hole to crawl out into "no man's land" and attack the German guns. In this scene, Vidor utilizes the cover of the darkness, much as Slim does, in

A poignant moment filled with love and sorrow, from *The Big Parade* (1925, directed by King Vidor for Metro-Goldwyn-Mayer). Renée Adorée is Melisande and John Gilbert is Jim Apperson (MGM/Photofest).

order to provide the scene with a sense of foreboding and tension. But then the darkness is contrasted with brief flashings of light in the sky, occasioned by the flying and exploding German artillery. Meanwhile, Bull and Jim worry about him.

They eventually realize that Slim has been injured in the shooting and bombing. They run out of the shell hole to rescue Slim but they find him dead. They become angry and decide to go after the Germans, seeking retribution. After Jim throws grenades toward the enemy, he eventually meets up with a wounded, dying German soldier who has been hit and who has taken refuge in a shell hole. In a remarkable scene, Jim overcomes his clear desire to kill the enemy soldier with a large knife; Jim opts to comfort him instead. The soldier asks for a cigarette and, even though it is last one, Jim retrieves his final precious cigarette from inside of his helmet where he had tucked it away. He gives it to the dying soldier and even lights it for him. War has, for a moment, been overcome by humanity. In many ways, the movie has been leading up to this scene.

Eventually, we witness the final battle scene, including a shot of Jim screaming in the shell hole, surrounded by chaos. The soldiers soon retreat from the front in unison, forming another "big parade" of trucks and infantrymen. Soon thereafter, Jim lies in a military hospital, his leg wounded from the same German attack that killed Slim. He talks with another injured soldier-patient and discovers that

Champillon, Melisande's town (and where the other soldier was wounded), was under siege and that it is only six kilometers north of where the hospital is located. Jim listens to another patient screaming wildly and decides that he cannot stay there any longer. He is desperate to find Melisande, and he escapes from his medical confinement through an open window, limping away on his crutch. Meanwhile, back near Champillon, Melisande stops in the "parade" of people leaving her decimated community and she looks back wistfully at the town. It is a sublime shot with the line of people departing on a muddy road and surrounded by fields waving in the breeze. Not long after the residents have left their homes, Jim arrives in war-torn Champillon and finds Melisande's house destroyed. We cut to a shot of Melisande and her townspeople silhouetted on the top of a hillside, moving steadily across the horizon line. We cut back to the village and the town is attacked once again and Jim is wounded yet again, this time destined to lose a leg once he reaches another hospital. A military ambulance arrives and they take him away on a stretcher.

As we learn from an intertitle, the war is soon over. Jim is sent home, an amputee and a changed man. We discover that Justyn is in a romantic relationship with Jim's brother Harry (Robert Ober). Jim passionately hugs his mother and Vidor inserts an interesting flashback scene here. His mom thinks of Jim at different stages of his childhood and then she thinks of his wounded leg. Jim tells his mother about Melisande and she advises him firmly that he must return to France and find her "no matter what." She has quickly realized, we can infer, that he will live his life as a sad and broken man without true love to rescue him from his disability as well as his traumatic memories of war. And she knows that Justyn has been romantically involved with Harry and that Jim should no longer pursue her.

In the moving final scene, Melisande tends the fields with her mother in the French countryside. She cries and then spies a silhouetted figure limping steadily down the nearby hillside. The approaching person seems familiar, even at such a great distance, and she somehow knows that it is Jim. As the figure comes closer, she runs to Jim and he hurries down the hillside path. The lovers are reunited, embracing and kissing madly. (This concluding postwar reunion will be echoed at the end of Vidor's later *So Red the Rose*.) The audience can quickly imagine them in their new happy life, having survived the horrors and losses of war.

Vidor later reported that "there was 12,800 feet in the cut" when the film premiered at Grauman's Egyptian Theater in Hollywood and the studio demanded that it be cut by 800 feet "so that they could get in another show every day." Vidor was already busy directing *La Bohème* but he wanted to control how the film was to be shortened. He later said that, when he was not working on his new film, he worked in his few spare hours in his at-home editing room, studying each splice in the movie and removing a foot and a half of celluloid before and after each original splice: "I did this so that the 800 feet came out, but did not affect the picture."[19]

A clause in Vidor's contract with the studio entitled the director to a fifth of the net profits. This led to an MGM attorney summoning Vidor for a meeting in which the studio's accountants exaggerated the cost of the picture and gave a strategically pessimistic projection of how it would do at the box office over the long term. The lawyer that Vidor had hired to represent him joined the studio lawyers in convincing him that it was in his best financial interest to sell his 20 percent share in the film to MGM. Vidor was busy making *La Bohème* and eventually consented to the deal. As he reported in an interview: "Later on I heard that the lawyer had accepted a big bonus for selling me out. It even got Congress involved, and they tried to prevent me from talking about it by paying me off again."[20] This would later be an enormous regret for Vidor, and yet, ever the optimist, Vidor managed to put the financial loss into perspective. In his autobiography *A Tree Is a Tree*, he reflected on the situation: "I thus spared myself from becoming a millionaire instead of a struggling young director trying to do something interesting and better with a camera.... Anyway, I like to take things as they come. The profits and losses are all in the same boat and that boat is a temporary affair."[21] And, of course, *The Big Parade* was the most influential success of Vidor's entire career.

The Big Parade had an enormous influence on the painter Andrew Wyeth, who first saw it as a boy and, as he claimed to Vidor in person, he saw it "180 times." Later in life, Wyeth wrote a heartfelt letter to the director, telling him of this remarkable influence that had lasted and shaped him since the very first time that he had seen Vidor's film. Wyeth wrote: "For years I have wanted to write and tell you that I consider your war film *The Big Parade* the only truly great film ever produced. Over the years I have viewed the film many, many times and [with] each showing the certainty of its greatness deepens.... I have always viewed it with awe and must tell you that in many abstract ways it has influenced my paintings."[22] Wyeth had absorbed imagery from the film and these memories had played a role in the creative visions that led to such masterly paintings as *Christina's World*, *Afternoon Flight of a Boy Up a Tree*, *Winter 1946*, *Snow Flurries*, and *The Patriot* (a portrait of the old soldier Ralph Cline). After receiving the letter, Vidor contacted Wyeth and they arranged to meet to have a conversation (along with the painter's wife Betsy) at the Wyeth home in Chadds Ford, Pennsylvania. Vidor brought along a camera and a cameraman and, with the Wyeths' blessing, filmed their conversation. Topics of their dialogue included *The Big Parade*, the intersections between painting and cinema, and the importance of landscape, symbolism, and the subconscious in the life of the artist. That recorded conversation became the basis of Vidor's final film in his career, the short documentary *The Metaphor* (1980) (see Chapter Twenty-Three).

As Wyeth told Vidor about his love of *The Big Parade*: "Now a lot of people say, Andy, why you do you look at this film so many times? I don't understand it. And all I can think of is: Well Christ, then they don't understand my painting."[23]

SEVEN

1926

La Bohème and *Bardelys the Magnificent*

"I realized that I must do something as different as possible from *The Big Parade*."[1] —King Vidor, 1926

La Bohème

Following the success of *The Big Parade*, Vidor entered the pantheon of Hollywood's greatest directors. He was no longer a filmmaker who showed promise; he was a director with a film that was a full realization of his artistic vision. The question loomed, "What would he do next?" After all, a director—no matter how successful—is only as big as their last movie, and *The Big Parade* was, indeed, a big picture. Vidor's next two films, however, had already been announced by the time of *The Big Parade*'s premiere in November of 1925. On October 10, 1925, MGM studio head Louis B. Mayer announced in *Moving Picture World* that Vidor's follow-up projects would be *La Bohème* and *Bardelys the Magnificent* (both 1926).[2]

At first glance, the selection of material would seem unnatural or ill-suited to Vidor's sensibility: both were French-set costume epics, the former a romantic drama set in the 19th century and the latter a swashbuckler set in the 17th century. Neither contained any of the themes or interests previously explored by Vidor and except for the fact that they were both slated to star John Gilbert, they did not seem like an attempt to build on the success of *The Big Parade*. Rather than using his newfound status to pursue a personal project, it seemed that Vidor was back to his routine of churning out assignments. This was likely the case, since Vidor had been attached to both projects publicly over a month before *The Big Parade* even premiered. While there was pre-release buzz in the air, the profits had not yet started to roll in. But they were no ordinary assignments: *La Bohème* and *Bardelys the Magnificent* were prestige pictures, and Vidor approached both productions with his characteristic attention to detail and atmosphere, bringing to them the eloquent cinematic techniques that he had been honing and for which he was so rightly celebrated.

La Bohème began as a project hand-tailored for Lillian Gish, one of the first big stars of the silent screen who debuted in D.W. Griffith's *An Unseen Enemy* (1912). In total, Gish and Griffith made forty films together over the next decade, including groundbreaking works such as *The Musketeers of Pig Alley* (1912), *Judith of Bethulia* (1914), *The Birth of a Nation* (1915), *Intolerance* (1916), *Hearts of the World* (1918), *The Greatest Thing in Life* (1918), *A Romance of Happy Valley* (1919), *Broken Blossoms* (1919), *True Heart Susie* (1919), *The Greatest Question* (1919), *Way Down East* (1920), and *Orphans of the Storm* (1921). After *Orphans of the Storm*, Gish parted ways with Griffith and starred in two movies for the independent company Inspiration Pictures: *The White Sister* (1923) and *Romola* (1924). By 1926, it had been two years since she had appeared on screen. She signed a new contract with MGM for $8,000 per week, with *La Bohème* as her first film.[3] After screening *The Big Parade*, she hand selected Vidor as her director along with Hendrik Sartov as her cinematographer, who had previously filmed her in Griffith's *Way Down East* and *Orphans of the Storm*.[4] Gish also brought her own particular production methods to the film, ones that she had learned from working with Griffith. As reported at the time in *Picture-Play Magazine*, "She rehearsed her production of *La Bohème* in its entirety in the accepted Griffith fashion. She was busy for weeks acting out her tragic role before the camera ground [rolled] a single time. When there were no settings ready, she went through the action on a bare stage with a table and a chair for props, just as is done in the spoken drama."[5]

La Bohème is based on *Scènes de la vie de bohème*, a serial by Henry Murger that originally appeared in *Le Coresaire* between 1845 and 1849 and was edited as a novel and published in 1851. Murger's work was later turned into two operas under the name *La Bohème*, one by Giacomo Puccini (1896) and the other by Ruggero Leoncavallo (1897). Though Vidor's film closely follows the structure of Puccini's opera, the credits for his film mention neither Puccini nor his librettists, Luigi Illica and Giuseppe Giacosa; instead, the screenplay is attributed to Fred De Gresac and as being suggested by *Life in the Latin Quarter* by Henry Murger, with continuity by Ray Doyle and Harry Behn, and titles by William Conselman and Ruth Cummings. Set in Paris during the winter of 1830, the story concerns a group of aspiring artists who share an apartment and struggle to make ends meet. One of them is the playwright Rodolphe (John Gilbert) who makes his living writing newspaper articles about animals. Living next door to him is Mimi (Lillian Gish), an embroiderer who sells her possessions to pay the rent. Mimi is pursued by Vicomte Paul (Roy D'Arcy), who hires her to embroider handkerchiefs to get closer to her. Mimi accepts the job but not Vicomte Paul's romantic advances. Rodolphe and Mimi fall in love and go on a romantic Easter outing in the countryside. Between romance and his play, Rodolphe neglects the writing of his articles. When Mimi delivers one to his editor, she discovers that Rodolphe has been fired because the article is so late. Returning home, she lies to Rodolphe and gives him money out of her pocket and pretends it is his earnings. She takes on extra needlework to pay their expenses. When Paul is in Mimi's room to pick up her work, she tells him of Rodolphe's play. Rodolphe sees them together and suspects them of having an affair. Later, after Mimi goes to the theater with Paul and again tries to convince him to help in getting Rodolphe's play staged, Rodolphe is convinced that their affair is real, and he turns violent. He then apologizes for hurting her; while he is out looking for a doctor, Mimi runs away and leaves a note that he should focus on his play. She asks that he take care of her pet bird. Eventually, Rodolphe's play is produced while Mimi works in a factory until she collapses. Dying, she grabs onto a passing carriage and drags herself through the streets to her old neighborhood to see her neighbors and Rodolphe one last time. As Rodolphe leaves her bedside to retrieve her pet bird to cheer her up, Mimi dies.

The ending is in stark contrast to the "love conquers all" finales of Vidor's earlier films such as *The Other Half* and *Love Never Dies*, when love was able to overcome medical illness beyond scientific probability. More than being mere deference to the original story, this contrast signals an overarching shift in the mood of Vidor's films that began with *The Big Parade*. The overwhelming optimism that characterized his earlier films was beginning to be replaced with a bleaker sense of realism. Vidor's upcoming crowning artistic achievement, *The Crowd*, is the perfect balance of optimism and pessimism. In the 1930s, *Street Scene, The Champ, The Stranger's Return, So Red the Rose, Our Daily Bread, Stella Dallas, The Citadel,* and even the melancholic Kansas sequences from *The Wizard of Oz* would all explore far darker themes than any of Vidor's films from the 1920s. These later films would acknowledge the realities of social unrest, economic depression, government corruption, medical ethics, hypocrisy, communities divided by their beliefs, individuals slandered by their neighbor, and in general a world of discord, unrest, and unease. These undercurrents came to the foreground in the 1940s and 1950s with *Duel in the Sun* and *The Fountainhead* and the noir-influenced *Beyond the Forest, Lightning Strikes Twice,* and *Ruby Gentry*. In contrast to the innocent victims of *Jack-Knife Man* and *Love Never Dies*, Vidor's late-career films focus on protagonists who are not the innocent heroes of Vidor's early days, but who are psychologically and morally complex characters. They are driven by unbridled desire and are very much responsible for their own downward spirals and for the webs in which they become trapped.

If John Gilbert's eyes were opened to the horrors of humanity in *The Big Parade*, in *La Bohème* his eyes are opened to the dangers of love and the destruction that one person can inflict upon themselves and their loved one. Love, the binding force in so many of Vidor's early films, is the dividing force here. Furthermore, Gilbert's character is not granted any catharsis; the closest catharsis the audience experiences is when Gish's character is dragged limp behind the carriage, near death, a moment of physical torture given to a body in so much anguish that it cannot even feel the pain. It is an unprecedented gesture in Vidor's filmography, one that at first seems like a mere melodramatic convention, but in the context of his larger body of work, reveals itself to be a defining stance. Perhaps it reflected his dissolving relationship and divorce with Florence Vidor; perhaps it was the source material. Maybe it was something deeper within the director that was changing, a broadening of his view of reality, but whatever the reason, this was a transitional film. Before *La Bohème*, Vidor was something of a pure idealist; afterward, while there always remained a trace of idealism that prevents us from calling him a cynic, his "innocence" had most certainly been lost.

The forest sequence from *The Big Parade* would come to be a trademark for Vidor, a crystallization of his theory of cinematic tempo. The cinematic high point of *La Bohème* builds on the musical formalism of *The Big Parade*. When Mimi and Rodolphe are at the Easter picnic, the two sneak off for a romantic reverie. Mimi dances into an open field and Rodolphe follows. What begins as a medium-long two shot, with Mimi on the left dancing and Rodolphe on the right standing still and entranced, both framed head to toe, suddenly shifts. Vidor's mobile camera begins to track forward towards Mimi as she continues to dance closer to Rodolphe, who just stands there staring at her. Suddenly, the camera stops and Rodolphe reaches out and takes Mimi's hands. There is a cut to the orchestra playing, far away, and then a cut back to Mimi and Rodolphe in the same position. As they begin to dance in unison, the camera backtracks, the couple moving forward towards the camera. It is a moment of cinematic ecstasy, with the cadence of the shots—a mixture of

Mimi Brodeuse (played by Lillian Gish) lies dying in bed as Rodolphe (played by John Gilbert) kisses her in King Vidor's *La Bohème* (1926, Metro-Goldwyn-Mayer) (MGM/Photofest).

editing and camera movement and non-movement—matching the propulsive, erotic impulses of the characters. As they dance in the field, the camera alternates between static long shots that capture the two bodies in motion amidst nature and closer mobile shots that pan to follow their movements. It is a marvelous orchestration of visual tempo, making full use of the technical potential of the cinema, and a perfect example of Vidor's artistry.

Despite Gish's celebrity, critics were harsh toward her performance. "For all her celebrated technique, Miss Gish seems absolutely incapable of getting under the skin of a character," Agnes Smith wrote in *Motion Picture Magazine*. "Her Mimi, except for some moments of gaiety, is the waif of *Broken Blossoms*. Unfortunately, the Mimi of the Latin Quarter was a joyous girl and not a cowed and beaten spirit. As played by Miss Gish, Mimi's meeting with Rodolphe is absolutely without feeling or imagination."[6] A gossipy *Photoplay* notice revealed how "[d]uring the making of *La Bohème*, Lillian Gish protested so hard against kissing Rodolphe, played by Jack Gilbert, that not a kissing scene was taken. Miss Gish felt that it was not in tune with her personality to play a part in which she was the object of passionate love. Then the picture was put together and run for a small group of critics. Their unanimous verdict convinced her that she was wrong, and for two whole days Lillian and Jack went through kissing scenes while King Vidor held the megaphone and stop watch."[7] *Variety* gave a mixed review: "The girls are going to go crazy over Jack Gilbert as Rodolphe, the lover, and the boys will like Mimi as played by Lillian Gish, although she gives a rather watered milk characterization."[8] And in *Picture-Play Magazine*, Sally Benson wrote with venom, "Miss Gish is as subdued and fidgety as a New England schoolma'am. Her shoes are heel-less, her bonnets Quakerish. She is still the little white flower of D.W. Griffith's *Broken Blossoms*."[9]

A later review from *Variety* offers a more level-headed opinion of the film: "From now on everything that King Vidor directs will be compared with his *Big Parade*. That will be a mistake, for a director, like an athlete, needs a change of pace occasionally, otherwise he goes stale. But the comparisons will be made nevertheless, just as everything that Griffith ever did or does calls for some comment regarding *The Birth of a Nation*. Thus a great many people will say of *La Bohème*, 'Well, it's not a *Big Parade*,' but that won't be doing Vidor justice. Vidor has turned out a picture in *La Bohème* that is as good as any director could have done with a tragedy in costume on the screen. That he has a picture that won't stand up as a $2 attraction isn't Vidor's fault, it's the fault of the story."[10]

Caught up in the rapture of *The Big Parade*, and distracted by Gish's legacy amidst an industry in rapid modernization, critics at that time seem to have missed the greatness of *La Bohème*, not taking notice of Gish's bodily performance—fluctuating between the ecstatic and the traumatic—and ignoring Vidor's use of "musical" tempo. In hindsight, however, it is a quiet masterpiece, a pitch perfect movie on nearly every level. And Vidor would later pay tribute to Gish's complete dedication to her film performance in his memoir, *A Tree Is a Tree*, with a fascinating anecdote:

Miss Gish was an artist who spared herself in no way. She threw herself wholeheartedly into everything she did, even dying. She wanted to know days ahead when we would film her death scene. She wanted to get in the mood and stay in it.... When she arrived on the set that fateful day, we saw her sunken eyes, her hollow cheeks, and we noticed that her lips had curled outward and were parched with dryness. What on earth had she done to herself? I ventured to ask about her lips and she said in syllables hardly audible that she had succeeded in removing all saliva from her mouth by not drinking any liquids for three days, and by keeping cotton pads between her teeth and gums even in her sleep ... [During her death scene she] neither inhaled nor exhaled. I began to fear she had played her part too well, and I could see that the other members of the cast and crew had the same fears as I ... The movies have never known a more dedicated artist than Lillian Gish.[11]

* * * *

Bardelys the Magnificent

Bardelys the Magnificent was an adaptation of the novel of the same name by Italian-born writer Rafael Sabatini. Sabatini is best known for his swashbuckling adventure novels, *The Sea Hawk* (1915), *Scaramouche* (1921), and *Captain Blood* (1922). All three stories had been adapted into feature films in the 1920s: *Scaramouche* (1923), directed by Rex Ingram and starring Ramon Novarro as the lawyer turned rogue with a thirst for justice and revenge during the French Revolution; Frank Lloyd's *The Sea Hawk* (1924), starring Milton Sills as a man wrongfully accused of murder and sold into slavery who escapes and becomes a pirate; and David Smith's *Captain Blood* (1924) starring J. Warren Kerrigan in the titular role of a doctor convicted of treason, sold into slavery but who (like in *The Sea Hawk*) revolts and becomes a pirate.

Bardelys the Magnificent was an earlier novel, Sabatini's third, originally published in 1906 when the author was thirty-one years old. The story tropes will sound familiar considering his later, more celebrated novels: set in seventeenth-century France, Bardelys (John Gilbert) is an aristocratic playboy who enters a competition with Compte Châtellerault (Roy D'Arcy) as to who can win the hand of Roxalanne de Lavedan (Eleanor Boardman, Vidor's second wife, who later starred in *The Crowd*). Bardelys and Châtellerault are loyal to King Louis XIII (Arthur Lubin) while Roxalanne's family are enemies of the King. When the King learns of Bardelys' intentions, he forbids the young man to pursue Roxalanne. Bardelys defies the King and sets out. Taking refuge in a barn, Bardelys discovers a dying revolutionary who is wanted for treason, Lesperon (Theodore von Eltz). Later, at a tavern, Bardelys is mistaken for Lesperon. Bardelys escapes and hides out at the de Lavedan castle, pretending to be Lesperon to win Roxalanne's heart. Bardelys' plan backfires when he is brought to trial as Lesperon and the only one who can confirm his identity is Compte Châtellerault, who refuses to do so. Sentenced to hang, Bardelys escapes and heads to Roxalanne's room. He signs away his estate to Châtellerault, concedes the bet and proposes to Roxalanne. Unfortunately, she married Châtellerault moments earlier in an exchange to spare Bardelys' life. The two men duel but are interrupted by the arrival of the King's soldiers who are there to arrest Châtellerault. However, Châtellerault stabs himself with his own sword before they can take him. Bardelys and Roxalanne are now free to marry each other.

Coming after *Scaramouche*, *The Sea Hawk*, and *Captain Blood*, *Bardelys the Magnificent* appears to have been made to cash in on the popularity of Sabatini's stories. Not content to be anything but the biggest and the best, MGM set out to make *Bardelys the Magnificent* the grandest Sabatini adaptation to date, putting one of their biggest stars, John Gilbert, in the role, and pairing him once again with Vidor. Like *La Bohème*, *Bardelys the Magnificent* is very much a star vehicle for Gilbert and less a personal project for Vidor. The film is built around Gilbert's star persona: he is the center of attention of every scene, and it seems intended to broaden his appeal from romantic lead to one who can also command action-adventure roles. There is swordplay aplenty, and Gilbert proves himself a worthy heir to the then-king of swashbuckling, Douglas Fairbanks. Whereas Fairbanks brought a lighthearted, comic flair and athletic exuberance to his roles, Gilbert displays a dashing, romantic charm that Fairbanks never had. The change of pace for Gilbert would turn out to be a one-time affair; after *Bardelys the Magnificent*, he would go into production on *Flesh and the Devil* (1926), the first of four films with Greta Garbo (and the start of their real-life highly publicized love affair) which would cement his reputation as the silver screen's ardent lover.[12]

Bardelys' escape from the gallows gives Vidor the opportunity for camera theatrics, the likes of which he had never filmed before. The castle courtyard, which would turn out to be the biggest set piece Vidor ever worked with, is filled with hundreds of extras. Like a conductor, Vidor organizes the spectacle magnificently between long shots and closeups. The long shots display a grasp of the epic that Vidor had never been able to explore before. The closeups show a visually adventurous and experimental side, such as the high-angle POV shot of spears being thrust into Bardelys' face, or the overhead shot of Bardelys trapped in a cage with spears poking in from all sides (a shot that is impressive not only for its extreme angle but also for the abstraction of the violence, with the assailants kept offscreen). Vidor also displays a comic sense of invention with the action choreography—Bardelys is able to escape the cage by climbing up through the gallows and standing on the spears meant to stab him. Next, he slides down the spears and crashes into the soldiers and uses one of their spears to pole vault himself over an advancing line of troops. Next, he repurposes the spear once more and uses it as a hook to pull himself up a wall. Reminding one of Griffith's Babylon sequence in *Intolerance* (which Vidor had witnessed first-hand), Vidor's camera rises vertically as Bardelys uses the spear to scale the interior wall of the castle. By not cutting, Vidor emphasizes the real-life proportions of the set. Bardelys' climb culminates in another direct overhead shot looking down as Bardelys climbs safely into a window (the high angle anticipates similar compositions atop the roof in both Hitchcock's *Vertigo* [1958] and *North by Northwest* [1959]).

An on-the-set photograph from the production of *La Bohème* (1926, directed by King Vidor for Metro-Goldwyn-Mayer). From left: cinematographer Hendrik Sartor, director Vidor, producer Irving Thalberg, and Lillian Gish (who plays Mimi Brodeuse) (MGM/Photofest).

The other standout sequence in the film is Bardelys and Roxalanne's romantic boat ride. Vidor builds on the visual rhythms from the Easter sequence in *La Bohème* and takes them to new heights. The two lovers are at opposite ends of the boat, looking at each other, passing through branches so low that the leaves caress their bodies, nature acting as a metaphoric stand-in for their hands. As Vidor cuts between their POVs, there is an erotic thrust created between the shots: the camera moves forward in one shot and moves backwards in the next, with the clash between the two creating a sense of propulsion that emulates the lovers' desire. It is arguably one of the most sensuous moments captured on film.

Critics were mostly positive. "A rip-roaring story … replete with distinctive touches. A most creditable piece of work," wrote *The Film Daily*.[13] "His is a more convincing and enjoyable Don Juan than John Barrymore's," commented *Motion Picture Magazine*. "For a swashbuckling romance of the Middle Ages, of the time of Louis XIII, I do not believe *Bardelys the Magnificent* could be improved upon. The direction was interesting and finished but not so brilliant as we expect of King Vidor since *The Big Parade*."[14] Mordaunt Hall, in *The New York Times*, was skeptical of the film's achievements compared to Vidor and Gilbert's earlier work: "An agreeable entertainment, one that is produced without stint and with an eye for beauty. It is a nice means of spending an hour and a half, but whether it will add much to the fame of either King Vidor or John Gilbert is doubtful. … [It] does not possess the stamina of the Fairbanks pictures. Mr. Fairbanks also has a happy way of taking the audience into his confidence, and one understands that the whole story is told with the hero's tongue in his cheek. On the other hand, Mr. Gilbert appears to take the exploits of the daring and handsome Bardelys with a little too much seriousness. … It all lacks the measured pace to be expected from a director of the calibre of Mr Vidor."[15] While Hall may have been right in his assessment that it was not a career-changer for either director or star, he seems to have been blind to the excellent rapport among Vidor, Gilbert, and Boardman as well as the subtle magnificence of the film. As Norbert Lusk wrote in *Picture-Play Magazine*, "The production is superb and true to the period, and King Vidor's direction yields not so much as a speck of criticism. It is perfect."[16]

Bardelys the Magnificent premiered on September 30, 1926. Earlier that month, Vidor had another spectacle planned of a different sort. He and Eleanor Boardman were to be married on September 8 at Marion Davies' house in Santa Monica. After

A romantic scene from *Bardelys the Magnificent* (1926, directed by King Vidor for Metro-Goldwyn-Mayer). The Marquis Bardelys (played by John Gilbert) embraces Roxalanne de Lavedan (played by Eleanor Boardman) (MGM/Photofest).

the announcement of the ceremony, Gilbert reportedly suggested that he and Garbo would also marry at the same time and make it a double wedding. On the morning of the wedding, Garbo left Gilbert standing at the altar. Boardman and Vidor, however, were married.[17]

Vidor reports in his autobiography that after he had made these last three films that were set (at least partly) in France (*The Big Parade*, *Bardelys the Magnificent*, and *La Bohème*), he and his new wife decided to visit that country. On the voyage there by steamship, they met F. Scott Fitzgerald, discovered that the writer had seen most of the director's movies, allowed him to be their tour guide in Paris, and became fast friends with him and his wife Zelda. Vidor and Fitzgerald even planned to make a film together, though it was never realized. Fitzgerald would go on to write a story about Hollywood titled "Crazy Sunday," originally published in the October 1932 issue of the magazine *The American Mercury*. One of its main characters, a famous movie director, was reportedly based on Vidor, or based quite possibly on a combination of different real-life persons including Vidor as well as Thalberg. Vidor would later return the "compliment" by directing the film *The Wedding Night* (1935), whose story by Edwin Knopf is loosely based on Knopf's friends the Fitzgeralds. In his memoir, the filmmaker said that it was unfortunate that Fitzgerald never had the chance to finish his novel *The Last Tycoon*, based on producer Irving Thalberg, since it was "the best novel of Hollywood" (it would later be adapted to film by Elia Kazan, released in 1976, and featured an all-star cast). Vidor also mentions that on that Paris trip after finishing *Bardelys the Magnificent*, bookseller and publisher Sylvia Beach introduced him to James Joyce, and he also met Ernest Hemingway at Beach's bookstore. And it was during this two-month visit to Paris when Vidor read a copy of *Variety* and learned that the movie industry had just switched from silent to 100 percent sound films. He was regretful as well as thrilled: "I realized that much magic would disappear from the screen. I also realized that new techniques would have to be discovered, invented, and established."[18]

Eight

1927–1928

The Crowd, The Patsy, and *Show People*

The Crowd (1928)

> "I think the one I'd least like to do over, or which gives me the least embarrassments, is *The Crowd*. It does reach a sort of purity in motion picture [story] telling that isn't dependent on dialogue or titles."[1]—King Vidor, 1963

> "Birth, youth, school, love, business struggles, married life, always against the background of the crowd—that is the motif.... Persons who want symbolism can find it in this picture; and persons who want human drama can find plenty of that, too."[2]—King Vidor, 1927

> "That's why I said I wanted to make more pictures. I'd learn more about myself. *The Crowd* is very definitely of myself. That was a great experience for me."[3]—King Vidor, late 1970s

On October 9, 1926, just one week after the premiere of *Bardelys the Magnificent*, Vidor's next film was announced in *Motion Picture News*: *The Glory Diggers*. It would feature "an original story by Irvin S. Cobb that deals with a great engineering feat—the building of the Panama Canal. Irvin S. Cobb was brought to California by Irving G. Thalberg, associate studio manager of Metro-Goldwyn-Mayer, some time ago to do a story of the gigantic project."[4] That same day, *Moving Picture World* carried a story with the same details.[5] The combination of Vidor, still riding high on the acclaim of *The Big Parade*, and Cobb, a highly regarded journalist and noted humorist whose stories were later the inspiration for John Ford's films *Judge Priest* (1934) and *The Sun Shines Bright* (1953), must have been tantalizing. Anticipation was certainly high for the film in the press, with it being selected by L.C. Moen of *Motion Picture News* as one of the "Likely Contenders for Leading Honors" among films for 1927: "The bigness of the theme, the plans being made, and the chance that King Vidor will make the most of it entitle this to a place among our prospects."[6]

As we now know, Vidor did not wind up making *The Glory Diggers* but instead proceeded with *The Crowd*. According to contemporaneous newspaper accounts, however, Vidor did not immediately abandon the Panama Canal project altogether. On Tuesday, May 17, 1927—before *The Crowd* had even been released—*The Film*

Daily announced that the project was now being "prepared by Laurence Stallings" instead of Cobb.[7] Stallings, in addition to being co-writer of the World War I play *What Price Glory*, was Vidor's scenarist on *The Big Parade*, and he had written the swashbuckling epic *Old Ironsides* for James Cruze as a follow up in 1926. The project was re-confirmed by *The Film Daily* a month later, on Tuesday, June 28, 1927.[8] A week after that, it was mentioned by *Variety*[9] as "a super special." The following week, on July 15, 1927, *Motion Picture News* announced that the film was now called *The Big Ditch*.[10] As late as Thursday, December 22, 1927, the film was still being reported as in production, with *The Crowd* star James Murray being attached as lead actor.[11]

After 1927, there would be no more mention of the film under either title in the trades. The film did get far enough along that Stallings met with Vidor over the script, which according to B.G. Braver-Mann was "a glorified account of how the late General Goethals and his men fought yellow fever during the construction of the Panama Canal." Braver-Mann writes that "a provision was made in the scenario script to show the close-up of an inoculation needle being thrust into a man's arm. Vidor objected to this close-up on the score of a purely personal dislike for the scene."[12] While *The Big Ditch/The Glory Diggers* would remain an unrealized project, it was not the last time that Stallings and Vidor would work together. The two collaborated on several films over the next two decades, including *Show People* (1928), *Billy the Kid* (1930), *So Red the Rose* (1935), *Northwest Passage* (1940), and *On Our Merry Way* (1946). But before making *Show People*, Vidor began work on the one film that, perhaps more than any other, would help to define his artistic career.

By the end of 1926, Vidor was 32 years old and had completed a decade in Hollywood. He had arrived in 1916, before the industry was even fully organized, and he sweated his way up the ladder from lowly gag writer to top director. His 1925 film *The Big Parade* was the talk of the town, and his two features of 1926, *La Bohème* and *Bardelys the Magnificent*, were hits. So the obvious question arose: when you are seemingly at the top of your game, where do you go from there? Eleven little words appeared on the front page of *The Film Daily* on December 3, 1926, and spelled out Vidor's future: "King Vidor will next make an original, *The Mob*, for M-G-M."[13] The film would arguably be Vidor's crowning achievement, and it was one of the most revolutionary films to emerge from Hollywood in the silent era. Today it is regarded by some film historians as the greatest work of American silent cinema.

The overall vision for this new project, which would also be called *One of the Mob*[14] before becoming *The Crowd*,[15] was rooted in Vidor's first feature, *The Turn in the Road*. Vidor had said of his debut, "This picture demanded the extreme of realism and naturalness in its treatment, for it deals with life of today as it is known by the average American. Its humor, pathos, suspense, and climax are drawn from everyday life. Over action or over characterization would ruin the picture."[16] Twenty-two feature films passed before Vidor was able to return to this vision and aesthetic. His "Creed and Pledge," originally published in January 1920, had so frequently been compromised by commercial demands and genre conventions that it seemed, at times, as though Vidor had conceded his personal artistic mission. With *The Crowd*, Vidor showed that he had most certainly not conceded; instead, he had waited until he had reached that advantageous point in his career when he had the freedom and the studio backing to do whatever he wanted. It was a unique moment that might not come again.

According to Vidor, it was a casual comment to MGM production chief Irving Thalberg that got the ball rolling. Intrigued by the potential title *One of the Mob*, Vidor got to work right away with Harry Behn, with whom he had collaborated on the writing for *Proud Flesh*, *The Big Parade*, and *La Bohème*. The two began listing the hallmarks of the ordinary person's life: birth and death, coming of age, falling in love, getting married, having children, contending with money worries and bad luck, etc. These were topics that were large in the universal sense but particular and quotidian in the everyday sense. In short, Vidor wanted to find the dramatic moments to which everyone in the movie theater could relate on a personal level, scenes pulled straight from their everyday lives. It would be a movie about life—nothing more nor less.[17]

Vidor reportedly gave this list of suggested life-events to the writer John V.A. Weaver, who had been contracted by MGM to help with the project. Weaver penned a 49-page story that was titled *The Clerk Story* and that included descriptions of ideas for sixteen different sequences. Vidor then developed his own fourteen-page "March of Life" treatment and, in the end, worked with Harry Behn in combining Weaver's story and suggestions with the director's own outline of potential scenes.[18] Both Vidor and Weaver wound up receiving co-writing credits and Behn remained uncredited (though Behn had received credit in earlier MGM publicity materials for the film while Weaver had not).[19]

The Crowd was the first movie to utilize major on-site filming in New York City. Vidor later told an interviewer, "I believe in filming *The Crowd* I was one of the first directors to journey from California to New York to shoot scenes with actors working on city streets and to use the normal flow of pedestrians and traffic for atmosphere."[20] According to Jordan Young's book on the film, shooting locations included the Equitable Building on Lower Broadway (the building in which John's office supposedly resides) as well as "New York Harbor, West 45th Street, Ninth Avenue, Times Square, the Marquis Street Theatre, the New York Telephone Building on West Street, Wall Street, Trinity Churchyard, Battery Park, South Ferry, and out on Long Island."[21]

The cinematographer was Henry Sharp, who would supervise the photography for such later films as Leslie Fenton's *Tomorrow, The World!* and Fritz Lang's *Ministry of Fear* (both 1944). The editor was Hugh Wynn, who also edited more than several of Vidor's films including *The Wife of the Centaur*, *The Big Parade*, *La Bohème*, *The Patsy*, *Show People*, *Hallelujah*, *Billy the Kid*, and *The Champ*. In terms of the tempo in filming and editing, Vidor had been inspired by D.W. Griffith to structure the montage of his scenes and sequences according to a definite

A romantic scene from the silent masterpiece *The Crowd* (1928, directed by King Vidor for Metro-Goldwyn-Mayer). John Sims (played by James Murray) embraces Mary (played by Eleanor Boardman) as they take the train home from their visit to Coney Island (MGM/Photofest).

sense of musical rhythm. He had already put that idea into full effect in his use of metronome-determined pacing in certain scenes (such as the Battle at Belleau Woods) in *The Big Parade*. For *The Crowd*, Vidor had repeatedly listened to one piece of classical music during his writing of the screenplay and had then asked for this piece of music to be played on the movie set: Tchaikovsky's Symphony No. 6 in B minor (the "Pathetique Symphony"). He even said that he had asked for the score of that symphony to accompany the film to theaters so that it could be played with live accompaniment throughout each screening, wherever possible.[22]

In his book on *The Crowd*, Jordan Young lists seven different endings that had either been filmed, planned, or suggested. In an interview, Vidor refers to six endings that had actually been filmed: "We shot six different endings for *The Crowd*.... There was a nice satirical ending that I liked best, with [the parents and] the boy sitting in a theatre audience, and the camera drawing gradually away from him until he was lost in the crowd again, just one of a million, no more identity...."[23] This was indeed the ending that became the "official" finale, though Vidor told film scholar Kevin Brownlow that the studio also sent an alternate "happy ending" to movie theaters, one in which the family celebrates Christmas in their home, with Mary telling John that she had never lost faith in him. MGM gave the theaters a choice in showing either the Christmas party ending or the director's preferred "satirical" theater ending. Vidor told Brownlow that, to his knowledge, the overly sentimental Christmas ending was hardly ever used.[24]

Perhaps the greatest compliment that could have been paid to this silent masterwork was the fact that the great Italian filmmaker Vittorio De Sica had once told Vidor that *The Crowd* had influenced him enormously—and therefore, at least indirectly, had influenced Italian neo-realist cinema. Vidor related in an interview later in life: "Last year [Vittorio] DeSica threw his arms around me and said, 'Oh, *The Crowd, The Crowd*! That was what inspired me for *The Bicycle Thief*."[25] The second greatest compliment that Vidor's film could have received may have been the praise of the distinguished silent cinema expert Kevin Brownlow, whose knowledge of silent cinema was encyclopedic and who chose *The Crowd* as the greatest American silent movie, despite such competing masterpieces as Charlie Chaplin's *City Lights* and *The Gold Rush*, Buster Keaton's *The General*, and D.W. Griffith's *Intolerance*, *The Birth of a Nation*, *Broken Blossoms*, and *Way Down East*. Brownlow offered the following tribute to *The Crowd* as part of the Foreword to Jordan Young's book:

> Admittedly, entertainment for its own sake can be valuable, but there's enough of the puritan in me to demand something more. And that's one reason why I love *The Crowd*. When a film of enormous social significance succeeds in being immensely entertaining, then as far as I'm concerned, the director has achieved near-perfection. *The Crowd* is one of the most eloquent of all silent pictures. It came out just before the Depression and yet it might have been made in the thick of it, so poignant is its picture of unemployment. It is surprising that it reached the public at all, for it broke all the rules of Hollywood.... *The Crowd* is practically plotless. And yet every incident is so brilliantly directed and acted that the film blazes to life. The shots are simple, yet full of emotional power; King Vidor treats his characters so lovingly and with such understanding that one cannot help but share his feelings. In a way, it's odd that this portrait of failure should have such uncanny intensity for it was created by a man for whom the American Dream came true.... *The Crowd* is the finest American silent film I have ever seen.[26]

Among the Hollywood "rules" that Vidor's film "broke" at the time, according to Brownlow, were the following: showing the casual imbibing of alcohol during the Prohibition, suggesting that work is dull, depicting a man's nervousness on his wedding night, featuring a woman announcing her pregnancy to her husband, and emphasizing the realities of poverty and failure in the Land of the American Dream.[27] We might also add the inclusion of the tragic scene in which John and Mary's young daughter is killed by a truck when she crosses the street after her parents have summoned her through the open window. The explicit presentation of the death of a child, followed by the parents' horror and grief and then mourning, was a shocking anomaly in the years of silent cinema. So the bold, convention-shattering nature of the film—in addition to its being a movie that is not centered on a unifying dramatic conflict—may be one reason why Thalberg and MGM took a year to release it.

But while *The Crowd* was not the box office hit that *The Big Parade* was, it eventually did well financially by earning more than double its production costs and returning a profit to the studio.[28] And though it was not without its occasional critics, *The Crowd* received generally high praise since its opening at the Capitol Theatre in Manhattan on February 18, 1928. A reviewer for *The Film Daily* summarized the film as "an average story of average people—just two out of the mob—but the director has demonstrated sincerity and humanness in its handling that mark the result as something well above the ordinary." Right after its release, Gilbert Seldes of *The New Republic* ranked the film as "the most interesting development in the American movie in years." *The Crowd* was also described as "tremendous in its simplicity" (*The Evening Journal*) and "an admirable cinema realization of an ambitious attempt" (*The Sun*). The more negative reviews emphasized the "somber" and even "macabre" effect on the audience (*The Daily Mirror*) and the film's "drab actionless story of ungodly length" (*Variety*).[29]

At the very first Academy Awards ceremony on May 16, 1929, *The Crowd* failed to be nominated for "Outstanding Motion Picture" (an award that went to William Wellman's *Wings*) nor for Best Cinematography (F.W. Murnau's *Sunrise* won). Neither lead actor James Murray nor lead actress Eleanor Boardman (Vidor's second wife) was nominated for acting awards (Emil Jannings won for *The Last Command* and Janet Gaynor for her performances in three films: *7th Heaven*, *Street Angel*, and *Sunrise*). Vidor had been nominated as Best Director for a Dramatic Motion Picture but lost to Frank Borzage (*7th Heaven*). *The Crowd* had also been nominated for being a "Unique and Artistic Picture/Production" but lost to Murnau's *Sunrise*.

However, time was certainly on the side of *The Crowd*. Over the decades, its status as an artistic triumph of the silent era has been cemented. In his book *Silent Films, 1877–1996: A Critical Guide to 646 Movies*, Robert Klepper praises Vidor's movie as "a masterpiece of artistic imagery" and rates it as superior to *Wings* and *Sunrise*.[30] And film historian Charles Silver summarized the greatness of the film in his program notes for the Vidor retrospective at the Museum of Modern Art in 1972:

> *The Crowd*, in its unassuming way, is as exemplary of the glories attained by the silent cinema in its death throes as is *Sunrise*, *The Passion of Joan of Arc*, or *The Docks of New York*. Its near-perfection reflects Vidor's singlemindedness of purpose at work on a project which is ambitious and within the range of his special talents. It is a film made with such conviction as to belie any charges of condescension toward "the little man." It is a film made with such craftsmanship, such economy of expression, as to establish Vidor's claim as a rival of Griffith and Keaton as the greatest American-born director of the silent era.... Vidor's film, however derivative technically, is so unique in conception ... that its basic originality cannot be challenged. We can only be grateful that Vidor was given the rare opportunity to freely pursue his inspiration and that Irving Thalberg for once felt: "M-G-M can certainly afford a few experimental projects." ... It has become a commonplace that the film contains some of the most memorable and accomplished sequences in all cinema. *The Crowd* has been used as a textbook for filmmakers from Hollywood to Moscow. Yet, its uniqueness is attributable more to its simple naturalism and pure humanism than to its accumulation of brilliant moments.[31]

Film scholar and film critic Richard Schickel, in his chapter on Vidor in his book *Matinee Idylls: Reflections on the Movies*, proclaims at the outset that "King Vidor was, I believe, the greatest silent film director America produced. His highest achievements in that form—*The Big Parade, The Crowd, Show People*—rank, in my estimation, with the best work of his European peers, the likes of Lang, Murnau, and Eisenstein." Schickel goes on to argue that the "central irony" of Vidor's long career in filmmaking is that "he remained a great silent film director through all the years he made sound films."[32] He points to clear examples of special scenes and sequences in the director's later sound era movies that stand out visually and dramatically but which do not use any dialogue (or minimal dialogue at best): the exciting irrigation sequence in *Our Daily Bread*; the graphic massacre of the Indian village in *Northwest Passage*; the spectacular confrontation between the ranch hands and the railway workers in *Duel in the Sun*; the scenes in *The Fountainhead* in which Howard Roark (Gary Cooper) first sees Dominique Francon (Patricia Neal) and later when he lustfully assaults her; the death of Rosa Moline (Bette Davis) in *Beyond the Forest*; and the montage of images of Pierre (Henry Fonda) observing the battlefield in *War and Peace*.[33]

Schickel gets to the heart of why Vidor, as Andrew Sarris once said, "created more great moments and fewer great films than any director of his rank."[34] Schickel puts this observation into context. Vidor was at his peak of cinematic artistry when it came to the visual and dramatic elements of the silent film, as demonstrated most tellingly by *The Crowd*, and more than several of his films in the sound era exhibit this type of consummate visual artistry while nonetheless suffering at points due to stilted or exaggerated dialogue (as with *The Fountainhead*), to weak or convoluted scripts (as with *War and Peace* and *Solomon and Sheba*), to the interference of overly zealous producers (as with *Duel in the Sun*), or to a combination of these.

Schickel also emphasizes Vidor's use of expressionism in many of his greatest scenes. He sees that style as rooted in the director's work in the silent era, not only due to Vidor's unique creative vision but also because of the very nature of silent cinema. And the director's brand of expressionism is nowhere more evident than in *The Crowd*, where certain elements of his artistry will be echoed in his later sound era films. While that film as well as *Our Daily Bread* and *An American Romance* highlight Vidor's concern with the everyday struggles of the "common" person, his visual and dramatic style is sometimes anything but naturalistic, even in such films where ordinary life and populist sentiment are highlighted in terms of the overall narrative. In fact, one can view the heightened emotionalism and stagy or exaggerated acting in some of Vidor's "talkies" (*Stella Dallas, Duel in the Sun, Beyond the Forest, War and Peace,* and *Solomon and Sheba* come to mind) as results of this inherent expressionism that was far better suited in many cases for his silent films.

The Crowd certainly contains many realistic elements such as the basic story and setting, along with the use of on-location shooting for many of the images of the city. But overall, the naturalistic sensibility of the story and setting as well as the many realistic scenes and sequences are in tension with the movie's expressionistic visual style in more than several shots or scenes. And it is perhaps this dialectic that contributes most of all to the film's unique artistic quality. The movie lulls us into a sense of objectivity and, at the right moments and with the right techniques, it distorts reality enough to allow us an entryway into the emotional lives of the characters. In his book on *The Crowd*, Jordan Young points to an intriguing unpublished exchange between Vidor and interviewer Nancy Dowd. Noting that several of the sets for the film reminded her of sets used by Fritz Lang, Dowd then stated: "Your sets are expressionistic, but at the same time they're real...." To which Vidor responded: "That would be natural. I'm not German, you see. I'm American."[35] It is this peculiar waltz between realism and expressionism that helps to define the essence of Vidor's artistic sensibility.

Vidor spoke often about the strong influence of German Expressionist filmmakers like Murnau and Lang on Hollywood directors of the 1920s, including John Ford, Frank Borzage, and of course Vidor himself. Schickel wrote, "But this was a man [Vidor] who liked to talk about how eagerly he had studied the work of Eisenstein and the Russian greats of the silent film, how much the UFA [Universum Film-Aktien Gesellschaft] films of Fritz Lang had meant to him and how he had tried to incorporate something of their spirit and vision in his work."[36] And Vidor once said, "In the case of *The Crowd*, I was very aware of the Germans: *Variety*, *The*

A symbolic shot from the silent masterpiece *The Crowd* (1928, directed by King Vidor for Metro-Goldwyn-Mayer). John Sims (played by James Murray) raises his arms amidst a sea of strangers ("the crowd") (MGM/Photofest).

Last Laugh, Metropolis, and so forth. That's camera movement, booms, perambulator shots and so forth.... German expressionism."[37]

Lang did not emigrate to the United States until 1933, though he had visited New York City and Hollywood in 1924 (to study American filmmaking) and his German films were highly influential throughout the 1920s. Murnau arrived in Hollywood in July of 1926, hired by William Fox to bring his artistic sensibility to the Fox studio. Murnau's first film for Fox, *Sunrise: A Song of Two Humans* (1927), was generally recognized as a masterpiece. It had an almost immediate effect on Vidor's filming of *The Crowd*, which competed against *Sunrise* in the special category of "Best Unique and Artistic Picture" at the first Academy Awards in 1929 (*Sunrise* won). Similarly, Ford and Borzage (like Murnau, directors at Fox studio at the time) demonstrated the strong influence of Murnau's expressionism—Ford in his 1928 films *Four Sons* and *Hangman's House*, as well as in later films such as 1935's *The Informer*, and Borzage in his *7th Heaven* (1927) and *Street Angel* (1928), as well as in many of his later films.[38] As Schickel points out, this type of expressionism—with its emphasis on a character's subjective viewpoint, along with the distortion of images of external reality in representing a character's emotional and psychological states—certainly remained a core element of Vidor's artistic vision since the time that this style impacted his making of *The Crowd*. (An interesting side note is that Murnau's film *City Girl* [1930], also done for the Fox studio, had been originally titled *Our Daily Bread*, the same title as Vidor's 1934 film.)

According to Schickel, Vidor's artistic bent toward the expressionistic was especially apt for the silent cinema: "This medium was not essentially a realistic one. Freed as no other fictional medium was from dialogue and its chief imperative, which was to make characters speak in demonstrably authentic tones, which in turn obliged them to naturalistic behavior, silent film was impelled to take flight from the realistic. In the hands of someone like King, whose natural bent was in this direction, a silent film could not help but transform reality, sometimes poeticizing it, sometimes rendering it in expressionistic terms."[39] For Schickel, then, the expressionist style was already in Vidor's creative bloodstream from the very start of his career. So the creative opportunities of silent cinema and the influence of Murnau and the other German Expressionist directors had only amplified this "natural bent."

Schickel gives a few clear examples of Vidor's "pre–Murnau" expressionist techniques in *The Big Parade*, including the heightened melodrama of Jim's departure from the village of Champillon, with Melisande clinging to the military truck, and the slow metronome-driven tempo of the battle scene set in Belleau Woods.[40] He then focuses on *The Crowd* and the way that the director's visual style tends toward the subjective. At the same time, he stresses, the dramatic style of the film elevates the characters of John and Mary to the level of the archetypal:

> *The Crowd* goes much further [than *The Big Parade*], much more openly, toward expressionism. And achieves something few films have ever achieved. Its protagonists, John and Mary, are representational figures, their very names suggesting in their commonness that they are

a modern Everyman and Everywoman, their tragedies the ones we all endure, their triumphs the small ones that briefly sustain all of us in our modest passages through life. And Vidor's style subtly yet perceptibly distorts their reality through his choices of angles, lenses, and the occasional forced-perspective setting, intensifying the symbolic nature of these characters and their little adventures. Yet they tear our hearts out. The devices that one might think would distance us from them somehow enhance our identification with them. The sheer alertness of the moviemaking, the tension of Vidor's aesthetic striving, imparts to this quotidian world a significance that mere realism could never achieve.[41]

Memorable uses of expressionist technique in *The Crowd* include the forced perspective shot of a wide-eyed, young John Sims (Johnny Downs, who would have a bit part playing a wounded Yankee officer in Vidor's *So Red the Rose*, 1935) when he climbs the staircase in his family's home after an ambulance arrives to carry away his father. Johnny realizes that his father has died (or is near death) and the manipulation of the camera position makes it appear that the people gathered behind Johnny in the doorway (one of many symbols of "the crowd") seem to be unnaturally distant. This technique heightens our sense of Johnny's emotions due to the focus on his face in the foreground in contrast with those in the far background. Another example of expressionism is the sequence in which the camera soars rapidly up the exterior of a skyscraper (actually achieved by a horizontal tracking shot in the studio) and then, after a dissolve from the exterior image of the building to one of the office interior, the camera tracks across the vast office in which John (James Murray) works, surrounded by a sea of fellow workers at their desks. The camera moves across this exaggeratedly large and populated space and then gradually lowers as we approach John's desk. This shot does not so much imitate a real office environment as it summons a sense of alienation amidst an atmosphere of uniformity, conformity, and routine. (Billy Wilder "borrowed" or at least echoed Vidor's idea for this setting three decades later for the office setting in his comedy classic *The Apartment*, 1960.)

The almost surrealist exaggeration of the office space is then repeated at the end of the film (in the satirical "official" finale) when John and Mary and their son roar with laughter while seated in a movie theater watching a comic scene. The camera then tracks backward quickly to reveal a theater (and its audience) that is far larger than the size of a conventional theater at that time. John and Mary are in close-up at first but then they disappear into "the crowd" when the camera retreats quickly to show an ocean of faces, ending finally with a shot from above that reveals only the tops of their heads, with even their facial identity having been "erased." A similar sense of estrangement-amidst-the-masses is evoked by the many earlier images of the city and its buildings, and particularly by the quick shots of moving pedestrians and cars in the streets, with some images dissolving into other images to create an almost kaleidoscopic, disorienting effect.

There is also the shocking, expressionist scene in which John and Mary's young daughter is killed by a speeding truck. The image of the child running across the street becomes super-imposed upon the image of the racing vehicle. The shot is

Eight. *The Crowd*, *The Patsy*, and *Show People*

both real and unreal at the same time. Then the people in the street gather quickly around the lifeless body while John rushes to his daughter to pick her up and bring her up to their apartment. The camera briefly captures the many gathered bystanders (yet another instance of "the crowd") from above, giving us another chance to experience John's feelings of being overwhelmed by forces in his life that are out of his control.

The story and sensibility of *The Crowd* echo the plight of the "common person" in Vidor's earlier *The Turn in the Road* as well as the focus on John Gilbert's "Everyman" character of Jim Apperson in *The Big Parade*. And *The Crowd* was a precursor to several of the director's later "populist" dramas in the 1930s and 1940s: *Street Scene*, *The Champ*, *The Stranger's Return*, *The Wedding Night*, *Our Daily Bread*, *The Citadel*, and *An American Romance*. As Durgnat and Simmon observe in their book on Vidor, *The Crowd* can be included among many populist movies of the 1920s and 1930s, both in the United States and in Europe, including Joe May's *Asphalt* (1929) and Frank Borzage's *7th Heaven* (1927).[42] The consummation of this trajectory in American cinema was undoubtedly John Ford's celebrated adaptation of John Steinbeck's novel *The Grapes of Wrath*, released at the start of 1940. In many ways, Vidor's *The Crowd* and his later *Our Daily Bread* (1934) are clear precursors of Ford's classic. And *The Crowd* was also the precursor of an important populist movement in international cinema, as noted earlier: Italian neo-realism, with Vittorio De Sica citing Vidor's classic as an inspiration for his own neo-realist classic *The Bicycle Thief*.

The greatness of a film that is composed strictly of vignettes of everyday dramatic situations, and particularly those of "ordinary people," depends substantially on the casting of its lead actors. In the case of *The Crowd*, Vidor worked with two gifted performers whose personal connections with the director went far beyond the studio. Lead actress Eleanor Boardman was Vidor's second wife and she had already acted in several of his earlier films: *Three Wise Fools* (1923), *The Wife of the Centaur* (1924), *Proud Flesh* (1925), and *Bardelys the Magnificent* (1926). She and the director divorced in 1933 and she retired from acting in 1935, living on until the age of 93. Sadly, on July 11, 1936, lead actor James Murray died from drowning after falling from the North River pier in New York City (only about six months after the death of John Gilbert, who died of a second heart attack after years of alcoholism, and less than a decade after the release of *The Crowd*). Murray's performance in Vidor's film had garnered nearly universal high praise and the combination of talent and tragedy in his life would stick with the filmmaker.

At the time of his death, the actor was penniless and his Hollywood career, once so promising after starring in *The Crowd*, had descended into chaos and then oblivion due to his drinking and lack of self-control. At first, MGM had assigned "handlers" to try to keep Murray out of trouble so that the studio could capitalize on his success, but to no avail. Vidor had offered him a role in *Show People*, despite his concerns about the actor's alcoholism, but Murray failed to appear on the set for three days and he was fired after being found asleep in a gutter on the studio lot. During the first half of the 1930s, the actor took small and bit roles (often uncredited) in many forgettable films as well as in a few more notable movies such as *Baby Face* (1933), *The Informer* (1935), and *San Francisco* (1936).

Vidor eventually bumped into Murray on the streets and barely recognized him. The director told the troubled actor that he was willing to give him the lead role in his planned film *Our Daily Bread*—playing a character named John Sims with a wife named Mary, in a clear sequel to *The Crowd*. However, Vidor warned the actor that he would need to quit drinking and to lose weight. Murray instantly became angry and rejected the director's offer. Later, Vidor would hear of the actor's demise, thinking that his drowning in the Hudson River had possibly been a suicide. But then an acquaintance of Murray who had been present at North Pier on that tragic day wrote to the filmmaker to inform him that the actor had in fact been clowning for an audience of people on the pier, all to earn a bit of drinking money, and he had accidentally slipped off the pier and drowned. The people present had at first thought that his falling off the pier had been part of the actor's performance.

Murray's pitiful decline and dramatic death had stayed with Vidor and, later in life, he wrote a treatment for a proposed script about Murray's career and demise. The movie was to be titled *The Actor*. At one point, according to the director, his treatment caught the attention of Francis Ford Coppola, who expressed interest in producing it. However, the project was never completed, especially after Coppola became immersed in the long chaotic production of *Apocalypse Now* (1979).[43] Vidor's "Screen Treatment for *The Actor*" includes a detailed observation of Murray that reveals the director's insightfulness about human nature, an insightfulness that no doubt assisted him greatly in his understanding of dramatic situations and in his direction of actors over the course of his career:

> I understand now the reason for my immediate reaction and conviction at first glimpse of James Murray. He symbolized the typical common man (one of the crowd) and yet his looks were far above average. He had a pleasing and expressive face. There was, however, something in his psychological make-up that wanted to keep him on a lower level. Oh yes, he was patently ambitious, he thought he would like to play leading parts, but something else in him of which he was not entirely conscious would come forth and make him afraid to take on the responsibilities that went with the top-level position of a star. On the one hand he appreciated my interest in him, my giving him the leading role in one of my films, but on the other he would blame me for pushing him up to a higher level than the one he felt he could live with. This is substantiated by the complete rejection of me when he contrived a disappearance as we waited for him for three days on his second film for me, *Show People*, and by the later scene on the bar stool when I discussed with him the lead in a third film [*Our Daily Bread*]. When I told him he would have to lay off the beer and booze before I would give him the part, his answer to me shows clearly that he had a certain anger for me for bringing him out of his comfortable complacency in the first place. Deep down he really saw himself as a bum no matter what an occasional temptation of success tried to say to him. This baring of his psyche is again proved at the time of his death. I think we have here the key to why so many actors and actresses who suffer a quick rise on the movie ladder to a glamorous life and wealth take

to the bottle and drug panaceas as a thrust at reality. This is done to counteract the illusionary character of their quick rise to fame and fortune. They feel their life as an idol is filled with holes, terrific holes. They know they are only playing a part.[44]

* * * *

The Patsy (1928)

Perhaps it was fate that Vidor made *The Patsy* while at the peak of his artistic and commercial success—or, more likely, it was his success that chose this fate for Vidor. After three back-to-back period pieces (*The Big Parade*, *La Bohème*, and *Bardelys the Magnificent*), followed by the everyman epic *The Crowd* and the unrealized spectacle *The Glory Diggers/The Big Ditch*, it might have seemed out of character for Vidor to direct a small chamber comedy/screwball love story like *The Patsy*. But it was precisely this prestige that caught the eye of William Randolph Hearst, who produced the film through his company, Cosmopolitan Pictures, for his mistress Marion Davies. *The Patsy* was written for the screen by Agnes Christine Johnston, a prolific screenwriter who spent much of her career at MGM, ultimately receiving credits for 89 shorts, films, and television episodes between 1915 and 1954. The script was based on a play of the same name by Barry Conners. Vidor recalled, "After the success of *The Big Parade*, Mr. Hearst never gave up until he had me directing Miss Davies. The approach came in the form of a request to do a favor for Mr. Mayer and, in addition, earn a substantial income. W.R. would always pay high when he thought anyone could do a good job for Marion."[45]

By 1928, Hearst and Davies had been making movies together for a decade. "In 1918 Hearst signed Davies to a contract with his newly-formed production company, Cosmopolitan Pictures, at $5 a week," wrote Karina Longworth. "Hearst's stroke of genius when it came to Marion Davies was to use what he had already proven had worked when it came to selling newspapers, and more than that, manipulating reality: If he wanted something to happen, he would report that it was happening, and then it would happen. And so Hearst put the weight of his newspaper empire into spreading the news about this amazing new star, Marion Davies, and then he found some movies for her to star in."[46] This relationship became fodder for Orson Welles who used it as the inspiration for *Citizen Kane* (1941), with Marion Davies as the model for Susan Alexander Kane (Dorothy Comingore), the opera singer with no talent for singing whose career is ramrodded forward by Kane's newspapers and private fortune. Unfairly, this mockery of Davies' life has too often supplanted her real-life story. Davies, when at her best (such as in her two silent films with Vidor), was among the silent screen's greatest comics.

While many of Davies' films for Cosmopolitan made use of her talent for impersonation, Hearst was too keen on placing her in dramas and period pieces instead of comedies, where her slapstick physicality and mimicry were better suited. Consider a brief list of her pre–*Patsy* roles: a pastor's daughter caught in a jewel heist/espionage drama in *The Dark Star* (1919); an heiress dreaming of pirate's booty in *Buried Treasure* (1921); Henry VIII's sister, Mary Tudor, in *When Knighthood Was in Flower* (1922); an Irish immigrant masquerading as a boy in nineteenth-century America in *Little Old New York* (1923); Princess Mary, whose relationship becomes an international crisis in *Yolanda* (1924); a woman who falls in love with a spy on the eve of the Revolutionary War in *Janice Meredith* (1924); an abused orphan girl in *Zander the Great* (1925); dual roles as a nineteenth-century socialite and an Irish musical hall girl in *Lights of Old Broadway* (1925); and a woman who disguises herself as her own niece in order to "test" her love's fidelity after his return from the Napoleonic Wars in *Quality Street* (1927). By contrast, Davies' role in *The Patsy* is exactly the sort of blank canvas that Davies needed to display her extraordinary comedic sensibility in all its glory.

Davies plays Patricia (Pat) Harrington, the black sheep of her family who is hopelessly in love with Tony (Orville Caldwell), but Tony is in love with her sister Grace (Jane Winton), who is in turn in love with the playboy Billy (Lawrence Gray). Patriarchal Ma (Marie Dressler) lords over the Harrington household and devotes all her love and energy to Grace; sheepish Pa (Dell Henderson, who played Mary's brother Dick in *The Crowd*) endures his wife's humiliation but silently sympathizes with Pat. At a yacht club dance, Billy woos Grace away from Tony in a speed boat, and Tony pursues in a rowboat with Pat. But Pat cannot catch up with Grace and Pat cannot convince Tony to pay attention to her. Pat contrives an imaginary "love interest" and asks Tony's advice; he suggests reading a book of witticisms. When that fails to win Tony over, she goes to Billy's house to make him jealous. Pat is heartbroken when that plan backfires at first, but after discussing their mutual feelings, the two embrace and kiss as the movie fades to black.

As frothy as the story may seem, when viewed in tandem with Vidor's other works, this Cinderella story is more than just a lighthearted reprieve from his previous movies. Like Vidor's best and more personal films, *The Patsy* is a thorough extension of his cinematic vision. When looking at his previous four films (*The Big Parade*, *La Bohème*, *Bardelys the Magnificent*, and *The Crowd*) as well as his whole body of work, one sees that *The Patsy* is right in line with Vidor's overarching concern with the struggles and triumphs of the common person. Like *The Crowd*, it also continues a line of social criticism that can be seen as far back as *The Jack-Knife Man*. More specifically, it builds upon the middle-class family satire of *Wine of Youth* and *Peg O' My Heart*, in which the younger generation refuses to conform to the standards of older generations. Pat, like Mary in *Wine of Youth* and the titular character in *Peg O' My Heart*, finds herself trapped in a world of social pretension and mannerisms that threaten to constrict and contain her. From the opening scene in which her slouching posture puts her at odds with the more "dignified" posture of the rest of her family, Pat's body reacts against her family's (and, more broadly, society's) attempts to control her. After reading a book of witticisms, she marches through her house stiff limbed (dehumanizing her movement like a robot) and repeating non sequitur jokes such as "The apple is famous in history, but it takes a grapefruit to stay in the public eye." Her mother and sister are horrified, thinking that Pat has lost her marbles (and to the silent delight of her co-conspirator father, who is in on the ruse). Refusing to play the part of the "younger sister," Pat's radical turn is as much an attempt to win the heart of Tony as it is a way to declare her own agency. Like Vidor, Pat is an independent spirit at heart.

Visually, the film is pure Vidor from its first frame, which is an overhead shot of the Harrington family eating dinner. Much like the famous shot of the soldiers walking in metronomic unison in *The Big Parade*, the Harrington family consumes their soup with synchronicity. Vidor's attention to bodily movement within the frame almost characterizes him as a choreographer as much as a composer of filmic frames. (Ironically, the musical is one of the few genres that Vidor never approached; the closest he came was his uncredited directing of the "Somewhere Over the Rainbow" scene in *The Wizard of Oz*.) Throughout *The Patsy*, Vidor uses bodily rhythms to create both narrative meaning as well as comedic moments, such as when the Harrington family arrives at their yacht club for a dance. Vidor's camera tracks parallel to the family, its speed in tandem with the steady pace of the group. Grace and Tony walk together, followed by Ma and Pa. It is Grace who is the outlier, a "fifth wheel," so to speak, who not only walks outside of the two-by-two formation but who also continually trips over the tassels of her own shawl, causing her to stumble repeatedly. Pat's body is rarely in tandem with anyone else's. Even in the opening sequence, a close-up shot reveals that Pat mimics her sister's movement, mocking her statuesque pose and mannered gesture. Later, when dancing with Tony, a close-up of her feet shows how out of synch she is with Tony—but mainly because he continues to stare at Grace and Billy who are dancing together. Pat, quite literally, dances to the beat of her own drummer.

Vidor's repeated use of windows/framing devices in *The Patsy* emphasizes both the performance and re-performance of its characters and their relationships, frequently drawing visual parallels to theater and cinema. Throughout the film, the Harringtons are always "on stage," aware of roles they are playing and how they are viewed by others. The dining room is only the first of many stages. At the yacht club, Billy pretends as a gag to be a waiter, tossing into the air celery that lands in Ma's cleavage, humiliating her (before she realizes he is rich, which changes her perception of the young man). Interrupting Billy and Grace in the living room, Pat walks back and forth past an open doorway, using off-screen space to literally try on different "hats," each time re-entering the frame under a different guise as though she were an actor stepping onto a stage. More pointedly, when she tries to seduce Billy in his own home, Pat is inspired by the framed photos of Hollywood stars on the walls, transforming herself first into Mae Murray and then Lillian Gish and finally Pola Negri, complete with a knife clenched in her teeth. Afterward she trashes Billy's home, as though to make it look like he had chased her around the room to arouse Tony's jealousy.

Marion Davies (left) stars as Patricia Harrington and Marie Dressler plays "Ma" Harrington in *The Patsy* (1928, directed by King Vidor for Metro-Goldwyn-Mayer) (MGM/Photofest).

The production also allowed Vidor to integrate his philosophical viewpoints with his production practice, fusing thought and action. The making of *The Patsy* was something of a group artistic experiment built on didacticism and collaboration, also anticipating Vidor's later ode to collective effort, *Our Daily Bread* (1934). In MGM press material at the time, titled "'School Sessions' Held by Director King Vidor," Vidor explained his concept:

> The school session idea is not new, but because there are few principals in *The Patsy* cast, we were able to develop it quite efficiently. I believe that any person in the motion picture business will understand and cooperate much more effectively with his co-worker if he knows what his job is all about and the difficulties he is facing. It is not possible for a cameraman to be a star, of course, but a star might very possibly be a good cameraman—and would be a better star if he was. I know that it helped me immeasurably to have my company know precisely what we were doing and to have them eager to offer suggestions. Miss Davies, for example, contributed at least 12 good comedy situations which we are using in *The Patsy*, and Marie Dressler contributed nearly as many. By making everyone realize that he or she are integral parts in the production ... and partially responsible for the success of the picture, I think that they all will do better work.[47]

The Patsy was the success that Hearst wanted for Davies, receiving rave notices. "Marion Davies does some really great comedy work," wrote *Variety*. "An excellent laugh picture."[48] Mordaunt Hall, in the *New York Times*, wrote that "[o]f all the varied Cinderellas who have from time to time graced the screen, Marion Davies, in an adaptation of Barry Conners's stage comedy, *The Patsy*, not only holds her own in the matter of vivacity and appearance, but she also elicits more fun than one would suppose could be generated from even a modern conception of the undying role. She is ably assisted by the adroit direction of King Vidor, the competent acting of the supporting cast and also by the wit with which Ralph Spence's titles are fired."[49]

The film even won over some critics of Davies who had previously been skeptical: "Among the pictures that I avoid have been those in which Marion Davies starred," wrote *The Film Spectator*. "They are exploited so ridiculously in the Hearst papers, and Marion herself jumps at us so constantly from the pages of these papers, that I am irritated in advance by her pictures, a frame of mind not conducive to fair criticism.... But the other night *The Patsy* squatted on my doorstep, so to speak.... It quite persuades me that Marion should sue somebody. I have seen her in so many parts that she should not have played that I have doubted if there were any part that she could play, and along she comes in this picture and gives one of the finest performances of a refined comedy role that it has been my good fortune to see in a long time."[50]

Among the biggest fans of the film in the press was its own star, Marion Davies. "I believe that *The Patsy* is the best comedy that I have ever had," she said in a *New York Times* article. "Mr. Vidor inspires the players who are associated with him. Not only has he a fine imagination and a philosophic turn of mind but he consistently refuses to take himself too seriously." Davies describes the collaborative nature of the set, such as the scene in which she passes by a doorway changing hats, which began with the simple direction "Peek around the curtains and we will figure out what to do." Davies was inspired by co-star Dell Henderson's hat, which happened to be lying around. From there, the gag was built.[51] Even more revealing is Davies' own interpretation of the director's sensibility: "Vidor's philosophy is to observe, to remember what he has seen and then reproduce it with a true human touch ... 'Watch, remember and reproduce'—that is the philosophy of King Vidor, and I think it is a philosophy all players as well as directors can well adopt."[52] "The human touch" of which Davies speaks is an enigmatic quality, for sure, but it is undoubtedly one of Vidor's touchstones, no matter how difficult to pinpoint it may be.

* * * *

Show People (1928)

Marion Davies and William Randolph Hearst must have been thrilled with the success of *The Patsy*, as they re-teamed with Vidor later that year for another comedy, *Show People* (1928). Like its predecessor, *Show People*'s comedic spectacles were built upon Davies's capacity for imitation and physical caricature. It also takes the notion of performativity even further, crafting a meta-narrative about the trials and tribulations of an aspiring actress new to Hollywood.

The project began with a request from Hearst to adapt a play by Guy Bolton called *Polly Preferred* (based on Bolton's earlier novel of the same name from 1923). Vidor could not even finish reading it as he disliked it so much. "Instead of trying to adapt the play, we just started writing a whole new story," Vidor said. "The play was called *Polly Preferred*, but it had nothing to do with the film. It wasn't even about Hollywood. The play was about a girl going to New York to go on the stage."[53] Bolton's name is not even in the final film credits. Another potential reason that Vidor wanted to stay away from Bolton's work is that, in 1925, he was sued for plagiarism by Ossip Dymow, who alleged that Bolton stole *Polly Preferred* from his own play *Personality*. Dymow won the suit, with Bolton admitting that it was "unconscious plagiarism."[54] Vidor enlisted the talent of previous collaborators Agnes Christine Johnston (screenwriter of *The Patsy*) and Laurence Stallings (the scenarist for *The Big Parade*) as well as Wanda Tuchock (who would go on to write a total of six films for Vidor between 1928 and 1932). The new scenario was a good-natured jab at Hollywood pretension, filled with backlot insight and access as well as plenty of self-referential humor. "We were thinking of giving the people we knew an inside joke," said Vidor.[55]

Davies plays Peggy Pepper, an aspiring actress whose father, Colonel Pepper (Dell Henderson, also the father from *The Patsy*), drives her from Georgia to Hollywood to pursue a career in the movies. Arriving in the big city, the first thing they do is drive to a studio and demand to see the president, whereby they are instructed to go to the casting office instead. When asked if she can act, Colonel Pepper instructs Peggy to perform the "various moods": "passion," "anger," "sorrow," and "joy." Whereas Peggy believes she is acting out serious dramatic emotions, the casting agent thinks she is joking and bursts out laughing. Peggy's audition lands her a job on a slapstick comedy set, where she is unsuspectingly belted with carbonated water in her face during a farcical dining room demolition. She is taken under the wing of her co-star, Billy Boone (William Haines, who had acted in three previous Vidor films, *Three Wise Fools*, *Wine of Youth*, and *The Wife of the Centaur*), and taught how to act in comedies. Peggy proves so successful in comedies that she is offered a job at High Art Studios as a dramatic actress. However, they do not want Billy to come with her. Along with the new job she is given a new name, "Patricia Pepoire," a new backstory that omits her slapstick roots, and a new romantic interest with a new co-star, Andre Telfair (Paul Ralli). Interrupting their wedding, Billy squirts Peggy in the face with carbonated water, reminding her of her roots and their shared experiences together, but Peggy sends him away. Ultimately, Peggy does not go through with the marriage to Andre. The film ends with Peggy on the set of a World War I film directed by none other than King Vidor. She secretly arranges for Billy to get a role as a doughboy and surprises him during the filming when they embrace on film.

Davies's elastic face and darting eyes are the real draw of *Show People*. More than two decades before Gene Kelly (as Don Lockwood) and Jean Hagen (as Lina

EIGHT. *The Crowd, The Patsy,* and *Show People*

An on-the-set photograph from the production of *Show People* (1928, directed by King Vidor for Metro-Goldwyn-Mayer). From left: Marion Davies (who plays Peggy Pepper), William Haines (who plays Billy Boone), director Vidor, and continuity writer Wanda Tuchok (MGM/Photofest).

Lamont) would lampoon silent cinema histrionics in *Singin' in the Rain* (1952), Davies parodies acting cliches, poking fun at both comedic and dramatic acting styles. Her wild facial expressions (the "various moods," as her father called them) during her audition recall Colleen Moore in *Ella Cinders* (1926) as she reads an acting manual and tries out different expressions. The slapstick film that Peggy makes shows her doing Mabel Normand–esque stunts, riding on bicycle handles, crashing and being thrown onto barnyard animals, and leaping off buildings. Vidor filmed these sequences at the actual Sennett Studios where Normand worked and where silent comedy was perfected, and the film includes an actual surprise cameo from the real Keystone Kops.[56] Davies's comedic timing is perfectly displayed during one of her "dramatic" sequences for High Art Studios, where the director instructs her to look left and imagine the man she loves (Peggy says, "I love you") and then look right at the man she hates (Peggy says, "I hate you"), which she is made to repeat with increasing rapidity.

Davies' most glorious expression of her physical comedy is the character-defining scene when Peggy is first blasted with the carbonated water. With arms outstretched, she takes the full blast of water, never once belying the surprise, shock, and humiliation that her character is feeling. Despite the circumstances, it is a rare moment of honesty from Peggy. And Davies, instead of satirizing her character, delivers the scene with absolute sincerity. As funny as it is, the scene is deeply moving, and shows the layers of meaning that Davies was able to convey as a performer. Not surprisingly, Hearst was opposed to the scene when he read it in the script; she was originally supposed to be hit by a custard pie thrown in her face. Vidor stressed to Hearst the importance of the act as an iconic slapstick gesture, and the carbonated water was selected as a compromise. Still, not wanting to risk further interference from Hearst, it was arranged for the *Los Angeles Examiner* to make a fake call to Hearst to pull him away from the set when the scene was filmed.[57]

Vidor is not above making fun of himself, either. Billy and Peggy attend a screening of Vidor's *Bardelys the Magnificent*, which Billy calls "punk drama." Later, Andre Telfair is shown wearing John Gilbert's costumes from *His Hour*.[58] Durgnat and Simmon note that these sorts of references show Vidor "acknowledging a reasonably down-to-earth viewpoint. Vidor can laugh at 'himself.'"[59] The authors also note that these jokes should not be viewed as serious critiques of either Vidor himself

A scene at the theater in *Show People* (1928, directed by King Vidor for Metro-Goldwyn-Mayer). Billy Boone (played by William Haines) and Peggy Pepper (played by Marion Davies) star in this masterful parody of Hollywood show business life (MGM/Photofest).

Eight. The Crowd, The Patsy, and Show People

or of Hollywood. They draw a comparison with Josef von Sternberg's *The Last Command*, made the same year, about an expat Russian royalty who faces humiliation as an extra in Hollywood (played by Emil Jannings, who won the first ever Academy Award for acting for his roles in this and 1927's *The Way of All Flesh*): "Social criticism is secondary [in *Show People*], so long as the system is free enough to allow individuals their choice, including the choice of opting out. Vidor's response to his workplace in 1928 could hardly be further from von Sternberg's in *The Last Command*, where the crowd of movie extras is exactly as bitter, and as lacking in freedom, as the prerevolutionary mass it impersonates."[60]

Angela Dalle Vacche views the politics of the film differently than Durgnat and Simmon, seeing them as more serious and in line with Vidor's other films:

> After dealing with issues of unemployment and social consensus in *The Crowd*, that very same year King Vidor went on to shoot *Show People*, a film about the Hollywood industry as a site of labor. Always on the side of Mickey Mouse or the little guy who can make it against all odds, Vidor criticizes egomaniac directors involved in pretentious Europhile costume dramas. Thus, he aligns himself with lighthearted and lowbrow comedies punctuated by pies flying from one face to the next. Laughter, here, is not about stupidity, but rather about a new culture of action and entertainment and pokes fun at Hollywood's clumsiness with highbrow foreign models and failing imitations.[61]

More than just a send up of Tinseltown, *Show People* is a fond remembrance of an industry on the brink of irreversible change. This was 1928, after all, the last real year of silent films in Hollywood. *The Jazz Singer*, a part-talkie, had premiered in 1927. *Lights of New York*, the first all-talking feature, appeared the following year. By 1929, sound would be the dominant mode of production. In this light and in hindsight, Vidor's use of cameos by such silent stars as Charlie Chaplin (who tries, and fails, to get Peggy Pepper's autograph), Douglas Fairbanks, and William S. Hart (in what would be his final appearance in a feature film) become especially precious. Davies, too, gets a cameo when she plays herself and Peggy spots her on the studio lot. Vidor's behind-the-scenes footage takes on an almost documentary quality, despite the comedic nature of the movie.

Show People was shot on the set of working studio backlots, with actual cast and crew performing their roles. Vidor may have intended *Show People* to be filled with "inside jokes," but more importantly he allowed the rest of us to be insiders on those gags. "*Show People* is one of the loveliest films ever made about Hollywood, and the perfect climax to Vidor's silent career," wrote curator Charles Silver. "It was intended to gently mock the career of Gloria Swanson.... The film effervesces with genial and warm satire culminating in the appearance of Vidor himself, a personal touch of considerable endearment."[62] For a director who began writing silent comedies, *Show People* is a fitting final silent film for Vidor, an elegy to his early days, a gentle mocking of his friends and colleagues, and a fond farewell to an art form that was in its final moments. By the time *Show People* was released to positive reviews in October 1928, Vidor was already working on his next project: a "talking picture."

Nine

1929
Hallelujah

"I don't imagine any picture ever was made with more wholehearted fun than was this one.... The story is based on events with which I was familiar as a boy at home in Texas."[1]—King Vidor, 1929

"I think it either will be one of the greatest hits of the year or one of the greatest flops. I'd certainly hate to have it turn out to be just one of those pictures.... The picture is, I hope, evidence of the correctness of my theory that the screen can do more than just narrate a series of events."[2]—King Vidor, 1929

"'Hallelujah' was shown in only a few cities of the South, because the exhibitors were afraid of race prejudice. Yet, at the theaters where it was shown, long lines waited to see it."[3]—Robert Dana, "King Vidor, Director of 'The Citadel,'" 1938

"I asked Vidor which had been his favorite film, and he said, without hesitation, 'Hallelujah.'"[4]—Our Film Correspondent, "King Vidor in England," *The Observer*, June 19, 1938

"In making 'Hallelujah' my interpretation or idea of the Negro was my Negro mammy.... I was born in the South, and as a boy, one of my first impressions of Negroes was that they were being mistreated by white men."[5]—King Vidor, 1939

"When we started *Hallelujah* in Memphis in 1929 we didn't know whether it was to be a silent film or a sound film or half of each."[6]—King Vidor, 1955

The screen is black. There is no sound. Faint scratches on the screen indicate that film is passing through the projector. Over the speakers comes the sound of rain and drums. Voices begin chanting. And then the MGM logo appears, with its silently roaring lion. The chorus sings the title of the movie as it appears on screen: *Hallelujah* (sometimes listed as *Hallelujah!*). There is something almost religious about the appearance of the title, with the mass of voices harmonizing its syllables. It is a fittingly divine introduction not only to a film whose narrative is laced with themes of spirituality, but also to King Vidor's first sound film. The carefully selected introduction of sound before image, as well as the simultaneous appearance of the title card and its aural proclamation, signals the director's interest in the interplay of sound and image.

Hallelujah's technical innovation has, since its first appearance, been intertwined with the film's complicated representation of race. Featuring an all-black cast (the second film of 1929 to do so, the first being *Hearts in Dixie*, released three months prior), *Hallelujah* tells the story of Zeke (Daniel L. Haynes), a southern cotton sharecropper who is lured into a gambling den by Chick (Nina Mae McKinney) and ends up committing murder. Despite trying to reinvent himself as a minister, Zeke is lured back into a life of sin by Chick, culminating in a double murder and a prison sentence for Zeke. Visually and thematically, the film exhibits many of the director's characteristic motifs. The story displays Vidor's continued interest in rural culture, close-knit communities, and small town life. The setting allows ample opportunities for the director to display his keen eye for naturalistic photography. He also films the manual and mechanical processes of the cotton industry with an almost newsreel sense of authenticity, blended with a romantic sense of idealization and perfection.

Hallelujah's controversy lies in its portrayal of black characters. While one may try to justify Vidor's intention to show black rural life in a major Hollywood production, the film reinforces racist stereotypes of the "happy slave," minstrel shows, and revivalist ecstasy. In interviews, Vidor explained that his long-standing desire to make *Hallelujah* goes back to childhood: "Our family employed one Negro woman and my father had mostly black men working in his sawmills. I saw very much of them as a group. I was very impressed with their music, their feelings, their attitude toward life, their feelings about religion, and their feelings about sex and humor. As long as I can remember I wanted to make a film about them."[7] Vidor's attitude about racial difference, however, expressed a patronizing view: "The American Negro is one of the greatest of actors for this very reason," Vidor is quoted in press materials for the film. "He is more sensitive to emotions than his white brother, and hence his acting has a naturalness that cannot be schooled. The same thing is true of the Negro singing in the pictures, in the 'blues' and spirituals.'"[8] Ignoring any aspect of training, he undermines the agency of the actors in his film and ignores their skills and accomplishments. This objectification is at the root of *Hallelujah*'s bigoted perspective.

Much critical attention has been devoted to the divisive reception of *Hallelujah*. Film historian Donald Bogle details the many opinions printed upon the movie's release by both black and white critics in his landmark book *Toms, Coons, Mulattoes, Mammies, and Bucks: An Interpretive History of Blacks in American Films*:

> *Hallelujah*'s view of black life was enthusiastically greeted by the white press.... Much of the Negro press, however, was less charitable. When *Hallelujah* had simultaneous premieres at the Lafayette Theatre in Harlem and the Embassy in the downtown white area, the black press denounced the racism inherent in the dual opening. Black patrons viewed it as a tactical move by MGM to spare the feelings of "swanky whites" who might not object to watching a screenful of darkies but who most certainly did not want to sit next to any in a theater. Of greater concern to some black critics, though, were the spiritual-singing, crap-shooting characters who were old types even in 1929.[9]

Judith Weisenfeld also compares and contrasts the initial reviews of *Hallelujah* in her book *Hollywood Be Thy Name: African American Religion in American Film, 1929–1949*. She notes that among the film's defenders was W.E.B. Du Bois, who took to the pages of the NAACP's publication *The Crisis* to advocate for *Hallelujah*. He "hailed the film as a 'great drama' and argued that the kind of African American religiosity portrayed ... must be understood as having developed as a universal human response to tragedy and disaster." He also "emphasized the universal human appeal of the story and noted the potentially positive consequence of the film's effective use of documentary-style sequences of black laborers."[10]

Among the voices critical of *Hallelujah* was that of acclaimed actor Paul Robeson, who took *Hallelujah* to task in *Film Weekly*: "The box office insistence that the Negro shall figure always as a clown has spoiled the two Negro films which have been made in Hollywood, *Hallelujah* and *Hearts in Dixie*," wrote Robeson. "In *Hallelujah* they took the Negro and his church services and made them funny.... Hollywood can only visualize the plantation type of Negro—the Negro of 'Poor Old Joe' and 'Swanee Ribber.'"[11] While they were not played for comedy, Robeson's characterization of the religious rituals as "funny" is an indication of the film's tendency towards caricature. Film historian Charles Silver's interpretation is in line with Robeson's:

> It could be argued that *Hallelujah* is, in its way, as important to the development of talkies as *The Birth of a Nation* was to the silent film fifteen years earlier. Unfortunately, the parallel between the two films doesn't stop there. Vidor, an unabashed Texan, carried much of the baggage of a Southern upbringing. On one level, *Hallelujah* clearly reinforces the stereotypes of Blacks as childishly simple, lecherously promiscuous, fanatically superstitious, and shiftless.... Certainly, Vidor could never be accused of the overt racial venom exhibited by Griffith in *The Birth of a Nation*. Yet the benefit of the doubt one might give to *Hallelujah* is partially negated by his *So Red the Rose* (1935) ... [in which] he converts the Blacks back into the happy singers they were before they became "uppity" and began to think of themselves as men rather than chattel.[12]

The film's problematic portrayal begins in the first scene, which introduces Zeke and his family as they pick cotton, smiling widely, and speaking with exaggeratedly improper grammar that is particularly incongruous with Haynes' eloquent and trained theatrical voice. The joy their faces express as they carry bags of cotton on their backs belies the reality of their labor. Racism, prejudice, and Jim Crow do not exist in Vidor's Southern fantasy—nor do any other races or ethnicities, for that matter. As Bogle commented, "Vidor, himself an idealist, had presented his Negroes in an idealized, isolated world. By having his blacks battle it out among themselves rather than with any white antagonists, he created an unreal universe and consequently divorced himself from real issues confronting blacks and whites in America."[13]

That night, after dinner, Zeke's family plays music and dances. As Vidor films close-ups of two children's feet as they tap dance, one can question the camera's viewpoint. What is the purpose of these shots? Are the grinning children performing

Nine. *Hallelujah*

Hallelujah (1929, directed by King Vidor for Metro-Goldwyn-Mayer) was a landmark film with a cast composed completely of African American actors. It was made during the transition between silent cinema and the sound era. From left: Fanny Belle DeKnight (as Mammy), Daniel L. Haynes (as Zeke), and Nina Mae McKinney (as Chick) (MGM/Photofest).

for their benefit or for the audience's? If it is the latter, then what is to distinguish Vidor's viewpoint from the perspective of a minstrel show attendee? Such exploitative overtones are present throughout *Hallelujah*.

Where *Hallelujah* excels are in its montages, which benefit from location shooting in Memphis and across the Mississippi River in nearby Arkansas.[14] There is an almost documentary realism to the way that Vidor films Zeke and his coworkers as they deliver the cotton to the gin and as it passes through the machines until it is processed into bales, which are then loaded onto wagons and brought to the riverbanks. There they are rolled across planks and onto steamboats. This sequence perfectly melds Vidor's interests in landscape, labor, and industrialization, which would culminate in his 1944 film *An American Romance*. Through Vidor's lens, this procedure is also romanticized; the labor is divorced from its actuality. As Zeke sits atop a bin of raw cotton, he sings and gestures broadly with his arms, while a group of nearby coworkers has formed a chorus to back him up. This, for Vidor, is the business of cotton: an occasion for song, a technical marvel and a capitalist metaphor. Nowhere in this scene do we sense the hardship of the workers or the exploitation of their labor. When Zeke walks off the riverboat, he has a wad of cash as though he is a rich man. One wonders whether Vidor believed this fantasy or whether he just does not care about—or understand—the reality of the situation.

As Zeke walks away with his money, he comes across a craps game behind some bales of cotton. Nearby, Chick dances for a crowd, slapping her knee and shaking her hips to a harmonica player. As Zeke watches, comments from the crowd are layered on the soundtrack, their faces never identified with their words. Among the most striking and audible is, "What a brown skin' bunch of sweetness she is." Disembodied from any character, the words serve to objectify Chick's performance, race, and gender (even her name is a symbol of her objectification). After she finishes dancing, Zeke says to her (in the film's typically caricatured dialogue): "You is just what I has got on my mind."

Zeke's visit to a juke joint is among *Hallelujah*'s crowning cinematic achievements. The camera tracks through the smoke-filled club, cutting between Chick singing, Zeke observing, people in the audience dancing, and even a drummer twirling sticks during a solo. Juxtaposing a variety of actions and characters, and alternating between close and long shots, Vidor expresses more vitality in editing and composition than movie musicals would for years to come. The shots of Chick are particularly evocative, with smoke swirling around her. The band members in the background are barely visible, like specters, their bodies lost in the haze and dim lights. Unlike the staginess of most Hollywood musicals during the early sound era, the camera eschews the traditional theatrical perspective and feels like it is in the middle of the action. Whereas Vidor's earlier films often expressed his interest in bodily movement, here his choreography moves beyond synchronous movement (as in previously discussed moments from *The Big Parade* and *The Patsy*) and incorporates multiple bodies moving in disparate ways within a single environment. Such a complex, sophisticated scene is remarkable considering the immaturity of the movie musical in 1929. Vidor's only other venture into the musical genre would be an uncredited contribution directing the "Somewhere Over the Rainbow" number in *The Wizard of Oz* (1939), but his fluidity and inventiveness in *Hallelujah* leads one to wonder what could have been if Vidor had further explored the genre in other movies.

At the juke joint, Chick goads Zeke into gambling away all the money from his family's cotton crop. Meanwhile, Zeke's brother, Spunk (Everett McGarrity), drives a carriage through town looking for Zeke. His search is another remarkable cinematic moment: a single tracking shot down a dark street and as the camera passes by bar windows, the soundtrack changes to reflect different goings on in each establishment. "Sound editing is far in advance of the time," film historian Scott Eyman notes. "A tracking shot of a wagon moving down the street, with the music changing from barrelhouse to blues depending on what bar the wagon is passing, must have been maddeningly difficult for the sound editors."[15]

Tragedy ensues when Spunk finds his brother. As Zeke wrestles with Chick's con artist partner, Hot Shot (William Fountaine), his gun goes off and Spunk is killed. Zeke returns home and finds spiritual rebirth as a minister. Despite being engaged to Missy (Victoria Spivey), Zeke runs off with Chick after she attends a revivalist meeting where Zeke is preaching. Zeke eventually abandons religion and works in a logging factory. When he discovers that Chick is planning to run off with Hot Shot, he pursues them, shooting and killing Chick. He then chases Hot Shot through a swamp, catching and killing him as well. Zeke's murder of Chick and Hot Shot in the moonlight is one of the finest sequences of the film. Lit by the moon, Zeke's pursuit is as chilling as it is impassioned, and the photography anticipates the poetic realism of film noir of the 1940s and 1950s and points the way for Vidor's own rustic noir movies *Beyond the Forest* (1949), *Lightning Strikes Twice* (1951), and *Ruby Gentry* (1952). After spending time in a prison work camp, Zeke is released on probation, walks the same dirt road where the film began, and rejoins his family.

Hallelujah displays a technical and artistic bravura that is a decade ahead of its time. Vidor's enlightened montage of sight and sound, blending silent footage with

An on-the-set photograph from the production of *Hallelujah* (1929, directed by King Vidor for Metro-Goldwyn-Mayer). From left: Daniel L. Haynes (who plays Zeke), Nina Mae McKinney (who plays Chick), and director Vidor. This film with an all-black cast was a landmark film during the transition between silent cinema and the sound era (MGM/Photofest).

synchronized sound footage, as well as his mixing of live sound and studio-produced artificial sound, displays a brilliance that belies its primitiveness. When trying to synchronize recorded sound with the footage, Vidor would instruct a projectionist to "make a grease-pencil mark on the rapidly moving film," but it would invariably be several feet off because of the delay between his command and the projectionist's mark.[16] Supplementing live recorded sound, Vidor and his crew had to create new sounds in the studio (what we would today call "foley"):

> We found ourselves making big puddles of water and mud, tramping through them with a microphone while a sound truck recorded the effect. Rotting branches and fallen trees were crawled over.... Never one to treat a dramatic effect literally, the thought struck me—why not free the imagination and record this sequence impressionistically? When someone stepped on a broken branch, we made it sound as if bones were breaking. As the pursued victim withdrew his foot from the stickiness of the mud, we made the vacuum sound strong enough to pull him down into hell.... In my first desperation with sound, I believed that this nonfactual use of it was ideally suited to my film.[17]

Despite these crude behind-the-scenes techniques, *Hallelujah* looks as polished as anything made a decade later in 1939, which is saying a lot considering how many sound films from 1929 visibly suffer from the same limitations that Vidor was able to overcome.

While *Hallelujah* was originally noted in the press for its all-black cast, that same cast did not benefit from the movie. As Bogle noted, "For most of the cast, *Hallelujah* was the beginning and ending of their screen careers. Hollywood had not yet found a place for the black performer. Of all the actors in the film, the one to meet with the greatest 'success'—and heartache—was its energetic leading lady, Nina Mae McKinney."[18] Haynes, who previously had been an understudy for *Show Boat* in New York, would not star in another movie; he had a few small roles (including one in Vidor's *So Red the Rose*), but ultimately he returned to the stage.[19] McKinney, who previously had been in the chorus of *Blackbirds* on Broadway, struggled to find work despite receiving an MGM contract, eventually emigrating to Europe in order to find roles.[20] Among her scant film credits are leads in the B-movies *Gang Smashers* (1938) and *The Devil's Daughter* (1939), and bit parts in Andre De Toth's *Dark Waters* (1944) and Elia Kazan's *Pinky* (1949) (in which a white actress, Jeanne Crain, plays the titular black character). According to press notes, many of the other actors in *Hallelujah* "are actual cotton workers from plantations near Memphis."[21] Scrolling through IMDB's cast list confirms Bogle's comments that film careers did not pan out for any of the actors, most of whom never had another credit.[22]

For all its problematic attitudes about race, *Hallelujah* remains a significant turning point in Vidor's career. More than just a technical masterpiece in the nascent sound period, it foreshadows many of the directions that Vidor would explore later in his career. Vidor would revisit the relationship of workers and land in *Our Daily Bread* (1934) and *An American Romance* (1944), albeit focusing on white protagonists. He revisited issues of race twenty-three years later with the far more progressive *Japanese War Bride* (1952), about the racism suffered by Japanese in America during and after World War II. In addition to the cinematographic connections to his later noir work, *Hallelujah* is also notable for having the darkest and most morally complex character in any of Vidor's work to date. Zeke's conflicted sense of self, desire, and spirituality is in stark contrast to the more admirable "everymen" of the director's earlier works; later films such as *Stella Dallas* (1937), *The Citadel* (1938), as well as his "noir trilogy" (*Beyond the Forest*, *Lightning Strikes Twice*, and *Ruby Gentry*) find their roots in *Hallelujah*. The melodramatic acting and fable-like construction connect it with such narratively disparate films as the father-son boxing drama *The Champ* (1931) and the Polynesia-set *Bird of Paradise* (1932). And Zeke and Chick would also be Vidor's most erotically charged relationship (in a moment of kink, Chick even suggestively bites Zeke's arm) until the Freudian western *Duel in the Sun* (1946).

More than just bridging the gap from silent to sound, *Hallelujah* suggests the many detours and directions that Vidor would take in the years to come.

Ten

1930

Not So Dumb and *Billy the Kid*

Not So Dumb

Not So Dumb (1930) was Vidor's third and final collaboration with Marion Davies. It was the least funny, lacking Davies's slapstick physicality as well as Vidor's inventive direction.[1] Coming after the rapturous fusion of sound and image of *Hallelujah*, *Not So Dumb* is strikingly static, exhibiting none of the previous film's experimentation or aural-visual montage. The film is an adaptation of George S. Kaufman and Marc Connolly's 1921 play *Dulcy*, a comedy about a wife whose attempts to influence a business merger involving her husband do not go according to plan over the course of a dinner party. *Dulcy* had previously been filmed in 1923 under the work's original title, directed by Sidney A. Franklin (future Academy Award nominee for Best Director of *The Good Earth* [1937]), and with Constance Talmadge in the titular role. The play would be filmed again in 1940, directed by S. Sylvan Simon and starring Ann Sothern.

For Vidor's film, *Hallelujah* scenarist Wanda Tuchock adapted the play, with additional dialogue by Edwin Justus Mayer, who would contribute to the script for Vidor's *So Red the Rose* (1935). Their script adheres closely to Kaufman and Connolly's text, with one notable change: instead of a wife, she is a fiancé. Vidor explained that this was at the command of Hearst: "He didn't want Marion playing a married woman. He feared that this would put her in some kind of category, and he wanted her to remain youthful."[2]

The movie begins with Dulcy (Marion Davies) and her fiancé Gordon (Elliott Nugent) waiting in the rain for a train to arrive with their houseguests for the weekend: Mr. and Mrs. Forbes (William Holden and Julia Faye) and their daughter Angela (Sally Starr). Gordon intends to close a business deal with Forbes for a stake in his artificial jewelry business. Unbeknownst to Gordon, Dulcy has taken matters into her own hands and invited an eccentric investor/golf fanatic, Van Dyke (Donald Ogden Stewart, better known as the Academy Award–winning screenwriter of *The Philadelphia Story* [1940]), as well as a Hollywood screenwriter, Leach (Franklin Pangborn). Dulcy wants to hook up Leach with Angela. Also around the house that weekend are Dulcy's brother Willie (Raymond Hackett) and an ex-con-turned-butler, Perkins (George Davis).

Dulcy's attempts to charm Forbes backfire one after another: when he asks for water, she insists upon a variety of beverages, none of which he wants; she arranges to be his bridge partner and then proceeds to talk incessantly during the game about how she does not know how to play; she disrupts a piano recital by crinkling wrapping paper from a box of chocolates; and a game of "detective" backfires when Dulcy hides Angela's pearls in the house and they go missing for real. Her surprise guests also backfire: Van Dyke is more interested in Mrs. Forbes than Mr. Forbes and Leach and Angela drive off to elope in the middle of the night. After Forbes breaks the deal with Gordon, Dulcy tries once more to intervene, arranging for Van Dyke to be Gordon's new business partner, a plan that goes awry after Van Dyke's brother arrives and reveals that his brother suffers from delusions and is not a rich investor. Forbes, however, does not believe that Van Dyke is a fraud and reverses his decision, making Gordon a partner in his company.

Much of the film's problem stems from the script being overly faithful to the stage play, which results in far too much gab, forcing Vidor to keep his camera stationary for most of the film. Occasionally Vidor tries to replicate his technique (used in *Hallelujah*) of cutting away from a speaker and splicing in silent footage. This occurs, for example, during the bridge game when Vidor alternates between close-ups of Dulcy talking and the bored face of Mr. Forbes, or during Leach's recitation of his new film *Sin*, when Vidor cuts to show Mr. Forbes, Willie, and Gordon asleep. However, even these instances are few and far between. One wonders if the repeated shots of characters disinterested in dialogue is Vidor's clever way of expressing his own disinterest and displeasure with the talkies. If that is the case, he does not find a way to overcome the obstacles presented by the new film medium.

Technically, the most innovative sequence is the piano recital, when Dulcy unwraps a box of chocolates, crinkles the wrapping paper under her arm, removes the wax paper, offers chocolates to guests, shushes other people who try to respond to her, and then explodes in applause before the piece is finished. The interplay of sounds and the sharp contrast in their tonal qualities recall Vidor's comments about overdubbing sound in *Hallelujah*: "Never one to treat a dramatic effect literally, the thought struck me—why not free the imagination and record this sequence impressionistically? When someone stepped on a broken branch, we made it sound as if bones were breaking."[3] Vidor's "impressionistic" approach to this scene is evident in the audio mixing, which keeps the piano low and overly amplifies Dulcy's noises to emphasize her disruption. Perhaps this, too, is another of Vidor's jabs at the talkies, with the commotion of eating representing movie audience members who are too busy munching on popcorn to hear the dialogue. Aural jokes such as this would be lost in the "silent" version of *Not So Dumb*, prepared "because some theatres were not yet equipped for sound. Kevin Brownlow saw the silent version in England and thought that it drags terribly because all of the gags are sound gags."[4]

When Hearst saw the finished film, he was not enthusiastic. He sent a memo of changes to be made, but MGM vice president Irving Thalberg refused. Hearst replied

Marion Davies stars as Dulcinea Parker and Franklin Pangborn plays Vincent Leach in King Vidor's *Not So Dumb* (1930, Metro-Goldwyn-Mayer). The screenplay is based on the 1921 stage play *Dulcy* by George S. Kaufman and Marc Connelly. This was Vidor's third and last film starring Marion Davies (MGM/Photofest).

to Thalberg: "All right old man. It's your funeral. I am only a pall bearer." Hearst's intuition was right: *Not So Dumb* was not a box office hit. "Vidor's two earlier comedies with Marion, *The Patsy* and *Show People*, had earned profits of $155,000 and $176,000," wrote David Nasaw in his book *The Chief: The Life of William Randolph Hearst*. "*Not So Dumb*, which cost less to make than either of them, ended up with a loss of $39,000."[5]

Despite the poor returns, some critics responded favorably. "Stirred up fairly constant chuckling from an audience," reported Mordaunt Hall in the *New York Times*. "Marion Davies, who is always at her best under the direction of King Vidor, shines…. The lion's share of the credit, however, must go to Mr. Vidor for his fine direction."[6] *Variety*, too, wrote favorably of the movie: "A continuously effective guffaw-inducer and tummy vibrator … a typically efficient King Vidor comedy effort, well dovetailed in dialog and keeping all the characters in their proper relationship and importance…. A dandy comedy all the way."[7]

Exhibitors Herald-World snarkily began their review of *Not So Dumb* with "It is too!" They continued by calling it "a thoroughly curious result. *Not So Dumb* almost measures up to an average program feature, but considered in the light of what might have happened—what should have happened—with the assistance of so many experts, the picture can hardly be called anything but a dud."[8] *The Wall Street Journal* commented, "A good deal of the cleverness and subtlety of the original play has been lost in translation. The present picture is only mildly amusing.... [Marion Davies] is supposed to be 'not so dumb' [but] many of her lines are very much so."[9] And *Inside Faces of Stage and Screen* was also dismissive of the movie: "Even the most conscientious of the reviewers cannot become too enthusiastic about this picture. It has its laugh moments, but these are more than offset by an exceeding dragginess which runs at intervals throughout the entire picture.... King Vidor's direction is clever but from a weak scenarization of the George S. Kaufman-Marc Connelly stage play."[10]

In sum, *Not So Dumb* is a minor film in Vidor's body of work, an underwhelming coda to his brilliant work with Marion Davies in *The Patsy* and *Show People*, and an impersonal work lacking his usual technical innovation and artistic flourish.

* * * *

Billy the Kid

> "To portray him as he actually was, or at least as he is described in books dealing biographically with his life, would be impossible on the screen."[11]—King Vidor, 1930

Only one year after his first foray into sound, Vidor found himself on the cusp of a new technical innovation in cinema: widescreen. Fox was busy filming *The Big Trail* (directed by Raoul Walsh and featuring John Wayne in his first starring role) in their 70mm "Grandeur" process. Entering the widescreen race with their own technology was MGM, who called their 70mm system "Realife." Unlike Grandeur and other larger format mediums, Realife did not require a special 70mm projector; instead, with only a few modifications, a standard 35mm projector could be upgraded to handle the new film. This necessitated that the 70mm film be reduced to a 35mm print that would be delivered to theaters. "A newly devised lens enlarges the image on the screen to the desired size," explained the *New York Times*. "[This] eliminates a potential expenditure of $40,000,000—a sum which, coming on the heels of the economic revolution of sound pictures and equipment, might have proved disastrous."[12]

Vidor was enthusiastic about the potential of Realife. "Close-ups are the easiest manner of getting around problems," Vidor said. "But why stop the camera and destroy motion? With the enlarged screen it is now possible to center on a number of characters at once, keeping them moving, getting all their reactions and thus continuing with your story."[13] In order to compare the two formats—as well as to create a standard 35mm version in the conventional and more widely projected 1.37:1 aspect ratio—Vidor shot two versions of the movie simultaneously. "Both cameras were right alongside each other when we filmed," he explained. "The 70mm seemed to see around each object. This sold me forever on wide screen films."[14]

For a story, Vidor chose a genre which was more suited to his romantic vision and his interest in rural communities, and which was new to him: a western. Previously, he had only worked peripherally in the genre: the Canadian frontier film *The Sky Pilot* (1921). Considering the popularity of western stories, both as low-budget cheapies as well as more prestigious A pictures such as James Cruze's *The Covered Wagon* (1923) and John Ford's *The Iron Horse* (1924), as well as the director's own Texas upbringing, it is surprising that it took Vidor until almost two decades into his career before he set his sights westward. Many of Vidor's motifs align with the genre's characteristics of naturalistic locations, expansive location photography and stories built around community, individualism, and the conflict between modernization and tradition. "The Western is the only type of story which has gone through the history of the motion picture without important change," Vidor said in an interview promoting his newest movie. "The drama of the West in the so-called wild days has a permanent appeal for all classes of theatregoers in these times when white-collar workers can't go galloping over endless plains but must take their thrills vicariously."[15]

For a story, Vidor chose to adapt Walter Noble Burns' 1926 biography *The Saga of Billy the Kid*. Returning were his frequent collaborators Wanda Tuchock (credited with continuity) and Laurence Stallings (credited with dialogue); additional dialogue was supplied by Charles MacArthur, co-author with Ben Hecht of the famous stage play (frequently adapted to film) *The Front Page*. The choice of material, however, proved problematic from the beginning. Billy the Kid was a legendary gunslinger. Born Henry McCarty in 1859, he later changed his name to William H. Bonney. A cattle rustler and veteran of the Lincoln County War, Bonney murdered at least eight men (including several sheriffs and deputies) and was eventually killed by sheriff Pat Garrett in 1881. Bonney was only 21 years old. Though the Production Code had not officially gone into effect (it would begin to "regulate" cinema morality in 1934), the Hays Office and other watchdog groups were still vocal about on-screen "decency." Though plenty of westerns had featured protagonists who killed, it was always in the name of justice and righteousness. William S. Hart, in his silent westerns, frequently played a "good-bad" man whose morality was a gray area; however, even Hart's characters were not of the same violent caliber as Billy the Kid.

Vidor encountered resistance from MGM immediately. Pitching the idea to Irving Thalberg, Vidor said in his autobiography, "I started by saying that Billy the Kid shot his first victim because of an insult to his mother. This bit of historical half-truth was emphasized in the hope of convincing Thalberg that all of the Kid's murders were understandable, if not entirely excusable."[16] Stallings also advocated to Thalberg that it was time for a grittier sense of realism. "The public, he [Stallings] said, was ready for honest brutality. He was right; it wasn't long before James Cagney rubbed half a grapefruit in his girlfriend's face. The movies were on the brink of a new era of violence."[17] A compromise was reached, with Billy turned into a guardian angel of the west, protecting ranchers from the evils of land barons and corrupt lawmen; his relationship with Pat Garrett became a buddy comedy, complete with in-jokes about their competing marksmanship (though they never threaten one another).

The film's distortion of historical fact became a point of controversy in the press. Even before the film had finished, the *Los Angeles Times* ran a preview with the headline, "Billy the Kid White Washed: Western Epic Gives Outlaw Clean Bill of Health."[18] Anticipating such criticism, Vidor opens his film with a message from the governor of New Mexico, Richard C. Dillon, that validates the film's portrait of Billy the Kid: "It seems to me that this picture of Billy the Kid, though it has taken liberties with the details of his life, presents a true drama of his career, and proves that this gunfighter of early New Mexico played his part of the West. Billy had a keen sense of justice which had been deeply outraged, and he set about with his gun and invincible courage to even up the scores, and in that way to restore to life on the range its personal liberty."

The first shot of *Billy the Kid* displays the film's finest qualities: a gorgeous long shot of a desert vista, bursting with location authenticity.[19] Even in the 35mm 1.37:1 reduction print (the widescreen version is, sadly, lost), the composition shows Vidor at his most painterly. What follows is the introduction of a wagon train led by John W. Tunston (Wyndham Standing) and Angus McSween (Russell Simpson). Arriving in New Mexico, they run afoul of land baron Donovan (James Marcus), who orders them to keep moving westward or he will steal their cattle. Ignoring the warning, Tunston and his people settle. Donovan begins murdering the settlers and stealing their cattle. During a community meeting, Donovan arrives and pushes for a showdown with Tunston. As one of Donovan's men draws two guns, from off screen there comes a shot which kills the gunman. The shot came from passerby Billy the Kid (Johnny Mack Brown, in his first western role, years before he achieved fame as a B-western regular), who intervenes and volunteers to protect Tunston and the settlers.

However unrealistic and melodramatic Billy's model of shoot-for-democracy is, this scene is significant in that it signals a new era of political interest for Vidor. Vidor's contract with MGM coincided with a shift in his stories towards more urbane social comedies and period pieces, *The Crowd* notwithstanding. And while *Hallelujah* showed a renewed interest in rural America, any political reading of that film is compromised by its naive and bigoted view of race and labor. All this makes this revisionist recasting of Billy the Kid as a defender of populism all the more intriguing. *Billy the Kid* is certainly Vidor's most virulent anti-capitalist film to date, as the gunslinger fights for the rights of the settlers to claim land, collectively organize, and exercise constitutional rights. However divorced from reality this may be, through Vidor's lens Billy the Kid becomes a democratic hero.

Violence continues to erupt between Tunston and Donovan. As Tunston tries to leave town to marry his fiancée, Claire Randall (Kay Johnson), Donovan's

King Vidor's first Western *Billy the Kid* (1930, Metro-Goldwyn-Mayer). From left: Frank Hagney (who plays Bert Grant), Wallace Beery (who plays Deputy Sheriff Pat Garrett), and John Mack Brown (who stars as William "Billy the Kid" Bonney). This movie was filmed using an early 70mm widescreen technology called "Realife" (MGM/Photofest).

men ambush him on the outskirts of town. The confrontation is the most majestic sequence in the film and features Vidor's finest framing and choreography. Even in the 1.37:1 35mm print that exists, one can see how brilliantly Vidor used the 70mm camera. As the two parties meet on the road, Vidor films them in an extreme long shot, symmetrically arranged on either side of the frame, a flat composition as though it were a painting. The desert buttes behind them dwarf the human figures: Donovan's posse is on horseback while Tunston's crew, except for him and Billy, are on foot. As Tunston tries to break through the line in his wagon, he is shot and killed. In another long shot, the posse rides into the distance, disappearing over the horizon, while the foot soldiers run behind firing into space, the futility of their gestures emphasized by the enormity of the desert landscape and the camera's distance.

After Tunston's death, McSween takes over the group. Donovan's raid on McSween's compound is the centerpiece of *Billy the Kid*, a twenty-three-minute siege that occurs over the course of several days as Donovan's men and sheriff Pat Garrett (Wallace Beery) trap McSween, Billy, and their followers in a single room. Long shots of Donovan's men crawling through grassy knolls and taking sniper posts on adjacent rooftops, as well as distance shots of Pat Garrett setting up in a hotel window across the street, show Vidor's most sophisticated command of spatial organization yet, integrating several different planes of action simultaneously. The battle itself is remarkably sober and unromantic and utterly distinct from the flash-bang shootouts typically associated with westerns. Much of the siege consists of men lying in wait, occasionally firing into the air, rarely seeing more than a fleeting glimpse of the enemy. As the days wear on, McSween's men suffer from dehydration. One of them chances going to the well but is riddled with bullets from off-screen; he struggles back to the compound with a single bucket of water before he dies. Despite a white flag offered by Pat Garrett, when McSween offers to give himself up to save his men, he is shot by Donovan, who is then shot by Billy. Such unheroic deaths are not the end of this bitter fight. As the rest of the men remain in the compound, Donovan's right-hand man Ballinger (Warner Richmond) decides to burn out the remaining followers. In a chillingly placid and beautiful long shot, burning barrels roll down the hill at night, the white flames the only illumination in the black night. Billy and his men try to escape in groups, enshrouded by smoke. However, Ballinger's men hide behind a wall and pick off several of them as they try to climb over a wall. Billy is one of the lucky ones and manages to escape into the night.

Despite the level of violence in this scene, Vidor restrains emotion and melodrama, emphasizing the uncertainty of the fight, the ennui of waiting, and the unpleasantness of death. The sequence stands among the most grim and fatalistic in any western. Durgnat and Simmon note in their book *King Vidor, American*: "Vidor never slickens the killings in *Billy the Kid*. When they occur on screen, life chokes out before any touchingly comprehensible last words, but after the screams of agony. He undercuts the moral acceptability of murder in Westerns through a frightening staging."[20]

Billy escapes to a desert cave, where Ballinger and Garrett pursue him. In another of the film's most striking uses of natural landscape as a framing device, Vidor places the camera inside the cave, with Billy off to the right side on a ledge, with most of the frame devoted to the cave's opening, the desert expanse in full view. Suffering from hunger, Billy succumbs to Pat Garrett's lure of cooking a steak outside of the cave and gives himself up. Taken into town for a hearing, Billy escapes custody, steals a rifle, shoots Ballinger, and then steals a horse and rides off into the night. Pat Garrett and Claire Randall witness Billy's escape. Pat shoots and deliberately misses and then observes: "There's something wrong with my aim lately. I've never missed so wide before." He then lends Claire his horse so she can catch up with Billy and marry him.

In real life, Billy the Kid did not have such a "happily ever after" ending. Instead of Pat Garrett letting him ride away, the sheriff was the one who shot him. Vidor said later in an interview that originally "we stuck to the historical ending, the death of Billy. Well, when we previewed it we found that the audience didn't want him to die. So we fixed it so that he would live, and to do that meant that we had to go back through the entire story, changing it so that it would appear justifiable that he should not die." This experience left Vidor unusually bitter, and it comes across heavily in the interview: "You see, the public doesn't want the truth. Why should I try any more to give it to them?"[21]

The story was not the only compromise made to Vidor's film. MGM's hope for a broad 70mm release never came to fruition. Ultimately, there were "only twelve theatres in the country that could run the wide screen material," Vidor recalled.[22] Critics in Los Angeles, however, were able to preview the 70mm version. Unfortunately, their initial reactions found several problems with both Vidor's direction as well as the technology. "It is to be regretted that a more suitable vehicle had not been secured for the introduction of this device [Realife]," wrote H. David Strauss in *The Billboard*. "The idea of *Billy the Kid* is so hackneyed and not so particularly well done that it makes the brilliance of this new projection and photography lose much of its luster."[23] Jay M. Shreck, in *Exhibitors Herald-World*, was initially enthusiastic, saying, "King Vidor has displayed real skill in adapting himself to this new pictorial medium. His direction throughout is of the usual high quality expected of him." He was critical of the process of reducing the 70mm film, which suggests that MGM's technology was not as well developed as they had thought: "Thirty-five mm film is used in projecting ... and in throwing the picture on a screen of such proportions there is at times a lack of definition. It is noticeable also that night scenes are extremely dark."[24]

Beyond the limitations of the Realife technology, critics were not impressed with the movie. "*Billy the Kid* possesses a few ingratiating moments and nothing more ... the rudimentary 1, 2, 3 yard-spinning structure ... no intelligence to use [Realife] ... just another western," wrote H.A. Potamkin in *Close Up*.[25] *Variety* echoed the same sentiments: "For those spots due to play it on normal or standard sized screen the picture is just another western, and not a good one."[26] And in *Motion Picture News*, Bill Crouch declared it as "spotty ... one wonders at times what it is all about."[27]

In short, *Billy the Kid* is a compromised film for Vidor. It is a return to the period drama, which he had not attempted since 1926's *Bardelys the Magnificent*, and would not try again for another five years with the Civil War drama *So Red the Rose* (1935). Its primary significance is for his early experimentation with widescreen photography, which he did not return to for another twenty-five years with *Man Without a Star* (1955).

Eleven

1931

Street Scene and *The Champ*

Street Scene

> "Elmer Rice [author of the 1929 play *Street Scene*] has managed, however, to achieve the screen's effect of changing scene while retaining the unity of play which the restriction of stage presentation imposes ... 'Street Scene' can serve as a lesson to screen as well as stage."[1]—"'Street Scene' Breaks Ancient Screen Mold," *Los Angeles Times*, July 26, 1931

> "You can never be real in sets; you can only be what people think is real."[2]—King Vidor, 1938

Street Scene (1931) is Vidor's boldest exploration of the formal limits of cinema. Coming after his experiments with sound in *Hallelujah* and 70mm widescreen cameras in *Billy the Kid*, *Street Scene*'s premise seems almost antithetical to Vidor's directorial style: an adaptation of the 1929 play by Elmer Rice (who also wrote the screenplay for Vidor's film) whose screen space is limited almost entirely to the same physical limitations of the stage: the exterior of a New York City tenement dwelling.[3] Over the course of two hot summer days, the tenants sit on the stoop, hang out in windows and pass by on their way home or on their way out. They gossip, sing, bicker about politics, flirt and fight. They argue about the past and dream of the future. Tensions boil and culminate in an off-screen murder. Premiering on the New York stage in 1929, it received the Pulitzer Prize for Drama that same year.

Whereas *Hallelujah* and *Billy the Kid* both attempted to expand cinema's palette in the crude early days of the talkies, *Street Scene* seemingly buys into the stereotype of "canned theater," merely filming the play rather than adapting it to the screen and privileging dialogue at the expense of the camera. Location photography had been key to Vidor's artistic statements and technical achievements in many of his earlier films, so his abandonment of such a characteristic component of his work is certainly an anomaly, considering that this was his first film for Samuel Goldwyn after the expiration of his MGM contract. Vidor was concerned about how to approach the material. As he reflected in his autobiography: "I feared that the static, immobile quality of that one stoop and that one section of sidewalk would offer little opportunity for movement." He then found inspiration in the oddest of places: a fly. "Why not look upon the front of the old tenement as the fly looks at the man's face? Let the camera be the fly. In *Street Scene* we would never repeat a camera setup twice."[4]

With characters always coming and going, it is Vidor's camera and the mammoth set that become the real stars of *Street Scene*. Vidor opens the film with a montage that recalls the "city symphony" genre—documentary portraits of urban life—such as Paul Strand's *Manhatta* (1921) or Walther Ruttmann's *Berlin: Symphony of a Great City* (1927). First, we see the skyline of New York in long shot; then the camera tilts down from the tops of the skyscrapers and pans across the roofs of the tenements below, a metaphoric camera movement that this will not be a story of New York's elite, but rather one of the common folk "down below." The camera continues panning until we see the street. Vidor cross-fades to a shot of children in the street dancing beneath an open hose held by firefighters, helping them cool off on what appears to be a hot day. This shot cross-fades to a closeup of a pick splitting ice and a man delivering ice; a chunk falls to the pavement, and a cat lapping it up is startled by two boys wrestling over it. Next, Vidor shows us a carriage driver whose horse will not budge, followed by a panting dog too hot to even stand, and finally a close-up of a fan blowing across a man sleeping on his fire escape. The camera moves across an open window to a streetlamp as it is lit, and then finally down to the stoop below, where the action of the film takes place.

Street Scene is a companion piece of sorts to *The Crowd*. *Street Scene* takes as its story a literal "crowd" of working class everypersons living in the same New York apartment building. The story evolves out of their passing remarks spoken and heard on the stoop and on the sidewalk in front of their building. *Street Scene* anticipates similar sidewalk-based narratives such as Rainer Werner Fassbinder's *Katzelmacher* (1969), in which a group of neighbors rally together over shared racism towards a Greek immigrant, and especially Spike Lee's *Do the Right Thing* (1989), in which a Brooklyn neighborhood's racial tensions explode on one hot summer afternoon. All three films use an ensemble cast and a very specific, limited setting as an allegory for larger social issues. The seemingly mundane passing remarks from the neighbors in *Street Scene* belie much more significant concerns: racism, anti–Semitism, sexism, nationalism, and classism are all at the root of their prosaic conversations.

At the center of the film's drama is the Maurant family: mother Anna (Estelle Taylor) who, dissatisfied with her marriage to Frank (David Landau), has begun an affair with the milkman; and daughter Rose (Sylvia Sidney), whose boss at the office is offering to kickstart her stage career in exchange for sexual favors. Meanwhile, Rose's neighbor Sam (William Collier, Jr.), a young student planning on going to law school, has a crush on her but is often bullied by another neighbor who is making unwanted advances on Rose, Vincent Jones (Matt McHugh). Eventually, Frank walks in on Anna and the milkman and he shoots them both, running out of the apartment building before the police arrive. Frank, hiding nearby, is eventually found by the police. Rose decides to leave the city and Sam asks to come with her, but she insists she wants a couple of years apart for each of them to grow before deciding whether to build a life together.

The scene in which Rose finds out about her mother's murder is one of Vidor's crowning achievements of mass choreography. The streets are packed in response to the shooting. An ambulance weaves its way through the crowd to the building. Overhead, the elevated train pulls into the station while people throng together below. Exiting the train is Rose, who sees the commotion immediately. In an extended long take, a camera on a crane moves backwards as Rose pushes her way through the horde and hurries down the street. Hundreds of extras fill the set as Vidor recreates a city neighborhood caught in a frenzy. From *The Big Parade* and *Bardelys the Magnificent* through *Hallelujah* and *Billy the Kid*, scenes of the masses were highpoints of Vidor's artistry. But the image of Rose in the street represents an apex of his direction, a sophisticated counterpoint of visual action and dramatic tension, one individual body moving in the same direction as the crowd but also struggling against everyone around her.

An on-the-set publicity photograph of the major cast members from *Street Scene* (1931, directed by King Vidor for Samuel Goldwyn Productions and distributed by United Artists). Shown are John Qualen (far left, as Karl Olsen), William Collier, Jr. (seated second from left, as Sam Kaplan), Estelle Taylor (seated center, as Anna Maurrant), David Landau (standing on top step, as Frank Maurrant), George Humbert (as Filippo Fiorentino), Beulah Bondi (far right, as Emma Jones), and Eleanor Wesselhoeft (in the window, as "Greta" Fiorentino) (United Artists/Photofest).

The film received rave reviews from critics. "The most gruesomely realistic setting ever contrived.... It is probably his best work—certainly the best he has done since the dimly remembered days of silence," raved Robert E. Sherwood.[5] "King Vidor has cut deeply into the East Side life and laid it bare with the skill of a surgeon," applauded *Motion Picture Herald*.[6] "An almost perfectly produced and acted picture. Not a flaw has slipped by the eye of director King Vidor. It's the pinnacle of his directorial career," wrote *Photoplay*.[7] "A fine achievement.... Proves the tremendous possibilities of sound and music wedded intelligently to the pictorial image," wrote Ralph Bond in *Close Up*.[8] And, in *Hollywood Spectator*, future screenwriter (and member of the later blacklisted "Hollywood Ten") Dalton Trumbo wrote, "One of the finest motion pictures I have ever seen; perhaps it is the finest ... dominated by an almost serene intelligence.... The direction of King Vidor is a thrilling piece of work, a blending of skill, restraint and imagination into a tremendously fine production."[9]

Among the dissenting opinions was that of Mordaunt Hall of the *New York Times*: "In comparison with the play [the movie] always seems to be more than slightly exaggerated. It is a good picture, but the acting lacks the naturalness of the original work and the lines [of dialogue] are invariably overstressed."[10] Acclaimed Argentinian writer Jorge Luis Borges was also critical of how certain characters come across as caricatures: "It has characters who seem true to life; it has others who are in masquerade. Basically, it is not a realistic work; it is the repression or frustration of a romantic work."[11]

Within Vidor's collective filmography, *Street Scene* stands out as a work that thoroughly embodies the director's vision, technical strategy, and thematic interest in the tension between the individual and the collective. As much as *The Big Parade* and *The Crowd*, *Street Scene* is a fundamental work in Vidor's oeuvre.

* * * *

The Champ

> "In the making of successful motion pictures, I feel that everyday emotions play the greatest part."[12]—King Vidor, 1935

Frances Marion was one of the most prolific and acclaimed writers of early Hollywood, with nearly 200 credits to her name, including three films as writer/director: *The Love Light* (1921), *Just Around the Corner* (1921), and *The Song of Love* (1923).[13] Beginning in 1912, her career includes work with leading directors in a variety of genres. Marion's screenplays include four of her greatest movies: *The Poor Little Rich Girl* (1917) directed by Maurice Tourneur, and *Rebecca of Sunnybrook Farm* (1917), *Stella Maris* (1918), and *Amarilly of Clothes-Line Alley* (1918), the latter three directed by Marshall Neilan. Her 1920s work includes *The Lady* (1925) and *Lazybones* (1925), both directed by Frank Borzage; *Lightnin'* (1925), directed by John Ford; *Stella Dallas* (1925), directed by Henry King (and which King Vidor would remake in 1937); *The Son of the Sheik* (1926) with Rudolph Valentino; *The Scarlet Letter* (1926) and *The Wind* (1928), both starring Lillian Gish and directed by Victor Sjöström; as well as *The Red Mill* (1927) starring Marion Davies, pseudonymously directed by Roscoe "Fatty" Arbuckle under the name "William Goodrich." Marion's work in sound was no less impressive, including adapting Eugene O'Neill's *Anna Christie* (1930) for Greta Garbo's first talkie as well as the prison drama *The Big House* (1930), directed by her husband George Hill, for which she received the Academy Award for Best Writing.

Her follow-up to *The Big House* was another crime drama, *The Secret 6* (1931); this was a frustrating experience, however, as the MPPDA's production code was just coming into effect and forced her to soften her ending with what she called "the proverbial happy ending" with the criminals being brought to justice, according to Cari Beauchamp's biography *Without Lying Down: Frances Marion and the Powerful Women of Early Hollywood*. As a consolation, Irving Thalberg of MGM "encouraged her to write an original story and gave her free rein, but added that he had been thinking about an 'old-fashioned western' for Wallace Beery, maybe set in Mexico." Visiting Tijuana, Marion found inspiration in the sight of a large man stumbling out of a bar with a little boy clearing the way for him and shouting, "Can't you see the champ needs some air?"[14]

And a film was born.

After shooting *Street Scene* for Samuel Goldwyn, King Vidor found himself at his former studio, MGM. Though an original story by Marion, the material must have felt familiar to Vidor, who a decade earlier had written and directed a similar film about the immutable bond between a downtrodden man and a young boy: *The Jack-Knife Man*. For *The Champ*, Vidor brought on his frequent collaborator Wanda Tuchock to write additional dialogue, with contributions from Leonard Praskins (who would pen Vidor's next film, *Bird of Paradise* [1932]).

The Champ is among Vidor's simplest and most direct works. Almost artless in its visual austerity, in *The Champ* Vidor expresses his sophistication not through impressive technical feats but with meticulously composed shots without distracting embellishments. His directorial style is sometimes completely transparent, his camera focused on making the most immediate connection between his two leading characters and the audience. In this way, it is somewhat of an unusual film for Vidor, a throwback to the straightforward charm of his earliest silent pictures such as the aforementioned *Jack-Knife Man*. More characteristic of Vidor is the film's sympathy for the social struggles of its marginalized characters and the sense of realism evoked by his images (despite its studio lot recreation of Tijuana).

The film's opening image is a reverse tracking shot of the titular "Champ," boxer Andy Purcell (Wallace Beery), and his son "Dink" (Jackie Cooper), jogging side by side on a dirt road in Tijuana as a car of jeering hecklers passes by. Father and son

An on-the-set photograph during the production of King Vidor's classic father-son drama *The Champ* (1931, Metro-Goldwyn-Mayer). Pictured are director Vidor (left) and star Wallace Beery (as Andy "Champ" Purcell). Beery won Best Actor Oscar for his role (sharing the award with co-winner Fredric March for his performance in the 1931 *Dr. Jekyll and Mr. Hyde*). Frances Marion won an Academy Award for Best Story. The film was also nominated for Best Picture and Best Director (MGM/Photofest).

are discussing the Champ's potential comeback and how he wants to buy his son a horse if he wins a match. Once they finish training for the day, the Champ's weakness becomes obvious: despite telling his son he would not drink, he heads for the nearest bar. That night, Dink and his friends go in search of the Champ because of their planned meeting with some boxing promoters and find him thoroughly drunk. Dink and his friend Jonah (Jesse Scott) try to sober up the fighter for the meeting and escort him there. At the meeting, the Champ belches and reveals his inebriation and the promoters decline to hire him for a fight.

That evening, Dink puts his father to bed. The sequence reveals Vidor's invisible artistry and shows how he seamlessly integrates silent-era techniques into sound cinema. The Champ sits on the edge of the bed as his son stands on the bed and struggles to get his father out of his shirt and coat, only to realize that he forgot to undo the bowtie. Dink tries to lift the bowtie over his father's face without untying it, which inevitably gets caught on his face. Vidor cross-fades to the Champ in his long johns, leaning on the bedpost and ready to fall forward; behind him, Dink rushes to throw back the sheets in time to pull his father back and have him fall into the bed. Acted without dialogue, the scene plays like a slapstick visual gag out of a silent movie and exemplifies the way Vidor grew as a visual storyteller. At a time in which other filmmakers were busy incorporating sound, Vidor's most sophisticated scenes from *Hallelujah*, *Billy the Kid*, and *The Champ* all incorporated pre-talkie techniques.

What is also remarkable about the sequence is Vidor's patience. Shown largely in two extended shots (with a couple of quick cuts at the start of the sequence for exposition), Vidor's camera is in no rush. The composition places the actors in the center of the frame and does not move, allowing the performers to interact in real time. The duration of the shot and lack of cutting build intimacy between characters and give an added, unspoken weight to the actions, as though this is not the first time that Dink has had to undress his drunken father.

Ironically, the actors did not feel such intimacy or camaraderie in scenes like this. Jackie Cooper later reported: "I really disliked him. It began the very first day on *The Champ*. There was to me no warmth to the man. He always made me feel uncomfortable. Beery was obviously angry. Vidor and [co-star Edward] Brophy and Vidor's assistant, Red Golden, were trying to make him do something.... They were accusing him of trying to upstage me.... He had apparently been going through his repertoire of mugging and broad gestures while I was supposedly in the foreground, doing or saying something vital to the action of the piece. Beery knew what he was doing, and he knew what Vidor, Brophy, and Golden were telling him. He couldn't get angry at them, so he got angry at me."[15]

In the morning, the Champ awakens before his son. A companion sequence to the night before, this one shows the father dealing with a massive hangover. Composed of largely a single take, the scene begins with a closeup of a curtain billowing in front of an open window, daylight streaming in. The camera backtracks and pans to reveal the Champ as he labors upright, scratches himself, and stumbles out of bed and across the room to the dresser. The camera pans to follow his movement as he picks up a pitcher of water, takes a drink, and then douses himself with it. Blinded by the water, he gropes for a towel that does not exist and then wipes his face with his shirt. Shadowboxing, he moves across the room. When he reaches the front of the bed, Vidor cuts to a closeup of Dink talking in his sleep about the horse that the Champ promised him. The single shot, long take of the Champ waking up lasts an impressive two minutes and forty seconds, the longest of many extended takes in the film. Vidor's use of non-montage sequences not only gives preference to the actors and their movements, but also emphasizes the weight of time and suggests an element of fatalism to their gestures.

Sneaking out to gamble, the Champ wins enough money to buy his son a horse, which Dink names "Little Champ." In its first race, however, the horse trips and loses. At the races, the Champ is recognized by his ex-wife, Linda (Irene Rich), who infers that the little boy who owns the horse is none other than her son, whom she has not seen since she lost custody during the divorce. Bribing the Champ with $100 before and $100 after, Linda arranges for him to permit Dink to visit her. Shortly thereafter, the Champ loses Little Champ while gambling. When he tries to win the horse back, he loses again, gets in a fight, and is thrown in jail. Dink witnesses his father fighting the authorities as they arrest him. When Dink visits the jail, the Champ orders the boy to move in with Linda and Tony (Hale Hamilton). Dink eventually runs away and reunites with the Champ shortly before he is set to fight the heavyweight champion of Mexico, Manuel Quiroga (Frank Hagney). Linda and

Wallace Beery as Andy "Champ" Purcell and Jackie Cooper as his son "Dink" in King Vidor's classic father-son drama *The Champ* (1931, Metro-Goldwyn-Mayer). Beery won Best Actor Oscar for his role (sharing the award with co-winner Fredric March for *Dr. Jekyll and Mr. Hyde*). Frances Marion won an Academy Award for Best Story. The film was also nominated for Best Picture and Best Director (MGM/Photofest).

Tony track Dink to the ring in time to watch the Champ's fight. Though he takes many blows from Quiroga, the Champ prevails and wins enough money to buy back Little Champ. On his way out of the arena, however, he collapses and Dink watches as his father dies. Dink runs to Linda who takes him in her arms as he cries out, "The Champ is dead, mama."

As a result of Vidor's straightforward directorial approach, the melodrama of the story (often a weakness of Vidor's films) is laid completely bare. While Beery and Cooper delivered remarkably sincere and affecting performances, critics at the time were quick to point out the film's tendency towards cornball humor. "The convincing, human and sympathetic directorial hand of King Vidor is in evidence throughout. *The Champ* is hokum but it's golden," wrote *Film Daily*.[16] "A maudlin tear-jerker.... It will probably be very popular, being good movie entertainment—but, oh! such bad, bad art!" wrote Herman G. Weinberg in *Close Up*.[17] Other reviews were more favorable. "[Vidor] has tackled this venture in a restrained fashion, always permitting the performances of Master Cooper and Mr. Beery to hold up a sequence that might have been banal and trite without them," wrote Mordaunt Hall in the *New York Times*.[18] And the Academy of Motion Picture Arts and Sciences awarded Beery the Oscar for Best Actor in a Leading Role (shared with Fredric March for *Dr. Jekyll and Mr. Hyde*) and awarded Marion the Oscar for Best Writing based on an Original Story. The film was nominated for Best Picture and Vidor was nominated for the Best Director Oscar (Vidor's third of five nominations in his career).

The Champ illustrates Vidor's engagement with popular entertainment and his career-long attempt to balance the demands of the studio with his more personal artistic ambitions. As he told the *Los Angeles Times* shortly after the film's release: "More and more, the dominant issue is becoming the money a picture brings, instead of the quality it contains. Afraid to experiment, relying on old rules that have been 'sure-fire box office' before, starving the intelligent audience to feed the moronic one, pictures are losing their spontaneity. There is so little freshness, so little zest anymore. The breath of life is missing in too many pictures."[19] While on the surface the film may seem among the more cinematically conventional, Vidor's use of extended takes and his integration of silent-era techniques show that he was searching for subtle ways to add that "zest" and "breath of life" that he felt was missing from movies. And *The Champ* typifies Vidor's sophisticated visual engagement with his scripts.

Twelve

1932

Bird of Paradise and *Cynara*

Bird of Paradise

Bird of Paradise (1932), arguably Vidor's most vapid film, is a pre-code Colonialist peepshow about an American sailor, Johnny (Joel McCrea), whose ship visits a reclusive South Seas island, where he falls in love with the daughter of the island's king, Luana (Dolores del Rio). Luana is destined to marry the island's prince and to be tossed into a volcano to appease the god Pele. Johnny rescues Luana from the marriage ceremony and the two escape to a nearby island for an idyllic romance. When the volcano begins acting up, Luana is captured by the islanders. Johnny tries to rescue her but is wounded by a spear. The couple are rescued by Johnny's shipmates. Johnny does not recover from his wound quickly and Luana is informed that the two of them have been cursed unless she gives herself to the volcano. Luana slips away and the film ends with her preparing for her ceremonial death.

The story is hokey exoticism at its best and racism masquerading as ethnography at its worst. Less interested in narrative than spectacle, Vidor focuses on location photography, half-naked bodies, and Production Code-breaking scenes of passion (implied and actualized) between Del Rio and McCrea. More interesting and dramatic than anything that wound up on screen, however, are two behind-the-scenes court cases that bookend the movie. The first is a lawsuit by author Grace Fendler, "who claimed that portions of *The Bird of Paradise* [by Richard Walton Tully] were plagiarized from a manuscript of her own called *In Hawaii*."[1] Tully's play, which was copyrighted in 1911 and premiered on the stage in 1912, was about "a doomed liaison between a young American and a Hawaiian girl ... a Polynesian variation of the Belasco/Puccini melodrama [*Madame Butterfly*]," wrote Christopher B. Balme. Balme also characterized the play as "explicitly exoticist, implicitly racist, and, perhaps most egregiously, it was a huge commercial success that was performed throughout North America for over a decade between 1912 and 1924 and was revived twice on the West End in London."[2] In February 1912, Fendler brought her plagiarism suit to the Manhattan Supreme Court, alleging that she had shown her manuscript to *Bird of Paradise* producer Oliver Morosco and asked "at least $25,000" in damages. Morosco denied sharing it with Tully and Tully denied ever having read it, insisting his first draft of the play dated to 1907.[3] The lawsuit dragged on for over a decade and was settled in August of 1928, when Fendler was awarded $781,891.10.[4] Two years later, however, the New York State Court of Appeals reversed the decision, declaring *The Bird of Paradise* an original work, paving the way for a screen adaptation. Reporting the legal turnaround, *Hollywood Filmograph* noted, "*The Bird of Paradise* is without doubt the most valuable piece of theatrical literary property as yet untouched by screen producers. With the recent innovations of color and sound, its artistic possibilities would seem endless."[5] Or so it would seem.

Legendary Hollywood mogul David O. Selznick was the head of production at RKO when Tully's play was going into production. He gave the script to King Vidor to read. Vidor tried, but had to report back to Selznick, "I can't read it. I finally got through the first act, but for the life of me I couldn't go any further." Selznick was no more a fan than Vidor, and he told the director, "I want Del Rio and McCrea in a South Seas romance. Just give me three wonderful love scenes like you had in *The Big Parade* and *Bardelys the Magnificent*. I don't care what story you use so long as we call it *Bird of Paradise* and Del Rio jumps into a flaming volcano at the end."[6] Vidor set out to deliver exactly what Selznick ordered, a flimsily plotted yet picturesque melodrama. Despite the film's crediting of three writers—Wells Root, Vidor's frequent collaborator Wanda Tuchock, and *Street Scene* co-writer Leonard Praskins—Vidor's memoir describes the film as going into production with not much more than the producer's barest outline. Wells Root did much of the writing just ahead of the cameras rolling, which created a messy shoot for script supervisor Elizabeth Wells to organize.[7] Filming on location in Hawaii—a stand-in for the film's nameless Pacific island location—proved disastrous. "When we first got there, there were no palm trees, so we had to have the telephone company move them down to where we were going to shoot. Then a tremendous storm blew all the leaves off the trees. The men had to crawl back up and nail them on. It also rained the entire time we were there," Vidor recalled. "So, finally we came back to California and went to Catalina and shot the rest of the stuff there."[8]

Further attempts at realism were abandoned by Vidor during production. *The New York Times* reported: "In spite of legend to the contrary, the natives were not regarded by King Vidor, the director, as an acceptable type of beauty for the American screen, and thirty-five girls who look as audiences want Hawaiians to look are dancing their way through native huts and streets on the RKO lot."[9] And dance choreographer Busby Berkeley, in only his third year in Hollywood, condescendingly ignored any attempts to accurately depict Hawaiian dances. "Berkeley says that Hawaiian hula dancers would be impossible in a film, as they spend hours slowly developing the figures of their ceremonials. 'No audience could possibly sit through it in a theater,'" Berkeley was quoted as saying in the *Washington Post*. "'The rhythm must be speeded considerably: the dreamy, slow Hawaiian tempo would be very lifeless on the screen. Yet no Hawaiian would understand or accept such directions.'"[10]

The resulting film is precisely what Selznick asked for and nothing more. It is

Delores del Rio (as Luana) and Joel McCrea (as Johnny Baker) in the South Seas romantic adventure *Bird of Paradise* (1932, directed by King Vidor and produced by Vidor and David O. Selznick for RKO Radio Pictures) (RKO Radio Pictures/Photofest).

filled with generic cliches, melodramatic improbabilities, and racist stereotypes. It falls into a series of South Seas–related films, including Robert Flaherty's *Moana* (1926), W.S. Van Dyke's *White Shadows in the South Seas* (1928), F.W. Murnau's *Tabu* (1931) (which began as a collaboration with Flaherty), Lewis Milestone's *Rain* (1932), and Charles Lloyd's *Mutiny on the Bounty* (1935). This series continued well into the 1950s and 1960s with Allan Dwan's *Enchanted Island* (1958) and Lewis Milestone's *Mutiny on the Bounty* (1962). *Bird of Paradise*'s colonialist perspective is evident from the get-go, with one of McCrea's shipmates referring to the island community as "happy, carefree people." They are viewed as primitive savages who exist as amusement for the white sailors (who throw alarm clocks and plates into the water for the natives to retrieve, as though they were dogs playing fetch) and whose non–Christian beliefs mark them as spear-throwing heathens to be feared. As one sailor remarks, "We'll never get out of there alive. Those people are savages."

As shown by their preproduction conversation, neither Vidor nor Selznick were all that invested in Tully's original story; instead, they were looking to exploit the bodies of stars Dolores del Rio and Joel McCrea and push the boundaries of the Motion Picture Production Code of 1930 (which was not enforced until 1934). Among the rules that *Bird of Paradise* breaks are the following:

Scenes of passion should not be introduced when not essential to the plot. In general, excessive passion should so be treated that these scenes do not stimulate the lower and baser element....

Seduction ... should never be more than suggested, and only when essential for the plot, and even then never shown by explicit method....

Miscegenation is forbidden....

Complete nudity is never permitted. This includes nudity in fact or in silhouette, or any lecherous or licentious notice thereof by other characters in the picture....

Dances which emphasize indecent movements are to be regarded as obscene....

Dancing costumes intended to permit undue exposure or indecent movements in the dance are forbidden....

The history, institutions, prominent people and citizenry of other nations shall be represented fairly.[11]

One need not look too hard to find examples of scenes that would not be permitted were this film to be made after 1934 when studios began applying Code rules. For much of the movie McCrea is shirtless and del Rio wears only a lei on top. Their relationship is unbridled sexual energy from their first meeting when Luana dives underwater to cut Johnny loose from a rope in shark-infested waters. As he comes to consciousness on the boat, she is waiting for him. Later that evening, she beckons him from the water to go skinny dipping (the actors do appear to be nude, though details are obscured by murky underwater photography). As they swim to shore, Johnny chases after Luana, forces himself on top of her and kisses her, after which she repeatedly points to her lips for more kisses; the roles are later reversed when Luana insists upon straddling Johnny and making him resist her to arouse her desire. In the film's kinkiest scene, Luana pours coconut milk into Johnny's mouth and then her own, the white liquid pouring down their lips onto their chests before they kiss.

More transgressive than any of this, however, is the fact that this is a relationship between persons of different races, a taboo explicitly prohibited by the Production Code. Joanne Hershfield views *Bird of Paradise* as "one of Hollywood's numerous ethnographic metaphors in which Western prohibitions against miscegenation are disguised as a tale of romantic love thwarted by the laws of nature.... Despite its depiction of interracial romance, *Bird of Paradise* ultimately prohibits breeding between Johnny and Luana on the basis of cultural taboos grounded in socioeconomic imperatives."[12] The "socioeconomic imperatives" that Hershfield refers to are the disparate worlds of the two protagonists. Luana must be sacrificed to the volcano in order that her village be saved from Pele, and Johnny must be able to return to the United States to start a family—a purely white family. His duty to his race is made clear by one of his shipmates: "The boy's whole life is wrapped up in his family. If he brings a native girl home, it will break his mother's heart." Luana is seen by the ship's captain as a sexual commodity, something for Johnny to exploit while at sea and to discard when he ships out. This undercurrent of racial superiority and sexism outweighs any notion that the interracial romance in the film is progressive.

Bird of Paradise's problematic representation of race is manifold. As was common at the time, most of the Pacific Islanders are not portrayed by actors from that region;

they are white actors from Hollywood in brown face. The film's one non-white star, Dolores del Rio, was Mexican. And as was common in her day, Hollywood cast her in a variety of different races and ethnicities from her start in the silent era: she was French in Raoul Walsh's *What Price Glory* (1926), Russian in *Resurrection* (1927), Spanish in Walsh's *The Loves of Carmen* (1927), French Canadian in *Evangeline* (1929), and Native American in John Ford's *The Fugitive* (1947). Coupled with the film's complete disregard for any cultural accuracy, *Bird of Paradise* is more exploitation than ethnography and exhibits racial prejudice that was, unfortunately, all too pervasive in Hollywood productions that attempted to "replicate" other cultures.

While critics at the time did not comment on the more problematic aspects of the film (though they, like the film's makers, were probably not even concerned or aware of them), they noted that the film was more of a titillating adventure than a picture of any substance. "Adaptation of old stage play picturesque and beautiful but theme is outdated and artificial," wrote *Film Daily*.[13] Norbert Lusk in *Picture-Play Magazine* wrote: "It enchants the eye and lulls the senses with the drenching loveliness of the tropics. Sad to say, it does not satisfy the mind and it falls short of being a noteworthy dramatic composition such as we expect of King Vidor."[14] "Frequently unconsciously humorous," commented Mordaunt Hall in the *New York Times*. *Hollywood Filmograph* did not appreciate even the more salacious aspects of the film: "When [Dolores del Rio] attempts to dance alongside some of the natives it is to laugh. Joel McCrea, as the strong manlike hero, is lifeless.... Some of the scenes are disgusting, especially when Luana sucks the lemon and forces the juice down Joel McCrea's mouth."[15]

The happenings on screen in *Bird of Paradise* are among the least significant in Vidor's career; the happenings off-screen, however, are significantly more important. The second behind-the-scenes lawsuit concerned Vidor himself. As he mused in his memoir: "On our homeward journey I exercised a latent talent for singing Hawaiian songs and accompanying myself on a guitar. Was it the need for a clear coordinator for my undisciplined imaginings, mixed with a good measure of appreciation? No matter how one analyzes it, I had fallen in love again. Not long after, Eleanor [Boardman] filed suit for divorce. In July 1932, Elizabeth [Hill] and I were married."[16] Hill would become an important collaborator, contributing to the scripts of five of his films: *Our Daily Bread* (1936), *The Texas Rangers* (1936), *The Citadel* (1938), *Northwest Passage* (1940), and *H.M. Pulham, Esq.* (1941). The two would remain married for forty-six years, until her death on August 21, 1978.

* * * *

Cynara

Vying with *Bird of Paradise* for King Vidor's most vapid film is *Cynara* (1932), a work of such mediocrity and conventional form that it lacks all but the smallest traces of Vidor's directorial vision and includes none of his thematic or philosophic concerns. The first of Vidor's films to be set in England, much of the setting and the characters seems alien to him. Largely studio-bound, the images lack the natural locations that are often key to his settings and the characters' interactions are so mannered they lack the warmth and casualness that are so often characteristic of Vidor's films.

The story of a married lawyer's infidelity with a young woman while his wife is away on a trip, *Cynara* also has the unfortunate distinction of basing its morals upon now-outdated standards that reveal the film's heavy-handed misogyny: the young woman, whose life ends in suicide after the older man breaks off their relationship, is seen not as a victim but as the root of the problem. Critics at the time were not offended by such a story. But viewed today, it is illustrative of the pervasive sexism that underscored narratives in popular entertainment. Produced by Samuel Goldwyn and written for the screen by *Champ* scenarist Frances Marion along with Lynn Starling, the film is an adaptation of the book *An Imperfect Lover* by R.F. Gore-Brown, which had previously been adapted to the stage by Gore-Brown and H.M. Harwood.

Cynara begins with British barrister Jim Warlock (Ronald Colman) preparing to catch a ship that is leaving for South Africa in an hour. As he says goodbye to his wife, Clemency (Kay Francis in an uncharacteristically submissive role, displaying none of the intelligence or strength she often brought to roles), she asks him, "Just what happened, that's all? What happened to you? Inside you, I mean. What she was like? What you thought? What you did?" As Jim begins to explain, the film transitions to a flashback. Clemency is leaving for Naples with her sister, Garala (Florine McKinney), who is looking to get over a recent breakup with her boyfriend. On her first night away, an old friend, John Tring (Henry Stephenson), takes Jim to an Italian restaurant for dinner. There, they meet two young girls, Doris (Phyllis Barry) and Milly (Viva Tattersall); John encourages Jim to join them in going to a movie. Jim and Doris begin an affair. When Clemency returns, Jim writes to Doris to call off the relationship and Doris commits suicide. Jim's letter is found next to Doris's body. He is called to testify at the inquest, where their affair becomes public knowledge. Professionally disgraced, he decides to move to South Africa alone. At this point, the frame narrative returns to the opening setting. After Jim leaves for the ship, John visits Clemency and convinces her that Doris's suicide was her own fault and that Jim should be forgiven. John admits partial blame for encouraging Jim's infidelity, but he ultimately places the blame on Doris: "She broke the rules" because she tried to "change the stakes in the middle of the game … you can't raise a man 10 shillings on a one shilling limit." He intimates that Jim might try to kill himself like Doris, though he does not think it is likely because "he's not a coward." The film ends with Clemency reuniting with Jim onboard the ship.

Ultimately, the film completely exonerates Jim for any of his actions: his wife left him alone; his friend encouraged him to flirt; and a young woman accepted his advances. As John Baxter notes, "The triumph of [Colman's] performance and Vidor's direction is that he makes the lapse seem more one of good taste than of morals."[17] *Cynara* finds no problem with Jim cheating on Clemency (even her name indicates the narrative's whitewashing of his action) or his manipulation and exploitation of Doris: the man is not responsible for any of his actions or their consequences. Jim's vindication is interesting in light of Vidor's own infidelity on the set of *Bird of Paradise* with script supervisor Elizabeth Hill, which culminated with Vidor's divorce from Eleanor Boardman. At the time of *Cynara*'s release, Dorothy Manners noted in *Movie Classic* the similarities between Vidor's film and his real life, and the way it shifts blame away from Jim's character: "King has handled with great sympathy toward (guess?) … the husband and the 'other girl.'"[18] The *Chicago Daily Tribune* also placed the blame with Clemency's character for leaving her husband alone, titling their view "A Warning to Blithe Ladies."[19]

The worldview of *Cynara* illustrates a significant change in Vidor's humanistic perspective expressed in his earlier movies and didactic articles. Recall the values espoused in his "Credo and Pledge" from 1920, which included the following: "I will never picture evil or wrong, except to prove the fallacy of its line. So long as I direct pictures, I will make only those founded upon principles of right, and I will

King Vidor's romantic drama *Cynara* (1932, Samuel Goldwyn Pictures). From left: Ronald Colman (as Jim Warlock), Phyllis Barry (as Doris Emily Lea), Kay Francis (as Clemency Warlock), and C. Montague Shaw (as the Constable). The screenplay is based on the 1929 novel *An Imperfect Lover* by Robert Gore-Browne (Samuel Goldwyn/Photofest).

endeavor to draw upon the inexhaustible source of good for my stories, my guidance and my inspiration."[20] With *Cynara*, Vidor might seem to have abandoned such lofty principles from his early days. On the other hand, one might simply view the film as merely "an assignment" or simply a "job of work," much like *Bird of Paradise*. It was never intended to be an expression of Vidor's own moral vision. The gender politics of *Cynara* are in line with *Bird of Paradise*, where sexual discourse is defined by class and socioeconomic privilege: just as that film viewed Johnny's relationship with Luana as a colonialist right of exploitation, *Cynara* allows Jim to have an affair and be forgiven regardless of the effects of his actions. *Cynara* views Jim, and the loss of his career and professional reputation, as the real victim.

Critics were largely positive and reinforced the film's worldview. "Beautiful balance of directness and simplicity.... A romantic tragedy built out of a minor bit of philandering," proclaimed *Variety*.[21] "King Vidor ... gives to his scenes effective and restrained guidance, with the result that the incidents move along at a pleasing pace.... The ending of the film is sensibly conceived," wrote Mordaunt Hall in the *New York Times*.[22] *Hollywood Filmograph* wrote: "King Vidor achieves a distinct triumph. His direction is superb. If it were not for his perfect understanding of delicate situations, the picture might easily have fallen short and not attained the classic distinction it has."[23] "Looks like a candidate for listing among the 'ten best' ... Colman is humiliated before the world and his wife ... before she comes to a more sympathetic understanding of his action," applauded *Film Daily*.[24]

Four decades later, when asked about the film, Vidor's response reinforced an autobiographical reading of the film, particularly his reference towards being able to "love" multiple persons, perhaps a thinly veiled reference to his own affair with Hill: "I see a reflection of my own character and attitude. Conditioned thinking tried to freeze everything like love and romance into a set category, with set responses. I know that my life work has been to upset this tradition.... If someone has love in their heart, they can love a hundred people, or even a thousand. Or, it can only be two or four."[25]

THIRTEEN

1933

The Stranger's Return

"It may be possible for Japanese directors to make films like [Josef von] Sternberg's, but we can't become the master like King Vidor who made *The Stranger's Return*."—legendary Japanese director Yasujiro Ozu, 1935[1]

The Stranger's Return was released in 1933 amidst the Great Depression, the same year that saw the arrival of *King Kong, Duck Soup, Dinner at Eight, 42nd Street, Queen Christina, The Private Life of Henry VIII,* and *The Invisible Man*. It is one of Vidor's finest—and most under-appreciated—films, the cinematic equivalent of a pleasant summer breeze. It certainly provided audiences at that time with escapist tranquility and amusement while also expressing the Jeffersonian ideal of the self-sufficient "yeoman farmer," an ideal that would soon be revived by Franklin D. Roosevelt, who was inaugurated only several months before the film's release. And in difficult economic times, those who had moved to the city from rural areas to find work—and who were making enough to afford a movie ticket—would have been treated to a relaxing return to their roots, even if briefly and vicariously. Small-town film audiences would have no doubt enjoyed this idyllic reminder of better, more self-reliant times in the countryside.[2]

Philip Stong adapted his own novel to the screen along with Brown Holmes, who had earlier contributed to the screenplays for the 1931 version of *The Maltese Falcon* as well as *I Am a Fugitive from a Chain Gang* (1932). Vidor certainly helped to shape the script, desiring above all to remain true to the novel, and in fact he later reported to interviewer Nancy Dowd that he had some difficulty in getting the author to remain as true to his own novel as Vidor wanted (Vidor, in fact, suspected that Stong's wife may have had a heavy hand in writing the original story).[3] Stong also played an uncredited role in contributing to the screenplay of his novel *State Fair*, leading to another film that was set in the rural Midwest and was being produced at the same time as *The Stranger's Return* (the 1933 version of *State Fair* being the first of three film versions of that novel's story). The film version of Stong's novel *Village Tale* was released in 1935.

The movie joins a few other rural films by Vidor in this period: *Hallelujah* (1929), *Our Daily Bread* (1934, made right after *The Stranger's Return*), and *The*

Wedding Night (1935). In these movies, the director shows a clear love of the land that was also evident in his own life. As Vidor told Nancy Dowd, referring directly to *The Stranger's Return*, "The farm has always been my favorite atmosphere. It's proven by the fact that I now live on one [i.e., his ranch in Paso Robles, California]. I used to be kidded a lot about some of the symbolism I used with the plow turning over the earth. It meant a new cycle of life, a new generation. There was a quality of metaphor."[4] Indeed, for some, the idea of rebirth or a new start might lie at the very core of the idea of America itself. In the very American genre of the Western, for example, there is a recurring theme (in many Western stories and films, anyway) of the Old West as the new home of a recently arrived homesteader or rancher looking for a second chance in life (typically a defeated Southerner in the post–Reconstruction era). Of course, challenges abound in trying to make that new start. And it is Vidor's own real-life love of the land, demonstrated most especially in these pastoral films of the 1930s—and echoed later by his glorious painterly landscapes in *Northwest Passage*, *American Romance*, and *Duel in the Sun*—that clearly disproves scholar John Baxter's thesis (in his book *King Vidor*) that nature and landscape take on the aspect of the adversarial and even "the demonic" throughout Vidor's oeuvre.[5] (In fact, Baxter undermines and contradicts this thesis at times by occasionally referring to Vidor's "ambivalence" about nature and even certain films' "celebration" of nature.)

The Stranger's Return centers on the joys and trials of an individual trying to make a new start. Picturesque tales of rural Americana were slowly starting to prove popular at this time, and Vidor's movie provides the kind of quiet glimpse of country living that can be found in such "folk" cinema of that time as John Ford's wonderful trilogy of films featuring the American king of rustic charm, Will Rogers: *Doctor Bull* (1933 again), *Judge Priest* (1934), and *Steamboat Round the Bend* (1935). Many of these "folk" films express a form of social and political populism and would find their culmination at the end of the Great Depression with such movies as Lewis Milestone's *Of Mice and Men* (1939) and Ford's *The Grapes of Wrath* (1940).

The Stranger's Return is set in Van Buren County, Iowa, though it was mostly shot in the Chino area of San Bernardino County near Los Angeles.[6] The film was photographed by William Daniels, edited by Dick Fant, and associate produced by Lucien Hubbard, who had also helped to produce *Wings* (1927), the first winner of the Best Picture Oscar. Meticulously crafted, this is a Pre-Code era movie and one of Vidor's best but least known films. Scott Simmon, co-author of the book *King Vidor, American*, ranks it as Vidor's most underrated work.[7] As Leonard Maltin observes in his movie guide, giving the film a superior rating, "Why this rich, mature, beautifully made film isn't better known is a mystery."[8] And as the legendary Japanese director Yasujiro Ozu declared in 1935, "It may be possible for Japanese directors to make films like [Josef von] Sternberg's, but we can't become the master like King Vidor who made *The Stranger's Return*."[9] More strangely, perhaps, Vidor never mentions the film even once in his 1953 memoir *A Tree Is a Tree*. One possible explanation is that, as he admitted later in life, he felt heartbroken after a brief romance with the film's star, Miriam Hopkins. Perhaps the memory of the movie was a painful one, and yet it is difficult to imagine that he would nonetheless completely neglect to mention this fine directorial achievement in an autobiography where most of his other films are discussed.[10]

The movie was released to generally favorable audience and critical acclaim, and it earned respectable profits at the box office. A *New York Times* review praised the movie for its direction as well as acting: "Having a full appreciation for honest dramatic writing, King Vidor has staged the novel excellently. Finally, the new film emerges as a shrewd, delightful and altogether effective entertainment, with a hearty and brilliant performance by Lionel Barrymore as the season's liveliest octogenarian."[11] A few critics praised the film for many of its merits and yet faulted it for being a bit "slow" and for centering on a love affair that brings little audience empathy.[12] It is a movie that certainly deserves greater popularity and appreciation and there had indeed been a bit of mystery as to its obscurity, as Maltin observed, but it is also Leonard Maltin who eventually solved the mystery.

Maltin once recalled that Charles Tabesh, who was Turner Classic Movies' senior vice president of programming, asked him to recommend any rare or unusual movies for a TCM film festival. Maltin recommended *The Stranger's Return* (1933). Maltin reported:

> Vidor never mentioned it in his autobiography, and I wonder if its commercial failure led him to make his next film (the ambitious *Our Daily Bread*) away from the studio system. *The Stranger's Return* has been out of circulation because MGM didn't renew its rights to the original story, by Philip Stong, the man who wrote State Fair. At Charlie's urging, Warner Bros. got to work and cleared the rights. But another challenge presented itself: when I borrowed the 35mm vault print from MGM for a showing at the Denver Film Festival some time back, there was a jump cut in the final scene. This was not so easily resolved. A fire long ago at the George Eastman House destroyed the original camera negative, so we had to use the same 35mm print—possibly the only one extant. Fortunately, I was able to consult the original editor's cutting continuity and learned that the missing footage was brief and didn't affect or alter the conclusion of the story. Whew! (I wasn't able to stay for the showing, but the next day several people stopped me on Hollywood Boulevard to say how much they liked it. I'm hopeful that TCM will assemble a complete print, using surviving 16mm footage, and present it to an even wider audience on their network.)[13]

Though the film was shown on television in the 1950s after having been sold by MGM to various television stations as part of a giant package of films, it was pulled from circulation in the early 1960s due (presumably) to the lack of renewed literary rights to Stong's novel. And so, according to Maltin, the film began to be televised again after Warner Brothers helped to clear the rights for Turner Classic Movies to show it in 2014. To date, the movie has not been released as an official DVD.[14]

There are clear connections with other Vidor films and not merely his other movies with rural settings. Lionel Barrymore would later play the cantankerous Senator Jackson McCanles in *Duel in the Sun* (1946). Beulah Bondi performed as the gossipy Emma Jones in his earlier *Street Scene* (1931). The bold mix of sentimental drama and broad humor and the consistent quality of the film come closest, in

Miriam Hopkins stars as Louise Starr in King Vidor's under-appreciated masterwork *The Stranger's Return* (1933, Metro-Goldwyn-Mayer). The screenplay was written by Philip Stong, who also wrote the 1933 novel on which the film is based (MGM/Photofest).

terms of general artistic comparison, with his film *The Champ* (1931). Both films, along with *Street Scene*, also feature fairly rapid editing between short takes, fine acting where the emotional range (from subtle to hammy) matches the mood and content of the given scenes, and effective combinations of static and moving camera. Vidor, much like Ford, is—when the situation calls for it—not afraid to transition quickly (and with almost Shakespearean audacity) between scenes of serious drama and scenes of over-the-top comedy or sudden exuberance. Both movies also recall Vidor's talent for bursts of eccentric humor that is evident in his films with Marion Davies. Donald Lyons and Glenn O'Brien observe in the introduction to their interview with Vidor later in his life: "And yet *Show People*, a zany Hollywood comedy, and especially *The Patsy*, a sort of Tarkingtonesque family farce ... show the same delight in self-assertive, irrational behavior—the same joy in human energy."[15] The same observation can certainly be applied to *The Stranger's Return* and *The Champ*, though the humor and energy is deftly interwoven with more serious or sentimental scenes.

As Simmon and Durgnat note in their book *King Vidor, American*, the title of the film is somewhat oxymoronic, though we do learn that its protagonist, city girl Louise Storr (Miriam Hopkins), is indeed a stranger to her paternal family's home, a farm known as "Storrhaven."[16] She has never seen her grandfather (Lionel Barrymore) before because her father George, Grandpa's eldest son, left the farm long ago after a dispute with him, never to return. And yet her arrival at the farm is also a type of return in that it is, after all, the only "home" she knows now that her father is dead, she has become divorced, and she cannot find any employment in the city ("there just weren't any more jobs"). And Grandpa Storr, as we soon see, is emphatic about blood-line continuity when it comes to the future of Storrhaven, and Louise is his only blood relative left. So her arrival is the return of the family line, as it were.

The audience can guess that part of Grandpa's joy in seeing his granddaughter for the first time has to do with his satisfaction in being able to turn over the farm to his blood kin, especially given his unhappiness with his house's other denizens, if he can convince her to stay there beyond his own death. Another part of his joy, we can surmise, has to do with his past grief over the long-ago loss of his son and his present opportunity to set things right, at least to some degree, in turning over the farm to his son's daughter. As Grandpa tells her soon after her arrival: "George never should have left." And, of course, there is his immediate pride in the fact that this sophisticated, beautiful woman is his granddaughter whom he has never seen.

In terms of the movie's theme of potential adultery (one of its themes, anyway), it harkens back to Vidor's *Street Scene* and *Cynara* (1932) and anticipates *The Wedding Night* along with *Stella Dallas* (1937), *H.M. Pulham, Esq.* (1941), *Beyond the Forest* (1949) and *Ruby Gentry* (1952). The theme of adultery may have been close to Vidor's heart in the sense that he allegedly had a secret affair with actress Colleen Moore in the 1920s around the time that they worked together on *The Sky Pilot* (1921) and while he was still married to Florence Vidor (they were divorced in 1924). In fact, the topic of broken marriages and relationships was undoubtedly on Vidor's mind during the making of *The Stranger's Return* since he divorced his second wife, Eleanor Boardman, only a few months before the movie was released. And Vidor admits that he had carried on a short-term romance with lead actress Miriam Hopkins during the making of this film, one that had left him broken-hearted.[17] In addition, in his book *A Cast of Killers*, author Sidney D. Kirkpatrick makes the case that Vidor was in love for decades with Colleen Moore, even though they would not meet again for forty years after their supposed affair. Vidor and Moore resumed contact in the 1960s and formed a film company together, Vid-Mor Productions, while collaborating on a screenplay based on the real-life William Desmond Taylor murder mystery. Vidor and Moore enjoyed a close friendship from the point of their reunion until the end of their lives, despite Vidor's long third marriage to Elizabeth Hill. Vidor died at his ranch in Paso Robles in 1982 and Moore died in Paso Robles in 1988.

While Barrymore steals the film in his performance as the crusty and iron-willed Grandpa Storr, the patriarch of his vast-ranging farm, and while it is his warm relationship with his granddaughter Louise (Hopkins) that provides the viewer with the most endearing scenes, it is Louise's dalliance with the married farm-owning neighbor Guy Crane (Tone) that proves to be the point of moral dilemma around which the plot eventually revolves. Guy is married to a conspicuously loyal, loving, and hard-working woman (Nettie, played by Irene Hervey) and the movie's audience (much like certain other members of Storrhaven) would most likely become troubled by the passion that Louise and Guy begin to demonstrate toward each other in such circumstances. We understand the reasons for their mutual attraction, and yet we are never comfortable with the ways in which that newfound affection occasionally veers towards fulfillment, especially since we find such easy empathy with Guy's wife Nettie. At one point, after a parlor conversation in which Guy and Louise reveal a shared interest in the theater, Nettie seems to sense Guy's infatuation and quickly guides him away when he stoops a bit too close to Louise as if he is about to kiss or embrace her, despite Nettie's presence. And yet Nettie remains patient and loving, also confessing to Louise a few moments later that she is not capable of satisfying Guy's need for a more culturally experienced interlocutor.

The film's mostly serene mood is established right from the outset. The credits begin while a slow, lilting song plays over shots of a flat countryside with the horizon line very high. After the credits, there are quiet shots of Storrhaven and its farm activity. The camera then zooms in on the front door and we then gain an interior shot with Beatrice (Bondi) bringing a bowl of food to the table. We are reminded of Vidor's famous shot in *The Crowd* in which the camera pans up a tall office building and then zooms in on a window, with a rapid transition to the next shot in which we are brought into the office interior in which our protagonist works.

Allen (Grant Mitchell) is the husband of Grandpa's other step-daughter Thelma (Aileen Carlyle) and the three are soon joined at the breakfast table by Grandpa Storr (Barrymore), who gives an overly quick and glum blessing and is clearly disgusted by the sight of the porridge-like cereal before him. He immediately leaves the table and walks out into the backyard to feed his meal to the chickens. Grandpa is immediately established as a comically crotchety character (one of many such characters played by Barrymore in his career) who then goes back into the kitchen to cook his own meal of fried eggs. Beatrice expresses concern for her stepfather's health and diet (a concern that we will later begin to doubt), to which he retorts, "I'd rather spend two minutes doing I want to do than a hundred years doing the things I *don't* want to do." His words are significant in that they express his brand of independent spiritedness and love of freedom, one that is soon echoed by the personality of his about-to-arrive granddaughter Louise.

Grandpa tells those gathered at the breakfast table that he has just received a telegram informing him that Louise will be arriving at midnight from New York City. It is quickly established by the others' gossip that she has recently separated from her husband. Grandpa and his whiskey-loving farmhand Simon (Stuart Erwin) meet the vibrant and beautiful Louise at the train station and make the car trip back to Storrhaven. Vidor uses an impressive chiaroscuro technique in the station scene that is almost Rembrandtian in its visual effect. Grandpa peers into the truck to speak with Louise, already seated, and his brightly illuminated face stands out moon-like against the surrounding darkness. When they arrive back at the farm, Grandpa introduces her to the rest of the house and we gain some clarity about the different relationships involved. Beatrice is the widow of Grandpa's nephew and Thelma is his step-daughter by his third marriage and Allen is Thelma's husband. We never hear about Grandpa's three wives (including the grandmother of Louise) and we also never hear about Louise's mother. We do hear a later reference to Grandpa's brother Jim.

In a following scene, Louise sits with Grandpa on the porch swing and their easy rapport is immediate. He tells her: "There's just two of us left now, us Storrs." He says about Beatrice and Thelma: "Not a drop of Storr blood in them." It is then established that Grandpa's son George, Louise's father, had long ago left the farm after a quarrel with his dad and had died not long ago. We also come to realize that Louise, who obviously takes after both her father and grandfather, was too proud to reach out for family help right after her dad died. Grandpa informs her that his own father had founded Storrhaven in 1830 and that she is a "fourth generation" Storr. Louise tells Grandpa that she finds the vistas familiar as she had seen photos of the farm that her father had taken with him.

Grandpa confides that George should never have left Storrhaven and that he (Grandpa) has rarely left his beloved home, only doing so in order to fight in the Civil War. So the viewer becomes enlightened about some of the complex family history and also gets a sense of Grandpa's emphasis on his inseparable bond with his land and farm and on the need for blood kin to stick together. There is an implicit contrast here, of course, between country and city lifestyles, given Louise's recent past. The city symbolizes to some degree the separation of Louise and her father from their familial home. And Grandpa's desire to turn Storrhaven over to Louise, if she will only stay, turns out to be as much about his need to have a similar personality take over the farm as his need to have that person be related by blood. In Louise, he gets both.

Grandpa then takes Louise to visit neighboring farmer Guy Crane and they have a comic quarrel about the boundary fence between their properties. We see that Guy is instantly attracted to Louise. Louise chuckles at their banter, clearly a discussion that has been recurring for years, and Guy clearly enjoys Grandpa's fiery spiritedness, even though the elder man eventually insults Guy's ancestors. Louise meets Guy's wife Nettie (Irene Hervey) and their young son Widdie (Tad Alexander) and we then transition to a splendid summery scene with sunny shots of Guy's farmhouse and property and birds chirping in the background. Nettie serves lemonade and cookies as they sit in the yard and she invites Louise and Grandpa for Sunday dinner.

There are wonderful little "grace notes" in the movie, those ornamental shots that provide subtle mood or atmosphere but that do not explicitly advance the

Pictured are Franchot Tone as Guy Crane and Miriam Hopkins as Louise Starr in King Vidor's romantic comedy *The Stranger's Return* (1933, Metro-Goldwyn-Mayer). The film also stars Lionel Barrymore as Grandpa Storr and Beulah Bondi as Beatrice (MGM/Photofest).

narrative. One such shot, emphasized by scholar-critic Jonathan Rosenbaum in his brief online review, shows a dog walking through an open door into a crowded church and then falling asleep beneath a pew, just as Grandpa falls asleep during the sermon (to Louise's amusement). As Rosenbaum puts it:

> A characteristic virtue of this character-driven adaptation of a Phil Stong novel set in farming country is a shot devoted to a dog wandering into a Sunday morning church service during the sermon, noticing that the place is full, and gradually sitting down under one of the pews. It's the sort of inessential detail that I wouldn't expect to find in any contemporary movie. I have no way of knowing whether or not this was scripted, but considering how little it has to do with the plot, I suspect it wasn't—that Vidor happened on such a shot as an afterthought. Apart from the economy of 30s features, this sort of meandering poetry seems increasingly rare in today's movies.[18]

Vidor uses clever camera motion in another scene where Guy and Louise dance amidst other moving couples while Beatrice sits and watches the couple with disapproving looks, given Louise's boldness in dancing so long and intimately with Guy, and particularly with his wife Nettie in attendance. When Louise takes notice of their scolding stares, Guy attempts to hide the fact by telling her that the women are simply jealous because she is from the city and is the new "heiress" of Storrhaven. The dance scene is cleverly executed by Vidor: it illustrates his talent for cinematic "rhythm" or "tempo" in terms of a fast-moving string of dialogue and shots.

There is a quaintly presented Sunday dinner scene at Guy's house, with Grandpa and Louise in attendance, and a tranquil after-dinner parlor conversation in which Guy and Louise reminisce about their experiences in New York City (Guy was there as a student and gave up a career as an agriculture teacher in order to return home and marry his childhood sweetheart Nettie). It is here that Nettie divulges to Louise that Guy gets a bit "lonely" out in the country and she observes that he may not be happy there. But Guy dismisses her concern and says that he likes to "keep his feet on the ground." Nettie clearly knows that she is not compatible with Guy in certain ways, given his past experiences and education. The stage has been set for the potential turbulence that Guy and Louise's affection might bring, particularly given the fact that Guy's family life is a stable and happy one.

Directly after their Sunday dinner, Guy drives Louise back to Storrhaven and urges her not to leave the farm. They speak of "big things, things that have a bearing on your whole life." He tells her that he needs to "stop this foolishness" and she asks, "What foolishness?" He then leans over to kiss her as the car wanders driverless for a few seconds into the field. They laugh about the kiss and speak of love, having surrendered to a momentary impulse. After this scene we witness pleasant shots of farm life, especially workers haying, and then a rather silly luncheon gathering of workers who, having returned from morning work for an abundant meal, become overly demanding to an obnoxious degree. Louise, helping the other women to serve the men, winds up slamming a cream pie into one worker's face, leaving everyone laughing. One may praise the scene for Vidor's careful orchestration of it, particularly in the way that the camera pans in following Louise around the table. Yet the comedy in the scene is a tad too stilted and the entire point seems to be that Louise uses her combination of service and spunkiness to show the men that she can "fit in," especially if she is going to take over the farm at some point. Some of Vidor's films suffer from the same type of exaggerated humor or melodrama in certain sequences, ones that do not always cohere with the scenes around them. Though with that said, the meal scene no doubt appealed to Depression era audiences who escaped to the cinema for distraction and a laugh. And the scene certainly reminds us of Vidor's talent for zany comedy as was demonstrated in his three films with Marion Davies.

Guy and Louise continue with their romancing, but Guy eventually tells her that he cannot break Nettie's heart. Guy tells Louise that she has been accepted by the men (supposedly her service at the luncheon table and the cream pie in the face of one of the workers were enough to do the trick), but she tells him that she is going back East. Apparently she feels that she does not want to endanger his marriage any further. When Louise then informs her grandfather that she is going back East, the elder Storr replies that she belongs there. He declares, "Storrhaven—it's worth fighting for, worth planning for. They'll never be able to get it away from us.... Farm's part of our minds—become part of our bodies.... Sometimes I think the big things of the past are more real than the little things that are right here."

He then starts pointing out Civil War "ghosts" that supposedly appear before him. Thus begins Grandpa's performance of feigned dementia which he puts into the form of preparing for an impending battle, as if re-living his time in the war. Louise expresses alarm at his sudden lapse of reason and the viewer is initially not sure of what is going on. But we soon discover that Grandpa is carrying out a deliberate strategy that will disclose to himself (and to others) Louise's compassion and loyalty as opposed to the greedy indifference of Beatrice and Thelma. Simmon and Durgnat compare this part of the film with Ben Jonson's *Volpone*, in which a man of wealth feigns illness for purposes of testing those who hope to inherit his fortune.[19] All of this comes to be demonstrated in front of three doctors as objective observers, doctors who had been called in to judge the old man's sanity. For Vidor fans, this scenario may call to mind Barrymore's later performance for the director. In *Duel in the Sun*, he is a similarly cranky patriarch who obsesses about his vast "empire" and about who will inherit it. Senator McCanles exiles his more rational and civilized son after a dispute between them, thus making the issue of inheritance all the more difficult. In Grandpa Storr's case, however, the choice is clear. The only challenge is making sure that Louise stays on to take over the farm.

After the witnessing of Grandpa's will by the three visiting doctors who realize his insanity is a pretense, Guy and Louise converse quietly on the porch. Guy expresses his desire for her to stay so that they can be "near to each other." Louise now knows it would be more than problematic. She then talks with Grandpa, who tells Louise that she will be wealthy when "normal times come back": i.e., when the crops come back and she can sell the corn. Knowing that remaining on the farm will be difficult for her with Guy nearby, Grandpa tells her: "A woman's heart does not ache so badly if her hands are busy." He says that he does not have much time left and that the farm will be hers sooner than she thinks: "When a man's 85 years old and the muscles of his heart and his life are stretched to the breaking point.... I've known that for a week. Perhaps tonight, tomorrow, the next day. Change comes. Well, you saved the very end of my life. That's the most important part. My house is in order. I'm tired. I'll go and set by myself awhile." He goes out to the porch, sits on the steps in the breeze, and sighs deeply. The very next day, a despondent Simon tells Louise that Grandpa is dead. He had left behind a letter detailing how everything should be handled after he has passed on. Simon tells her: "Lots of times he didn't do or say the things he wanted to because he thought they seemed so darned silly."

In the final sequence of the film, we see that Louise will indeed take over the farm as she sits at the table with the others, taking Grandpa's seat and saying grace. There are then beautiful shots of the tree-lined farm filled with tractors and workers in the foreground and with dust filling the frame. There is a shot of Louise and Simon standing in the dust from the tractors. Guy arrives in his car and they share a laugh about the image of Grandpa chuckling up in Heaven. He tells her that he has accepted a teaching position at Cornell and that Nettie seems happy about it. "Strange pattern it makes, doesn't it?" she ponders. "The city girl comes to the farm to stay and the farm man goes to the city." He replies, "It's the only way to work this out, Louise. I'm not crying about it." She responds, "Sometimes we like to think that we're entitled to all we can get out of life. Well, when you come right down to it, I don't suppose either of us would really break up Nettie's house, would we, Guy?" To this he bids her farewell and calls her "a grand girl."

In many ways, this comedy-laced drama revolves around the tension between the restraint of moral obligation and the unrestrained surge of romantic passion. In this case, Louise and Guy learn to refrain from their obvious love for one another because of his duty to his wife and son and because of Louise's duty to take over the family farm in a way that does not disrupt a close-knit community (including the family next door). And, of course, Louise's love for Guy will be satisfied in knowing that he is satisfied in carrying out his loving obligations to Nettie and his son. In fact, Vidor puts it this way himself when reflecting on the film with interviewer Nancy Dowd, especially after she refers to the final lines of the movie: "Philosophically, the emphasis is all on duty and obligation, and nobody has the courage to say, 'This is what I'd like to do.' It is always the dichotomy of conflicting forces, the dichotomy of following something from a vague sense of duty, or else being honest and true with yourself."[20]

Guy and Louise would clearly love to have followed a different path in life, one that they could have shared together as a couple, if only they could have met far earlier before Guy married and had a child. But with Guy's family life a reality, one centered upon his own love and respect for Nettie and Widdie, romantic desire must give way to familial love and obligation. And the rightness of this choice is no doubt illuminated by the fact that Guy tells Louise that Nettie is happy that they are going to Cornell so that Guy can pursue something that he was not able to pursue beforehand. We can guess that Nettie is not happy simply because this decision will take him away from Louise: she has loved Guy enough to realize that the farm life did not allow him to express his full personal potential, and she realized this even more after city girl Louise arrived at Storrhaven. Likewise, taking over the farm will permit Louise to fulfill her own sense of obligation to her beloved grandfather, and perhaps to her father too. And it will also allow her to fulfill her life in ways that were not possible back in the city. In this sense, the story reflects one essential idea of America, that of a place where new starts and second chances are possible, where human life (as in Nature) can be regenerated.

Fourteen

1934–1936

Our Daily Bread, So Red the Rose, The Wedding Night, and *The Texas Rangers*

Our Daily Bread (1934)

> "It is difficult for many young people to realize that the early 1930s were a period of real crisis for the United States, with widespread unemployment and depression.... I wanted to take my two protagonists out of *The Crowd* and follow them through the struggles of a typical young American couple in this most difficult period.... Then I read a short article by a college professor in *Reader's Digest*. It proposed the organization of co-operatives as a solution to the unemployment problem.... Here was the nucleus of my story."[1]—King Vidor, 1953

Our Daily Bread was released in 1934 and, along with the prior year's masterful *The Stranger's Return* and the following year's *The Wedding Night* and *So Red the Rose*, belongs to a quartet of countryside dramas by Vidor. *Our Daily Bread* is the second part of his planned "war, wheat, and steel trilogy." He came up with the idea for the story after reading a *Reader's Digest* article on agrarian-based "co-ops" (co-operatives), and both he and his wife Elizabeth Hill wrote the script. Unable to find studio or private funding, Vidor approached the banks with the assistance of his friend Charlie Chaplin, one of the owners of United Artists, and Chaplin provided Vidor with the "releasing contract" (a contract that guaranteed major distribution once the film was made). However, as the director reports in his autobiography, the banks were not keen on financing a film that portrays banks in a negative light. So Vidor was forced to mortgage almost everything that he owned (house, car, savings) to finance the movie himself.[2] It was a clear example of independent filmmaking long before the emergence of such "indie" directors as John Cassavetes.

The film is, like the director's earlier *The Crowd*, a precursor to later neo-realist cinema. It has been praised as an earnest socio-political "document" that reflected its time: the Great Depression. The film depicts the plight of a poverty-stricken couple and their founding of an agricultural community in which labor and resources are bartered for the sake of the shared benefit of the common good. Vidor's film is a bold example of personal filmmaking that echoes the courage he summoned to follow up his first smash hit *The Big Parade* with *The Crowd*. The director certainly deserves credit for his brave independence in making such a movie at a time when its story and themes were still raw in the public psyche, and most especially considering the great financial risk that he was taking. *Our Daily Bread* resulted from the same type of social consciousness and moral conscience that gave rise to *The Crowd*. In fact, the lead characters in *Our Daily Bread* have the very same names (John and Mary Sims) as those in *The Crowd*, so this is Vidor's imagining of what may have happened to that couple after the earlier story concluded. In addition, Vidor initially offered the lead role of John Sims to James Murray, the star of *The Crowd*, after meeting him on the street by chance. But Murray had sadly slipped into the depths of chronic alcoholism by this point and he immediately and angrily rejected the offer when Vidor told Murray that he could have the role as long as he quit drinking and lost some weight.[3]

The film is noteworthy in terms of its cinematic craftsmanship mostly because of its mesmerizing final sequence after John Sims (Tom Keene), having recklessly fled from his wife Mary (Karen Morley) and his community with his new "sweetheart" Sally (Barbara Pepper) in tow, discovers that a nearby stream is flowing—seemingly miraculously given the harsh drought that has been killing their crops. He instantly coordinates the lightning-quick irrigation project that allows the vital water to flow to the sunbaked fields and thereby to rescue the crops. The entire sequence requires a suspension of belief for many reasons: the fact that the stream is flowing and feeding the nearby power plant, only a few miles from the commune, despite no rain and a horrible drought; the immediate response and impromptu ditch-digging that involves all of the heat-ravaged commune members working at a tireless, almost superhuman pace; and the fact that they have been told with nearly magical precision and prognostication by Chris (John Qualen) that they have exactly five days until the crops will die unless some type of "miracle" occurs (which, as we now see, it in fact does). On top of that, there seem to be no errors made amidst such an intricate project taking place over two miles of challenging terrain: they dig the aqueduct for all their worth and then the water flows seamlessly from source to destination while taking sharp turns at certain points. When the water begins to overflow one of these turns, a worker simply lies in front of the surging water as if he were Superman and uses his body to divert it back to its proper channel. It is all unbelievable, and even more so than the far-fetched scene earlier in the film when the men of the commune intimidate the serious land bidders so that the co-op members acquire their desired land for a mere $1.85 while the other bidders quietly accept defeat. But this is a movie, after all. And though this is a far different type of film than the traditional Golden Age Hollywood fare of the time, the documentary-like "realism" of the film does not jibe well with such scenes where the credibility of the storyline is stretched beyond the breaking point.

The social and political philosophy that underlies the vision of *Our Daily Bread* could not be more different from the hyper-individualist, anti-collectivist worldview

Fourteen. *Daily Bread, Red the Rose, Wedding Night, Texas Rangers*

A shot of many members of the farming co-operative in King Vidor's populist rural drama *Our Daily Bread* (1934, produced by Vidor and distributed by United Artists). The film is a sequel to the director's silent classic *The Crowd* (1928) and the two lead characters share the same names as the two lead characters in that earlier film. Standing: Henry Hall (as Frank). Kneeling at center, to the right of Hall: John Qualen (as Chris Larsen), Tom Keene (as John Sims), and Karen Morley (as Mary Sims) (United Artists/Photofest).

advocated in Vidor's later adaptation of Ayn Rand's 1943 novel *The Fountainhead* (see Chapter Twenty). The members of the farming co-operative in *Our Daily Bread* bring what they can to the table to create a self-sustaining community. This community is organized around the principle expressed by Karl Marx's famous dictum "from each according to his ability, to each according to his need." An example of this is when John selects people to live on his farm. Each of the men tells John what he can do, whether he is a tailor, a violinist, or a contractor. Initially, John takes the men who can do the most manual labor related to farming. However, John ends up taking everyone. This turns the society into a functioning collective in which each individual brings what he can and gets what he needs. There is an effective shot in the film in which the tailor, after opening his shop, lists what he has and what he wants. *The Fountainhead* is based on Rand's anti-socialist and anti-collectivist philosophy, but John's commune does not appear to corrupt individuality in the manner that Rand would assume it would. Individuals in this collective are still able to maintain their individuality.

What *Our Daily Bread* clearly critiques is the type of unregulated capitalist economy that prompted these characters to form a collective in the first place. When the economy is decimated, as in the Great Depression, the collective seems to be a viable alternative that allows for survival during this life-challenging time. The main point of *Our Daily Bread* is not that collectivism functions better than capitalism, but rather that, when capitalism fails, a collective is a viable method of survival. John is a man who does not seem highly intelligent but who inspires these people to help each other sustain themselves temporarily on this farm. This relationship provides mutual benefits and it is not "parasitic" in the way that Randian Objectivists might initially interpret it.

The most plausible way to view the co-operative in the movie is in terms of organic unity: a "body" that consists of many different "parts" or individuals, all operating within a functional whole. These parts vary, but they serve a shared purpose in helping the community, and therefore the parts themselves, to subsist. The group benefits the individual and vice-versa. The individuality of those living in the commune is not necessarily lost but is vital for the common good that in turn helps to sustain the individual members. *Our Daily Bread* demonstrates a principle of proportional equality in that each member of the group helps to maintain the collective as a whole by caring for the individuals who compose the collective. Given the

King Vidor's populist rural drama *Our Daily Bread* (1934, produced by Vidor and distributed by United Artists). Pictured are Karen Morley (as Mary Sims) and Tom Keene (as her husband John Sims). The movie was financed almost entirely by Vidor when he failed to gain studio funding for the production. United Artists distributed the finished film (United Artists/Photofest).

FOURTEEN. *Daily Bread, Red the Rose, Wedding Night, Texas Rangers* 151

economic situation in which sheer survival is the primary goal, self-interest is best sustained by the good of the group and the collective benefits are returned to the individuals who have contributed to the common good. The commune in *Our Daily Bread* functions according to this type of proportional equality, but it is not necessarily achieved in a manner where the collective negates the value of the individual, as Rand assumed. Therefore, *Our Daily Bread* shows a group of people trying to sustain themselves amidst adversity and who utilize their individual skills to achieve the benefit of the group as a whole. Self-interest is not abandoned but it is, in fact, the instinct that drives the co-operative. John's commune is not a mass-minded mob of those who sacrifice their lives and happiness for the group. Such a collective is incentivized because people work for their shared good in a way that benefits the individual in a time of crisis. The individual's interests and desires and freedoms are not eliminated, but they are rather channeled in a way that sustains all individuals in the group.

It is perhaps not surprising, given the social and economic dynamics at work in *Our Daily Bread*, that the movie was misunderstood by some on both sides of the political spectrum. It was labeled as "capitalistic propaganda" by some at Moscow's annual film exhibition after its release, even though Vidor's movie won second prize at the event. At the same time, William Randolph Hearst's publishing company called it "pinko" in one of its reviews and the *Los Angeles Times* refused to advertise such a "far left" film. Nonetheless, in his autobiography, Vidor tells us that his film was treated fairly by the critics and that it was not a box office failure: "Nobody lost any money on the venture; we were well compensated by a fair return for our efforts, and by the greater satisfaction of having turned out a film which was true to our intentions and faithfully depicted our times."[4]

Vidor used a metronome in his filming of the memorable ditch-digging scene in which the co-op members create an irrigation system in record time. This scene encompasses the climax and finale of the movie. But whereas the director used the metronome in *The Big Parade*'s battle scene in order to create a slow, haunting, tense, fatalistic tempo, he created a rapid-fire pace for the hurried irrigation scene. This heightened pacing builds tension and engages the viewer in the frenzied determination of the workers. As in both films, the metronomic rhythm shapes the movements of the many characters on the screen while, at the same time, the patterns of their motions help to determine the way in which the scene will be later edited (as well as later enhanced through the accompanying music by composer Alfred Newman, who had worked with Vidor on *Street Scene*). Vidor's words about the significance of this scene in his autobiography are well worth noting: "I believe that the climax of *Our Daily Bread*, like that of parts of *The Big Parade*, is an example of film sense in its most comprehensive form.... Digging a long ditch in straight, pictorial action without the use of rhythmic design to integrate it could have been boring.... Unified into a musical pattern, however, the episode held an emotional interest for the full eight hundred feet of its length."

Today, *Our Daily Bread* may appear to many to be something like a curio in a museum, but it is a testament not merely to the spirited populism of the 1930s but also to Vidor's passionate commitment to his art and vision. And the director appears to have had quite happy memories of making it, apart from its complete lack of box office appeal. That is perhaps due as much to the close-knit community of people who helped him make it (his cast and crew) as to the fact that the movie's lack of a big budget challenged him to resort purely to the bare bones of his cinematic artistry, a challenge that he had in fact enjoyed. As Nancy Dowd wrote in her program notes for the Museum of Modern Art's wide-ranging Vidor retrospective in 1972: "*Our Daily Bread* was shot on an abandoned golf course near Hollywood. Because Vidor was trying to ration every penny for production essentials, all the usual studio glamour was abandoned. Tents were used as dressing rooms, and the silent scenes were shot last to save the expensive rental of sound equipment. Vidor recalls that the co-operative nature of the film affected the cast and crew. They worked together in a communal spirit that overshadowed the hardships of low budget productions."[5]

* * * *

So Red the Rose (1935)

Later in life, Vidor referred to *So Red the Rose* as a "very good film," though he may be in the minority with that view.[6] Like certain other movies by the director such as *The Fountainhead* and *War and Peace*, it is a work that has its moments and that exhibits expert craftsmanship in many parts but which, at the end of the day, gets pulled down by the weight of its own clunky narrative and stilted dialogue. It also is a film that is problematic because of its use of clear racist stereotypes (the same problem that plagues *Hallelujah*) and because the story is pervaded by a general sense of nostalgia for the Old South, though the latter sentiment is certainly inherited from the novel by Stark Young that serves as its basis.

The movie was produced by Douglas MacLean for Paramount and its screenplay was written by Laurence Stallings and Maxwell Anderson (along with Edwin Justus Mayer) who had co-written the highly successful World War I play *What Price Glory?* Of course, Stallings was the scenarist for Vidor's first big box office and critical success, *The Big Parade*, which was based in part on Stalling's popular autobiographical novel *Plumes*, published in 1924. Stallings also worked on other Vidor films: he co-wrote the treatment for *Show People* (with Agnes Christine Johnston), contributed dialogue to *Billy the Kid*, and co-wrote the screenplay for *Northwest Passage* (with Talbot Jennings). Stallings also wrote the screenplay for John Ford's *The Sun Shines Bright* (1953), the re-make of Ford's earlier *Judge Priest* (1934) that had starred Will Rogers (it was one of three Ford films that Rogers starred in before his untimely death).

So Red the Rose can easily be compared with those two Ford films because all three are set in the Civil War era (Vidor's film takes place during the war and the Ford films just after the end of the war), all three express some nostalgia for the Old South and Confederacy, and all three contain clear instances of brazen racial stereotyping. One might make the argument that Ford's two films, based on writer Irvin S. Cobb's series of Judge Priest stories, use blatant racial stereotypes in order to subvert them, given that the basic storylines also include anti-racist elements. But this may be a charitable reading, given the degree of the derogatory depictions of African American characters (including one played by Hattie McDaniel in the earlier Ford film and one played by Stepin Fetchit in both of the Ford films). Suffice it to say that *So Red the Rose* includes the same type of stereotyping and nostalgia for the Old South but reveals little or nothing that could lend itself to the possible interpretation that Vidor and his screenwriters intended to undermine the stereotypes within the narrative. And so, even given the era of its release, the racism in *So Red the Rose*, like the racism in *Hallelujah*, is problematic and one can perhaps blame the combined forces of Paramount, Vidor, the screenwriters, and the source material.

There are some beautifully photographed scenes and sequences in the film and these can be credited to both Vidor and his cinematographer, Victor Milner. During his career, Milner had been nominated for ten Oscars and he won for his photography in Cecil B. DeMille's *Cleopatra* (1934). Other classic films for which Milner had served as cinematographer include *Trouble in Paradise* (1932), *Design for Living* (1933), *The General Died at Dawn* (1936), *Union Pacific* (1939), *The Lady Eve* (1941), *The Palm Beach Story* (1942), *The Strange Love of Martha Ivers* (1946), and *Unfaithfully Yours* (1948). Vidor's movie was edited by Eda Warren who had also served as editor for *The General Died at Dawn*, *The Big Broadcast of 1938* (1938), and *I Married a Witch* (1942).

So Red the Rose did not do well at the box office. Reportedly, after the commercial failure of Vidor's film, studios swore off making any Civil War era romances for a few years, at least until William Wyler's antebellum *Jezebel* (1938) and, of course, Victor Fleming's *Gone with the Wind* (1939). While it remains a lesser Vidor work, the movie does include more than several charming as well as moving scenes and it boasts a splendid performance (often comedic) by Walter Connolly, who plays plantation owner Malcolm Bedford. Just before acting in Vidor's film, Connolly had starred as the titular character in Edward Sedgwick's *Father Brown, Detective* (1934). Connolly's role in *So Red the Rose* may be compared with other amusing family patriarchs played by Eugene Pallette in Gregory La Cava's *My Man Godfrey* (1936), Donald Crisp in John Ford's *How Green Was My Valley* (1941), and Lionel Barrymore as Grandpa Storr in Vidor's earlier *The Stranger's Return* (1933). Memorable scenes with Connolly include his quiet, supportive farewell to his son Edward (Harry Ellerbe) when the young man decides to go off to war after hearing of the death of his friend in battle. Effective comic scenes include the one in which Bedford is awakened and enraged by Union soldiers who force him out of bed so he can help them (to find their way back to the proper route to Vicksburg) as well as when he decides to join the fight after being shamed by the Union soldiers. Connolly's most hilarious scene centers on him trying on multiple old hats, including top hats, to see which will best match his antiquated and outrageous military uniform. And then there is his quiet, poignant death scene on the sofa after returning from battle and after nursing his final mint julep. Connolly's superb performance is yet another clear demonstration of Vidor's talent for working with capable actors and giving them the space to make the best of their roles.

Bedford's daughter Valette (Margaret Sullavan) criticizes her distant cousin Duncan (Randolph Scott) for refusing to go to war to fight for the Confederacy. One is reminded of Justyn toward the beginning of *The Big Parade*; it is Justyn who, in her enthusiasm for the enlisted men who march off to war, triggers Jim into enlisting. Duncan initially resists joining the military not so much because he is a pacifist (he clearly demonstrates otherwise later in the film) but because, as he makes clear, he does not believe in killing other Americans. He tells Valette that he went to school up north and has friends there. He eventually changes his mind when he brings Valette's mother Sally (Janet Beecher) to search for her son Edward on the battlefield. Sally had awoken with a vision of her son crying out to her and, convinced of its truth, she is adamant about undertaking the search. Just after they have arrived at the battlefield, Confederate officers carry the corpse of Edward past them on a stretcher. The timing stretches credibility but the scene is haunting. Duncan leaves Sally to return to her plantation alone. He has seen enough and he now forsakes his earlier dedication to the ideal of "one America" and rides off to assist the Confederate cause.

In many ways, the heart of the film revolves around Duncan's change of heart and then, later toward the end, his return to his old values. Many a drama includes a moral awakening or spiritual epiphany that results in a radical change of view (sometimes a change of worldview). One of the most iconic moments of moral transformation in the history of American cinema takes place in John Ford's classic Western *The Searchers*. Ethan Edwards (John Wayne) has been searching for his niece Debbie (Natalie Wood), who had been abducted by the Comanche chief Scar (Henry Brandon) when she was just a girl after her immediate family had been massacred by Scar's tribe. Ethan swears vengeance against Scar but, the longer the search continues (it goes on for more than several years), the more he also seeks to kill Debbie, should she still be alive, due to the fact that she would have become assimilated by the chief's tribe by this point. Ethan would rather have her dead than as one of the enemy, believing that her soul would have become tainted. Ethan's racist mission to "save" Debbie by murdering her is immediately, almost miraculously reversed when he finally finds Debbie, who has indeed been assimilated as one of Scar's young wives. Ethan chases her to the entrance of a large cave and picks her up in his arms. Rather than killing her, however, he immediately and almost subconsciously embraces her, perhaps remembering the moment earlier in the film when he picked up the much younger Debbie in his arms just after returning "home" from

FOURTEEN. *Daily Bread, Red the Rose, Wedding Night, Texas Rangers*

his apparent wandering years following his service to the Confederacy in the war. Ethan's dramatic change of heart is that moment to which the entire film has led and it is indeed a powerful, archetypal moment.

Such an immediate change in morality and psychology occurs in real life, of course, but it also serves a given film narrative without needing to bother about the details leading to such a change. Such transformations can, of course, be the result of subconscious emotional needs that cannot be easily analyzed or portrayed. However, suffice it to say that Duncan's changes of heart in *So Red the Rose*—from being a critic of the war to being a man who joins the war because he is bent on vengeance, then the eventual change back to his old value of putting humanity first—are not depicted in the profoundly moving way in which Ethan's epiphany is shown in *The Searchers*. We know that Duncan becomes instantly converted once he sees his cousin Edward's body being dragged off the battlefield, also realizing how it must affect Sally. But the transformation lacks the required degree of emotional power, even if we can safely assume that Duncan has felt torn about his opposition to the war over time.

Duncan's awakening on the desolate battlefield brings to mind other moments in Vidor's works when similar changes occur. There is, of course, Jim's sudden desire to enlist in the army in *The Big Parade*, especially after being caught up in the communal fervor of his town's patriotic parade (and not to mention Justyn's support of those going off to fight). There is John in *Our Daily Bread*, who becomes enamored with Sally and suddenly decides to take Sally and leave his wife and the commune behind, only to experience a sudden change of heart a few minutes later. He notices the sound of the power plant humming and immediately returns to help his people build an irrigation system. There is Dr. Andrew Manson in *The Citadel*, who forsakes his values once he becomes caught up in the high society of London but then returns to his former ideals after witnessing the botched fatal surgery performed on his old friend Denny. There is Langdon Towne in *Northwest Passage*, who joins Rogers' Rangers for the sole purpose of making maps and recording frontier life in his sketch book—but who soon becomes transformed into a ruthless Indian-killer. And there is Pierre in Vidor's adaptation of *War and Peace*, who shares Duncan's opposition to war—though for Pierre, it is a resistance to war in general while Duncan resists the particular war that involves Americans killing Americans. Pierre never winds up joining the fight as Duncan does, but he does travel a great distance to visit his friend Andrei at the battlefield so that he can see what war is like with his own eyes. Before that, he shunned the war entirely.

Duncan eventually arrives back at the Bedford plantation in uniform, hunting Union POW escapees. Just before this, Valette has decided to help one of the wounded escapees and she puts him in bed to rest. Duncan discovers that she has been hiding the Union soldier and, after expressing sudden outrage and the desire to take him away, nearly forcing the injured soldier out of bed, Valette pleads with Duncan and he experiences an instantaneous change of heart. He switches uniforms

Randolph Scott (as Duncan Bedford) and Margaret Sullavan (as Valette Bedford) in King Vidor's Civil War drama *So Red the Rose* (1935, Paramount Pictures). The screenplay is based on the novel of the same title by Stark Young (Paramount Pictures/Photofest).

with the soldier as quickly as he has switched moral perspectives. Then, after emerging from the bedroom, he is accosted by his own Confederate army members (who obviously do not recognize him) and taken away. In the end, Duncan manages to escape and return to the Bedford plantation.

Valette almost magically hears him calling her, just as her mother had heard her son calling her from the battlefield, and she runs toward his voice. They see one another across a nearby stream and then, moving to a wooden bridge not far away, they cross the bridge from opposite banks, run to one another, and embrace. Despite being distant cousins, they obviously have loved one another for a long time without making their mutual love known. Valette has seen the horrors of war firsthand and Duncan has had his humanity restored. We know that they can now live happily ever after and restore the plantation to its former glory, despite the slave rebellion that occurred while Duncan was away. Luckily for her, Valette had appealed personally to the slaves and quelled the revolt. She had told them that she did not want them to be slaves but that they still needed to work for their sustenance, even if they were free, and that the plantation is their longtime home. The leader of the revolt, Cato (Clarence Muse), surrenders to Valette's emotional appeal when she reminds him of the way that he had cared for her when she was a little girl. Cato's change of heart is as sudden as that of Duncan on the battlefield and he helps to restore order. Apparently, given this happy ending, Duncan and Valette can enjoy their life together on their old plantation. The slaves, who will soon be free once the war has ended, can work as hard as they always did, but as a job and not as forced slavery. And somehow the movie's finale seems to imply that the audience should be happy with that situation.

* * * *

The Wedding Night (1935)

The Wedding Night is, in many ways, a throwback to the sort of folksy, naturalist, rural-set films with which he began his career. "I have always attempted to adhere to the 'earthier' themes in the pictures I have directed in Hollywood," Vidor wrote in a column for the *New York Times* at the time of the film's release. "My belief has always been that simplicity is beauty, and I am trying to find beauty in every-day people whom we meet and know in our daily lives."[7]

Set in small-town Connecticut, *The Wedding Night* is about a burned out New York City novelist, Tony Barrett (Gary Cooper), who visits an inherited family property to find inspiration for a new book. His wife, Dora (Helen Vinson), decides to return to New York. The story by Edwin Knopf is said to be loosely based on Knopf's (and Vidor's) friends F. Scott and Zelda Fitzgerald. Fitzgerald had written a story about Hollywood titled "Crazy Sunday" and it was originally published in the October 1932 issue of the magazine *American Mercury*. One of its main characters, a famous movie director, was reportedly based (at least in part) on Vidor, whom Fitzgerald had met on a voyage to France right after the director had finished making *Bardelys the Magnificent*. By directing the film *The Wedding Night* (1935), one could say that Vidor was "returning the compliment" to his old friend Fitzgerald.

Tony's neighbor, Manya Novak (Anna Sten), whose family are Polish immigrants who run a nearby tobacco farm, helps him around the house. Tony and Manya begin to fall in love, but their relationship remains unrequited as Tony is still married to Dora and Manya is engaged to Fredrik Sobieski (Ralph Bellamy) through an arranged marriage/property deal organized by her father (Sig Ruman). Gossip continues to surround Tony and Manya, which culminates on Manya's wedding night when her husband, inebriated, bursts into Tony's house to attack him. Manya intervenes and is knocked down the stairs, killing her.

Like Vidor's earliest melodramas, *The Jack-Knife Man*, *The Sky Pilot*, and *Love Never Dies*, *The Wedding Night*'s strength lies in its straightforward, folktale-type narrative and picturesque photography. Vidor integrates location photography of the tobacco fields with evocative studio-bound recreations of New England. The interior of Tony's country home is lovingly photographed by Gregg Toland, the future cinematographer of *Wuthering Heights* (1939, for which he won an Academy

Award), *The Grapes of Wrath* (1940), and *Citizen Kane* (1941). Toland's nighttime photography, capturing the soft shadows cast by lanterns and fireplaces, makes palpable the warmth felt by Tony and Manya.

Coming one year after Frank Capra's *It Happened One Night*, *The Wedding Night* finds itself in the heart of the 1930s screwball comedy cycle, and despite the fatalistic, morbid ending, there are a number of lighthearted moments early in the film when Vidor seems to be channeling the visual strategies of this emerging subgenre. In post 1934 Hollywood, filmmakers had to be creative in order to work around the Production Code, and in screwball comedies, sexual tension and physical contact could not be explicitly expressed. In *The Wedding Night*, Vidor uses rustic rituals as flirtation devices, such as when Tony is unable to light the woodstove in the kitchen. As Manya shreds paper and bends over the stove to add kindling, Tony tilts his head, both checking out how she lights the stove and "checking her out" in a sexual fashion.

As Manya helps Tony make his bed, he begins telling her intimate personal details: "I hate people who tuck in the blankets, mind you. I like mine loose so my feet can express themselves." Later, he points to the quilt and says, "I count these patches when I'm going goofy at night." Such information seems to be a coded invitation for her to spend the night. Vidor films much of this conversation in an extended long-take, the duration of the scene emphasizing their chemistry and building the tension. Visually, Vidor uses a bedpost to vertically bisect the frame, signifying the separate worlds to which they belong. After they are done making the bed, Tony reaches across to shake her hand, the long-awaited moment of physical contact. As soon as he touches her hand, she informs him that she can no longer bring milk in the morning, as her father and fiancé are angry with her for spending so much time with Tony. She then turns and walks out of the frame; the camera remains stationary for a moment as the emptiness of her side of the frame expresses her sudden absence from Tony's life. Such a sequence illustrates Vidor's command of bodily choreography within the cinematic frame as well as the sophisticated simplicity of his direction.

The romantic conflict at the heart of *The Wedding Night* is a loose reworking of similar plots in earlier films. Just like Jim Warlock in *Cynara*, Tony is a husband who finds a new love interest while separated from his wife; that Tony is an artist whose romance kindles while he is on-location for work particularly recalls Vidor's own relationship with Elizabeth Hill during the shooting of *Bird of Paradise*. Unlike *Cynara*, however, Vidor's sympathies in *The Wedding Night* seem more evenly distributed among Tony, Dora, and Manya (Fredrik, on the other hand, comes off as a drunken, possessive brute). When Tony asks for a divorce, he also asks Dora to think of Manya. Her response gives voice to the emotions that Clemency Warlock was not allowed to vocalize: "Wives can't think of Manyas.... All Manyas are alike to wives, no matter how sweet they are.... I'd like to scratch her eyes out and call her names. And tell you how much I've had to put up with, how you've let me down. You better

FOURTEEN. *Daily Bread, Red the Rose, Wedding Night, Texas Rangers*

go to bed before I do. We'll talk in the morning." Unlike *Cynara*, in which the wife completely exonerates the husband, here in *The Wedding Night*, Tony is not let off the hook. The screenplay, by Edith Fitzgerald and based on a story by Edwin Knopf, is decidedly less sexist in its worldview and more sophisticated and empathetic towards its characters than Frances Marion and Lynn Starling's script for *Cynara*.

The Tony-Manya relationship also seems like a reimagining of the Johnny-Luana conflict in *Bird of Paradise*. In that film, Luana was not permitted to pursue her relationship with the American sailor because of her obligation to her tribe; similarly, in *The Wedding Night*, Manya must go through with her marriage to Fredrik (which comes with a piece of land purchased from Tony by her father) as prescribed by custom. As Durgnat and Simmon note, "Her plight comes over as entirely her community's fault." It seems most likely that this was a matter of melodramatic convention rather than an explicit critique of Polish culture. Durgnat and Simmon observe that "it's hard to say how far Goldwyn, or Vidor, wanted Polish 'alienness' to bear the brunt of the blame" and that "maybe it's unfair to expect some such sophistication from the film at a time when rural America, ravaged by Depression, rejected renewed immigration so violently that the Johnson-Reed Act virtually stopped further immigration after 1929."[8]

On the set, Vidor encountered difficulties with his two stars. Cooper had risen to stardom in the twilight of the silent era with *The Winning of Barbara Worth* (1926) and *Wings* (1927), and his characteristic slow-style of speaking made him among the most distinctive, naturalistic, and charming actors in the talkies—in such films as Josef von Sternberg's *Morocco* (1930), Rouben Mamoulian's *City Streets* (1931), Frank Borzage's *A Farewell to Arms* (1932), and Ernst Lubitsch's *Design for Living* (1933). Anna Sten was an actress from Kiev whom Goldwyn had tried turning into a star in two previous Hollywood films, *Nana* (1934) and *We Live Again* (1934). Despite their respective experience in front of the camera, behind the scenes both actors posed problems. Vidor recalled: "Gary [Cooper] began to stutter and stammer and interrupt himself. He spoke very slowly at times and he was also having trouble just remembering his lines."[9] Sten, not a native English speaker, was still challenged learning the new language. Vidor later reported: "Rather than a director, I felt like a dentist, trying to pull the syllables out of her mouth before the parallel gesture had passed by. Between Cooper's mumbling and Sten's slow process of translation, I was having a fine time."[10] Considering these obstacles, it is remarkable that Vidor elicited such smooth performances from both actors and such on-screen chemistry, as their connection seems much more believable than, say, that between Ronald Colman and either Phyllis Barry or Kay Francis in *Cynara*.

Critics responded to the stark drama of *The Wedding Night*. Andrew Sennwald in the *New York Times* wrote: "With the assistance of King Vidor, Hollywood steps out of its emotional swaddling clothes ... [A]n uncommonly adult style ... displays an unusual regard for the truth and it is courageous enough to allow an affair which is obviously doomed to end logically in tragedy ... a satisfying compromise between

Mr. Vidor, the realist, and Mr. Goldwyn, the romantic."[11] Norbert Lusk, in the *Los Angeles Times*, used the film to discuss Vidor's success in transitioning to sound and his ability to maintain a personal style across the technology jump: "A poignant, absorbing film ... with uncommon intelligence and sympathy.... [Vidor] is one of the very few whose work has not been robbed of individuality by the intrusion of speech. The same quiet, deep, unstrained quality of emotion is here evident, and his sensitive, discriminating use of detail in its proper place, neither overemphasized nor understated. Nor is there any director who recognizes and uses the forces of nature to form the background of a mood or even to motivate it as unerringly as Mr. Vidor."[12] And in the *New York Herald Tribune*, Richard Watt, Jr., aptly captured the director's signature feeling: "Persuasive is the Vidor touch that the regular events of the picture take on an air of authenticity and poignancy while all of the characters seem to live and breathe with high validity."[13]

* * * *

The Texas Rangers (1936)

In December of 1935, just after the U.S. premiere of *The Wedding Night* in November, Vidor gathered about a dozen fellow Hollywood filmmakers at his home to discuss the formation of a director's union that would give them a stronger voice in the industry. This was especially needed when the major studios began making severe pay cuts in the face of the Great Depression and their own losses in profits. The directors who attended this gathering included Frank Borzage, Howard Hawks, Henry King, Ernst Lubitsch, Lewis Milestone, and William Wellman. By January, the new Screen Directors Guild had been incorporated with twenty-nine founding members who elected Vidor as their first president. One of his chief tasks was to persuade many other filmmakers to join with them, and he succeeded, even while remaining actively involved in his own directorial work. As Durgnat and Simmon say of the newly formed union: "Two years later, it had grown to some six hundred, including virtually every active director and assistant director. Under the name it took in 1960 (after incorporating television directors), the Directors Guild of America remains a key Hollywood bargaining and professional unit."[14]

Around the time of the founding of the Guild, Vidor began work on his next western, *The Texas Rangers*. The 1930s is a fairly barren decade for the Hollywood western, mostly filled with mediocre B-Westerns and bookended by two films that sought to redefine the genre. The first tried but failed: Raoul Walsh's artistically and technologically innovative—but commercially disastrous—film *The Big Trail* (1930), which introduced both John Wayne in his first leading western role and, more significantly, 70mm "Grandeur" widescreen photography that captured in painstaking realism a cross-country trail drive. The second film became an influential milestone: John Ford's *Stagecoach* (1939), also starring Wayne. Ford and

FOURTEEN. *Daily Bread, Red the Rose, Wedding Night, Texas Rangers* 161

his screenwriter, Dudley Nichols, had both won Academy Awards for their work on *The Informer* (1936), Ford for direction, Nichols for screenwriting. With *Stagecoach*, they combined a pulp story by Ernest Haycox, "The Stage to Lordsburg," with inspiration from Guy de Maupassant's "Boule de Suif" and created a film that, like their source material, was a perfect blend of high- and low-brow, an artistic and politically-minded drama, beautifully photographed, that packed more action and punch than any serial or B-western shoot-em-up. Excepting Walsh's *The Big Trail* (and the occasional film such as Edward L. Cahn's *Law and Order* [1932]), Hollywood had not seen such adult westerns since the silent days just over a decade before.

Released midway between *The Big Trail* and *Stagecoach*, King Vidor's *The Texas Rangers* (1936) plays out like an A-budgeted B-western: a silly piece of hackneyed sagebrush hokum whose visual authenticity harkens back to Walsh's film (and Vidor's own widescreen experiment, *Billy the Kid*) but falls far short of the art-and-action fusion that Ford achieved. Vidor and his wife Elizabeth Hill are credited with the story and Louis Stevens with the screenplay, based upon data furnished by Walter Prescott Webb's book, *The Texas Rangers*. Their script hardly seems like an historical recreation, or even a loving endorsement, of the Texas Rangers, particularly as most of the film is spent with its protagonists using their position in the Rangers as leverage in order to go back to their previous occupation: that of outlaws. Like with *Billy the Kid*, Vidor seems interested in exploring an anti-hero protagonist in *The Texas Rangers* but due to Production Code constraints (which would not permit glorifying criminality) he was stuck with a character who is neither hero nor anti-hero, neither outlaw nor lawman.

The Texas Rangers begins with a prologue set to a montage of the western frontier: roaming buffalo, cattle, Native Americans, gun-toting desperados on horseback, and then finally a shot of the titular group riding in line across the landscape. Meanwhile, the narrator states, "To the Texas Rangers, this picture is dedicated." The film then cuts to a stagecoach driven by Wahoo (Jack Oakie), which is held up by a masked bandit. In the next scene, we see Wahoo around a campfire playing guitar and singing as his partners split the loot from the stagecoach. To his right is Jim Hawkins (Fred MacMurray), the bandit who held up the train; to his right is Sam (Lloyd Nolan). Hearing voices from an approaching posse, the trio douse the fire and split off into the night. The following morning, we see that Jim and Wahoo have reunited but have not found Sam. Lacking their third member, the two decide to go back to their old routine of robbing stagecoaches. Wahoo is shown driving a coach and beside him riding shotgun is a Texas Ranger. When he stops to water the horses, Wahoo gestures for Jim to call off the holdup and put away his gun and remove his bandana. The duo decides to join the Texas Rangers to better inform their stickups. Jim tells Wahoo: "Look, hard head, there's a lot more to this job than forty bucks a month and chuck. A lot more. I can't tell you just yet, I have to figure it out first. But listen, there ain't a game in this world that wasn't made to be beat, if you're dealing the cards."

On their first job as Rangers, they catch Sam fording stolen cattle across a river and team up with him, planning to let him in on their scheme. Returning to their barracks, they come across a cabin under attack from Native Americans. They shoot away the attackers, but not soon enough to save the life of a mother and father. Jim and Wahoo take the boy Davey (Bennie Bartlett) back to their leader, Major Bailey (Edward Ellis). Bailey's daughter Amanda (Jean Parker) looks after Davey and falls in love with Jim, who initially is resistant to her attention.

On their next mission to gain the trust of Major Bailey, Jim and Wahoo risk their lives to save the Rangers from Native Americans who have them pinned down from a mountain top. As the Native Americans roll large boulders down towards the Rangers, Jim and Wahoo work their way up. Wahoo is wounded, but Jim makes it to the top, then shimmies down a tree, steals a horse, and returns with more Texas Rangers to run off the remaining Native Americans.

Jack Oakie (left, as Henry B. "Wahoo" Jones) and Fred MacMurray (as Jim Hawkins) in King Vidor's second Western, *The Texas Rangers* (1936, Paramount Pictures). The screenplay, co-written by Vidor and his wife Elizabeth Hill, was based on events described in Walter Prescott Webb's 1935 book *The Texas Rangers: A Century of Frontier Defense* (Paramount Pictures/Photofest).

Jim is rewarded with a mission to clean up Kimball County and arrest Jess Higgins (Fred Kohler, Sr.). Jim plans to replace Higgins with Sam. Wahoo refuses to go along with the plan, so Jim kicks him out of the gang. After arresting Higgins, Jim breaks off the deal with Sam, decides to go straight, and pursues a relationship with Amanda. When Sam becomes notorious as the "Polka Dot Bandit" because of his handkerchief, Major Bailey orders Jim to apprehend him. Jim refuses, and Bailey says he knows about Jim's criminal past and arrests him on an outstanding warrant. Wahoo and Davey plan to apprehend Sam themselves, but Davey is caught trying to deliver a message to the Rangers and he is kidnapped. Wahoo is shot by Sam. Bailey lets Jim out of jail to avenge his friend, and Jim single-handedly rescues Davey and shoots Sam.

FOURTEEN. *Daily Bread, Red the Rose, Wedding Night, Texas Rangers* 163

The convoluted plot of *The Texas Rangers*, with its duplicitous outlaws masquerading as lawmen, is as melodramatic as any B-western from the same time period, only more overwrought and extended (an inflated 98 minutes). Durgnat and Simmon commented: "[I]t contains what amounts to two B Westerns: 'The Texas Rangers Wipe Out the Injuns' and 'The Texas Rangers Wipe Out a Monopolist.'"[15] They also note how closely the narrative resembles another genre popular at the time: the crime film. Whereas pre–Code films focused on the law breakers, in a Post-Code Hollywood, films shifted the focus to the law enforcers. Durgnat and Simmon call attention to "*Bullets or Ballots* and *G-Men* (both released shortly before *The Texas Rangers*), in which [Edward G.] Robinson and [James] Cagney are tamed into heroic government agents.... In the course of *G-Men*, Cagney grows from outlaw to FBI man—the contemporary version of *The Texas Rangers*' pattern."[16] The relationship to the crime genre is also hard to ignore when one hears Fred MacMurray's voice, who speaks his lines with hardboiled menace and a modern, urban grittiness (for contemporary viewers, it is difficult to hear his voice without thinking of his later performance as Walter Neff in Billy Wilder's 1944 *Double Indemnity*).

The Texas Rangers' strength lies in its photography. Vidor said in an interview at the time of the film's release, "Most people don't get much real action in their daily lives, but they would like to if they could. Seeing action on the screen gives release to this universal desire for adventure and the outdoors."[17] Vidor learned from *Billy the Kid* the vital impact that location photography can give to westerns. And though he was not able to film in Texas, he was able to take his cast and crew away from the studio backlot. "We shot this film up near Gallup, New Mexico," Vidor recalled. "Then we worked in Santa Fe for a while at the Ranger headquarters there and in Santo Domingo, between Santa Fe and Taos. We built a couple of interiors up there so that we could work in bad weather."[18] The film's finest sequences would have benefited from 70mm widescreen photography, but even in 1.33:1 there is something vivid and dynamic about the compositions and their real locations. The background buttes and overhanging clouds tower over the characters, giving the scenes a solemnity and weight that belie the lightness of the script.

Vidor's choreographic direction is, arguably, one of the hallmarks of his style, and it is evident throughout his career, but never so much as in his outdoor epics. His placement of bodies within the frame is dynamic, and their movement within the frame (as opposed to montage) is Vidor's primary manner of constructing his sequences. Vidor's most noticeable advancement in *The Texas Rangers* is his use of deep focus photography, a technique by which objects close to and far away from the lens are equally in focus. This was Vidor's second collaboration with cinematographer Edward Cronjager, who had previously shot *Bird of Paradise* and who would ultimately be nominated for seven Academy Awards, although he never won. Vidor and Conjager's most impressive shots in this film include the shot of Jim and Wahoo peering down on Sam running his cattle across the river; Jim and Wahoo looking down the mountain at the attack on Danny and his family at their cabin; and the mid-film climactic battle between the Rangers and the Native Americans, with hundreds of riders and horses on both sides rushing at each other. While the script never rises above B-level cliches, these are the scenes in which Vidor's expertise—and the film's A-level budget—shine through.

Some publications were charmed by the film. "Far above the common run of western vehicles.... Vidor has drawn a vivid picture of the trying times of the period, at the same time combining fictional entertainment far reaching in appeal," wrote the *Motion Picture Herald*.[19] "First-rate semi-historical entertainment ... rich in comedy and thrills," wrote the *Film Daily*.[20] Others, however, saw through the glossy surface and called out the film's low quality plot. "A glorified horse opera ... it has vigor and a certain quote of excitement, but it lacks the epic qualities for which it undoubtedly reached," wrote *Modern Screen*.[21] *Variety* criticized the film: "What appears to have been intended as an epic of the Southwest is just a fancy hoss opry ... it could have taken at least a 15 minute slicing." *Variety* also made note of "boulders that are too obviously paper-mache."[22] And the *New York Times* wrote, "[P]retty maudlin stuff ... simply a revival of a decadent cinema form, generically referred to as 'cops and robbers.'"[23]

Billy the Kid and *The Texas Rangers* were nascent westerns for Vidor: primarily visual experiments over narrative frameworks whose stories did not match their pictorial sophistication. Vidor's next forays into frontier stories would be much more substantial and rank among three of his finest films: *Northwest Passage* (1940), *Duel in the Sun* (1946), and *Man Without a Star* (1955).

Fifteen

1937
Stella Dallas

One of Vidor's most popular and endearing movies was *Stella Dallas* (1937), produced by Samuel Goldwyn. Though, according to Vidor's memoir *A Tree Is a Tree*, he almost wound up making the film version of Mark Twain's *The Adventures of Tom Sawyer* for David O. Selznick instead. In September of 1936, Selznick, the producer of Vidor's earlier film *Bird of Paradise* (1932) and later movie *Duel in the Sun*, had asked Vidor to direct *Tom Sawyer* and, furthermore, demanded that he begin preparations almost immediately. However, Vidor had just promised his wife (and himself) a relaxing leaf-peeping trip to Connecticut at the start of that October, especially given his hard work in the prior summer months, and so he steadfastly refused the initial offer due to its timing. When Vidor returned from this autumn vacation, he heard no more from Selznick (until a year later), and so he soon began work on *Stella Dallas* for Goldwyn.[1] One can only assume that Vidor would have delivered a magnificent film version of the Twain story, given his deep love of Americana and the American landscape, his admitted appreciation of the author, his experience in mixing comedy and pathos, and his proven ability to direct child actors (most clearly demonstrated in *The Champ*).

Stella Dallas may have very well ended up being a William Wyler film, who had been lined up by Goldwyn to direct the melodrama. The only problem was that Wyler had become delayed in finishing his *Jezebel* with Bette Davis, and so Vidor was brought in as Wyler's replacement. Vidor's film is a re-make of the 1925 silent tear-jerker directed by Henry King, also produced by Goldwyn, and starring Ronald Colman and Belle Bennett. It was based on the 1923 Olive Higgins Prouty novel of the same title. That original story has also been the basis of a stage play (1924), a long-running popular radio soap opera (1937–1955), and a later film re-make in 1990 titled *Stella*, starring Bette Midler and produced by Samuel Goldwyn, Jr. Set in the factory town of Millhampton, Massachusetts, the story follows Stella Martin (Barbara Stanwyck, in one of her best roles), the ambitious daughter of a poor mill worker.

The movie is the type of exaggerated melodrama, bordering on something like a soap opera, that Vidor eventually became known for by the end of his career, especially with such later films as *Duel in the Sun*, *The Fountainhead*, *Beyond the Forest*, *Ruby Gentry*, and his Biblical epics *War and Peace* and *Solomon and Sheba*. These films involve highly charged emotions and overly dramatic histrionics in more than several scenes. In *Stella Dallas* there likewise tends to be overly expressive acting and plenty of stagy or stilted dialogue, as if the actors were performing on a stage. And there are some sudden, almost surreal juxtapositions between light-hearted, even silly comic scenes and more somber, heartfelt scenes. And yet *Stella Dallas* rises to the top of the list of Vidor's melodramas due to the expert directing, the story itself, and Stanwyck's dedicated performance. No less than the legendary Japanese filmmaker Akira Kurosawa ranked the film as #16 on his list of 100 favorite films.[2]

Stella quickly seduces Stephen Dallas (John Boles), a man who works in an office at the local mill and whose father, a successful banker, had committed suicide after losing his fortune. Despite Stephen being without wealth after the death of his father, Stella pursues him anyway, having read about his background in the local newspaper. The camera allows us to see (along with Stella) the newspaper article telling of his father's death two years prior and referring to Stephen as "a Harvard man and a crew man." The article reports that he has disappeared, no doubt to go off and make a life for himself somewhere else. The paper also refers to the very recent marriage of a Helen Dane whose wedding took place in a "swanky Paris church" and who was "a major figure in the tragedy." One question stands out on the page: "What Had the Suicide of Banker Dallas to Do with the Recent Wedding of Beautiful Helen Dane?"

But Stella knows exactly where Stephen has landed and no doubt senses his potential, given his background. When Stephen walks by her house at the beginning of the movie, Stella is in the front yard pretending to read a book of poetry titled *India's Love Lyrics*. They make quick eye contact. Her brother Charlie (George Walcott) soon rushes past her, taunting her about her flirtation with the passerby. She in turn insults him by calling him a mere "mill hand." We know right away that this will be a story about a romance between members of different social and economic classes, not unlike Vidor's later films *Duel in the Sun*, *Beyond the Forest*, and *Ruby Gentry*. The female characters in these movies do not seem to have the emotional capacity to rise above these class differences and, more importantly, to overcome desires that lead them away from a path to long-term happiness. In the interesting case of Stella, she stubbornly clings to a sense of identity that eventually impels her to push away the one person in her life whom she truly loves. As we shall see, she seems to be far more willing to sacrifice than to change.

Stella cleverly arranges to bring her brother's lunch to the mill factory. Rather than bringing it directly to her brother, she intentionally winds up in the office where Stephen Dallas currently works. Just before her arrival, we see Stephen in his office, reading the very same newspaper pages that Stella (and we) had been reading. He is writing a letter to his "Dearest Helen" to offer congratulations on her wedding and to say that he had intended to write to her for a long time. He then crumples up the letter and discards it. We now know that he had been romantically linked with

Helen and that this relationship ended when Stephen left home after his father's suicide. He does not seem to be overly upset at re-visiting the news about the death. Stella then arrives in the office, and they are soon led to arrange their first date.

They go to see a silent movie. After they leave the theater, she tells him that she wants to talk and act like him, no longer hiding her class difference. He tells her, "Don't be like someone else. Stay as you are. Don't pretend." Authenticity and personal identity become key themes of the film. He admits that he had been very lonely and unhappy until she had walked into his office and his life. They embrace and kiss, but she stops him and responds, "You won't have any respect for me." Then they fully embrace and kiss. When she returns home, her father is angry that she has stayed out all night, but Stella informs her family that she and Stephen had quickly gotten married that very night. We can only guess that Stella's desire to escape her lower-class family and Stephen's deep loneliness have compelled them to do what seems to be, at best, entirely hasty and capricious. They do not know each other yet, but they are desperate for happiness.

Stephen and Stella have a daughter named Laurel (nicknamed "Lolly"), but they eventually separate after it becomes evident that they are emotionally and socially incompatible. In the eyes of her husband, Stella is simply too crass and impetuous on

Ed Munn (played by Alan Hale, Sr.) and Stella Dallas (played by Barbara Stanwyck) laugh on a train after Munn pulls a prank on his fellow passengers in the mother-daughter drama *Stella Dallas* (1937, directed by King Vidor for Samuel Goldwyn Productions and distributed by United Artists). The screenplay is based on the 1923 novel of the same title by Olive Higgins Prouty (United Artists/Photofest).

too many occasions, though she certainly proves to be a loving and doting mother. Stephen follows his work to New York City for a long time, and Stella stays behind to devote herself to the care of Laurel (Anne Shirley) while also enjoying the company of her jovial, prankish, uncouth, and frequently intoxicated pal Ed Munn (Alan Hale, Sr.). Ed seems to covet Stella but settles for mere friendship, knowing that she is married. Laurel grows into a beautiful young woman, her parents eventually divorce, and Stephen re-marries after striking up a romance with Helen (Barbara O'Neil), the woman he once loved and who is now a widow with three sons. And Stella, after realizing at one point that her boorishness and vulgar fashion taste have deeply embarrassed Laurel in front of her friends at school, asks her former husband and his new wife to adopt Laurel so that she will have the things in life that she deserves. Stella becomes the archetype of the self-sacrificing mother, recalling the sacrifices made by her own laboring and self-denying mother (Marjorie Main).

Since Stella deeply loves her daughter, we are convinced that she does this so that her daughter will live a better life and so that Stella will never again be an embarrassment to her. But Laurel does not want to part from her mother, feeling that Stella needs her and would agonize without her. Laurel returns home from visiting Helen's mansion to tell her mother that she will never leave her. Stella, who has been alerted to the situation via a telegram from Helen, tries to keep her daughter's best long-term interests in mind while stifling her heartache in forcing her daughter away. She deceives Laurel by pretending that she plans to go off to South America on vacation with Ed Munn. Stella's pretense is successful, and Laurel returns to her Helen's house and accepts her new life there with her father and his family.

In fact, this is only one of several acts of deception that Stella engages in. At the outset, she initially deceived her future husband Stephen about her own socioeconomic class. Later on, after they have married and had a baby, Stella again deceives Stephen when she begs him to bring her out on the town and she dances with Ed Munn. Her husband wants to leave after a while, but she pretends that she has left her handkerchief at Munn's table so that she can join her new friend and not leave the party. These earlier pretenses are done out of sheer self-interest. Deceiving Laurel is done purely for Laurel's sake, of course, and brings loss and pain.

Does Stella finally deserve her fate in not having her daughter in her life anymore? She smiles broadly at the end, in a now famous scene in which she walks away from the window where she has watched (from outside in the rain) Laurel's wedding in progress. This might be short-term satisfaction because of her deep love for her daughter, especially knowing that Laurel is embarking on a better social and economic life. But we know that Stella will be miserable and solitary without her daughter, and we know that at some point Laurel will miss her mother deeply. Stella has always tried to be true to herself, even if it meant losing her husband, but perhaps she could have tried to adapt just enough so that she would not have to alienate herself completely from the social world that she now deems necessary for Laurel's future happiness.

The movie is ultimately uneven at best, chiefly due to Stella's contradictions. It depends on the viewer, of course, as to whether these contradictions prove to be engaging or irritating. It must be conceded that, no matter the verdict regarding the overall film, Stanwyck gives a bravura Oscar-nominated performance, and she expresses these contradictions effectively. Stella holds true to being the type of woman she really is and refuses to change, even if it costs her Stephen and Laurel. She stays true to Stephen's advice to "stay as you are" and "don't pretend." But in the end, who is she really? She does stay true to her love for her daughter, even if it ironically means losing her daughter. She surrenders her own long-term happiness for the sake of Laurel's long-term welfare—not unlike, say, Tom Doniphon's similar sacrifice for the love of Hallie in John Ford's *The Man Who Shot Liberty Valance* (1962). But Stella's authenticity is called into question, at least to some degree, because of her acts of deception in winning over Stephen and in forcing Laurel back to her father's house. Authenticity would seem, on the surface, to conflict with pretense. In the end, when rejoicing at Laurel's new marriage, does Stella maintain a sense of integrity and dignity? It is doubtful. She has intentionally surrendered the one person whom she has truly loved, saying at one point, "I don't think there's a man living that could get me goin' anymore. Oh I don't know, I guess Lolly just uses up all the feelings I got and I don't seem to have any left for anybody else."

As pointed out by Durgnat and Simmon in their book *King Vidor, American*, the "unresolved problem" of the film is that Stella turns into a non-credible character all too often. One would think that this woman is not so lacking in social self-awareness that she does not come to realize how ludicrous her clothes and behavior sometimes really are and how they are perceived critically and mockingly by others. Can Stella be self-aware enough to seduce Stephen and to sacrifice for the sake of Laurel and yet she has no clue that it is her crassness that has jeopardized both relationships in her life?[3] She seems to be almost as crass in her resolution to deceive (and hence lose) Laurel as she is in her choices of attire and social persona. Why is Stella unable to come to an awakening and curb her penchant for outrageousness, at least for the sake of a daughter who truly loves her?

This is the question that in fact motivates the audience to stick with the story and to find out whether Stella does in fact come to such an awakening. And the loss of Laurel seems to be the price she must pay for her refusal to change. What appears to be a suddenly happy ending—we see Stella's moment of happiness when she turns away from the window and from Laurel's wedding—is in fact quite pathetic. In staying true to part of herself (her social bearing, her taste in fashion, her manner of speech), she loses the other, more essential part of herself (her continuing role as a loving mother). When she willingly surrenders Laurel to her ex-husband and his second wife, she is as obsessed about social and economic status as she was at the outset in trying to escape her dreary life through seduction and manipulation. She ignores Laurel's pleas and confessions of love and decides that mother knows best.

And perhaps the most pitiful aspect of this situation is that, at the beginning

Barbara Stanwyck as the title character in *Stella Dallas* (1937, directed by King Vidor for Samuel Goldwyn Productions and distributed by United Artists). Stanwyck was nominated for an Academy Award for Best Actress in a Leading Role and Anne Shirley, who played her daughter Laurel, was nominated for the Best Supporting Actress Oscar (United Artists/Photofest).

of the movie, even while surrounded by her poor laboring family, Stella exhibited very little of the outrageous fashion and behavior that eventually define her. The more that she had become immersed in a higher social milieu, the more she had felt driven to turn herself into a spectacle. She recurringly views her fashion "sense" as the expression of who she really is. And yet, as Durgnat and Simmon also point out, Stella seems to have at least a temporary awareness of her unrefined persona when her ex-husband visits and she tries to impress him by wiping off her lipstick and cutting the ribbons from her dress. Stephen views her anew but it is only a momentary act of being, in her own eyes, inauthentic. Durgnat and Simmon rightly observe: "Instantly she's the 'high-class' woman he was always desiring. Her inability to continue along this line is owing less to any martyr complex than to individualist spunk."[4] The greatest mistake she makes is sacrificing her truest sense of self (as mother) for the sake of her most superficial sense of self.

Does all of this create a complex character or a ridiculous one or a little bit of both? It is Stanwyck's performance and Vidor's direction of her that make the film work to the degree that it does, in spite of our annoyances with Stella and her contradictions and her faulty choices. And just when we might lose interest in the title character because of her recurring uncouthness and volatility, the director pulls us back into the story again through his use of highly dramatic and well-timed close-ups that strategically highlight Stanwyck's expressiveness and Stella's inner emotions. Vidor plants his close-ups selectively, depending on the emotional tempo of the scene. He observed in his book *King Vidor on Film Making*: "Big head close-ups are a most effective accent but I believe that their effectiveness can be dissipated if their use is overdone."[5]

One of the most powerful uses of the close-up is when the camera zooms to Stella's face while she is sleeping in the train berth and she wakens to hear the girls in the nearby compartment talking about her. This is the moment of Stella's deepest shame in having realized how much she had embarrassed her daughter while visiting her at school. Laurel also hears the girls talking and, realizing that her mother has also heard, climbs into her mother's berth to cuddle with her. This leads to another close-up on Stella's face as she embraces her beloved daughter. There is also the poignant close-up of Stella at the end of the film, when she witnesses Laurel's wedding through the window. And there are also occasional close-ups of Laurel in the film, such as when her stepmother Helen tells Laurel that she will come to live with them at her father's house and Laurel declares that she could never possibly leave her mother. These close-ups all work well because they are well timed and not over-used.

Credit for the film's effective visual choices and compositions must be given both to Vidor and his head camera man, Rudolph Maté, whom Vidor praised highly.[6] Maté had also been the cinematographer on William Wyler's superb film *Dodsworth* the year before (1936). And he would go on to supervise the photography on such classic films as *Foreign Correspondent* (1940), *The Westerner* (1940), *To Be or Not to Be* (1942), *The Pride of the Yankees* (1942), and *Gilda* (1946). Maté also went on to direct many films of his own, including the classic film noir *D.O.A.* (1949).

Thanks to both story and camerawork, the viewer is typically aligned with Stella's perspective throughout the movie, and we gain a sense of nervous discomfort and tension due to the embarrassment that we feel for her at times. Stella only seems to get worse, despite our on-going hopes. And there are also scenes of attempted humor that do not really work very well and that only make the viewer cringe rather than laugh, especially due to our partial identification with the title character. There is a bit of exaggerated silliness on a train when Ed Munn pulls the churlish prank with the itching powder. And there is the scene in which Ed shows up at the house highly inebriated, bringing a turkey for the holiday meal. Even Ed becomes ashamed for his drunken foolishness once he realizes that Stephen Dallas has arrived. Ed's behavior has now humiliated Stella and Laurel at a crucial moment, and that humiliates Ed.

In fact, *Stella Dallas* demonstrates that Vidor is particularly adept at depicting scenes of social embarrassment. There is also Laurel's deep sense of humiliation at the lunch counter with her friends, when she is horrified to see (in a mirror) that it is her visiting mother, in outlandish clothes and acting crudely, who has been the object of her friends' ridicule. Laurel runs away, traumatized. Earlier in the film, Stephen is embarrassed by Stella's antics at the dance party. Then there is the highly embarrassing party itself, after Stella has gone to great pains to throw a grand celebration of Laurel's birthday and none of Laurel's many invited friends show up.

The tempo of *Stella Dallas* is an intricate one since it is a film that waltzes rapidly between comedy and pathos at different points. While the editor of the film is listed as Sherman Todd, who would go on to edit John Ford's *The Long Voyage Home* (1940) and Sam Wood's *For Whom the Bell Tolls* (1943), Vidor claimed much of the credit for the montage. In his interview with Nancy Dowd, Vidor answered in the affirmative when asked whether he did the cutting himself. He noted that while producer Samuel Goldwyn sometimes tried to intervene in the editing at times, the producer did not alter any scenes in a substantial way, especially since Vidor worked well and closely with the assigned editing assistants for this film.[7] Vidor also mentioned that, on this film as well as others, he often "cut with the camera" in the sense that he filmed as economically as possible, refusing to shoot a scene in multiple ways and from different angles and distances. By refusing to create an excessive amount of footage with alternate shots and by sticking to what was only necessary for telling the story, Vidor prevented the producer from later editing the film differently than the way Vidor had strictly envisioned. Vidor recalled: "I tried to cut with the camera, as Jack [John] Ford used to do. I didn't take a lot of extra shots. There weren't a lot of ways to put the picture together.... I would usually decide right there on the set what shot I was going to use...."[8]

Many have praised Barbara Stanwyck's performance, even if they did not like the film in its entirety, though more than several critics have thought that she was miscast in the title role. The director who had initially been assigned to the film, William Wyler, had reportedly wanted Ruth Chatterton for the title role, but she allegedly rejected the offer, having just portrayed a troubled wife only a year before in the Wyler-directed and Goldwyn-produced *Dodsworth*. Though he was rumored to have considered both Marion Davies and Miriam Hopkins for the lead role, Vidor wound up quite satisfied with Stanwyck. When asked what he thought of Stanwyck's performance, Vidor replied, "I thought it was wonderful.... It is very difficult with that sort of performance to keep from going overboard in getting funny and comical. She was such a good actress, and she has such an appealing voice and knows how to handle it. She seemed to get sympathy in spite of the broad strokes of her character."[9]

Sixteen

1938–1939

The Citadel and *The Wizard of Oz*

The Citadel (1938)

> "In *The Citadel* I collaborated with my wife [Elizabeth Hill] who wrote part of the adaptation. During the shooting of the picture she worked with me on set.... The film has a more closely knit dramatic form than the novel. It has a stronger dramatic drive, and its tempo and pace are much faster."[1]—King Vidor, 1939

The Citadel was based on A.J. Cronin's award-winning novel that was published only the year before in 1937. Cronin based his story on his own personal experiences as a doctor in the coal-mining countryside of South Wales (just as he had for his 1935 novel *The Stars Look Down*, which was adapted to film in 1940, with direction by Carol Reed and a screenplay co-written by Cronin). The novel was one of the first to center on topics in the field of medical ethics and the story was said to be a motivating influence on the founding of the National Health Service, a publicly funded healthcare system in Britain.[2] Cronin once summarized the goal of his novel: "I have written in *The Citadel* all I feel about the medical profession, its injustices, its hide-bound unscientific stubbornness, its humbug.... The horrors and inequities detailed in the story I have personally witnessed. This is not an attack against individuals, but against a system."

Vidor's film adaptation is one of the director's finest works, ranking alongside his *The Big Parade*, *The Crowd*, *The Champ*, *The Stranger's Return*, *Northwest Passage*, and *Duel in the Sun*. It is also probably Vidor's best acted sound era movie, thanks to the superb performance given by Robert Donat as Dr. Andrew Manson as well as the work of the splendid supporting cast. While the storyline becomes a tad disjointed once its main character goes to London with his wife and gradually loses sight of his ethical principles and ideals, the movie as a whole demonstrates Vidor's consummate artistry in terms of dramatic characterization, visual composition, and careful tempo. *The Citadel* could be said to be Vidor's *How Green Was My Valley* (1941), as it were, and it may even be the case that the latter movie, directed by John Ford, may have been influenced by Vidor's film—if Ford had indeed had time to watch it amidst the several superlative films that he was making around this time (there is no evidence of that, however). Certainly the near-perfect first half of *The Citadel*, set in a rural village in Wales, reminds one of Ford's masterpiece in terms of both setting (Wales) and cinematic quality.

The Citadel was nominated for Academy Awards for Best Picture, Best Director, Best Actor, and Best Screenplay. While it won none of those Oscars, alas, it was awarded Best Film for 1938 by the New York Film Critics Circle and Best Film for 1938 by the National Board of Review. As film historian Charles Silver wrote about the movie, "*The Citadel*, except for a few small lapses, is one of Vidor's most perfectly crafted films. It is one of two Vidor films to be nominated for the Academy Award for best picture of its year (the other was *The Champ*). It is the kind of movie one expects from William Wyler or David Lean at their best. It has none of the rough edges of obviously flawed works like *Hallelujah* and *Our Daily Bread* to betray the fact that there is a human being trying to breathe life into it."[3]

The movie was produced by Victor Saville for MGM. The screenplay was written by Ian Dalrymple, Elizabeth Hill (Vidor's third wife), and Frank "Spig" Wead, the former naval aviator who turned to writing novels and screenplays after a devastating and crippling spinal injury in 1926 due to an accidental fall at his home. Wead was the author of many screenplays, including those for John Ford's *They Were Expendable* (1945) and Victor Fleming's *Test Pilot* (released the same year as *The Citadel*, in 1938). He was also the subject of Ford's film *The Wings of Eagles* (1957), portrayed in that film by John Wayne. The expert cinematography for *The Citadel* was supervised by Harry Stradling, who also directed the photography for Tim Whelan's *The Divorce of Lady X* and Anthony Asquith's *Pygmalion* (co-directed by Leslie Howard), both also released in 1938. Stradling would go to work with Hitchcock on his *Jamaica Inn* (1939), *Mr. and Mrs. Smith* (1941), and *Suspicion* (also 1941), along with later classics such as *Easter Parade* (1948), *The Barkleys of Broadway* (1949), *In the Good Old Summertime*(1949), *A Streetcar Named Desire* (1951), *Johnny Guitar* (1954), *A Face in the Crowd* (1957), *Gypsy* (1962), *My Fair Lady* (1964), and *Hello, Dolly!* (1969). *The Citadel* was edited (in collaboration with Vidor) by Charles Frend, who had edited *Sabotage* for Hitchcock in 1936 and who would edit *Goodbye, Mr. Chips* (1939, also starring Donat) and Gabriel Pascal's *Major Barbara* (1941, and co-edited with David Lean). After 1941, Frend turned his attention to directing films.

With an expert cinematographer and editor on hand, Vidor also benefited greatly from an excellent cast of both leading and supporting actors, undoubtedly his best cast until *Duel in the Sun*. Lead actor Robert Donat, one of the best British actors of the cinema in the 1930s, had already performed in *The Private Life of Henry VIII* (1933), *The Count of Monte Cristo* (1934), and Hitchcock's classic *The 39 Steps* (1935). He was nominated for a Best Actor Oscar for *The Citadel* but lost to Spencer Tracy (*Boys Town*). However, the very next year Donat beat out Laurence Olivier, Clark Gable, and James Stewart to win Best Actor Oscar for his superlative role in *Goodbye, Mr. Chips* (1939). Vidor often called Donat "one of my top favorites" among male actors (along with Spencer Tracy). Vidor recalled later in life that when he first met Donat at a hotel before preparations for the film had begun, he had been expecting someone like Douglas Fairbanks or Errol Flynn but instead saw a frail man carrying a briefcase. Donat had long been very sickly, having suffered severely from asthma (he would eventually die from a brain tumor as well cerebral thrombosis at age 53). Vidor recalled in an interview later in his life that the actor spoke softly and seemed to reserve his energy and voice for his acting.[4] He recalled the actor in a conversation with film scholar Richard Schickel:

> I had seen Robert Donat on the screen as a romantic type of hero, and when I met him he was far from that. He had a concave chest and slender little arms, but as he started to get interested in the film, he blossomed out and filled out—he had ways of making himself look robust. And he was the only actor I ever knew who wanted to go out looking for locations with the director. He wanted to know all about the scenes; he wanted to look at them too—and study the people. We went to Wales together. And he laid out his entire emotional rise and fall, how he would play each scene. It was interesting that he would have a mirror right on his lap and keep working on his makeup—the makeup around his eyebrows and hair and all that—right up until the cameras were going, and then he'd drop it and immediately give a superb performance. I never was more pleased with anybody's performance than I was with his.[5]

Vidor looked back upon the production of *The Citadel* as one of the most satisfactory experiences of his career, particularly due to the opportunity to work with Donat along with a superb supporting cast of British actors, including Ralph Richardson, Rex Harrison, Emlyn Williams, Francis Sullivan, Cecil Parker, and Felix Aylmer. Vidor also benefited greatly from having made the film at MGM's Denham Studios in England, and especially having worked there with Ben Goetz. As Nancy Dowd wrote in the program notes for the 1972 Vidor retrospective at the Museum of Modern Art, Goetz was "a man of great integrity whom Vidor had described as the ideal studio executive." She also notes that Goetz had assisted Vidor with handling casting, scripting, and production challenges and even involved MGM in a legal case in order to permit Rosalind Russell to play Manson's wife Christine (the initially announced choice, Elizabeth Allan, sued the studio when they decided to replace her with Russell and also after they decided to replace her with Greer Garson in *Goodbye, Mr. Chips* the following year). Dowd notes that, with the help of Goetz, "King Vidor had for the first and probably the last time the opportunity to make a film without compromise." She also notes that Donat and Vidor became close friends after the making of the movie and that when "Donat's infant son was evacuated to the United States at the height of the war, he asked Vidor to become the child's godfather. The similarities between the two men are obvious: a quiet, profound dedication to an art governed both lives."[6]

The first half of the film follows Cronin's novel with a fair degree of faithfulness. Before the picture begins, we read an opening message on the screen: "This motion picture is a story of individual characterizations and is no way intended as a reflection on the great medical profession which has done so much towards beating back those forces of nature that retard the physical progress of the human race." We see a train racing through a valley. Manson is on his way to the village of Blaenelly to

Ralph Richardson (left, as Dr. Philip Denny) and Robert Donat (as Dr. Andrew Manson) star in King Vidor's drama *The Citadel* (1938, Metro-Goldwyn-Mayer). The film, centered on a love story as well as issues of medical ethics, was based on the 1937 novel of the same title by A.J. Cronin. It also features Rosalind Russell, Rex Harrison, and Emlyn Williams (MGM/Photofest).

accept an assistant's position with the ailing old town physician, Dr. Edward Page (Basil Gill). He sits eagerly on the edge of his seat in the train compartment and watches intently the quickly passing scenery while raindrops pelt the window. We see rapid shots of the depressing landscape and a coal mining town and laborers. The train arrives in the station in the village of Blaenelly, his destination, and he is greeted by a coachman, who tells him "the last assistant only stayed ten days" because the work is too hard and he alludes to one other unidentified reason ("you'll find out"). We soon find out what that reason is: Dr. Page is far more ill than had been conveyed in his letter (bed-ridden for the long term, in fact) and his wife (Dilys Davies) is a neurotic, stingy busybody. She offers Dr. Manson his first meal in the house after his long trip but gives him only a piece of bread and a few tiny scraps of bacon and a glass of water. Meanwhile, she consumes her own plate full of superior food along with a pint of ale.

His dinner is interrupted when he is summoned for his first assignment in the village: a sick woman surrounded by her large family. Manson tries to assure the family that she will get better, but he looks skeptical. He returns to the office and the vibrant, gregarious Dr. Philip Denny (Ralph Richardson) arrives along with his dog Hawkins. Richardson brings a charismatic breath of life into the proceedings as everything has thus far been rather dismal for Manson. Denny cynically asks why Manson has decided to move there for such a job, given that there is no hospital, clinic, or x-ray technology. After hearing about Manson's recent patient visit, Denny advises him to keep an eye out for typhoid in that neighborhood. Manson exclaims, "Typhoid! Of course!" When they next meet up at Denny's office, Manson admits to him that he had been correct: it was indeed typhoid. Denny asks his new friend to look through his microscope and shows him the bacteria that is causing typhoid in an area of the village where, Denny theorizes, the antiquated underground sewer system is leaking into and polluting the local well water. Denny tells Manson that the village council refuses to pay for a new sewer, and so he suggests that they should dynamite the main sewer to force the village to make the needed change for the sake of the residents' health and lives. Manson is rather stunned by his proposal. Denny says that boiled water is what is needed for the patients for the time being.

Manson then visits the local elementary school and meets the teacher Christine Barlow (Rosalind Russell), where their eventual romance and then marriage first begins. (Russell is a peculiar choice for the role of Christine, since she is the only American in the cast, but she does an adequate job and succeeds in several scenes when she is called upon to burst into tears.) Manson scolds her for allowing children with the measles to come to school. She tells him that the students who attend school can at least get nutrition from the glass of milk that they are offered each day in school. Manson tells her that milk is not what they need to overcome their illness. But at this point, the straightforward Miss Barlow gives him some spirited resistance and Manson tells her firmly that he will report her to the regional medical authorities. The rural Welsh schoolroom scene reminds one of similar schoolroom scenes in *How Green Was My Valley*. After this point, we witness a series of dramatic and powerful events.

Manson is called upon to deliver a baby that does not respond to his slaps. He gives the baby to a family member and goes to comfort the ill mother, telling her softly "It's a boy" but not having the heart to tell her that the baby is dead. The mother manages a weak smile. But, after deliberating for a moment, he suddenly rushes into action and calls for pans of warm and cold water. He then begins to splash and smear the infant with the water, hoping wildly to revive it. The old woman in the room frowns and tells him firmly, "The child is dead. It is God's will. Let it alone." But he continues and then begins to breathe into the baby's nostrils and mouth. Eventually the infant is revived and begins to cry. The women in the room stare in astonishment, having witnessed what they believe is a miracle. After leaving the house, Manson greets the father on his way in the door and tells him that both the mother and child are fine. After being thanked, Manson looks up and smiles and declares quietly, "Thank God, I'm a doctor!" He begins to sense, perhaps, that lives could be saved in certain circumstances in which one must simply have faith to try anything possible and not always follow the conventional procedure. Otherwise, he would have given up on the baby who was showing no signs of life. However, directly thereafter, he passes by the window of a nearby house where he can see a family singing over a visible corpse, as if to temper his exuberance and remind him of the high mortality rate in the village. A large quarantine notice on the front door reads, "Typhoid Danger: Risk of Infection."

Then comes the rousing scene when, in the middle of the night, he rushes into Denny's house, waking him and telling his friend that he is ready to dynamite the main sewer so as to prevent further typhoid, given that there is already an epidemic. He and Denny get drunk (the older doctor is an obviously hard-drinking man) and they sneak off into the village, along with Hawkins the dog, and perform the illegal action. There is a wonderful shot with the camera looking up out of the sewer at Denny's and Manson's faces. There are six explosions and Hawkins begins to bark and does not want to leave. Denny runs to retrieve the dog, and they make their escape as the townspeople rush into the streets. We must here ponder a major ethical question: Despite the criminality of their destructive act, was the blowing up of the sewer justified by serving a higher purpose, for the sake of preventing more sickness and death due to the typhoid contagion? The two medical men did not endanger any lives and their action resulted in the greatest good for the greatest number of people, but were they morally permitted to engage in such a crime for the sake of the common good? We can assume that the movie wants us to answer in the affirmative. Denny and Manson seem satisfied after their crime and we soon see Manson bicycling and whistling through the village in daylight, passing by the construction of the new sewer. They had forced the community's council to act for the health and lives of the residents, even if it had required devious means to their end.

There are soon many patients in his office, including Miss Barlow, the teacher, who complains of a sore throat. He has fun teasing her for a few moments and holding down her tongue with a depressor a bit too firmly, checking her throat. She then praises him for having saved the Morgan family's baby and he tells her, "When I first arrived here, I thought the practice of medicine was bound by ethics and textbooks. I've learned differently, thanks to you." He apologizes for having scolded her in her classroom, telling her that the milk she gave the children was indeed good for them, and she returns the apology. She mentions that she knows Denny and, immediately following, says that "everyone is delighted about the new sewer." She has easily figured out who dynamited the old sewer.

Soon thereafter, Manson gets into a heated argument with an imperious Mrs. Page about five pounds that he was given by Mr. Morgan as a bonus for having saved his infant. The doctor's wife is enraged that he did not report the received money to her so that he could hand over his share. She had found out about the money from a snitching banker after Manson had deposited the money into his account. Manson forces her to apologize, threatening a defamation lawsuit, and tells her that he was offered a job on his own by the mining company directors, but that he had refused it out of respect for Dr. Page.

SIXTEEN. *The Citadel* and *The Wizard of Oz*

Dr. Andrew Manson (played by Robert Donat) treats a sick woman as her family watches in King Vidor's drama *The Citadel* (1938, Metro-Goldwyn-Mayer). The film was nominated for four major Oscars: Best Picture, Best Actor (Robert Donat), Best Director (Vidor), and Best Adapted Screenplay (Ian Dalrymple, Elizabeth Hill, and Frank Wead). It won the Best Picture Award from the New York Film Critics Circle and from the National Board of Review (MGM/Photofest).

Manson applies for a job with the coal-miners' medical aid society in the nearby town of Aberalaw. After being "interviewed" by the society board and the representatives of the miners, he lies to the society that he is engaged to be married. Mr. Owen (Emlyn Williams), the chair of the society, has made it clear that the miners prefer a married doctor, given that he must make house calls and they do not want any possible seduction of their wives or daughters. Andrew then returns to his village and convinces Christine to marry him, telling her that it is the only way for him to acquire the position. After she surprisingly agrees, he confesses that he had already told the society that he was engaged, and she laughs. We wonder whether this act of deception on the part of Manson signals a moral defect, despite serving the purpose of helping him to arrive at a happy situation: the new job, which will benefit both the miners of Aberalaw and himself, as well as his new marriage. While seeming to be a "noble lie" of sorts, it does serve as a minor precursor to the later moral decline that Manson will suffer after he moves to London with Christine and succumbs to a materialistic lifestyle and the temporary loss of his ideals.

We then see a powerful, well-directed, and well-edited sequence in which Manson saves a coal miner during a collapse of the coal mine. There are quick camera shots of the stone ceiling cracking and moving and then poignant close-ups of the miners who are looking on. Next, there is a scene with the lead doctor of the workers' medical aid society who tells Manson not to be too strict with the men who ask for certificates that declare them temporarily unfit to work. Many of them have been asking for the doctor-signed certificates so as to take a break from the hard work. Manson vents his anger about this to his wife and she reminds him of his principles and inspires him to keep researching with the expensive microscope given to him by Denny as a gift. We then watch the married couple carrying out research and we see the lab animals, who seem to be treated well.

Mr. Owen of the medical aid society arrives to inspect Manson's research. Manson tells Owen about his hypothesis that the workers are suffering from tuberculosis caused by the silicon dust from the anthracite in the coal mines. A group of miners soon come to his office to take back their medical cards that designate Manson as their physician. It has become obvious to the workers, based on gossip about Manson's research, that his work to prevent future illness and to save their lives is also a threat to their jobs. His wife soon arrives in tears and tells her husband that a group of miners ("representatives of the committee") barged into his laboratory, broke their medical equipment, and took the lab animals, putting all of the guinea pigs into a bag. She reports that the vandals had accused them of torturing the animals, obviously a ruse to end Manson's research. At least indirectly, this scene raises yet another ethical question in the field of medicine: whether animal experimentation for research is morally justified. We soon witness a moving scene in which Manson is "put on trial" before the medical aid society. They ask him to carry on merely as a doctor and to give up his research. They clearly think that he is a danger to their jobs, particularly if the government should get involved in the regulation of the coal industry for the sake of the workers' health.

Disillusioned, Manson and Christine move to London where there is a quick collage of images to depict his new life. He establishes his own medical practice in a poor area of the city but he soon finds it difficult to attract paying patients. He finds himself in the position of treating a female socialite for "willful hysteria" and then bumps into his old medical school buddy, Frederick Lawford (Rex Harrison), who is now a physician for the wealthy. Manson is soon introduced to high society and his practice begins to thrive, often from treating upper class patients for what seem to be psychosomatic symptoms. With his newfound money, he buys Christine a fur coat and speaks of future gifts. He soon gets into an argument with her after she begins to suspect that he has quickly forgotten his original dedication to the common good. While they are picnicking on a hill, Christine tells Andrew, once he has begun to suffer his moral decline after being enticed by the financial rewards of helping the wealthy: "Remember the way we used to talk about life? It was an attack on the unknown, an assault uphill, as though you had to take some citadel you couldn't see but you knew was there." She makes it clear that she does not want a life of wealth and luxury and that she misses their old lifestyle together, one built on basic shared values. Soon thereafter, they meet Denny who has come to visit them in London. Denny proposes his new idea of forming a medical association and only accepting what patients can afford so that a more universal form of basic healthcare can be provided for those who need it the most. Manson rejects the proposal and Denny, like Christine, now sees how much Andrew has changed since arriving in London and after catering to the rich for so long.

The second half of the movie, set in London, is a bit disjointed, not merely in terms of its contrast to the first half of the movie but in terms of how much ground it covers in an overly rapid fashion: Manson's economic rise, his moral descent, his marital woes, and then his eventual awakening and return to his original ideals. Denny, still fighting for the cause of improving healthcare for the poor and the working class, is severely injured by an automobile right in front of Manson's apartment after they have a quarrel. Manson asks the arrogant, high society surgeon Charles Every (Cecil Parker) to perform the operation and he botches the job, despite it being a rather simple surgery. Poor Denny dies on the operating table and,

An on-the-set photograph taken during the production of King Vidor's drama *The Citadel* (1938, Metro-Goldwyn-Mayer). From left: director Vidor, Robert Donat (who plays Dr. Andrew Manson), and Ralph Richardson (who plays Dr. Philip Denny) (MGM/Photofest).

afterward, Manson berates Every and states matter-of-factly that Every murdered Denny through sheer incompetence. It is here that Manson experiences his moral awakening and quickly returns to his original mission. He soon works with Richard Stillman, an unorthodox American tuberculosis expert who helps Manson to save a girl's life but who is castigated by the medical profession for not being a licensed physician and for not seeking the official approval of the medical society. Due to his alliance with Stillman, Manson's license to practice is jeopardized.

At a tribunal before the medical council, he gives an impassioned defense of Stillman and his new methods. Superbly performed by Donat in this climax of the movie, his speech to the council is a condensed and partly paraphrased version of the heartfelt speech given by Manson near the conclusion of Cronin's novel. After mentioning the names of those great men of medicine like Pasteur, Ehrlich, and Haffkine, researchers who were not officially qualified physicians, he asks those medical professionals gathered in the room to "put their house in order": "If we go on trying to make out that everything's wrong outside of the profession and everything is right within, it means the death of scientific progress.... I have made mistakes, mistakes I bitterly regret, but Stillman isn't one of them."

There are two major departures from Cronin's novel in the second half of the movie. In the book, Christine dies after being run over by a bus and it is a stranger, not Denny, who dies at the hands of the incompetent surgeon. In Cronin's story, it is suggested that Manson will unite once again professionally with Denny. By making Denny the victim of Every's botched surgery and by allowing Manson and Christine to walk off together happily at the end of the film, Vidor's film adds dramatic power to the story, not to mention the expected happy ending. With *The Citadel*, the director achieved, thus far in his career, a type of consummation of the creative trajectory that had led him from his two silent masterpieces, *The Big Parade* and *The Crowd*, through his artistic triumphs of the earlier 1930s, including *Street Scene*, *The Champ*, and *The Stranger's Return*.

* * * *

The Wizard of Oz (1939)

Directly after finishing *The Citadel*, Vidor was soon called upon by MGM to take over the directing of unfinished scenes in *The Wizard of Oz* (1939), the famous adaptation of Frank L. Baum's children's fantasy novel, when its director Victor Fleming needed to leave the production and begin work on *Gone with the Wind* (also 1939). Vidor completed the job beyond the call of duty and took no credit for his significant contributions. What is clear is that the wonderful work that Vidor accomplished in these scenes demonstrates the type of concentrated artistry and accumulated talent that he had practiced in a focused way throughout his making of *The Citadel*. In terms of his supervision of the cinematography, music, tempo, and acting in completing these scenes as a favor for both Fleming and MGM, Vidor's contributions exhibit the work of a confident master working at the peak of his powers.

Things could have resulted far differently for Vidor. He had originally been called upon by David O. Selznick to consider directing *Gone with the Wind* after George Cukor had left the initial production due to some disagreement. Vidor had already made his own compact version of that Southern Civil War romantic drama with *So Red the* Rose back in 1935, though not with any great box office success as a result. After spending a few days ruminating upon the long, ponderous, convoluted script, Vidor passed on Selznick's offer and agreed instead to finish *The Wizard of Oz* while Fleming took over *Gone with the Wind*. Vidor filmed most of the black-and-white Kansas scenes, including the tornado sequence and the iconic scene where Dorothy (Judy Garland) sings her classic song "Somewhere Over the Rainbow." Vidor related his involvement to interviewer Richard Schickel:

> Victor Fleming was a good friend, and he took me around to all the sets that had been built and went through the things. He left that night, and I took over—it was, as I remember, about two and half weeks, three weeks possibly. Which included the "Somewhere Over the Rainbow." It's run all the time, and whenever I hear it, I get a tremendous kick out of knowing that I directed that scene. I always wanted to do a musical film. I wanted to keep the movement going, just as we had in silent pictures....
>
> I did some of the cyclone scenes, and "We're Off to See the Wizard"—working with Bert Lahr, Ray Bolger, Jack Haley and Judy Garland. But I did not want any credit, and as long as Victor was alive, I kept quiet about it.[7]

It is perhaps typical of Vidor's character that, for the sake of his friend Fleming, he took no official credit for having created what were undoubtedly the most well-known, widely seen movie scenes that he ever directed.

One can certainly recognize certain ways in which Vidor's uncredited assignment echoes aspects and moments of his overall career. The Kansas scenes have the type of folksy, rustic charm that can be found in Vidor's earlier "countryside trilogy" of the 1930s: *The Stranger's Return*, *Our Daily Bread*, and *The Wedding Night* (and not to mention the scenes of *The Big Parade* set in the French countryside). The depiction of the cyclone as the force of Nature (as well as Super-Nature) that spins the entire story into pure fantasy recalls the youthful start of Vidor's life in filmmaking: his recording of the 1909 Velasco hurricane that became known as "Hurricane in Galveston." His directing of the young Judy Garland as Dorothy echoes the way in which he deftly elicited wonderful performances from Jackie Cooper in *The Champ* and the young Anne Shirley as Laurel in *Stella Dallas*. The living room confrontation scene between Dorothy, Aunt Em (Clara Blandick), and Uncle Henry (Charley Grapewin), on the one hand, and the diabolical Elvira Gulch (Margaret Hamilton), on the other, puts one in mind of the way in which Dr. Andrew Manson (Robert Donat) confronts the selfish Mrs. Page (Dilys Davies) in *The Citadel*.

Furthermore, the glimpse of the easy-going camaraderie of Dorothy's three farmhand friends Hickory (Jack Haley), Zeke (Bert Lahr), and Hunk (Ray

Bolger)—who later become her dream companions—bears a loose resemblance to scenes with Jim Apperson (John Gilbert) and his pals Bull (Tom O'Brien) and Slim (Karl Dane) in *The Big Parade*. We can almost envision those three actors transplanted into the roles of the three farmhands in the Kansas scenes as well as the roles of the Tin Man, the Cowardly Lion, and the Scarecrow in the magical land of Oz. And while Vidor would never make an outright musical per se, his expert handling of the famous "Somewhere over the Rainbow" scene does recall other musical scenes in his career: the song and dance numbers in *Hallelujah* and the slave-singing episodes in *So Red the Rose*, not to mention a scene in his later *War and Peace* in which the occupants of horse-drawn carriages traveling through the wintry Russian landscape burst into exuberant song. Finally, while Vidor never made a pure fantasy or science-fiction film, his crucial involvement in adapting the magical story of *The Wizard of Oz* may be viewed as fitting for a director who remembered well the very first movie he had seen as a boy: Georges Méliès' pioneering scifi-fantasy short *A Trip to the Moon* (1902).

Seventeen

1940

Comrade X and *Northwest Passage*

Comrade X

Comrade X (1940) finds Vidor in geographically, stylistically, and politically foreign territory. A mashup of trending screwball comedy and rising anti–Communist sentiment, *Comrade X* is perhaps the strangest film in Vidor's entire career. His second of three films set in Russia (the first was *His Hour*, the third would be *War and Peace*), and his only rom-com outside of his three Marion Davies movies, it is an uneven experiment that never fully manages to negotiate the dividing line between idealism and amusement.

Its story—about an American journalist in Russia blackmailed into marrying a streetcar driver to smuggle her out of the country—was initially slated to be "a remake of the Samuel and Bella Spewack play, *Clear All Wires!*, first filmed in 1933 with Lee Tracy," reported the *New York Times*. "The new scenario, according to the studio, has been extensively rewritten by Ben Hecht and Charles Lederer."[1] While the film *Clear All Wires!* does involve an American journalist in Moscow, its plot about a falsified assassination has nothing in common with Vidor's film; the final writing credits omit the Spewacks entirely and credit only Hecht and Lederer, as well as Walter Reisch for the original story.

Comrade X, however, is heavily influenced by another movie which was cowritten by Reisch: Ernst Lubitsch's *Ninotchka* (1939). Made the previous year, it famously cast Greta Garbo in her first comedic role, and it went on to receive four Academy Award nominations: Best Picture; Best Actress (Garbo); Best Writing, Original Story (Melchior Lengyel); and Best Writing, Screenplay (Charles Brackett, Walter Reisch, Billy Wilder). The story is about a Soviet agent, Ninotchka (Garbo), sent to Paris to ensure the sale of jewels taken during the Revolution, and who winds up being seduced by Count Leon d'Algout (Melvyn Douglas), who wants the jewels returned to their original owner. Caught between romance and ideology, Ninotchka eventually defects from Russia to be with Leon. Ninotchka's rigid persona and total indoctrination are the source of the film's comedy and its politics; by extension, her capitulation to "love" at the end is a coded endorsement of capitalism over communism.

Comrade X is fueled by this same political dichotomy as *Ninotchka*, as well as the same clichés and assumptions about communism and life in Soviet Russia. It similarly tries to rebrand a lead actress formerly known for dramatic roles. In the case of Vidor's film, it is Hedy Lamarr, an Austrian-born actress who catapulted to stardom with her erotic performance (and nude scenes) in the Czech film *Ecstasy* (1933). She appeared in no other films until she arrived in Hollywood, where she made *Algiers* (1938) wherein she falls in love with jewel thief Charles Boyer, followed by the Indochina romance *Lady of the Tropics* (1939) with Robert Taylor, *I Take this Woman* (1940) in which she plays a suicidal woman who marries her doctor (Spencer Tracy), and the oil drilling adventure *Boom Town* (1940) opposite Tracy and Clark Gable. Casting her against type, *Comrade X* downplays her exoticism and presents her as a working woman (a streetcar driver). "Hollywood had it all wrong," Vidor told the *Los Angeles Times*. "We never should have played her as a vamp. I had a long talk with her at the start of the picture and it came to me that she is just a sweet, simple kid—happy, girlish, even a little boyish. She'll be that as a Russian streetcar conductor in *Comrade X*, straightforward and not slinky. I think we've got it!"[2]

Originally Robert Montgomery had been slated to be Lamarr's co-lead, "but was called off when the war became too hot," as Montgomery had famously enlisted with the British military in 1939 to fight.[3] In his stead, her *Boom Town* co-star Gable was selected to play McKinley B. Thompson, the American reporter stationed in Moscow. When his butler, Vanya (Felix Bressart), discovers his secret camera, Vanya realizes McKinley is also the notorious "Comrade X" who is sending covert messages out of the country, and who is wanted by the secret police. Vanya then blackmails McKinley to get his daughter, Theodore (Lamarr), out of the country. Posing as a devout Communist to win her affection, McKinley marries Theodore. When the police discover the camera in Vanya's room, McKinley and Theodore are also taken in for questioning and arrested as enemies of the state. McKinley uses a photo of the police commissar committing a murder as leverage for him, Theodore, and Vanya to get out of prison in exchange for the negative. After they steal a taxicab, they are pursued by the police. The trio sneak aboard a train transporting a general's tank on its way to military maneuvers. Once the train arrives at its destination, they kidnap the general and commandeer his tank. The other Russian tanks see the star on the general's tank and follow it, unaware that it has been hijacked. Theodore drives the tank and leads the others first over a cliff, and then through a river, before giving a false order for the followers to turn around. McKinley, Theodore, and Vanya keep driving across the border until they are in Romania and can surrender. The film ends with the three protagonists back in the USA watching a baseball game. "The Dodgers are murdering the Reds!" says Theodore. "A-ha! Counterrevolution!" replies her father.

Other than *Ninotchka*, the primary influence on *Comrade X* is a series of screwball comedies—zany romantic romps distinguished by their rapid-fire dialogue mixed with slapstick pratfalls—that were in vogue from the mid–1930s through the 1940s. Decades later, this cycle of films was aptly labeled by philosopher Stanley

Cavell as "the Hollywood Comedy of Remarriage" in his book of the same name. His book focused on *It Happened One Night* (1934), *The Awful Truth* (1937), *Bringing Up Baby* (1938), *His Girl Friday* (1940), *The Philadelphia Story* (1940), *The Lady Eve* (1941), and *Adam's Rib* (1949). Cavell's designation is based on Shakespearean scholar Northrop Frye, whose "The Argument of Comedy" divides comedy between an "Old" style focused on a heroine "who may hold the key to the successful conclusion of the plot" and the "New" style that "stresses the young man's efforts to overcome obstacles posed by an older man ... to his winning the young woman of his choice." Cavell tells us: "What I am calling the comedy of remarriage is, because of its emphasis on the heroine, more intimately related to Old Comedy than to New, but it is significantly different from either, indeed it seems to transgress an important feature of both, in casting as its heroine a married woman; and the drive of its plot is not to get the central pair together, but to get them back together, together again."[4]

Comrade X fits Cavell's general qualifications for a comedy of remarriage. While McKinley and Theodore are married early in the film, their marriage is based on blackmail and McKinley's falsehood that he shares Theodore's political beliefs. When she discovers the truth, she is appalled. The rest of the film is about how, through these extraordinary circumstances, Theodore and McKinley fall in love with each other for real, and Theodore's defection to the United States—and abandonment of her political ideals—is a symbolic "remarriage." Nor is this Theodore's first marriage; she mentions how she turned over her first husband to the police as a political traitor, which makes McKinley's masquerade all the more precarious and Theodore all the more dangerous. And while McKinley's ruse gets them out of jail, it is ultimately Theodore's ability to drive the tank that allows them to escape across the border to safety.

Visually, *Comrade X* is one of the least identifiable of the director's works. It is largely confined to interior spaces, such as hotels, meeting rooms, a jail cell, and, for the finale, inside a car and tank. Vidor mostly sticks to long takes that, befitting the screwball genre, privilege the dialogue-heavy script by Hecht and Lederer. For the tank sequence, Vidor finally gets to take the camera outside, and the sequence is one of the funniest and most memorable in the film, an old-fashioned mechanical farce of vehicles toppling over that harkens back to Mack Sennett and his Keystone Kops, whom Vidor had previously honored in *Show People*. The tanks themselves were "copied from photographs in an official Soviet Army book," reported the *New York Times*. "The big tank was designed by studio technicians and emerged a monster 30 feet long and 12 feet high, bristling with guns. It was built mostly of wood but was practical. Gable and Miss Lamarr spent eight jarring days in it, galloping merrily over a special course on the studio's back ninety acres."[5]

Critics mostly responded positively to the film. "Packed with laughs and funny situations," declared *Film Daily*.[6] "Hilarious hokum, but does give Hedy Lamarr a rare chance to act.... It out—Mack Sennet's Mack Sennet [*sic*]," wrote Lionel Collier.[7] *Variety* was also enthusiastic: "Cracking vigorously and lustily at Communism

Clark Gable (as McKinley "Mac" Thompson) and Hedy Lamarr (as Theodore/"Lizzie") in King Vidor's romantic comedy *Comrade X* (1940, Metro-Goldwyn-Mayer) (MGM/Photofest).

and its precepts, with broadest strokes and not-too-subtle satire ... typical Sennettian slapstick chase of armored tanks across the border to safety for a wild climax.... Vidor deftly milking every ounce of comedy and satire from the material provided."[8] The *New York Times* enjoyed the satire but was underwhelmed in comparison to the director's other films. "Seldom has a film—with the exception of Charlie Chaplin's *The Great Dictator*—satirized a nation and its political system with such grim and malicious delight as does this Yuletide comedy.... Obviously, the boys at Metro were laboring under the influence of their own *Ninotchka*," wrote Bosley Crowther. "Unlike *Ninotchka*, however, *Comrade X* lacks an even comic pace.... King Vidor's direction is competent, but not—as we have come to expect—inspired."[9]

A more politically engaged and insightful review came from David Platt in the *Daily Worker*, a newspaper published by the Communist Party USA. While one might expect him to disagree with the film's message, Platt offers more than just an ideological disagreement and places *Comrade X* within the larger context of MGM's politics throughout the 1930s, revealing a troubling history:

> M-G-M has used its jungles against Negroes, sandstorms against Mohammedans and Hindus, joss houses against China, portraits of King Henry VIII and Venetian Palazzos to exalt the select of Europe ... to obscure men's minds.... I can think of only three or four

outstanding progressive films released under the banner of M-G-M in the past twenty-five years. Eric von Stroheim's *Greed* (1924) comes to mind, Victor Seastrom's *The Wind* (1927), *Anna Christie* (1930), Fritz Lang's *Fury* (1936) and Pearl Buck's *Good Earth* (1936) but that is all.... Vidor is now back in the arms of the men of Wall Street who supervise the movie industry. The director of *The Crowd* who has fought for an independent movie for years has gone over to their side completely. It is hard to believe, but it's true that *Comrade X* was directed by King Vidor. It is his worst film, one from which he will not quickly recover. Vidor got tired of the struggles and sold out bag and baggage to the fellows who hold the purse strings ... [and] a studio that is capable of producing an anti–Soviet film like *Comrade X* alongside of an anti–Negro, pro–Confederate film like *Gone with the Wind* ... [The same] producer of the pro–Fascist film *Gabriel Over the White House* and the anti–Soviet film *Ninotchka*.... Metro-Goldwyn-Mayer has also had some peculiar dealings with the National Socialist Party in Germany. It explains their failure to make a single anti-Nazi film between the time of Hitler's accession to power and the Munich betrayal.[10]

Platt's review is insightful and invaluable because it offers evidence that deeper political readings of Hollywood films were being published at the time, and that critics were not merely complacent participants in the publicity machine. Platt's review also points towards a growing conflict in Hollywood that would tear apart the industry and would deeply implicate Vidor: the rising tide of anti–Communism that would culminate in the blacklist.

Comrade X was released in December of 1940. Less than a year later, in September 1941, Vidor would be identified in print as a Communist by Eugene Lyons, a "former N.Y. Times correspondent in Moscow and [then] present editor of *American Mercury*," in his book *The Red Decade: The Stalinist Penetration of America*.[11] Lyons pointed to *The Daily Worker* as evidence of Vidor's politics: "*The Daily Worker* increasingly reported the soul of Hollywood. There you found the record of the ideological emanations of the awakened conscience of the movie capital-ists, collections for 'progress,' the blossoming of ever new organizations, the special showings of Spanish propaganda films, the gay parties and publicity stunts for the cause. There you read interviews with Clifford Odets, William Dieterle, King Vidor and any number of others whose opinions, by some coincidence, fitted into the current drives backed by the *Worker*."[12]

The accusation did not lead to any blacklisting of Vidor, who continued to work regularly for major studios throughout the 1940s and 1950s (MGM and Warner Brothers) as well as independent producers such as David O. Selznick (for *Duel in the Sun*, released in 1946). Ironically, Lyons' accusation, along with the release of *Comrade X*, coincides with a stark political shift for Vidor. In the mid–1940s, he helped to found the Motion Picture Alliance for the Preservation of American Ideals, described by John Cogley in his *Report on Blacklisting* as "a militantly anti–Communist, pro-free enterprise group.... Earlier, leaders of the Alliance, at the peril of being branded disloyal to the industry, had endorsed the finding of Senator Jack B. Tenney's California Un-American Activities Committee."[13] Also on the committee was the virulent anti–Communist novelist Ayn Rand, whose novel *The Fountainhead* Vidor would adapt for Warner Brothers in 1949.

A slight film in Vidor's canon, *Comrade X* is nonetheless significant for the ways in which he turns his back on the anti-capitalist politics of *Billy the Kid*, the pluralism of *Street Scene*, the collectivism of *Our Daily Bread*, and the populism that pervaded so many of his earlier films.

* * * *

Northwest Passage

King Vidor's *Northwest Passage* (1940) is a colorful, expertly crafted adventure yarn based on Kenneth Roberts' epic novel published in 1937 but first serialized in the *Saturday Evening Post* in 1936. The story, both frontier saga and heroic odyssey, deals with the military and trailblazing exploits of Major Robert Rogers and his soldiers. Vidor brought in Laurence Stallings to work with him on the screenplay that would have covered both halves of Roberts' novel, including Rogers' later life spent in London and in Michigan, where he hoped to lead an expedition to discover the fabled inland route to the Pacific. Vidor observed: "Part Two of the book was an examination of the disintegration of a man who had been built up into a strong heroic figure in the first part."[14] As Vidor recalled in his memoir *A Tree Is a Tree*, he and Stallings began work on the script after "preparatory production activities had been going on for two years" (location scouting, construction for shooting around Lake Payette in Idaho, etc.) and after various writers had attempted unsuccessfully for nearly three years to adapt Roberts' epic, two-part novel. However, the producer of the film, Hunt Stromberg, did not approve entirely of the script in progress and assigned a new screenwriter, Talbot Jennings, to replace Stallings. Then, as Vidor described it in his autobiography: "I found myself with an arbitrary starting date. One of the big sets had been built near the edge of the lake in Idaho and, on a certain day of the summer, the level of the lake would begin to fall. The water's edge would then recede so rapidly that in the space of a few days it would be impossible to get the lake and the fort in the same setup. It was decided to determine upon a definite departure date from Hollywood whether the script was finished or not. With the first half of the story, or prologue, in completed script form, we had enough pages to keep us busy for many weeks."[15]

Vidor reported that, after three months of production, the studio failed to deliver the second part of the script which would have covered the second half of Roberts' novel. Vidor had filmed the first half of the story, dealing with the journey of Rogers and his men to raid the Abenaki village of St. Francis, Quebec, on behalf of the British in the French and Indian War. With high costs already incurred due to the challenges of on-location shooting and an unfinished script for the second half of the story, the studio and producer decided to call it a day and limit the scope of the narrative to what had already been shot.[16]

Northwest Passage is far from being a traditional Western, yet it expresses several of the genre's essential elements. Vidor had already dabbled in oater terrain with *Billy the Kid* (1930) and *The Texas Rangers* (1936), but unlike fellow directors such as John Ford and William Wyler, he had not made any Westerns in the silent era. However, perhaps because he was a native Texan with a keen interest in the history of the Old West, Vidor came to the sound era Western with a sense of familiarity, especially in terms of his feel for the Western landscape. He would go on to direct *Duel in the Sun* (1946), the epic soap opera on the range that, along with Ford's *My Darling Clementine* (1946), helped to initiate the diverse period of the post–World War II Western. And in the later phase of his career, Vidor would make a last valiant effort in the genre with his *Man Without a Star* (1955).

Northwest Passage is set in New England and Quebec during the French and Indian War of the mid–1700s. It deviates, therefore, from the traditional setting of the Western (i.e., post–Civil War era and territory west of the Mississippi). But the film deserves comparison with Vidor's other Westerns (as well as those of other directors) because it is a frontier adventure story of raw courage and perseverance in which a band of soldiers forge their way through the early American wilderness while battling Indians and the French as well as Nature. Major Rogers (Spencer Tracy) and his army of brave men do everything in their power to adhere to a code of honor while surviving against enemies and the elements. *Northwest Passage* invites special comparison, perhaps, with those other *quasi*–Westerns which likewise challenge the boundaries of the genre due to unconventional aspects of setting or story—movies such as Victor Seastrom's *The Wind* (1928) or Ford's *Drums Along the Mohawk* (1939). The latter film, a cinematic "cousin" of sorts to *Northwest Passage*, is also an early Technicolor Indian-fighting adventure set in the colonial era and in the Mohawk Valley of central New York State.

Between the years 1939 and 1941, Hollywood witnessed an "A-Western Renaissance" after studios and filmmakers became convinced that the genre afforded opportunities to mirror a contemporary culture amid dramatic transition and self-definition. This movement in American film history included such movies as John Ford's *Stagecoach* (1939), Henry King's *Jesse James* (1939), Michael Curtiz's *Dodge City* (1939), Cecil B. DeMille's *Union Pacific* (1939), George Marshall's *Destry Rides Again* (1939), William Wyler's *The Westerner* (1940), Wesley Ruggles's *Arizona* (1940), Curtiz's *Virginia City* (1940), and Raoul Walsh's *They Died with Their Boots On* (1941). American cinema in the 1930s had been populated by countless B-Westerns, ranging from the "singing cowboy" films of Roy Rogers to the many low-budget shoot-em-ups starring John Wayne. But in 1939, movie studios were ready to return to the type of investment in the Western that could be seen at the decade's outset with such glorious epics as Raoul Walsh's *The Big Trail* (1930) and Wesley Ruggles's Oscar-winning *Cimarron* (1931). After 1941, however, with the Japanese attack on Pearl Harbor and America's entry into World War II, studios tended to pump more of their A-production money and energy into war films rather than horse operas.

An on-the-set photograph of director King Vidor (left foreground) conversing with Spencer Tracy (who stars as Major Robert Rogers) in the frontier adventure drama *Northwest Passage* (1940, Metro-Goldwyn-Mayer). The screenplay, by Laurence Stallings and Talbot Jennings, is based on Kenneth Roberts's 1937 novel of the same title (MGM/Photofest).

Westerns and other forms of frontier or pioneering adventures, when taken seriously, were able to reflect the collective memory of economic hardship experienced by the average movie-goer throughout the Great Depression. At the same time, their typical depictions of nation-building expressed a revival of optimism in the late 1930s, given that the Depression was ending. And so brighter days for America lay ahead. Since many A-Westerns took the form of trail-blazing and community-building epics, they reminded audiences that America had emerged gradually and successfully from a savage wilderness and a constant struggle against adversity, therefore inspiring hope. Frontier films provided a sense of idealistic faith for many who had become tired of their weary lives after almost a decade of economic devastation.

In addition, the fundamental battle between good and evil that was played out repeatedly in the Western genre captured the interest of many who had the war in Europe on their minds, especially with the real possibility of American involvement looming on the horizon. At least in hindsight, the surge in A-Western movie production in the late 1930s can be connected to the complexity and spirit of its era, given the Western's capacity to reflect prospective as well as retrospective attitudes about America's social, political, and economic situation. In addition, and at their most basic level, Westerns provided simple escape from the everyday worries of those who were coping with the effects of a national economic disaster and the prospects of American immersion in an international war against the aggressive Axis powers. And finally, such frontier films also helped to restore a nostalgic sense of one's authentic origins for those Depression-era folk who had migrated to the cities looking for work. The rural Old West or Old America became a symbolic substitute for rural America in general.[17] As film scholar-theoretician André Bazin observed about the rise of the A-Western at this time: "This phenomenon can be explained by the widespread publicity given westerns between 1937 and 1940. Perhaps the sense of national awareness which preceded the war in the Roosevelt era contributed to this. We are disposed to think so, insofar as the western is rooted in the history of the American nation which it exalts directly or indirectly."[18]

Northwest Passage certainly belongs to those history-minded Westerns and frontier films that expressed such concerns at this time. Though the classical Western of this period had something to say about the expansion as well as resurrection of the American "project" in the immediate post–Civil War Reconstruction era, movies such as *Northwest Passage* and Ford's *Drums Along the Mohawk* brought the story of America back to the colonial period. *Northwest Passage* is an especially intriguing example of a high-quality, landscape-oriented, A-production frontier film made during the above-mentioned "renaissance." While the adventures portrayed in the novel and film were undertaken in northern New England and the St. Lawrence River region, the filming was done chiefly around Payette Lake in Idaho and in the forested mountains of Oregon.[19] The movie exhibits the kind of appreciation for the natural world that recalls the influences of nineteenth-century American landscape painting—especially that of the Hudson River School (Thomas Cole, Asher Durand, Albert Bierstadt, Frederick Edwin Church) and Rocky Mountain School (Albert Bierstadt, Thomas Moran)—as well as the influence of landscape photography of this period (chiefly Carleton Watkins).

Vidor was certainly attuned to such artistic influences. Around the time that Vidor directed *Northwest Passage*, he became more interested in the art of painting. Vidor is one of many great directors (including John Ford and Raoul Walsh) who had been influenced by American landscape painters, including those who were masters of depicting scenes of the Old West (Frederic Remington, Charles Russell and Charles Schreyvogel, among others). Vidor's own interest in the intersection between painting and film eventually became crystallized in his last film, the short documentary *The Metaphor* in 1980, which focused on his interview with painter Andrew Wyeth. The two great visual artists discussed their respective art forms, including the fact that Vidor's silent classic *The Big Parade* had had an enormous impact on many of Wyeth's works (see Chapter Twenty-Three). And, along with his masterful and symbolic use of color in his later films *American Romance, Duel in the Sun, War and Peace,* and *Solomon and Sheba,* it is *Northwest Passage* that may well be Vidor's most "painterly" movie. As he told Nancy Dowd regarding the deepening of his interest in painting just before he made *Northwest Passage*:

> You see, for years we thought in terms of black and white. Suddenly we moved into color, and my color sense had been neglected all those years. I had heard of cool colors and warm colors, but I had to learn what they meant because I didn't want to depend on anybody to tell me all of that. I learned that greens, blues, reds, and a few other colors had a strong influence on the mood of a scene. I became interested in buying paintings and going to art galleries, but John Marquand gave me a set of paints and I sat down and started painting. That was where I learned the most. I started to paint pictures as soon as I knew I was going to do this film…. I studied up on perspective and that was about the only thing I knew…. I knew a lot about composition from my work in black and white and this experience helped me quite a bit with my painting. I seemed to be influenced by Impressionism. I did a lot of work with forced perspective in my films, so this interest in art really did carry over into my pictures.[20]

Apart from its rich aesthetic tapestry, *Northwest Passage* presents in graphic fashion the suffering and struggle of colonial soldiers undertaking frontier battles during the French and Indian War (1754–1763), an extension of the war between Britain and France (eventually known as the Seven Years' War). Major Rogers leads a band of determined colonial soldiers who fight for the British against the French and their Native American allies. Rogers is a model of the stoic military leader who must conceal his own sympathies and weaknesses to inspire his men to persevere. The title of the novel and film reflects the historical Rogers' later life after his active military career, when he was appointed by King George III as a royal governor in a fur trading area of Michigan. One of his primary missions was the organization of expeditions to discover and chart the legendary "Northwest Passage" that would provide a trading route across the continent.[21] The combination of Rogers's earlier military accomplishments and his later involvement in frontier exploration, plus his writings about such events and deeds, makes him an apt symbol of America's early efforts in realizing its idealist project of nation-building—even if, in real life, Rogers may have sometimes sympathized more with the British than with the colonists, especially during the course of the American Revolution. While he was at one point convicted by the British of being a traitor who had supported France (though he was later pardoned), suspected by American leaders of being a spy for the British, and then died a broken alcoholic in debt, Rogers lives on in history and legend as a man who had a deep faith in the idea of an expansionist America.

The movie's bold display of Technicolor artistry at an early stage in the use and development of that technology must have certainly impressed its original audiences—as did *The Wizard of Oz* (to which Vidor contributed its black-and-white Kansas scenes, including the famous "Somewhere Over the Rainbow" scene) and *Drums Along the Mohawk* the year before. Certain scenes of men paddling canoes down sapphire-blue rivers and against emerald-green forests remind one of landscape paintings by Bierstadt and color-soaked illustrations by N.C. Wyeth (as in the latter's contributions to an edition of Cooper's *The Last of the Mohicans*).[22] The studio's choice of using Technicolor, however, gave Vidor more than a few headaches when it came to the ways in which the deep colors of his on-site settings did not always translate as intended onto film, especially when the first rushes were seen. As Susan Glover tells us in her essay "East Goes West: The Technicolor Environment of *Northwest Passage* (1940)":

> The film was one of the earliest to use the new Technicolor process on location. The cinematography was credited to William V. Skall and Sidney Wagner, and their work earned an Oscar nomination. According to Rudy Behlmer it was to have been MGM's first feature in the

Walter Brennan (left, as "Hunk" Marriner) and Spencer Tracy (as Major Robert Rogers) star in King Vidor's frontier adventure drama *Northwest Passage* (1940, Metro-Goldwyn-Mayer). The screenplay, by Laurence Stallings and Talbot Jennings, is based on Kenneth Roberts's 1937 novel of the same title (MGM/Photofest).

new three-strip Technicolor process. (By the time it premiered, two other films—*Sweethearts* [1938] and *The Wizard of Oz* [1939] had appeared.) ... One problem with filming the natural environment was, ironically, the ubiquity of the color green. All color processes to that point that been unable to accurately reproduce hues of green, and considerable work went into finding a dye for the green Ranger uniforms that, on film, would blend in to the green of the natural surroundings. In his autobiography Vidor recalls the early production tests, when the dull green of the Rangers' uniforms appeared on the film as a "brilliant Kelly green" ...[23]

Northwest Passage begins in Portsmouth, New Hampshire, and then brings its viewer to an early version of the "Western" frontier, that of the northern New England region surrounding Lake Champlain and extending upwards into the terrain around the St. Lawrence River in Quebec. The landscape plays a dual role as inspiration and obstacle. Rogers' Rangers must travel vast distances through dangerous territory, haul their boats over hilltops, trudge through swamps, ford raging rivers, and above all, seek to survive in rugged terrain where food is scarce. *Northwest Passage* depicts the rigors and dangers of the wilderness in a manner that is more explicit than most other Hollywood Westerns of this era. Here, Vidor clearly reveals the great beauty of the terrain, but also the ways in which the suffering involved in the attempt to trek through that land leads to madness and death.

It is a sense of spiritual faith that is the only thing left to give the Rangers (or at least most of them) a remnant of hope. Many are on the verge of complete mental and physical collapse, and a few have already crossed that threshold. Their sense of duty, dreams of an expanded civilization, and hatred of a common enemy keep Rogers' men going. The story of American expansionism has its dark underbelly and Vidor's film does not shy away from that side of the tale, showing both the romantic power of the mythic ideal and the deadly consequences.

The production of *Northwest Passage* involved countless hurdles that echoed to some degree the ordeals faced by Rogers' frontiersmen. Shooting began in Idaho in June 1938, but filming ceased soon thereafter and was postponed until the following spring, mainly due to "logistical and management problems." Technicolor technology had been enhanced during the months in between the two shoots, so the footage from the previous summer (under the direction of W.S. Van Dyke) was not used and Vidor took over as director when filming recommenced in the spring.[24] Other obstacles ranged from inoculating the entire cast and crew against tick fever to reshooting scenes because of changes in the physical environment (such as fluctuating foliage colors and water levels).[25] In another example of the obstacles faced, part of the on-site filming in the summer of 1938 involved the initial shooting of the thrilling scene in which the Rangers create a human chain across perilous river rapids. The filming was started at the Yellowstone River; the task proved too dangerous for cast and crew and the rest of the scene was shot on the MGM studio lot using a massive water tank.[26]

Northwest Passage begins with an emphasis on geography, giving a "lay of the land" in a literal sense: a series of maps of colonial North America during the time of conflicts among the British, the French, and their Indian allies. Maps and map-making, in fact, figure prominently in the plot and remind us of an essential theme in the story of American expansionism: the collective drive to conquer and organize natural spaces. The narrative officially begins in colonial Portsmouth in 1759, and one may recall the opening of Ford's *Drums Along the Mohawk*, which starts with the wedding of Gil (Henry Fonda) and Lana (Claudette Colbert) at Lana's elegant European-style family home in Albany. Here a clear contrast is drawn between the cultured, commercial, colonial East on the one hand, and the raw frontier wilderness, on the other.

We see men on the Portsmouth waterfront, preparing the rigging of a ship and laboring at other tasks. One worker who sits on a crossbeam spots the Boston stagecoach arriving. We now see that it carries young Langdon Towne (Robert Young), who has returned home from Harvard after going there at his family's wishes to study for the clergy. He is returning not as a graduate, however: he has been expelled for having drawn a negative caricature of the University president. We learn that Langdon is an aspiring artist who wishes to practice his vocation at all costs. He resembles a Byronic hero to some degree: highly passionate and dedicated to his cause (painting), rebellious, creative, artistic, and rather undisciplined. Langdon is quickly established as a willful but sensitive young man who is a symbol of civilized life, but who will soon be thrown into the wilderness to face adversity, despite his cultured and creative personality. He will learn the kind of discipline that makes true heroes.

Above all, Langdon desires to develop his craft as an "American" painter by portraying, not the civilized colonist, but the Indian as he exists in his natural setting. Toward the beginning of Roberts' novel, Langdon explains his mission to the father (Louis Hector) of his future bride Elizabeth (Ruth Hussey): "Because nobody knows how they look ... [T]hey're a peculiar warm color, and they'd lend themselves to harmonious, bold, striking designs. I think I could use them against the foliage, against the sky and the water, in a way that's never been done before." Elizabeth's father remains deeply doubtful of such artistic aspirations and advises Langdon that "common nature" is an unfitting subject for a serious painter.[27] But the enthusiastic Langdon, dedicated to his creative passion, remains persistent; that focus on his artistic vocation and interest in Native American life is also emphasized in the film.

After arriving back in Portsmouth, Langdon runs into "Hunk" Marriner (Walter Brennan) who has been put into the stocks for, as the accompanying sign states, "Disloyal Conversation." Given Langdon's report about his expulsion, there is a parallel to be drawn here: both men are not afraid to flout authority in their desire to speak their minds. They are especially apt exemplars of the archetypal Easterner who becomes a Westerner, particularly since they are men who are constrained and frustrated by the conventions of a rigid Puritan lifestyle in old New England. Langdon and Hunk yearn for freedom, yet they wind up seeking it in a regimented existence amidst savagery, wilderness, and war.

It does not take long before our "Romantic" protagonist lands in serious trouble again after he insults a representative of the Crown while highly inebriated at a local tavern. Langdon and Hunk (who has come to his friend's rescue) escape, even though Langdon must leave his beloved Elizabeth behind. They make their way by canoe to a small outpost on the frontier, Fort Flintlock, where they meet Major Rogers and help him in sobering up a drunken Indian guide. Langdon soon tells Rogers that he has drawn maps of western territories because he wants to go there to paint Indians "as they really are"—saying this even as, ironically, the viewer of this film is given a wholly negative and stereotypical portrait of an Indian. Langdon appears initially to be sympathetic with "the red man." He and his sidekick Hunk are, at this point in the film, heading to Albany (supposedly where "the West" begins) so that he can travel with traders and fulfill his dream of seeing and painting the "real" West.

Rogers wants Langdon to join his company because he desperately needs a man who is good at drawing as the mapmaker for his next expedition. He tells Langdon that he may be a bit too educated for the rough woodsmen who make up the Rangers, but Hunk retorts: "He's not *that* educated." Langdon scoffs at Rogers' invitation: "I want to paint live Indians, not dead ones." Rogers then explains why Langdon may someday need to kill the native he may be painting, due to the real threat involved. Langdon aspires to portray the Native American as he truly exists, but Rogers lectures him that this is merely some romanticized dream. As we will soon see, Langdon proves Rogers right and the artist winds up killing Indians rather than merely depicting them.

As Armando José Prats points out in his book *Invisible Natives: Myth and Identity in the American Western*, Langdon's initial artistic goal and his subsequent forsaking of that goal during his Indian-fighting adventure are especially symbolic of the ways in which the Native American is referenced in Hollywood Western narratives—referenced, but only to be vanquished, forgotten, and erased via these movies' various forms of "cultural appropriation."[28] Prats, in fact, uses *Northwest Passage* as his chief cinematic example in introducing and outlining his book's overall argument about the treatment of the Indian in American Western films.[29] As revealed by his sketchbook when shown later to Major Rogers, Langdon has been content to render drawings of his beloved Elizabeth and of Rogers and selected other Rangers. But the Indians against whom he is fighting are never depicted, dead or alive.[30] Langdon gradually comes to view the natives existing "as they are" through Rogers' eyes: as savage enemies, possibly deceitful scouts, or hopeless drunks who have been partially assimilated to white society (like Rogers' inebriated and inarticulate guide Konapot).[31]

After being lured into the company of the Rangers after a drunken night, Langdon and Hunk become "accepted" to some degree by the rough-hewn Rangers. They soon venture as new soldiers through a wild but majestic terrain that poses danger as much as it affords beauty. The idea of the landscape as an obstacle to be conquered emerges specifically when we witness the Rangers toiling to transport their boats over a hillside to avoid being spotted by the French and their Indian allies. These enemies are camped just down the shoreline, obstructing their voyage, and the men groan and sweat as they lift their boats with a massive rope. Vidor shows us each step of this burdensome task, including the eventual lowering of the wooden vessels down the hillside as the boats finally slide into the river, now beyond the place where the French ships are waiting. Rogers has outwitted the enemy with his trademark determination and his expert coordination of collective labor.

Soon thereafter Rogers tells his men what their mission really is, using a map painted on the stone face of a hillside. They have been assigned by their British superiors to destroy the Abenaki village of St. Francis in Quebec, given the destruction wrought by the Abenakis' past raids on the whites. Rogers clearly explains why they need to go after the Indians, calling forth one of the Rangers who describes in brutal detail how the Abenakis had torn his brother's skin upwards from his belly and then hanged him from it while he was still alive. This description of torture cements in the men's minds the fact that the Indians are animalistic savages who need to be destroyed. Ruthless revenge becomes a duty and a matter of justice, not merely a desire.

On the surface, the attack on the Abenaki appears to be justified, given what Rogers and his Ranger have to say about the savage deeds of their Indian enemies. It is this surface-level view that undoubtedly led George Fenin and William Everson, in their landmark survey *The Western: From Silents to the Seventies*, to point out that this film holds a special place in the genre because of its unrelentingly negative depiction of the Indian enemy: "*Northwest Passage* has a place in the general history of the Western for being one of the most viciously anti–Indian films ever made.... The Indian's side of the question is never presented."[32] Or, as Prats has argued, the Indian perspective is presented here, but through the words of Rogers and his men— and so presented only through a distorting, appropriative, and deeply biased interpretation that renders the native's genuine viewpoint completely absent.

However, as Susan Glover argues, things are not quite so simple as they would at first appear, and that is because, while we *hear* about the Abenakis' brutality through the words of Rogers and his selected Ranger, the movie *shows* us the brutality of the Rangers. The scene of the massacre of the Abenaki village, while ludicrously artificial at certain moments, is graphic enough to make the viewer wince at the fierce violence waged by Rogers' men. Rogers is shown hurling a hatchet at a barking dog at the start of the massacre, a grotesque act for any animal lover in the audience, even if we know that Rogers needs to keep the dog quiet while his men position themselves for the attack. While the film concentrates on the military goal of the Rangers in the face of an Indian enemy, and while it certainly elevates the Indian-fighter Rogers to the level of stoic hero, it also intriguingly communicates the alleged savagery of the enemy in words, a clear distancing device, while demonstrating the bloodthirsty vengeance of the hero and his men in direct, penetrating images. The viewer

The violent sequence in which Rogers' Rangers attack and massacre the Abenaki village of St. Francis in King Vidor's frontier adventure drama *Northwest Passage* (1940, Metro-Goldwyn-Mayer). From left: Spencer Tracy (as Major Robert Rogers, in the foreground with hatchet in hand), Robert Young (as Langdon Towne), Walter Brennan (as "Hunk" Marriner), and Donald MacBride (as Sergeant McNott, in the background between Tracy and Young). The fifth actor is unidentified (MGM/Photofest).

experiences a narrative in which Indian *violence*, the very motivation for the revenge massacre, is presented in a deliberately detached manner (i.e., "merely" verbally) and the Rangers' acts of violence are conveyed in immediate, horrifying imagery. Such an observation certainly qualifies, at least to some degree, the criticism that *Northwest Passage* is *purely* "anti–Indian" and therefore racist in its overall intentions. At the very least, there is an implicit dynamic in place here between the different modes of presenting these opposing perspectives, one that complicates the film's presentation of its basic subject matter.[33]

Vidor proceeds to provide regular glimpses of the glorious landscape as the Rangers journey to St. Francis and avoid detection by the French and Indians. We then witness the massacre of the Abenakis at St. Francis. As the survivors trek homewards after the destruction of the Indian community, the men suffer from extreme hunger. There were no substantial provisions to be found at the village they had destroyed and they have only a few kernels of corn to sustain each man. At one point during the battle at St. Francis, a Ranger named Crofton (Addison

Richards) had begun to show signs of having suffered the severe psychological effects of such a brutal existence. He was about to kill a native child, but another Ranger prevented him, saying the child is "too young" and must simply be taken prisoner. As if to channel his rage, Crofton savagely attacks a dead adult Indian with a hatchet. After the battle, the increasingly deranged Ranger shows himself to be more than disturbed, mocking the hunger of his comrades and carrying a mysterious bundle around with him as if it were a sack of treasure. Not long thereafter, he steals away to feed off the contents of his treasured sack: the head of the Indian corpse that he had viciously decapitated. We are not shown this gruesome event, of course, but the horror of this scene is increased by the fact that Vidor leaves the act of cannibalism to the power of the viewer's imagination. Eventually Crofton runs off a cliff in a suicidal frenzy, leaving a stunned Rogers to offer a eulogizing salute to a formerly loyal member of his band.

Despite the splendor of the natural scenery around them, the Rangers have suffered greatly from lack of food and expenditure of energy in conquering a hostile foe. They would gladly trade the beauty of their surroundings for a bit of sustenance. Fort Wentworth, their long-desired destination, proves to be a deserted outpost. Rogers rushes ahead to investigate the fort, finds it empty just before the men arrive, and for once expresses signs of weakness, breaking into a momentary crying jag before he hears his men approaching. An exemplar of stoic dignity, Rogers quickly regains his composure, or what there is left of it, and then demands that the men march into the camp. They are starved and exhausted, at the threshold of death's door, with the dream of food having kept them going up until this point. Fort Wentworth has been their last hope. Rogers then cites the Biblical example of Moses, who allegedly went hungry for forty days without food and water, and cites a few verses from Scripture (a paraphrased amalgam of Isaiah 40:3 and Isaiah 43: 19-20): "The voice of Him that cryeth in the wilderness. Prepare ye the way of the Lord. Make straight in the desert a highway for our God. Behold, I will do a new thing. Shall ye not know it? I will make a way in the wilderness and rivers in the desert. And the highway shall be there, and a way. And wayfaring men, though fools, shall not go astray therein." We might recall here other examples of faith-oriented encouragement or consolation in movie Westerns, examples such as the handing of a Bible to a dying man in Ford's *The Searchers* and the reliance on scripture-reading in Ford's *3 Godfathers*.

In the end, of course, hope is answered, and British soldiers now appear in boats, arriving to help the ragged Rangers after Rogers had earlier sent a few of his men back to their starting point to seek help. Rogers tells his men in their dilapidated attire to stand proud and straight with eyes front. We suddenly transition to the near future: the surviving Rangers march into town to great fanfare, with the citizens out in the streets to greet them. The British commander wastes no time in giving Rogers his new orders—to find the fabled Northwest Passage—and asks him to read them to his men before the townspeople. Langdon and Hunk, however, have decided that they will not join the men on their next adventure. Langdon tells his sweetheart Elizabeth, who had been patiently waiting for him all this time, that Rogers and his men are now marching off to make history. When Langdon's fiancée asks Rogers if a Northwest Passage really exists, he tells her, "There's bound to be." And Rogers promises Langdon, before departing: "I'll see you at sundown, Harvard." Langdon looks on as Rogers and his men march off and he proclaims to Elizabeth: "That man will never die."

The film concludes with a shot of Rogers silhouetted against the sky at the end of a dark road—not unlike the concluding iconic shot in Ford's *Young Mr. Lincoln* (1939). The chiaroscuro image reminds us that the road ahead will be a mixture of darkness and light—but as long as the light exists, there will be a mission to fulfill and a nation to build. Once again, the memory of suffering and sacrifice is combined with a sense of optimistic faith and historical destiny to do justice to the complex story of American expansionism. And yet, the film clearly *shows* us—even if it does not *say* so—that the story of America and its "Myth of Conquest" are inevitably intertwined with death and loss, with racism and conflict. We may want to cheer on Rogers at the end of the film as he embarks on his new mission, but we also witness the refusal of Langdon and Hunk to join him, opting for a settled and civilized existence. We also suspect, given the movie we have just watched, that Rogers' upcoming adventure will involve great suffering, the oppression of others, and the loss of human lives.

In many ways, the challenging complex production of *Northwest Passage*, including the many logistical obstacles and the exercise in the use of Technicolor for a landscape-oriented film, served as practice and precursor for Vidor's great achievement in directing *Duel in the Sun* a half-decade later. Taken together, these two "epics" demonstrate that this filmmaker, who had mastered the nuances of black-and-white photography throughout the 1920 and 1930s, did not shy away from the artistic challenges of a new medium of cinematic expression, just as he had successfully transitioned to the sound era with such films as *Hallelujah*, *Street Scene*, and *The Champ*. In the 1950s, Vidor would make full expressive use of Technicolor in his films *Man Without a Star*, *War and Peace*, and *Solomon and Sheba*.

Finally, the making of *Northwest Passage* gave Vidor the opportunity of working with a man whom he regarded as one of the greatest actors he had ever directed: Spencer Tracy. Despite the rigors and tensions suffered by both men during the production, Vidor admired Tracy's acting so much that he wanted the actor to star in his later *An American Romance* (1944), a very personal film whose story, created by Vidor, was intimately connected to his overall vision. Unfortunately, Tracy was busy with another film (*A Guy Named Joe*) at the time that the studio wanted Vidor to begin shooting. So a lesser actor, Brian Donlevy, was chosen and his casting was, according to the director, one of the reasons for the failure of *American Romance*.[34] But Vidor maintained his deep respect for Tracy and later wrote of him in his book on filmmaking:

> Tracy along with [Robert] Donat just about head my list of the best actors I've worked with. Everything that Spence did came over with tremendous conviction. This was his biggest asset. Like [John] Gilbert, he had to deal constantly with emotional problems.... He played strong courageous parts with absolute conviction and yet physically—and emotionally—he was hardly a strong, courageous man. While working in Idaho on a tough location for *Northwest Passage*, he repeatedly threatened to leave the location and return to Los Angeles before the job was finished.... I am sad to have to say that what gives many actors' work interest and vitality is the conflict between their own tumultuous emotional lives and the outer role they are playing.[35]

In the end, thanks to Vidor's masterful direction as well the solid acting of professionals like Tracy, Brennan, and Young, *Northwest Passage* rose above its troubled production and unfinished script. It can be viewed today as a highly satisfying though flawed masterwork in early Technicolor film artistry and the evolution of historical movies.

Eighteen

1941–1944

H.M. Pulham, Esq. and An American Romance

> "If the motion picture is anything, it is for everyone.... I am probably the only sculptor, if I can call myself a sculptor, who ever found himself inside his piece of marble and had to cut his way out."[1]—King Vidor, 1943

H.M. Pulham, Esq. (1941)

> "There is not a scene in the entire picture in which Robert Young (Pulham) is either not present or depicted. Because of this peculiarity of the story I had to keep an experimental point of view all the time."[2]—King Vidor, 1941

Before *H.M. Pulham, Esq.* went into production, Vidor was called away to take over direction of *The Yearling*, an adaptation of Marjorie Kinnan Rawlings' novel about a young boy's compassion for a young deer. Spencer Tracy, one of Vidor's favorite actors who had just worked with him on *Northwest Passage*, had been cast in the lead role and Victor Fleming was originally slated to direct but left the project early on. With its rural setting, the story must have seemed a perfect fit for Vidor. Unfortunately, the project was beset with problems from the start, including coping with the excessive heat and swarms of insects when the initial cast and crew went on location in the Juniper Prairie Wilderness area in the Ocala National Forest of Florida. The story was set amidst cornfields, and while still in pre-production, Vidor encountered difficulties with the necessary growing of corn (the "script called for this small acreage in many stages of height and growth") and the use of multiple deer at various ages ("in the time required to make the picture, the little fawn would grow up and become a deer..."). Additionally, as Vidor recalled in his autobiography, "many script revisions were necessary. Production of *The Yearling* was not resumed until three years later ... and Clarence Brown took over the directorial helm."[3] Gregory Peck had eventually replaced Tracy, who bowed out of the project. Of course, the film would go on to be nominated for Oscars for Best Picture, Best Actor (Peck), Best Actress (Jane Wyman), Best Director (Brown), and Best Cinematography. It won the latter award.

Vidor returned to start the production of *H.M. Pulham, Esq.* The film is the culmination of Vidor's inquiry into the American "Everyperson"—his attempt to distill drama from ordinary, shared experiences, an artistic trajectory that dates back to *The Turn in the Road* (1919), *The Big Parade* (1925), and especially *The Crowd* (1928), whose quotidian narrative *H.M. Pulham, Esq.* most closely resembles. Even more so than in *The Crowd*, Vidor has stripped the narrative of melodramatic devices and the visuals to the most basic—almost mundane—elements. Based on a novel of the same title by John P. Marquand, the script was written by Vidor and his wife, Elizabeth Hill. Harry Moulton Pulham, Jr. (Robert Young), is a middle-aged businessman whose life has settled into a comfortable routine of upper-class luxury, financial stability, and a contented but passionless marriage to Kay (Ruth Hussey, who also acted with Young in *Northwest Passage*). He lives in his old family mansion in Boston and makes a living managing investments that belonged to his father. As he starts to write his own biography for a college reunion, he remarks to himself, "Looks like a tombstone, doesn't it? Maybe I'm dead and I don't even know it." Writing his own biography, along with a phone call from an old flame, Marvin Myles (Hedy Lamarr), sparks a series of flashbacks going back to his birth and continuing through his college days at Harvard, experiences in World War I, and his work at an advertising agency with college friend Bill King (Van Heflin), where he first met Marvin. In between flashbacks, Harry calls Marvin and arranges to meet for a drink. Seeing her across the lobby, he decides to cancel the date and instead sends two dozen American Beauty roses to her and buys an orchid for his wife. The next day, he urges his wife to run away with him so they can rekindle their romance, but she says no. Harry makes another date with Marvin in her hotel room, but instead of starting an affair, they tell each other about their family and business lives. As Harry returns to his office that afternoon, his wife is waiting in a car out front and agrees to go away with him for the sake of their marriage.

The film's opening is one of the director's most expertly crafted sequences, a characteristically Vidorian rhythmic montage of Harry's morning routine. Set to metronomic orchestral music on the soundtrack, a series of close-ups show us Harry's world. Walking down the stairs; a dog waiting at the bottom (its tail wagging to the beat); unfolding a napkin at the table; a newspaper headline, "Roosevelt Warns Nazis"; ritualistically cracking a hardboiled egg; breaking off a corner of a piece of toast and feeding it to the dog; and adding cream and sugar lumps to his coffee. Vidor films these shots as disembodied gestures, close-ups of his hands and feet, mechanized and dehumanized. The first time we see Harry is a medium shot of him kissing his wife and saying, "Goodbye, dear." She repeats the same phrase to him; both are disinterested in either the kiss or the words. So practiced is this routine that Harry even counts the breaths it takes him to walk to his job, twenty-five of them. The montage is mostly without dialogue and displays Vidor's continued use of silent film techniques. The use of the metronome not only informs the editing pattern, but as in *The Big Parade*, it informs the choreography of the actors' movements before the camera, as well.

Unlike so many of Vidor's domestic narratives, *H.M. Pulham, Esq.* exhibits a decided lack of melodrama—or comedy or tragedy, for that matter. Even Harry's decision to leave New York—and, by extension, Marvin—is handled as a matter of practicality and family responsibility. After the death of Harry's father, he returns home to run the family business. When she visits, the cosmopolitan Marvin is turned off by the stuffy, upper-class milieu of Harry's social circle, as well as by the New England puritanism of his family (she is not even allowed to drink alcohol within his home, and she does so in secret). She says that she could not conform to his world, and he does not want to leave his family, thus ending the relationship. Later, he and childhood friend Kay decide to marry after she observes how unhappy both of them secretly are. Even Harry's World War I experience (filmed on the same set as *The Big Parade*) is distilled to a civil discussion about surrender during a cigarette break with a German officer; after declining to surrender, Harry even offers the rest of his pack to the German, admitting that he probably will not be around to smoke the rest of them.[4] And then there is the unresolved tension of Harry and Marvin's romance that lingers at the end of the film.

Doomed extramarital affairs are a recurring theme in Vidor's films, such as in *Hallelujah*, *Street Scene*, *Cynara*, and *The Wedding Night*. What makes *H.M. Pulham, Esq.* different is that the specter of marital infidelity which hangs over the whole picture is, ultimately, never consummated. It is clear that the flame between Harry and Marvin has not died, but they both have separate lives and are not about to jeopardize them. Unlike the melodramatic fantasy of *Love Never Dies*—in which Tilly's husband commits suicide, allowing her to reunite with old lover John—*H.M. Pulham, Esq.* offers no such convenient conclusion. Harry and Kay drive off, supposedly to a happier marriage, but even the director is unconvinced of this resolution. "That's why I might have bought this book, because the idea of going back to an old, cold love and trying to revive it has always been a fascinating theme to me. It happened in my own life in a very sad way," Vidor recalled.[5] "I am not sure if that is a happy ending or not. I think it was an honest ending, though."[6]

Vidor's everyman-protagonists, curiously, do not always come from lower or working-class backgrounds. Harry is a child of wealth like Paul Perry (Lloyd Hughes) in *The Turn in the Road*, James Apperson (John Gilbert) in *The Big Parade*, Mary Sims (Karen Morley) in *Our Daily Bread*, and Tony Barrett (Gary Cooper) in *The Wedding Night*. What is interesting about *The Turn in the Road*, *The Big Parade*, and *The Wedding Night* is that all three protagonists had trials that shook them from their privilege and forced them to see the world through different eyes. Even Tony Barrett is forced to confront his cosmopolitan perspective by writing a book about immigrant farmers, an act which reconnects him with the land, with literature, and with love. Unlike in Vidor's earlier films, Harry does not undergo any perspective-altering experiences. Even his time in New York and relationship with Marvin cannot shake him from the sheltered affluence that he grew up with. His worldview—philosophically and literally—does not change from the start of the film to the end. Looked at from this angle, it is understandable that Vidor challenges the relative happiness of the film's ending. For all of its comfort and security,

Eighteen. *H.M. Pulham, Esq.* and *An American Romance*

Robert Young (as Harry Moulton Pulham) and Hedy Lamarr (as Marvin Myles Ransome) in the romantic drama *H.M. Pulham, Esq.* (1941, directed by King Vidor for Metro-Goldwyn-Mayer). The screenplay, by Vidor and his wife Elizabeth Hill, is based on the novel of the same title by John P. Marquand (MGM/Photofest).

Harry's existence is among the bleakest and most meaningless in all of Vidor's films.

In contrast with Harry is Marvin, a modern, independent woman whose free will and metropolitan tastes are divergent from many of Vidor's female characters whose lives reflect the conservative tastes of their respective times. Often they are tied to conceptions of the "home" in both positive (*Love Never Dies*) and negative (*Cynara*, *The Wedding Night*) ways; single women who defy social norms are punished for their moral transgressions in *Bird of Paradise*, *Cynara*, *The Wedding Night*, and *Stella Dallas* (actual death in the first three, and a more spiritual death in the fourth). The character Marvin most reminds us of is a grown-up version of Sylvia Sidney's Rose Maurrant from *Street Scene*, another female character who rejects a romance that would mean compromising and settling down. Marvin can arguably be seen as a turning point for Vidor's female protagonists, as his late 1940s and early 1950s films are distinguished by a series of strong women in central roles whose behavior breaks with gender convention: Jennifer Jones in *Duel in the Sun* (1946), Dominique Francon in *The Fountainhead* (1949), Bette Davis in *Beyond the Forest* (1949), Ruth Roman in *Lightning Strikes Twice* (1951), Shirley Yamaguchi in *Japanese War Bride* (1952), and Jennifer Jones again in *Ruby Gentry* (1952).

It is unfortunate that in *H.M. Pulham, Esq.* the character of Kay, Harry's wife, is given such little screentime. While not villainized like the wives in *Cynara* and *The Wedding Night*, she is portrayed as vain, passionless, and more interested in the convenience of a marriage to someone in her social class. Her decision to go off with Harry at the film's ending comes across as an unmotivated reversal of her character. Is it a practical consideration, an attempt to save a marriage in order to prevent divorce? Or is it a sincere effort to find romance? The film offers no clarification and is more interested in Harry's unrequited feelings for Marvin than in how Kay feels about her own life.

Entering his second decade of sound cinema, Vidor continued to experiment with sound in *H.M. Pulham, Esq.* "There were several innovations in *Pulham* that have since become rather standard technical processes," Vidor remarked. "Previously, the reading of a letter had been managed either by a close-up which permitted the audience to read the letter themselves, or else the character read it aloud. In *Pulham*, I had the actor read silently, with the text in the voice of the writer coming over the sound track. Another experiment was to have the offstage voice in a telephone conversation sound natural and normal and close to the ear, without subjecting it to tinny and 'distance' effects."[7]

The film received two National Board of Review Awards in 1942, one for star Robert Young and another for Charles Coburn who plays Harry's father. *Variety* called it "a surefire moneymaker."[8] *The Film Daily* praised it as being "[in] the ranks of the year's top-notch films.... Imparts further lustre to the already shining name of King Vidor. Without exception, the sequences have that rhythmic flow which spells mastery in handling both story values and cast talent.... The genius of Vidor is likewise prominent in the manner in which he has developed the retrospective character of the screenplay into a tight, swift-moving, and enthralling entity."[9] Bosley Crowther, in the *New York Times*, was unstirred by the movie: "Vidor has permitted his film to lose ironic point. And although he has handled certain details and etched character with clarity ... he has failed to make *H.M. Pulham, Esq.* either a credible social comment or an account of a truly pathetic life. It is mostly a long-drawn whimper from a fellow for whom you can't hold much regard."[10]

* * * *

An American Romance (1944)

> "Three years ago, some sixteen years afterwards, when the emotional need of the nation was to lift war production to its highest level, my chance came to tell the story of steel.... We worked three years on this picture, the most difficult technical problem I ever encountered."[11]—King Vidor, 1944

> "King Vidor's films take the myth of America as their starting point and look at people trying to live it."[12]—Margaret and William E. Hrezo, 2010

An American Romance joins *The Crowd, Our Daily Bread,* and *Truth and Illusion* as one of Vidor's most personal projects, one based on a story conceived by the director—and a story that is an archetypal expression of how he conceived of America and the American dream. A film about the idea of America itself was a timely one, considering that the United States had recently emerged from the Great Depression of the 1930s, only to become actively involved (in December of 1941) in World War II. Similar to his later film version of *War and Peace, An American Romance* is an epic story that contains many magical moments and impressive scenes which, along with the less magical scenes and sequences, fail to cohere into a superior movie. Also like his later adaptation of the Tolstoy novel, Vidor would later blame part of the failure of *An American Romance* (which he originally wanted to title simply *America*) on the casting of the lead actor (Brian Donlevy as Stefan Dubechek, though his name becomes Americanized as Steve Dangos). And then there is the fact that both movies have rather clunky first halves that detract from their superior second halves. As Dangos, Donlevy spends a good part of the movie, up until he succeeds in business, acting as a bumbling, bewildered immigrant, with all too many shots of him looking puzzled. And in addition, Donlevy's accent simply does not work, especially in the first half of the film, and does more to annoy and detach the viewer than to elicit the audience's empathy and engagement. Henry Fonda as Tolstoy's Pierre luckily only had to suffer an early scene as a befuddled, highly inebriated partygoer; otherwise, his character is simply aloof rather than silly in much of the rest of the movie. In the case of *An American Romance,* Donlevy spends a good portion of the movie acting rather silly and using a stock facial expression signaling his perplexity. In the end, the failed attempts at frequent humor, especially in the first hour or so, seem to degrade rather than to amplify the lead character. Vidor and his screenwriters, working from his original story idea, attempted to bring sporadic levity to this portrait of a struggling immigrant. As originally conceived, the movie is a bold, unique, ambitious experiment, one that Vidor envisioned as the ultimate expression of his ideals and of his conception of America. But in execution, the results simply did not bake just right in the oven.

Vidor later blamed the commercial and critical failure of the film on the clumsy editing of the movie by the studio after it was out of the director's hands. However, would we have wanted to experience a longer movie if a large part of it simply did not work? And though Spencer Tracy, Vidor's original choice to play Dangos, is a far superior actor than Donlevy, it seems difficult to picture Tracy performing in many of the scenes that depict Dangos as a bumbling, grimacing fool. One might even go so far as to say that Donlevy gave the best performance that could be expected of an actor, given the story and dialogue and the type of expressions and reactions and broad humor that Vidor demanded for the role. And Donlevy is more convincing in the second half of the film as his character becomes a caring father who rises to the top and who then becomes more assertive and, in the face of compromising with his workers, outright dictatorial. It is indeed difficult to view Tracy or any other famous leading actor of that time as Dangos, given the parameters of Vidor's conception of the character. In fact, in the superior second half of the film, the actor is quite good and so is the directing, with some of the best scenes Vidor had yet created. Rather than blaming a good part of the failure on Donlevy and studio interference in the editing (it originally premiered at 151 minutes and was cut to 122 minutes), it may have been more apt if Vidor and MGM had found a way to condense the lumbering first hour into an extended flashback so as to get more quickly to Dangos' rise in the steel industry and his subsequent supervision of automobile and airplane production.

The movie was one part of Vidor's trilogy that he called "War, Wheat, and Steel," the three themes that made up his story of America. This trilogy also included *The Big Parade* as the first part and *Our Daily Bread* as the second. Vidor's vision in the third film revolves around a parallel between the refinement of earth and minerals into metal (and then metal into industry) and the refinement of Dangos from an Ellis Island immigrant into an American citizen and then a top American industrialist. Most interesting is Vidor's strategic and symbolic use of color (in this case, Technicolor). The first part of the story, set in Minnesota's Mesabi iron range, consists mostly of reds and browns and beiges that echo the earth and landscape. Then the color palette shifts to frequent blues and grays and silvers as we become immersed in Dangos' career in the steel and automobile industries. So in this sense, and given the great care that Vidor and cinematographer Harold Rossen took in composing their impressive images of the rural and urban landscapes, the film is very painterly and recalls the director's highly expressionist use of Technicolor in his earlier *Northwest Passage* and most especially in his very next film: *Duel in the Sun*. Rosson, whose career in movies began in 1915, had directed the photography on *The Wizard of Oz* and would also work with Vidor on *Duel*.

Like his later *War and Peace*, *An American Romance* is a movie of impressive cinematic moments that do not ultimately cohere into a greater whole. There are the remarkable documentary-like sequences bringing the viewer to an iron quarry, to a ship carrying the ore to port cities, to the mills of Pittsburgh where the iron ore is melted into steel, and to the automobile and airplane assembly lines. These sequences are expertly crafted in terms of photography and montage and may have functioned more effectively if Vidor had simply included them in a documentary on American industry. There is also the thrilling scene where Dangos escapes a river-like outpouring of fiery molten steel with the quick thinking and help of his fellow workers. Other scenes that work well, especially as parts of the portrait of early twentieth-century America, include a brief glimpse of an old-time baseball game as well as a scene in which Steve's wife Anna (played ably by Ann Richards) watches with her young son as a butterfly emerges from its chrysalis. The boy questions his mother about this little miracle of Nature and she attributes the beauty and magic to God. This is a typically Vidor-ian spiritual moment. There is also an intriguing scene in which Dangos tries to get his hand-cranked car started after it breaks down on the way to his son's high school graduation and he gets help from a teacher, Howard Clinton (Walter Abel), who is also on his way to the ceremony. Mr. Clinton will wind up assisting Dangos with his invention of a crank-less automobile and, after they become business partners, he will share in his financial success.

Perhaps the center-point of the film is the high school graduation (class of 1918) of Dangos' son George (Bob Lowell), who gives an idealistic, patriotic speech as valedictorian. As part of that sequence, just before the speech, we witness a young woman getting hilariously carried away as she sings in a high-pitched voice while accompanied by a boy on violin. Here is a scene in which Vidor effectively achieves the infusion of humor into his story. George's brief speech can be viewed as Vidor's typically optimistic message of faith and hope and it emphasizes the idea of America as a land of freedom and opportunity as well as a land of immigrants:

> My preceptors, parents, classmates, and friends: On this graduation day, we stand upon the threshold of a new world, a world of strife and struggle. We're about to take our places in this world. The future belongs to us, the future of the America that we are about to inherit. The right to be Americans was won for us by others. Most of us are sons and daughters of foreign-born parents who came from distant lands to find opportunity and freedom. We must learn the deeper meaning of America. We must help write the living present as others before us have written the glowing past. You will find us ready to take our places by your sides, you who are already fighting life's battles. We march forward strong and brave, knowing that there is nothing that is impossible in this land for us and our children. We believe in the fundamental principles of democracy and we believe in the preservation of it. We face the future with hope, with faith, and with courage. We will not fail you.[13]

An American Romance would go on to be a commercial and critical failure for Vidor. Given that it was a personal project connected closely with his moral vision and idea of America, the period in the aftermath of the film was temporarily depressing for the director. But ever the optimist, and thanks to David O. Selznick, he would soon be asked to direct a movie with a stellar crew and an all-star cast and the highest production values possible: *Duel in the Sun*, which would go on to become the "biggest" Western movie made to date.

Meanwhile, just before beginning work on *Duel in the Sun*, the Motion Picture Alliance for the Preservation of American Ideals (MPAPAI, also known as MPA) was formed in 1944, chiefly constituted by conservative Hollywood directors, actors, and writers. Vidor joined this group and its political cause of defending the motion picture industry in the face of what they perceived to be communist as well as fascist influence. It was perhaps fitting that Vidor, directly after trying to depict his own "mythical" story of what he perceived to be the nation's ideals, felt called upon to join forces with friends and colleagues who sensed a threat to "the American way." Apart from Vidor, members included John Wayne, Ayn Rand, Ward Bond, Walter Brennan, Gary Cooper, Cecil B. DeMille, Walt Disney, Victor Fleming, John Ford, Clark Gable, Leo McCarey, Robert Montgomery, Ronald Reagan, Ginger Rogers, Barbara Stanwyck, and Robert Taylor. The group's "Statement of Principles" included the following:

> In our special field of motion pictures, we resent the growing impression that this industry is made of, and dominated by, Communists, radicals, and crackpots. We believe that we represent the vast majority of the people who serve this great medium of expression.... Motion pictures are inescapably one of the world's greatest forces for influencing public thought and opinion, both at home and abroad. In this fact lies solemn obligation. We refuse to permit the effort of Communist, Fascist, and other totalitarian-minded groups to pervert this powerful medium into an instrument for the dissemination of un–American ideas and beliefs. We pledge ourselves to fight, with every means at our organized command, any effort of any group or individual, to divert the loyalty of the screen from the free America that give it birth. And to dedicate our work, in the fullest possible measure, to the presentation of the American scene, its standards and its freedoms, its beliefs and its ideals, as we know them and believe in them.[14]

As time went on, the Alliance would become more active in the Hollywood "blacklist" effort, especially due to the persistent efforts of those like Ward Bond and Ayn Rand. Vidor seems to have gradually lost interest in being a member. Rand would later write a pamphlet (*Screen Guide for Americans*) on behalf of the group in 1947. Of course, Vidor would go on to work closely with Rand when he directed the film adaptation (released in 1949) of her bestselling philosophical novel *The Fountainhead*. One might easily peg Vidor as a political conservative due to his membership in the Alliance, but as Durgnat and Simmon point out in their book *King Vidor, American*, he was never easy to classify, especially politically. After all, he was the director of two very different movies with very different political messages: *Our Daily Bread* and *The Fountainhead*. And in 1940, he had labeled himself as a "rabid Roosevelt supporter."[15] It may be fair to say that Vidor most always championed both individual liberty as well as the common good and aligned himself with the political cause that seemed to work best at realizing both—just as, in *An American Romance*, he celebrates Dangos' triumph of individualism through capitalism (creativity, innovation, self-reliance, competition) while also making a case for the value of workers' unions and their right to collective bargaining. It is, in fact, Dangos' son Teddy (Stephen McNally) who joins with the company's labor representatives to challenge his father and make a convincing argument that everyone fails if the workers are not allowed the opportunity to organize and argue for their interests. Balancing individual freedom and the common good may be difficult at times and it requires sacrifices on either side of the equation, but ultimately, it seems that Vidor believed that the balance was always worth the effort. The board room scene in which Teddy speaks for the workers while also paying respect to his father's great business achievement may be the best example of how we can understand Vidor as the very same director who made both *Our Daily Bread* and *The Fountainhead*.

NINETEEN

1946

Duel in the Sun

"And the motion picture is bigger than I; bigger than any group of men; it is as big as all humanity.... No man can lay down principles to govern it."[1]—King Vidor, 1926

"Emotions have existed ever since the creation of man and have been the cause of practically every act, either good or bad, that man has committed.... Emotions are not limited to a few but are universal."[2]—King Vidor, 1935

Back in September of 1936, several years after they had worked together on the 1932 film *Bird of Paradise*, David O. Selznick offered Vidor the job of helming the movie version of Mark Twain's *The Adventures of Tom Sawyer*. But Vidor had already planned an early October leaf-peeping trip in Connecticut with his wife at the time and could not begin preparations for the movie exactly when Selznick wanted him to start. After his trip, Vidor heard nothing else from Selznick and he began work soon thereafter on *Stella Dallas*. A year later, according to Vidor's memoir, Selznick called him to offer the same job once again, but this time Vidor had already committed to filming *The Citadel*.[3] In late 1944, the two men talked briefly about a possible remake of Vidor's silent melodrama *Wild Oranges*, to star Gregory Peck and Ingrid Bergman, but it remained a mere idea.[4] Finally, in 1945, the producer and director, who had once been neighbors and who socialized together, joined forces to make what Selznick intended to be the next *Gone with the Wind*. The big budget production, high expectations, and grandiose story summoned the director to the heights of his creative vision and technical mastery—and gave him the opportunity of working with an army-sized crew and a stellar cast.

RKO had purchased the rights to Niven Busch's novel of the same title in 1944. The studio had originally planned for John Wayne and Hedy Lamarr to star in it, with Busch adapting his own novel for the screen. Joseph Breen, the head of Hollywood's Production Code Office, read the planned screenplay and objected to the original script for including "a story of illicit sex and murder for revenge" without offering any redemptive view that would morally condemn such story elements. Busch had originally wanted to cast Jennifer Jones, but she was under contract to Selznick (whom she would later marry in 1949). Selznick wound up buying the rights to the novel from RKO and produced the film, casting Jones in the key role of Pearl Chavez. Selznick then hired King Vidor to direct and the producer wrote the screenplay, based on an adaptation by Oliver H.P. Garrett and with help from Vidor.[5]

This was Vidor's fourth sound era Western—following his earlier *Billy the Kid* and *The Texas Rangers*, along with the quasi–Western *Northwest Passage*—and certainly his finest work in the genre. There are flaws, of course, including some choppy editing and over-baked melodrama, though both weaknesses can be blamed far more on Selznick than on Vidor. But it could be argued that in this movie, Vidor demonstrated the cumulative peak of his artistry, especially in technical terms, and prepared the director for his later large-scale productions of *War and Peace* and *Solomon and Sheba*. And the commercial and critical failure of *An American Romance*, despite Vidor's highest hopes for such a personal project, no doubt motivated him to show Hollywood what he could do when he had the proper budget, crew, and cast of stars. Vidor must have been looking for redemption of sorts after his disappointment with the overall reception of *An American Romance*, the project in which he had invested so much time and energy. In fact, one might even view that previous film, along with his more successful *Northwest Passage* before that, as having provided the kind of experimental exercise in bold Technicolor, sweeping narrative, and novelistic tempo that made *Duel in the Sun* so successful, despite its weaknesses. And, of course, many of these weaknesses were not due solely to any mistakes on the part of Vidor alone. Selznick had given him this grand-scale opportunity but unfortunately the producer's meddling in the production on a regular basis made it such a frustrating experience for Vidor that he eventually walked off the set toward the end of the production. Other directors such as William Dieterle and Josef von Sternberg were already involved in the production and contributed to certain scenes or helped to finish the movie after Vidor quit toward the very end (though they remained uncredited). Nonetheless, despite the intense pressure from Selznick and the rigor of supervising a cast and crew of hundreds, plus the usual constraints facing any auteur working within the confines of a big studio blockbuster production, Vidor clearly rose to the occasion (and beyond). Vidor reflected on the film in his memoir *A Tree Is a Tree*:

> The picture started out to be a moderate-sized Western with an unknown cast. When we had finished, it was just about the most super-duper-Technicolor ever made.... If David [Selznick] wanted an actor, nothing would stop him until he had the performer under contract ... As *Duel in the Sun* got into production, David had visions of making it into a kind of *Gone with the Wind* in a Western setting. Preliminary sketches of ranch houses and streets were set aside and new ones were ordered. Beginnings and ends of scenes were added, sequences were enlarged, and previous estimates for cattle, cowboys, and cavalry had to be revised accordingly. Episodes were added where none had been before. Experts were called in as consultants on Western folklore, dancing, and customs. Everything that had ever happened west of the Rocky Mountains was considered for the script. Every worker, down to the humblest laborer on the set, was instilled with the Selznick spirit.[6]

NINETEEN. *Duel in the Sun*

If ever there were a movie to illustrate what film critic and theorist André Bazin meant by a "super-western," it is *Duel in the Sun*. In his essay "The Evolution of the Western," in the second volume of his *What Is Cinema?*, Bazin states:

> Let us call the ensemble of forms adopted by the postwar [post–World War Two] western the "superwestern." For the purposes of our exposé this word will bring together phenomena that are not always comparable. It can certainly be justified on negative grounds, in contrast to the classicism of the forties and to the tradition of which it is the outcome. The superwestern is a western that would be ashamed to be just itself, and looks for some additional interest to justify its existence—an aesthetic, sociological, moral, psychological, political, or erotic interest, in short some quality extrinsic to the genre and which is supposed to enrich it....[7]

Above all, a "super-western" tends to be novelistic in terms of its lengthy, elaborate narrative and accompanying character development, and *Duel in the Sun* certainly fits the bill. Aesthetically bold, morally complex, psychologically charged, and erotically daring, this movie was released around the start of a phase of visually as well as psychologically expressive Westerns that emerged between the end of World War II and 1950. *Duel in the Sun* is one of a number of major Western films made at that time, ones that utilize the conventions of the genre while also deepening and complicating the characters and dramatic situations that are framed by those familiar patterns. And just as Vidor's earlier *Stella Dallas* (1937) served as a precursor of sorts to later post-war film noir, especially in its heightened melodrama and psychological tensions along with the moral ambivalence of its titular character, *Duel in the Sun* set the standard for later "noir Westerns" such as *The Furies, Johnny Guitar, 3:10 to Yuma*, and *Forty Guns*. *Duel in the Sun* was also the clear precursor of such later, highly psychological Westerns as Ford's *The Searchers* and *The Man Who Shot Liberty Valance*.

The second half of the 1940s marked an important transition point in the evolution of the Western film. This gradual transformation of the genre was undoubtedly due to new audience expectations, the result of the "maturing" of America's public self-consciousness both during and after the nation's multi-faceted wartime experience. Despite the Allied victory and a revived sense of "American exceptionalism" in some quarters, many Americans were nonetheless aware of the costs in human life and the bleak lessons about human nature that World War II had occasioned. A skeptical and even pessimistic sensibility often lay beneath the public roar of military triumph, and this tension was clearly reflected in the postwar use of the Western genre in a more critical, de-mythologizing manner. Hollywood producers were certainly aware of their audiences' increasing need for more complex "adult" movies that reflected the public's gradual disillusionment with traditional myths of unfailing heroes and inevitable communal progress. Filmmakers were conscious of their roles in conveying the collective awakening that had taken place. This phase of Western filmmaking included John Ford's *My Darling Clementine* (1946), Elia Kazan's *The Sea of Grass* (1947), Howard Hawks' *Red River* (1948), Ford's *Fort Apache* (1948) and *She Wore a Yellow Ribbon* (1949), Raoul Walsh's *Colorado Territory* (1949), Delmer Daves' *Broken Arrow* (1950), and Anthony Mann's *The Furies* (1950).

Lionel Barrymore (as Senator Jackson McCanles, left) and Joseph Cotten (as his son Jesse McCanles, foreground right) in the rousing confrontation with the railway workers in King Vidor's "super-Western" *Duel in the Sun* (1946, produced by David O. Selznick for his Vanguard Films company). The screenplay, co-written by Selznick, is based on the novel of the same title by Niven Busch (Selznick Releasing Organization/Photofest).

The genre had always blended history and fiction in recreating the kind of struggles amidst adversity that took place (most often) in colonial as well as Reconstruction Era America. The Western's usual depiction of courage and hardship, along with its recurring emphasis upon the conflict between good and evil, had resonated with audiences at the beginning of America's involvement in the war. But starting in 1946, many Western movies offered more expressive ways of presenting its stories of struggle and conflict, stories that frequently centered upon morally ambiguous characters and psychologically complex situations. This deepening of the genre in response to the war and its aftermath also paralleled audiences' heightened interest in film noir and in narratives that recognized the irrational aspects of human existence. It was especially in the immediate post–World War II period that the Western became a popular narrative vehicle for the exploration of human instincts, emotions, and desires. The protagonist had to contend with the inner battle between his ego and id while also confronting external adversaries. The struggle to control his repressed libido or will-to-power sometimes became as challenging as his struggle for survival or justice. The Westerner slowly came to recognize that his own psyche might be as chaotic and labyrinthine as the wilderness surrounding him.

Nineteen. *Duel in the Sun*

Duel in the Sun deals with the rivalry between two brothers, Lewt (Gregory Peck) and Jesse (Joseph Cotten), and their love for the seductive "half-breed" Pearl Chavez (Jennifer Jones), recently arrived at the ranching empire of the brothers' father "Senator" Jackson McCanles (Lionel Barrymore). Pearl's father Scott Chavez (Herbert Marshall) has been recently sent to prison and to his eventual execution for having killed his cheating wife and her lover, and so his daughter goes to live with the Senator and his wife Laura Belle (Lillian Gish), the distant cousin and long-ago lover of Pearl's father. Set against a Technicolor-soaked landscape constructed of both on-location shots and studio settings, Vidor's film deals, first and foremost, with the Freudian tension between instinctual self-expression and its counter-force, the repression of subconscious impulses, along with the racial and class differences between Pearl and the McCanles family.[8] And given that the movie begins with the sultry dancing of Pearl and with the subsequent shooting of her adulterous mother by her jealous father, we realize immediately that we can expect a narrative built around themes of unbridled desire and explosions of previously bottled-up passion.

An on-the-set photograph of three Hollywood legends during the production of King Vidor's classic Western *Duel in the Sun* (1946, produced by David O. Selznick for his Vanguard Films company). Walter Huston (left, who plays Jubal "The Sin Killer" Crabbe) and Lionel Barrymore (right, who plays Senator Jackson McCanles) catch up with pioneering filmmaker D.W. Griffith, who visited the set to see three of his former actors (Huston, Barrymore, and Gish) (Selznick Releasing Organization/Photofest).

The film's "Preface" opens with an image of Squaw's Head Rock, a mysterious stone formation that resembles the profile of a human face staring off across the desert below a sunset-hued sky. This is also where the movie will end, returning full circle. A narrator tells us that this will be a story set in Texas in the 1880s and built around the conflict between evil and pioneer morality. (Though set in Texas, most of the movie was shot near Tucson in Arizona as well as in the Wildwood Regional Park in Thousand Oaks, California.)[9] We then hear the narrator refer to the doomed lovers who died in the shadows of the great stone face. We transition to the image of a wildflower growing amidst the rocks and the narrator interprets the wildflower as a symbol of Pearl Chavez (Jennifer Jones):

> Deep among the lonely sun-baked hills of Texas, the great and weather-beaten stone still stands. The Comanche called it Squaw's Head Rock. Time cannot change its impassive face, nor dim the legend of the wild young lovers who found Heaven and Hell in the shadows of the rock. For when the sun is low and the cold wind blows across the desert, there are those of Indian blood who still speak of Pearl Chavez, the half-breed girl from down along the border, and of the laughing outlaw with whom she here kept a final rendezvous, never to be seen again.... And this is what the legend says: A flower, known nowhere else, grows from out of the desperate crags where Pearl vanished. Pearl, who was herself a wild flower, sprung from the hard clay—quick to blossom and early to die.

A noir-like sense of fatalism then hangs over the story: we have been told in advance of Pearl's death at a young age. We then witness Pearl dancing outside a noisy cantina and a man strolls over and speaks with her, hinting lewdly that she is more attractive than her mother. He then enters the cantina and, inside the vast space, the camera wanders through the crowd until it fixes upon Pearl's Mexican mother, who dances wildly on a stage amidst a watching crowd. She eventually traverses the tables and bar counter and flirts with the man who has just spoken to Pearl outside. Meanwhile, Pearl's father, Scott Chavez (Herbert Marshall), endures the rude remarks of his fellow poker players about his wife. He then takes notice of her erotic dancing and the fact that she leaves with the man who clearly desires her. Pearl follows them and expresses grief when her mother leads the man into her nearby home. Seeing her father emerge from the cantina, she tries to stop him from going home and finding her mother with the man, but she fails to do so. But before taking leave of his daughter, he apologizes to her for the disappointing life that he has helped to create for her, clearly insinuating that his marriage to her wild mother had been an awful mistake. She watches as her father barges into the home, knowing full well what he will find. We witness his murder of the man and then of his wife, but only indirectly: we hear their voices and the pistol shots, and we see the rapidly moving silhouettes of the victims as they beg him for their lives.

We soon find Pearl's father in jail, telling the authorities that he does not regret the killing and that he deserves swift justice. Pearl sits in the jail cell with her father and he tells her about his first love, his distant cousin Laura Belle McCanles (Lillian Gish). He tells Pearl to go to the McCanles ranch and that she will have a home there. Pearl bids farewell to her father before his execution. Vidor then opens "Act Two"

A wounded and bloodied Pearl Chavez (played by Jennifer Jones) crawls across the rocks to reach her lover "Lewt" McCanles (off-screen, played by Gregory Peck) in the violent final sequence of King Vidor's classic Western *Duel in the Sun* (1946, produced by David O. Selznick for his Vanguard Films company). Several years later, Jones starred in Vidor's Southern romantic melodrama *Ruby Gentry* (1952) (Selznick Releasing Organization/Photofest).

with a grace note: the image of the setting sun and a stagecoach being led by horses through the countryside. Pearl exits the coach and is met by Jesse McCanles who questions her, but she resists. They ride off to the sprawling McCanles ranch and are greeted by Jesse's mother, Laura Belle, who observes fondly that Pearl looks just like her father. Jesse's father, "the Senator," arrives and treats Pearl with contempt for being Scott Chavez's daughter. Pearl is then introduced to Laura's other son, the wild Lewt (Gregory Peck, playing against type).

Night falls and Pearl wanders around the ranch house while Laura plays the piano. Laura tells Pearl about her sons, explains how she met the Senator, and confides that neither she nor Pearl's father ever found happiness. We then switch to the Senator and Lewt playing chess and, when talking about Pearl, Lewt shows interest in her. Later that night, Lewt visits Pearl's room, where he assaults her. Meanwhile, elsewhere in the great house, the Senator and Jesse and Laura sit and converse about the railroad, given that surveyors have come to the ranch to ask about using part of the McCanles property for the railway route. Jesse told the surveyors that they could come onto the ranch to see about building there, but the Senator is vehemently opposed and angry at Jesse for having suggested such a thing. Jesse says goodnight and then intimates that he may be leaving the ranch soon.

On the following day, while Pearl swims in a pond, Lewt arrives to harass her until she emerges from the water. Pearl stays in the water until it is dark and then returns to the ranch with Lewt. Pearl is soon questioned by Laura about where she has been, but Lewt enters and lies to his mother, telling her that they had been swimming together. Later that night, Pearl is woken up by the ranch servant Vashti (Butterfly McQueen), who tells Pearl that Laura wants to see her in the sitting room. Laura introduces Pearl to Jubal Crabbe, a frontier preacher played by a typically charismatic Walter Huston, an actor whom Vidor later praised in superlative terms when he reflected on his making of the movie.[10] Crabbe, at Laura's urging, delivers a fiery sermon on how Pearl should avoid temptation, all the while glaring at her with covetous eyes and gestures.

We soon experience a rousing, memorable sequence that demonstrates Vidor's mastery in directing a multitude of actors amidst a swirl of action and conflict (as he did in *The Big Parade* and *Northwest Passage* and as he would on an even larger scale in *War and Peace* and *Solomon and Sheba*). The Senator has sounded the alarm to call all hands on deck to ride and confront the railway workers. There are impressive shots of the Senator and his men riding quickly to the edge of the ranch empire where the workers are gathered. Parallel editing is used to great effect with shots of the railroad laborers intercut with those of the Senator leading his men on horseback. The Senator's army of ranch employees arrive at the railroad track under construction and the Senator confronts his old friend Lem Smoot (Harry Carey, one of the silent cinema's cowboy heroes), now a railway enforcer. Lem warns the Senator: "Jackson, you and I fought to build this State of Texas and I aim to see these men perform their duties, peacefully and as authorized." The Senator retorts, "Is that so? Well, I'm gonna shoot any trespasser that comes on my property. If you don't like that, Lem Smoot, you can lump it: you and the State of Texas." Jesse boldly tells his father he is in the wrong because the railway men are unarmed and they have a legal decree permitting them to build the track. To demonstrate this symbolically, Jesse moves to stand on the side of the railway workers. Jesse asks his father, "You mean to shoot down unarmed men?" The Senator responds, "Just like the rattlesnakes if they cross that line." But, just as the Senator is about to start shooting as promised, the U.S. cavalry appears, signaled by flags and bugles. The Senator backs down, saying, "I once fought for that flag. I'll not fire on it." He then angrily sends Jesse away because of his betrayal.

Jesse and the Senator return to the ranch, where Jesse bids farewell to his tearful mother and goes to say goodbye to Pearl, but he finds her with Lewt. Jesse leaves but she chases after him and he tells Pearl that he loved her, but that he cannot do anything with Lewt in the picture. Lewt and Jesse have a brief confrontation about Pearl before Jesse leaves. Time passes and it is evident that Pearl and Lewt have grown closer. They go for a swim, where she asks if they will be married. Lewt lyingly assures her that they will. The Senator soon throws a party where Lewt and his father talk about Pearl and his conduct with her. We hear news about Jesse's success in Boston and that he now has a new wife. Pearl and Lewt get into a fight about the idea of marriage, and she scolds Lewt for having not told anyone about their marital "plans." Lewt now makes it clear that he does not want to get married. Angrily disappointed by Lewt, Pearl exits the party and is met by a gentle man named Sam Pierce (Charles Bickford), who consoles her, clearly enraptured by her beauty. She returns to the party with him and they dance. After the party, Pearl and Sam ride off to Sam's ranch to have a look at his horses. Sam suddenly asks Pearl to marry him, and she appears troubled by this, recognizing his basic goodness and calling herself "trash." Pearl then tells him that she will indeed marry him, and we can immediately sense that it is an act of vengeance against her beloved Lewt.

Jesse eventually returns to the ranch by train with his new wife and her father. On the train, going through the Spanish countryside, Jesse meets a worker from his

A sneering Pearl Chavez (played by Jennifer Jones) aims her rifle at her lover "Lewt" McCanles (off-screen, played by Gregory Peck) in the violent final sequence of King Vidor's classic Western *Duel in the Sun* (1946, produced by David O. Selznick for his Vanguard Films company). The movie earned Jones an Oscar nomination for Best Actress and Lillian Gish was nominated for a Best Supporting Actress Oscar for her performance as Laura Belle McCanles (Selznick Releasing Organization/Photofest).

ranch. The man tells Jesse that Pearl has agreed to marry Sam Pierce. Jesse and his wife talk about Pearl and Jesse confesses that he was in love with Pearl. The night before his wedding, Sam Pierce drinks in a bar, celebrating, when Lewt comes in and confronts him about marrying Pearl, calling Pearl his girl. Sam defends Pearl, Lewt shoots him dead, and Lewt is soon wanted for murder with a bounty on his head. A funeral is given for Sam soon thereafter and Pearl and Laura attend it together, sitting by Sam's grave.

Later, back at the ranch, Laura and her husband sit by the fire. She tells him that they must have raised Lewt wrongly, recognizing his villainy and knowing that he murdered poor Sam Pierce. The Senator does not concur, knowing that Lewt has taken after his father. Soon thereafter, we see Lewt, on the run, meeting up with his father at a pre-arranged location. They converse against the bold colors of a setting sun. The Senator gives Lewt money and tells him that he cannot visit the ranch for some time. They say farewell for a time and there is a breathtaking shot of Lewt going in one direction and his father's carriage in another, silhouetted against the crimson sunset.

Lewt passes through a town where he sees an announcement about the arrival of a freight train that is carrying a cargo of explosives. Lewt sets a trap for the train and it crashes and explodes, killing two of the train workers. From a nearby hillside, he watches the disaster that he has caused and rides away, whistling "I'll Be Working on the Railroad." This is a scene that Selznick had proposed in order to shock the audience and show Lewt to be one of the worst villains ever put on the screen—and even more of a shock, considering that it is the typically heroic Peck who is playing him (one thinks here of the same casting-against-type of Henry Fonda as the archetypally evil gunslinger in Sergio Leone's later Western *Once Upon a Time in the West*). Vidor protested vehemently against the inclusion of this scene, but Selznick insisted that it remain in the film. In his memoir *A Tree Is a Tree*, Vidor later claimed that the producer may have been correct, seeing that the film eventually became a box office success, despite receiving initially poor critical reviews.[11] But the scene ultimately proves unnecessary, especially since Lewt is already wanted for murdering Sam Pierce.

Lewt eventually returns to the ranch and breaks into Pearl's room. Pearl points a gun at him and tells him that she is going to kill him. After a tense moment, Pearl collapses in his arms. Meanwhile, Sheriff Hardy (Charles Dingle) and his men have come to the ranch searching for Lewt. The sheriff tells the Senator that someone has seen Lewt heading back to the ranch. Sheriff Hardy asks to visit Laura in her room and the Senator reluctantly consents. He finds Laura bedridden and looking at family photos. The sheriff then knocks on Pearl's door, where Pearl pretends to be asleep as Lewt hides behind the door with his gun. The sheriff departs from the ranch with his men. Lewt and Pearl talk about the future, about owning a ranch together, and getting married. They are the same morally troubled pair of lovers as before, except now we know that Pearl has the callousness to ignore Lewt's murder of Sam. Lewt turns to leave and Pearl explodes, screaming and begging him to take her with him.

We soon witness Laura in bed and talking to the Senator about their sons and her lost love, Pearl's father. She talks about the failure of her relationship with the Senator, who rants about how Laura Belle ran away from him before they got married and how the Senator, having rushed after her mad with jealousy, suffered the horse-riding accident that crippled him. Then, finally, the Senator confesses that the failure of their marriage was his own fault and admits that he never should have rushed after Laura Belle with revenge in his heart when she ran away years ago. He had obviously been jealous of her love for Pearl's father at that point in her life. The love of Laura Belle for her husband has reached its limit after she has dealt for so long with his ruthlessness and icy ambition.

> LAURA BELLE: "I never had the courage to discuss it with you before, but it doesn't matter now. I paid for my mistake. You've hated me all through the years."
> THE SENATOR: "*You* paid? What about *me*? What about me with these legs? As useless as a hog-tied steer. And all because you couldn't stand to be mistress of the biggest ranch in Texas. And why, huh? Why? I'll tell you why. Nobody needs to tell me who you was running away to that night. Nobody needed to tell me you was running to Chavez."
> LAURA BELLE: "It's not true. It's not true. I was running away, but not to Scott."
> THE SENATOR: "Well, true or not, you left me. And true or not, I went after ya, like any lovesick, half-baked boy."
> LAURA BELLE: "I'd give anything, anything to undo it."
> THE SENATOR: "I loved you, Laura Belle. Yes, I loved you. Kept on saying to myself all through the years that I hated you, until I finally did hate ya. In my heart, I knew all the time it wasn't your fault. It was my fault. It was my jealousy made me like I was. Hard and cruel like, till I guess you had to leave me. I never should have gone out after you that night. But when I found out you was gone, I got to thinkin' you was goin' to him and I couldn't stand it. I swore I'd stop ya and bring ya back."

In this stagy and yet touching scene, the dying Laura Belle crawls across the expanse of her bed to offer her affection to a husband who is absorbed in his own sudden release of guilt and emotion. After his confession of guilt and her attempt to embrace him, Laura Belle falls from the bed to the floor, dead, while having tried with her last breath to express her love for her emotionally stunted husband. The Senator takes a stilted moment to notice almost casually that she has fallen by the side of his wheelchair. It is a sublimely melodramatic moment bordering on the ridiculous, charged with a surplus of sentimentality and over-acting and yet, at the same time, elevated by the co-presence of these two screen legends, Gish and Barrymore.

Barrymore and Gish, two screen titans by this point, clearly relished this opportunity to act together after having worked for D.W. Griffith in the early Biograph years. They both appeared, for example, in Griffith's 1913 *The Battle at Elderbush Gulch* (along with fellow *Duel* supporting actor Harry Carey). Vidor had also worked as an extra for Griffith at one point early on. One memorable story from the production of *Duel in the Sun* is that the legendary Griffith, no longer an active filmmaker, visited his old friends on the set while Gish and Barrymore were filming a particular scene together (perhaps the very bedroom scene discussed above, though the exact scene was never specified). As Vidor later told the story in an interview, the presence of Griffith on the set made Barrymore so nervous that he began to forget his lines. Sensing the trouble that Barrymore was having, Vidor alerted Griffith to the problem and the "Old Master" agreed that it was time to leave.[12]

Jesse returns to the ranch for his mother's funeral. Vashti tells Jesse about what he missed and how his mother had died. Jesse then decides to have Pearl moved off the ranch. Jesse goes to the barn, where he finds Pearl and tells her that he is going away. Jesse invites Pearl to come to Boston with him and his wife so that she can learn how to live a better life in a civilized society. They leave together, but while Jesse is at the hotel with Pearl, he receives a message from Lewt. Lewt tells Pearl that if she does not return to the ranch, he will come to town to retrieve her. Jesse responds to the messenger by telling him to tell Lewt that Jesse will be waiting for him. And this, of course, leads to an expected confrontation, one in which Lewt shoots his own unarmed brother, though not (as it later turns out) fatally.

The famous, emotionally charged conclusion, one concocted by Selznick for full melodramatic effect, involves the mutual killing of these two immoral lovers, Pearl and Lewt. Selznick clearly wanted the complete reverse of the typical happy Hollywood ending, and one that clearly troubled Hollywood censor Joseph Breen because no overall redemptive lesson had been offered after so much lust and violence had been presented.[13] Lewt summons Pearl by messenger, informing her that he is hiding out by Squaw's Head Rock in the desert. The image of Pearl riding her horse dissolves into the shot of a glaring sun. Pearl reaches the rock and finds Lewt there above her, at a distance. Lewt motions for her to come to him, but Pearl starts to walk away with her rifle. She then hides and shoots at Lewt who starts to shoot at her in turn. A gunfight ensues until Lewt shoots Pearl in the chest. Wounded, she takes cover and shoots at Lewt. He appears to be shot, calling out to her and imploring Pearl to climb up to him. Pearl drags herself upwards and across the rocky terrain to Lewt, where she tells him that she had to kill him. She says her final goodbye as they are both fatally wounded. The camera zooms out from the pair to a long shot of Squaw's Head Rock, exactly where the movie began.

Due to Selznick's constant intervention in the production, with countless daily script changes and suggestions for scene re-takes and bringing in other directors for consultation, Vidor quit his job for the first time in his career. But, as Vidor later told an interviewer, he did so toward the very end when most of the movie had already been shot and there were only a few days of shooting left to do.[14] Vidor maintained sole directorial credit, despite the partial involvement of other directors such as Von Sternberg and Dieterle, chiefly because he had supervised 85–90 percent of the finished movie and because the Screen Directors Guild frowned on Selznick's suggestion of listing several directors' names in the credits.[15] Nancy Dowd asked Vidor later in his life whether he was "discouraged about filmmaking" after the decision by

Pearl Chavez (played by Jennifer Jones) in a tense embrace with her lover "Lewt" McCanles (played by Gregory Peck) in King Vidor's classic Western *Duel in the Sun* (1946, produced by David O. Selznick for his Vanguard Films company). Some critics had nicknamed the movie "Lust in the Dust." The screenplay, co-written by Selznick, is based on the novel of the same title by Niven Busch (Selznick Releasing Organization/Photofest).

MGM to edit *An American Romance* without his assistance and then after the interference of Selznick throughout the making of *Duel in the Sun*. Vidor replied, "Yes, I was. I wasn't tired of filmmaking, but I was tired of all the people who just seemed to get in the way all the time."[16]

Vidor also admitted that he was not involved in the editing of *Duel in the Sun* and that his original conception of the film had been in complete conflict with Selznick's grandiose plans that ultimately shaped the overall project. The director summarized the conflict: "I started out with a vision of a very intense story, very similar to Zinnemann's *High Noon*. That was what I was striving for. I wanted just plain good acting, with no blown-up or overacted scenes.... But Selznick wanted this overly dramatic thing that just grew bigger and bigger, as was his style."[17] Vidor would go on, however, to associate with Selznick several years later when he directed Jennifer Jones again (now Mrs. David Selznick) in *Ruby Gentry* (1952). This time, Selznick was not an official producer but rather an advisor, so Vidor was more successful in rebuffing any attempted interventions. Vidor also worked briefly on a few segments of Selznick's television project "Light's Diamond Jubilee" and, most interestingly, later chatted with the producer about a possible movie based on certain works of the German-born writer Hermann Hesse, author of the mystical cult novels *Steppenwolf* and *Siddhartha*.[18] Given Vidor's own life-long interest in spirituality and individuality—the two recurring themes of most of Hesse's writings—Selznick's unrealized suggestion of the director taking on such a project is an intriguing one.

If anything, *Duel in the Sun* is an epic, glossy piece of entertainment whose story centers on the moral dangers that can result from a lack of spirituality in one's life. If any character serves as the spiritual and moral center of the movie, it is not the preacher Jubal Crabbe, known as "The Sin Killer," but rather Laura Belle.

Twenty

1948–1949

On Our Merry Way, The Fountainhead,
and *Beyond the Forest*

> "I like to think of the films as being immortal, if possible. And as much as you put yourself into your films, that is immortal. The immortal self is the divine birthright that we are given. I think everyone has it, but most people don't have the opportunity to find it. It takes an artist to find it, and it takes a good artist. That's why I said I wanted to make more pictures. I'd learn more about myself...."[1]—King Vidor, later 1970s

On Our Merry Way (1948)

On Our Merry Way is an omnibus film whose quality is far less than the sum of its parts would suggest. A co-production between Benedict Bogeaus and Burgess Meredith, the film was an anthology styled in the vein of *If I Had a Million* (1932) and *Tales of Manhattan* (1942) and intended to showcase a variety of stars in front of and behind the camera. Today Meredith is better known for his Oscar-nominated role of Mickey, the curmudgeonly trainer in *Rocky* (1976), but at the time, Meredith was best known for his portrayal of George in Lewis Milestone's film of John Steinbeck's *Of Mice and Men* (1939). In the mid–1940s he also experimented with screenwriting, adapting *Diary of a Chambermaid* (from a novel by Octave Mirbeau and a play by André Heuzé, André de Lorde, and Thielly Nores). The 1946 film, based on his screenplay, was directed by Jean Renoir and produced by Bogeaus and it starred Meredith and then-wife Paulette Goddard. Bogeaus was an entrepreneur who began in real estate and moved into radio before landing in Hollywood in the early 1940s. Before *On Our Merry Way*, he had already produced André de Toth's southern gothic thriller *Dark Waters* (1944), setting the tenor for much of his career: low-budget genre fare from top-tier auteurs whose careers were fading. Bogeaus' later films include Robert Florey's amnesia noir *The Crooked Way* (1949), Jacques Tourneur's exotic jungle noir *Appointment in Honduras* (1953), and a fertile ten-film collaboration with Allan Dwan.

For *On Our Merry Way*, Bogeaus and Meredith tapped Arch Oboler for an original story. Oboler was best known at the time for his horror radio series *Lights Out*.

The script would be written by Lou Breslow and frequent Vidor collaborator Laurence Stallings, with an additional episode by novelist John O'Hara, one written especially for an episode to co-star real-life buddies James Stewart and Henry Fonda. Directing duties would be split among Vidor, Leslie Fenton, and John Huston.

Real-life husband and wife Burgess Meredith and Paulette Goddard star as Oliver and Martha Pease. Martha is an abstract artist, and Oliver pretends to be a newspaper columnist known as the Roving Reporter, ashamed to admit that he really only works in the want-ad section. Martha encourages her husband to do better with his column and suggests the topic "What influence has a child had on your life?" Posing as a representative of the newspaper's owner, Oliver convinces the editor to let him take over as Roving Reporter for the day. As a bookie chases him around the city over a debt, Oliver interviews subjects whose stories are shown in flashback. Two jazz musicians (Stewart and Fonda) with a broken-down van attempt to rig a talent show so that the mayor's talentless son wins and they can use the money to fix their van. An aspiring actress (Dorothy Lamour) and an aging silent film star (Victor Moore) are fired because of a spoiled child star. And two magicians (Fred MacMurray and William Demarest) try and hold a runaway child for ransom. Each of the stories has a happy twist ending: the musicians are able to get their van fixed, the actors receive new contracts, and the magicians are able to leave their con games behind and return to the stage. When Oliver submits the story, he is fired. At home, he finds all of his furniture repossessed. His wife reveals that she knew about his real job and gambling debts all along, and that her suggestion for the article was simply a hint that she was pregnant. In the film's final happy twist, Oliver's boss informs him that he likes the story and that he is the new Roving Reporter.

The film is as hackneyed and flimsy as the theme of Oliver's column. The film's many behind-the-scenes troubles not only compromised what wound up on the screen, but they are far more interesting than what wound up on the screen. Perhaps because of its patchwork production, *On Our Merry Way* lacks any cohesive style or message; and unlike *If I Had a Million* (which had six directors), *On Our Merry Way* only had three (or four, depending on how one counts) and lacks the directorial diversity of its predecessor. Fenton (formerly an actor with parts in Howard Hawks' *The Road to Glory* [1926], Raoul Walsh's *What Price Glory?* [1926], William Wellman's *The Public Enemy* [1931], and John Ford's *Air Mail* [1932]) was responsible for the MacMurray and Lamour episodes; his direction is serviceable if unremarkable and nondescript.[2] The Stewart-Fonda episode was begun by John Huston, but according to Stewart biographer Marc Eliot, he "change[d] his mind at the last minute, citing a project about to go into production that he said he had somehow 'forgotten about.' ... In a panic, they turned to George Stevens, Jimmy's director in *Vivacious Lady*, who agreed to do it as long as he didn't get any on-screen credit."[3] Vidor directed the Meredith-Goddard frame narrative, which is certainly the most inspired bit of the film and evinces a distinguishable Vidor style. The metronomic opening sequence of Oliver and Martha waking up and making breakfast recalls the opening montage of *H.M. Pulham, Esq.* Durgnat and Simmon suggest that when Martha criticizes the Roving Reporter, "Vidor might well have been in sympathy with the wife's complaint that the public is tired of entertainment divorced from 'the way people really live,' but his functional style here never engages that idea."[4]

Vidor's most significant contribution to the film was a fourth episode starring Charles Laughton as the Rev. John B. Dunne, who suffers a crisis of faith. This segment was unfortunately cut from the film after its initial release. The sequence begins with the scatterbrained minister spilling water over himself while doing dishes. Late to his sermon, Dunne steps onto the pulpit but realizes he has forgotten his notes and does not know which hymns are supposed to be sung. His sermon meanders, and the congregation is uninterested (some fall asleep). That night, he writes a letter of resignation. On his way home during a storm, a small boy under a tree begs Dunne to see a dying man in a nearby house, but the boy insists that the minister should not say who sent him. As Dunne recites the story of David and Goliath, his faith in the gospel returns. After, he sees a picture of the boy in the house and learns that he had died many years before.

It is interesting that while faith was such a deeply personal topic for Vidor, he rarely approached it directly in his films. *The Sky Pilot* and *Hallelujah* are his only other films that feature ministers as protagonists, though Dunne differs greatly from the protagonists in those films. The minister in *The Sky Pilot* stands up to a hostile community, wins them over, and heals a crippled woman so she can walk again; the minister in *Hallelujah* gives in to temptation, cheats on his wife, and commits two murders. The crisis suffered by Dunne in *On Our Merry Way* is decidedly more internal and less melodramatic, and his loss of faith is as much directed towards himself as it is towards the gospel. Vidor would only directly touch on religious themes in two more films, the Biblical epic *Solomon and Sheba* (1959) and *Truth and Illusion: An Introduction to Metaphysics* (1964). Given more development, the Laughton episode could have become the basis of a significant film.

The segment, alas, turned out to be the most controversial part of the film. "According to the Bogeaus company, the Laughton episode, directed by King Vidor, is believed to be too serious for the general tenor of the picture," reported the *New York Times*, "and Bogeaus expects to use it later as the nucleus for another feature."[5] That plan involved selling the excerpt to David O. Selznick, but the deal never materialized.[6] *Variety* reported:

> The bank which financed the original film claims it owns a share of the leftovers. As a result, Bogeaus can't get the financing necessary to complete a picture out of the old scissored parts.... His idea now is to shoot a beginning and an end for the Laughton footage and issue it as a feature in itself. Security-First National Bank of Los Angeles, which financed *Miracle*, claims, however, that it has a first lien on anything left over from the shooting of the film, just as it does on the film itself. It has no objection, of course, but it wants to get out of the new pic whatever of its coin it may not bail out of the original. That's agreeable to Bogeaus except for one thing, no bank will advance him the money required for the additional shooting and editing while another bank has a first lien on the resulting picture.[7]

Cutting the Laughton episode was not the only change in the film, as it ultimately went through two other titles. "Effect of a picture's title on its b.o. [box office] draw was perhaps never more clearly demonstrated than in the case of Benedict Bogeaus' *On Our Merry Way*, formerly labeled *A Miracle Can Happen*. Pic … had three openings under the old tag," reported *Variety*. "It did fairish biz in Detroit, but flopped miserably in New York and Philly. Producer and distrib, as a result, decided to pull it while they figured out the reason…. It was decided that the title must be at fault, that the word 'miracle' was probably confusing people. They didn't know whether it was a religious picture, or what. As one UA exec declared: 'The word 'miracle' in a title is like building a fence around the theatre."[8] Another interim title was *Along Came Baby*.[9]

The name change was not enough to save the movie or to turn it into a hit. As *Variety* commented, even with the new title, "biz is still not extra-special."[10] As for Vidor, he only liked the part of the movie that was cut: "I felt the Laughton episode was most effective and thought it absolutely ridiculous that it wasn't included in the film."[11] As John Baxter noted, "Today Vidor chooses to ignore the film and pointedly omitted it from his filmographies."[12] No mention of it was made in *A Tree Is a Tree* or in his career-length discussion with Nancy Dowd and David Shepard. Vidor invested little of himself in *On Our Merry Way* before going on his own merry way to Warner Brothers, where he was hired to direct an adaptation of Ayn Rand's controversial novel *The Fountainhead*.

* * * *

The Fountainhead (1949)

The Fountainhead is one of Vidor's most recognized films, chiefly because it is based on the bestselling novel by Ayn Rand. Unfortunately, it is also one of Vidor's weaker films and this can be blamed chiefly on Rand herself, who insisted on not only writing the screenplay but on obtaining the studio's guarantee that not a line of her script would be altered without her express approval. Due to clunky dialogue and a plot that is too abstracted from the drama of everyday life, the movie lumbers along to its "soaring" final scene in which Dominique Francon (Patricia Neal) rapidly ascends the exterior of a skyscraper-under-construction in an open workman's elevator, the city stretched below, Max Steiner's "heroic" music swelling, with her new husband Howard Roark (Gary Cooper) waiting at the top of his newest architectural triumph. This final scene echoes the tracking shot up the exterior of the towering building in *The Crowd*.

After its release, *The Fountainhead* was roundly criticized by many reviewers for being "boring," "inept," "asinine," "loquacious," "bombastic," "pretentious," "wordy," "cold," and "unemotional." Looking back on it today and in the context of Vidor's entire body of work, one could say that Vidor did the very best that he

Twenty. *On Our Merry Way*, *The Fountainhead*, and *Beyond the Forest*

could, given the limitations of Rand's story and screenplay—plus the fact that he was forced by Warner Brothers to stay as faithful to the script as possible. The novel's repetitive use of speeches and conversations about the dangers of mass-minded collectivism and the value of individuality may work for many of her readers on the printed page (and the same goes for her other influential, bestselling novel *Atlas Shrugged*), but this repetition and didacticism do not translate well into cinema. In the film, Vidor's use of symbolic imagery often rises to heights to which the dialogue in Rand's screenplay can only aspire.

In fact, it is difficult to imagine any of the great Hollywood directors of the time (Ford, Hawks, Hitchcock, Curtiz, Welles, etc.) who could have done much better under the circumstances. The camera work, lighting, production design, and the performances of the lead actors are as good as they could be and help to compensate a bit for the flaws of Rand's plot and script. A few film critics and historians in recent years have expressed appreciation for the film, viewing it in hindsight as a noir-like expressionist melodrama that aptly captures the spirit of Rand's self-indulgent soap opera of ideas. And according to this perspective, Vidor was just the right choice for making the film, not so much because he (like Rand) had a philosophical bent toward the principle of individuality, but because several of his prior movies had utilized the form of amplified melodrama and symbolism that were already inherent in Rand's novel and screenplay. Such reviewers appreciate Vidor's artistic courage in having executed such a challenging project in such a uniquely stylized manner. In his 2011 review of the film, Emanuel Levy described it as a "highly enjoyable, juicy Freudian melodrama."[13] David Thomson summarized it as "one of the most beautiful and mysterious of films."[14] And David Kehr wrote the following review in 1985: "King Vidor turned Ayn Rand's preposterous 'philosophical' novel into one of his finest and most personal films (1949), mainly by pushing the phallic imagery so hard that it surpasses Rand's rightist diatribes and even camp ('I wish I'd never seen your skyscraper!'), entering some uncharted dimension where melodrama and metaphysics exist side by side. The images have a dynamism, a spatial tension, that comes partly from Frank Lloyd Wright (whose life Rand appropriated for her novel) and partly from Eisenstein, yet the pattern of their deployment is Vidor's own: the emotions rise and fall in broad, operatic movements that are unmistakably sexual and irresistibly involving."[15]

Once one accepts the parameters of the material, one can appreciate better Vidor's creativity in having made the best of it, once he had accepted the assignment. Vidor's penchant for playing off the tension between naturalism and expressionism worked (to varying degrees of success) for earlier films ranging from *The Crowd* and *The Stranger's Return* to *Stella Dallas* and *Duel in the Sun*. Those stories were rooted in the type of drama that could summon a certain level of emotional engagement on the part of the viewer. But Rand's story is already too unnatural, stilted, and overly intellectual. Her characters are not so much archetypal as hackneyed and full of platitudes. *The Fountainhead* leaves many viewers feeling cold because the

Patricia Neal (as Dominique Francon) and Gary Cooper (as her lover, the architect Howard Roark) in King Vidor's *The Fountainhead* (1949, Warner Brothers), an adaptation of Ayn Rand's controversial bestselling novel of the same title (first published in 1943). Rand also wrote the screenplay and obtained the studio's guarantee that nothing in her screenplay would be altered without her express approval (Warner Bros./Photofest).

symbolism that drives the dramatic situations becomes overly conspicuous, subsuming any possible emotional alignment with the characters.

With all of that said, there was no shortage of talent in support of Vidor in making *The Fountainhead*. The movie benefits as much as possible by its casting of Gary Cooper as architect Howard Roark, champion of anti-conformism, and Patricia Neal as his like-minded lover, the architecture critic Dominique Francon. Rand had wanted Gary Cooper to play Roark all along as he was an actor she had long admired. However, Vidor had initially desired a lead actor who was more dynamic: "I didn't think Gary Cooper was proper casting for it, where I felt it should be someone like Bogart or James Cagney."[16] At one point Alan Ladd was considered for the role. Cooper's wife had read Rand's recently published novel and persuaded her husband to do the same. After doing so, Cooper signed a contract with Warner Brothers under the condition that he be given the role of Roark.[17] Rand praised Cooper's performance, along with the entire movie, after the film's release, describing it as a faithful adaptation of her novel. Later, Rand criticized almost everything about the movie, including the acting and directing—everything except for her screenplay, of course. Vidor came to appreciate Cooper's performance, recognizing that it had the kind of quiet dignity and subtle expressive power that compensated a bit for some of the film's more bombastic elements. Indeed, given the melodramatic extremes that were generated by the screenplay, an actor such as Bogart or Cagney might have made the film far "campier" than it already is. Cooper's typically understated demeanor tends to temper ever so slightly the movie's otherwise exaggerated and didactic tone.

Rand also wanted Barbara Stanwyck for the role of Dominique and the actress had lobbied intensely for the role, even persuading Warner Brothers to purchase the rights to the novel so that she could star in the film version. She appealed to Rand herself, but in the end, Vidor reportedly thought that the star of his earlier *Stella Dallas* was too old for the role and the studio supported his decision without notifying Stanwyck, who consequently terminated her contract with Warner Brothers (it was Rand herself who phoned Stanwyck to break the news about the casting decision). Other actresses such as Bette Davis, Lauren Bacall, Gene Tierney, and Veronica Lake had been interested in or considered for the role of Dominique.[18] The studio nonetheless greenlighted Vidor's choice of Neal, who had only started acting in films. The year 1949, in fact, saw the release of the young actress's first four films: *John Loves Mary*, *The Fountainhead*, *The Hasty Heart*, and *It's a Great Feeling*. Neal only had a brief cameo as herself in the latter film, but interestingly, Vidor also had a cameo in that movie, also playing as himself.

The Fountainhead was produced by Henry Blanke who also produced Vidor's *Beyond the Forest* (both released the same year in 1949). Blanke was a German-born producer who had worked as an assistant to Ernst Lubitsch in Hollywood and who had many titles to his credit as an associate producer (including *The Maltese Falcon*, 1941). He later produced such notable films as *Of Human Bondage* (1946), *The Treasure of the Sierra Madre* (1948), and *The Life of Emile Zola* (1937). The highly dramatic music for *The Fountainhead* was composed by long-time Warner Brothers composer Max Steiner, who had created the scores for such classics as *King Kong* (1933), *Gone with the Wind* (1939), *Casablanca* (1942), *Now, Voyager* (1942), and *The Searchers* (1956). The editor of *The Fountainhead* was David Weisbart, who also worked on such other notable Warner Brothers films as *Mildred Pierce* (1945), *Night and Day* (1946), *Dark Passage* (1947), *Johnny Belinda* (1948), *The Glass Menagerie* (1950), and *A Streetcar Named Desire* (1951). He also produced Nicholas Ray's classic *Rebel Without a Cause* (1955).

The Fountainhead showcases some excellent camera work and masterful use of lighting, especially the chiaroscuro effects in the nighttime scenes. The film demonstrates Vidor's great talent for visual artistry when he is working with the right cinematographer. In this case, he joined forces with Robert Burks, who also supervised the photography for Vidor's *Beyond the Forest*. After working on these two consecutive films, Burks would go on to begin a long-term partnership with Alfred Hitchcock, beginning with *Strangers on a Train* (1951). They would also collaborate on *I Confess* (1953), *Dial M for Murder* (1954), *Rear Window* (1954), *To Catch a Thief* (1955), *The Trouble with Harry* (1955), *The Man Who Knew Too Much* (1956), *The*

Wrong Man (1956), *Vertigo* (1958), *North by Northwest* (1959), *The Birds* (1963) and *Marnie* (1964). Burks won the Oscar for Best Color Photography for *To Catch a Thief* after having been nominated for his cinematography on *Strangers on a Train* and *Rear Window*. It is evident from the two Vidor films as well as these Hitchcock classics that Burks shared Vidor's instinct for creating a certain visual tension between naturalism and expressionism. As noted by Christopher Beach in his book *A Hidden History of Film Style, Cinematographers, Directors, and the Collaborative Process*, in his work for Hitchcock on *The Wrong Man*, Burks had helped to push the director away from his initial desire to use a strictly documentary-like visual style for that movie. Burks created noir-like and expressionist visual techniques for evoking the moods and psychological states of that film's characters.[19] In most of the movies that he shot for Hitchcock, the cinematographer helped to establish a subtle and consistent middle ground between the realistic and the symbolic. Vidor had already demonstrated such an artistic tendency and so his work with Burks on *The Fountainhead* was an apt pairing that succeeded up to a point, given that the story was already imbued with archetypal characters and highly symbolic situations.

What is most illuminating about Vidor's work on *The Fountainhead* is two-fold. First, the film shows that Vidor was persistent and creative enough to execute and complete the production despite the challenges of dealing with Rand and her script as well as with other dramas taking place behind the scenes. Secondly, a comparison and contrast between Vidor's and Rand's philosophical interests may help to highlight some of the intellectual underpinnings of the director's overall worldview.

Vidor certainly had his challenges during the production. Rand not only managed to obtain the studio's assent in making sure that no alterations to her script would be made without her express approval, but she also reportedly visited the set frequently so that she could be assured that the studio lived up to its agreement.[20] A conflict between Vidor and Rand did arise when the director decided (quite wisely) that Howard Roark's courtroom speech toward the end of the film was simply too long and that certain parts of his "lecture" to the jury should be eliminated. Gary Cooper also felt that this concluding monologue (the longest in film history up to that time, according to Durgnat and Simmon) was too lengthy and awkward.[21] Initially, Vidor has asked Rand to "coach" Cooper through the speech but the actor's questions about the monologue only prompted Rand to revise and expand it for the purpose of clarification.[22] As the story goes, Rand appealed to the studio to stick to their agreement and Warner Brothers convinced Vidor to film the speech as it was written by Rand.[23] Vidor reported later in life, "I didn't like the ending at all, I didn't go for it and I tried to get away from it but they had a contract with the authoress that they couldn't change the ending ... [However] I felt there was enough interesting stuff to be playing with architecture, Frank Lloyd Wright, and so forth to interest me."[24] Vidor objected most of all to the idea that Roark would ultimately be acquitted of the crime of destroying (by means of dynamite) a building that he had initially designed but that had then been modified substantially by a committee of conformist architects (according to the devious plan of hyper-collectivist Ellsworth Toohey, played in caricatured fashion by Robert Douglas). An excerpt from Roark's self-defense gives a sense of the overall style of Rand's screenplay:

> The great creators—the thinkers, artists, scientists, and inventors—stood alone against the men of their time. Every new thought was opposed, every new invention was denounced. But the men of unborrowed vision went ahead. They fought, they paid, and they suffered, but they won. No creator was prompted by a desire to please his brothers, for they rejected the gift that he offered. His truth was his motive, his own truth, and his own work to achieve it in his own way.... My ideas are my property. They were taken from me by force, by breach of contract. No appeal was left to me.... The world is perishing from an orgy of self-sacrifice. I came ... in the name of every man of independence still left in the world. I came here to state my terms. I do not care to work or live on any others. My terms are a man's right to exist for his own sake.[25]

Rand had also requested that the studio hire the legendary architect Frank Lloyd Wright to design the special architectural elements of the film, especially given that Wright had been the chief inspiration for Rand's character of Roark. Rand appealed directly to Wright but the architect, in his typically bombastic manner, killed the possible deal outright when he demanded a fee of $250,00 along with final decision-making authority over the movie's script and casting (and thus "out–Randing" Rand, as it were). While the author then suggested other notable architects such as Louis Kahn and Richard Neutra, the job finally went to studio art director Edward Carrere who also worked on such films as *White Heat* (also 1949), *Sweet Smell of Success* (1957), *Elmer Gantry* (1960), and 1967's *Camelot* (for which he won an Oscar).

And so Vidor walked a fragile tightrope of sorts during his making of *The Fountainhead*, just as he had walked such a tightrope when dealing with David O. Selznick during the production of *Duel in the Sun*. In addition to coping with Rand as well as the studio chiefs, Vidor also knew that his two lead performers were having a romantic affair during the making of the movie. He took advantage of their chemistry together, of course, but he must have feared that any major change in their real-life emotional drama might possibly disrupt the production. Of course, Vidor was no stranger to on-set romances, especially given his own relationships with a few of his past leading actresses (including Eleanor Boardman and Miriam Hopkins). Because Cooper was married during his affair with Neal, the couple suffered some backlash from the public when their relationship became known around the time that the movie was released.

The special confluence of intellectual and artistic forces occasioned by the collaboration between Vidor and Rand is worth discussing further. Vidor, Rand, and Cooper had belonged to the controversial anti-communist, anti-fascist Motion Picture Alliance for the Preservation of American Ideals, formed in 1944. This group also included such other movie business luminaries as Ward Bond, Walter Brennan, Cecil B. DeMille, Walt Disney, Victor Fleming, John Ford, Clark Gable, Hedda Hopper, Leo McCarey, Ronald Reagan, Ginger Rogers, Barbara Stanwyck, and John Wayne. In 1947, Rand published a manifesto titled *Screen Guide for Americans* that elaborated on the principles of this conservative Hollywood group. Part of this pamphlet read: "The purpose of the Communists in Hollywood is *not* the production of political movies openly advocating Communism. Their purpose is *to corrupt our moral premises by corrupting non-political movies*—by introducing small, casual bits of propaganda into innocent stories—thus making people absorb the basic principles of Collectivism *by indirection and implication*. The principle of free speech requires that we do not use police force to forbid the Communists the expression of their ideas—which means that we do not pass laws forbidding them to speak. But the principle of free speech does not require that we furnish the Communists with the means to preach their ideas...."[26] It was this Alliance that, as Merrill Schleier writes in an essay on *The Fountainhead*, "invited the infamous House Un-American Activities Committee (HUAC) to Hollywood to help them rout out Communists from the film industry."[27] Rand was obviously quite active in this Alliance, but it is not apparent that Vidor was active at all, or that he remained active after first joining.

Gary Cooper (as architect and individualist Howard Roark) aggressively embraces Patricia Neal (as Dominique Francon) in King Vidor's *The Fountainhead* (1949, Warner Brothers), an adaptation of Ayn Rand's controversial bestselling novel of the same title (first published in 1943). Cooper and Neal carried on an off-screen affair during the production and Vidor captured their romantic chemistry in his film (Warner Bros./Photofest).

Vidor certainly looked upon his making of *The Fountainhead* as a fortuitous one because the story expressed, at least generally speaking, his life-long faith in the primary value and foundational nature of the human individual. However, this is not to say that we should equate the director's philosophical perspective with that of Rand. As he stated in the Vidor episode of Richard Schickel's television series *The Men Who Made the Movies*: "In *The Fountainhead*, the divinity (almost) of the artist is another theme which I've always been interested in: [the idea] that the whole universe springs from the individual and what he's conscious of. And that's the reality. What he is not conscious of does not exist. Strange that they selected me to direct it because this is a thing that I was always playing with and thinking about. Although I didn't entirely agree with Ayn Rand's approach to it."[28]

In terms of the intellectual premises of Rand's novel *The Fountainhead* and how it relates to Vidor's own worldview, we should say a few more words about Rand and her overall perspective. The movie was indeed a meeting of the minds of two very different individualists. Her life story is even more intriguing than the lives of the characters in her novels and her passion for the cinema was rooted in her youth. Ayn Rand is a name that she adopted as a young woman. She was born Alisa Zinov'yevna Rosenbaum in 1905 in Saint Petersburg, Russia to a middle-class Jewish family. Her father was a successful pharmacist and provided well for a time in caring for his wife, his oldest daughter Ayn, and her two younger sisters. But Rand grew up in Russia at a very turbulent time. She witnessed the "bloodless" revolution of 1917 against the Tsar, led by Alexander Kerensky, whom Ayn much admired. Soon thereafter occurred the Bolshevik Revolution in which Vladimir Lenin and the Bolsheviks took power and established Communism as the dominant political philosophy. Lenin and the Bolsheviks prized the value of the state over that of the individual and they even went so far as to confiscate private property and private businesses in the name of the state and the common good. Rand's father lost his business in this way, and the family felt forced to flee to the Crimea (on the northern coast of the Black Sea) to escape the oppressive Bolshevik forces. Rand went to high school in the Crimea but then returned to Saint Petersburg when she was sixteen. She attended and graduated from a technical university there and mainly studied philosophy and history. Her favorite philosopher was the ancient Greek philosopher Aristotle and she was also influenced by the German thinker Friedrich Nietzsche, though she later came to disagree with some of his ideas about individuality (she primarily regarded him as an "irrationalist"). Her favorite writers were the Russian novelist Fyodor Dostoevsky and the French novelist Victor Hugo. She then fell in love with the cinema and studied screenwriting for a short time.[29]

It is not surprising that Rand, who had prized the principle of individual freedom since a very young age and who had been appalled by the Bolshevik take-over, desired strongly to leave Russia and flee to America, a country that she had always dreamt about because it was founded on the values and principles that she treasured. And so she acquired a visa in 1925 for the purpose of a six-month trip to the United

States to visit relatives in Chicago. Once arriving in the United States, Rand decided to stay, not surprisingly. Rand later said that when she arrived by ship in New York City, she fell in love with the city's majestic skyline of modern skyscrapers, testaments in her mind to the greatness of American capitalism and to what humans could achieve if they are free to use their reason in the ways they wish. One thinks here of Johnny Sims' arrival in New York City by ship in *The Crowd*. Certainly Vidor shared Rand's love for America and for American freedom and democracy.

Rand then traveled to Chicago to visit her relatives, told them of her dream of becoming a Hollywood screenwriter, and set off for Hollywood with a bit of borrowed money in her pocket. Her great self-confidence, independence, and determination are personality traits that the heroic protagonists of her novels tend to share. In a great stroke of luck, upon arriving in Hollywood, she was spotted by the legendary film director Cecil B. DeMille, whose movies she had seen in Russia. According to Rand, DeMille drove through the studio gates on his way to make a film when he saw poor Ayn waiting around, as she had not been allowed to enter. DeMille took an immediate liking to this young Russian emigrant whose dream was to become a screenwriter, and he drove her onto the studio grounds to the set of the movie he was making (*The King of Kings*, 1927) so that she could witness movie-making first hand. She soon began working as an extra in movies and as an editor of screenplays. She quickly improved her English and she became an American citizen in 1931. Rand soon wrote a fairly successful play that was produced on the Hollywood stage in 1934 and that opened on Broadway in New York a year later. It was titled *Night of January 16th* and used a creative device not previously seen in a stage production. The play focused on a court trial and each night when the play was performed, audience members were randomly selected to serve as the on-stage jury and to arrive at their own verdict. Their verdict would determine which of two different final scenes would be performed. Paramount Pictures made a movie version of the play in 1941, starring a young Robert Preston and with a screenplay co-written by Delmer Daves. Rand's first novel, titled *We the Living*, was published in 1936. It is the story about an independent woman's life in Communist Russia and it was soon made into a two-part Italian film (released in 1942) starring Alida Valli and Rossano Brazzi.

Rand then set down to work on *The Fountainhead*, a massive and highly detailed novel that took her seven years to write. It was published in 1943. It is the story of an idealistic, independent-minded architect named Howard Roark who is forced to leave architecture school when he refuses to design buildings in the traditional Neoclassical and Beaux-Arts styles that the teachers demanded of their students. He goes to work at a quarry, where stone is mined from the earth for use in construction projects. He would rather work here than to study at a school where he would be required to surrender his personal goal of creating unique, revolutionary architecture. He eventually goes to work for an older architect who had once shown evidence of designing the type of creative, anti-traditional architecture to which Roark is dedicated. He learns enough from this architect to strike out on his own, and over time Roark's architecture gains great praise from some and much criticism and condemnation from others.

One man who detests Roark and his architecture is the rather far-fetched character of Ellsworth Toohey, a popular newspaper columnist who is a socialist and who resents anyone who tries to rise above the common standards of mainstream society. Toohey believes in collectivism, in putting the values and interests of society above those of the individual. He resents those, like Roark, who are not afraid to use their artistic talent and freedom to create works that are completely new and individualistic. At one point in the novel, Toohey persuades a man he knows to hire Roark to design a temple in the city; but before the temple is constructed, Toohey interferes and has other, more traditionally minded architects alter Roark's design and make the building far less bold and daring than Roark had envisioned. Roark is infuriated that the building has not been constructed as he designed it, and he destroys the temple using dynamite, something he knows how to use from his days working in the stone quarry. This act of vandalism is featured in the film and leads to the famous courtroom scene and self-defense discussed above.

Roark is the ideal man, according to Rand's philosophy. He is a creative and heroic individual who puts himself and his own artistic vision first, refusing to conform to the standards and expectations of society and tradition. And as in other novels by Rand, he is surrounded by other characters who are either inspired by his independence, pride, and self-confidence or who resent this type of person for not conforming to the standards of mainstream society. Rand refers to these mediocre and resentful characters as "second-handers," those who seek to undermine the individualists while also (rather hypocritically) benefiting from the results of their productivity.[30]

Rand tells us that the "ultimate value" for human beings should be an individual's own existence or life. While humans are born with the potential to think and to use their reason or intelligence, they are also born as creatures that must continually *choose* to use this power of rationality. Humans can easily decide to give up on the job of reasoning, to un-focus our minds in a lazy fashion and act as little more than the other animals: concerning ourselves merely with the pleasures and pains and immediate sensations of life and not rising above that level in order to exercise our intelligence. Focusing our mind and using our rationality for productive work that will improve our lives is what *virtue* is all about, according to Rand. Rand tells us that the one "fundamental right" of a human being, the right upon which all others are based, is a human individual's right to their own life, which entails the freedom to preserve and to improve their own life. The way in which we realize or implement that fundamental right to life is through our right to property. Democratic laissez-faire capitalism is the ideal political condition for the person who chooses continually to use their reason to live a more stable and productive life. That is because such a political-economic system provides and protects our individual rights and liberties. Without individual freedom, according to Rand, we would sacrifice our lives to the whims or arbitrary choices of others, especially those who might oppress and exploit us, even if they claim to do so "in the name of God and religion" or "for the good of society." This is the problem with both altruism and collectivism, which are really flip sides of the same coin, according to Rand: altruism asks us to sacrifice our lives for others, including strangers, and collectivism asks us to sacrifice our lives for the group or society, which really amounts to the same thing. Only a political-economic system that protects individual rights and liberties will allow for the type of personal freedom needed to make necessary choices in how to best preserve and improve one's own life. Even love and friendship should be viewed as selfish, but in a very positive sense, according to Rand. A relationship in which another person offers me nothing at all in terms of my personal happiness is not genuine love or friendship, according to Rand. It would be a sacrifice of my time and energy, and an irrational one at that.

Vidor and Rand shared a definite emphasis on the grounding principles of individuality and individual freedom in the face of conformism and mass-mindedness. Vidor was certainly no fan of Communism or fascism, to say the least. And both Rand and Vidor practiced this philosophy in their own lives in somewhat similar ways. Rand dared at times to criticize the mainstream conservative "establishment" that often embraced her. She became an outspoken critic of the ways in which she thought that the United States veered increasingly toward the type of socialism and collectivism that she had witnessed as a girl in Bolshevik Russia. She even appeared many times in televised interviews with the likes of Mike Wallace and Phil Donahue, firmly voicing opinions that stirred waves of controversy. Vidor, in a similar manner, was bold enough to break out of the conventional Hollywood "box" with such radically different films as *The Crowd*, *Our Daily Bread*, and *An American Romance*. Even his first big hit, *The Big Parade*, while making a gargantuan profit for MGM, was certainly not the typical movie of its time: far longer, far more multifaceted (war, romance, comedy, family drama), and far more stylistically innovative than many other silent films. For the sake of making *Our Daily Bread*, as we have seen, he sold off almost everything he owned to finance the movie himself. In this sense, Vidor was really a precursor of the later independent film movement in America. In addition, even while he worked within the Hollywood system on studio assignments, Vidor managed to inject many of his films with his individual style. And finally, like Rand, Vidor did not shy away from sharing his views on his films, his art form, or his personal philosophy with the public at large, whether it was in countless interviews (in print and on film), in his 1953 autobiography, in his 1972 book *King Vidor on Film Making*, or in his documentaries *Truth and Illusion* (1964) and *Metaphor* (1980).

On the other hand, Rand and Vidor diverged sharply when it came to their views on religion. Rand was an avowed atheist, viewing religion as not only delusional but as a clear example of mass-minded collectivism. Vidor was a devout monist whose spiritual philosophy was rooted in Christian Science. For Vidor, individuality and spirituality go hand in hand and God should be viewed as the Supreme Individual through which all other forms of individuality originate. His prioritizing of the individual as the primary source of "reality" depends very much upon the equation of individuality and divinity. (See Chapter Twenty-Three for a more detailed view of Vidor's spiritual philosophy in relation to his later documentary *Truth and Illusion*.) For Rand, the individual is primary because there is no God to ground our subjective freedom and because Nature is a deterministic force that would otherwise rob us of the very freedom that makes us truly human. According to her, humans are innately free simply because we are born with the capacity for rationality and self-consciousness.

Politically, Rand opposed the very "New Deal" politics of Franklin Delano Roosevelt that Vidor had supported in the 1930s. His *Our Daily Bread*, for example, is not a defense of communism as a preferred economic and political system, but rather an example of what a community can do temporarily when it needs to survive in a desperate situation and when it has a shared goal of mutual sustenance. (See Chapter Fourteen for a discussion of *Our Daily Bread*.) The co-operative in *Our Daily Bread* echoes the type of collective effort that was championed by FDR's national policies as a way out of the Great Depression. Vidor was certainly no opponent of those successful programs such as Social Security and Medicare that were created under FDR and that continued because they provided a basic "safety net" with which the United States might survive future economic emergencies. Rand, however, condemned these basic policies. A government that takes from one group of people, against their voluntary consent, to give to others, is little more than a "criminal," "parasite," and "looter," according to Rand.

While Vidor may have been a Republican for a good part of his adult life, he was undoubtedly a conservative who, while prioritizing personal liberty, did not view human life as operating in a vacuum or on some ideal level playing field. Unlike Rand, Vidor clearly did not view the shared goal of a common good to be antithetical to individuality or individual freedom. His classic *The Crowd* emphasizes the plight of the individual who struggles to obtain a modicum of financial security and happiness in the face of "the mob" and "the system" and yet who comes to realize that his happiness is dependent on the happiness of others, starting with his family. The ending scene of *The Crowd* might show Johnny Sims and his family as being awash in a sea of faces in a crowded theater, but they are happy and laughing—together. Vidor's film *Our Daily Bread* is a testament to his faith in the importance of the common good in the service of sustaining the individual when life and livelihood are threatened. And his film *An American Romance* has something to say about the value of labor unions in a capitalist system. Rand, on the other hand, viewed the power of unions as another instance of anti-capitalist collectivism. Needless to say, all three of the above-mentioned films were Vidor's three most personal projects and over which he had the most creative control, compared with his other movies.

At the end of the day, Rand viewed individuals in "atomic" fashion, as being radically separate, independent, self-reliant, and (ideally) self-sufficient. For her, the singularity and independence of the individual is a feature of objective reality. Vidor had a much more "organic," holistic, and idealistic perspective, according to which individuals are reflections of a greater spiritual reality, one in which morality is determined not merely by a person's own rational self-interest but by the Universal Good itself. This may make for an indefinable moral standard, one that Rand would have rejected as "mystical" and therefore irrational, based more on emotion than reason. But for this philosophical filmmaker who always looked back to his roots as a Christian Scientist, there is always a dimension of human life that transcends the boundaries of human ethics—that of the spiritual and the divine—and it is our recognition of such an dimension, one that goes beyond the limits of mere rationality, that makes us fully human and that gives meaning and purpose to the other areas of our lives. (Again, see Chapter Twenty-Three for more on Vidor's spiritual philosophy in connection with his later documentary *Truth and Illusion*.)

* * * *

Beyond the Forest (1949)

The repression of desire and its subsequent explosion, sometimes in perverse or violent ways, had long been a theme in Vidor's work dating back to his silent films such as *Wild Oranges* and *His Hour*. This theme certainly became explicit in his recent films *Duel in the Sun* and *The Fountainhead*. In the early sound era, Vidor had continued to explore sexuality: sex and murder are deeply intertwined in both *Hallelujah* and *Street Scene*; inter-racial romance and sexual taboos were pushed to the boundaries of the Production Code in *Bird of Paradise*; and extra-marital affairs became central topics in *Cynara*, *The Wedding Night*, and *H.M. Pulham, Esq*. *Duel in the Sun* marked a new era in explicit psychosexual themes for Vidor, one that set the stage for the eroticism in *The Fountainhead* and in his subsequent trilogy of "Americana noir": *Beyond the Forest* (1949), *Lightning Strikes Twice* (1949), and *Ruby Gentry* (1952). The rustic, small town communities that Vidor so admired and romanticized in his earlier films now become sites of sexual, gender, and class oppression. The women at the center of these dramas transgress social boundaries to achieve their goals. Unlike many examples of film noir from this period, ones that focus on male figures of authority and power (private detectives, police officers, reporters, or criminals), Vidor reverses the gendered narrative of film noir and privileges the femme fatale as the protagonist. Another unifying and distinguishing trait of these movies is the depiction of the domestic housewife, so often the moral counterpoint to the femme fatale or dangerous woman. In contrast, *Beyond the Forest* presents us with Rosa Moline (Bette Davis), the most fascinating of all film noir housewives in that she is both heroic and destructive, depending on the viewer's perspective and the character's specific situation.

Beyond the Forest was Vidor's second film for Warner Brothers, following *The Fountainhead*. The story comes from a 1948 novel of the same title by Stuart Engstrand, which *Kirkus* called "a not too well written book that has trashy undertones and overtones."[31] The script was adapted by Lenore Coffee, the Academy Award–nominated co-writer of *Four Daughters* (1938). She was a very prolific screenwriter and script doctor whose career began with *The Better Wife* (1919), written for Clara Kimball Young, and whose last feature was *Cash McCall* (1960) with Natalie Wood and James Garner.[32]

"This is the story of evil," reads the film's scrolling prologue. "Evil is headstrong—is puffed up. For our soul's sake, it is salutary for us to view it in all its ugly nakedness once in a while. Thus may we know how those who deliver themselves over to it end up like the Scorpion, in a mad frenzy stinging themselves to eternal death." Before we meet Rosa, a narrator introduces us to Loyalton, Wisconsin, over shots of the deserted town: empty streets, black smoke pouring out of the mill's incinerator, a horse tied up outside of the blacksmith's shop. These are images one would typically associate with Vidor: a montage of American symbols embracing community, nature, and industry. The camera's movement—via ground-level tracks and overhead cranes—move from the outskirts to the inside of town, suggesting an attraction, a suction, that pulls one deeper into the heart of the town, cinematically capturing the sense of entrapment felt by Rosa Moline. The montage ends in the courthouse, where the town has gathered to see Rosa on trial for murder. We meet the jurors and the townspeople before we even see Rosa, who pops up from out of the frame with her jet-black hair. She responds to an off-screen accusation, "Why should I kill him? Someone tell me that. Why should I want to? It was an accident." The delayed introduction to Rosa playfully heightens the shock of seeing Bette Davis with atypical raven's hair, and it is the first of many examples of how the film tantalizes the audience, putting Rosa on display for her immorality but also deriving great pleasure from the spectacle. It is a contradiction that the film never fully reconciles and that also enraged the Production Code Office—and which the censors could not fully sanitize.

From here the film flashes back to a fishing trip in the country with Rosa and her husband, the town doctor Louis Moline (Joseph Cotten), and the lodge caretaker Moose Lawson (Minor Watson). Louis is called back to the city to deliver a baby; meanwhile, Rosa feigns a twisted ankle so she can stay behind. After getting Moose drunk, she sneaks away to the main lodge for a rendezvous with Chicago playboy Neil Latimer (David Brian). The next morning, as the two play a game of pool, Neil laughs when Rosa says to him, "I want you to marry me." She slaps him and the two embrace in a passionate kiss. Such a combination of lust and aggression echoes the tension between Pearl and Lewt in *Duel in the Sun* and between Dominique and Roark in *The Fountainhead*. It also serves as a precursor to the relationship between Boake and the titular character in *Ruby Gentry*.

Back in Loyalton, Rosa becomes jealous by the arrival of Moose's daughter,

Carol (Ruth Roman), mistakenly assuming that she is involved with Neil. Fed up, Rosa demands that her husband collect outstanding debts from his patients; she takes the money and heads to Chicago to see Neil. She arrives at his office but is unable to make an appointment to see him. Later, he arranges to pick her up at her hotel. In the car, he announces he is engaged to another woman. Returning to her husband Louis, she announces that she is pregnant. At Moose's birthday party, Neil arrives and tells Rosa that he has changed his mind and wishes to marry her. The two plan to run off to Mexico and Moose threatens to tell Neil that she is pregnant. On a hunting trip the following morning, Rosa shoots Moose, which ties back to the trial at the start of the movie.

After the jury rules that the killing was an accident, Rosa suffers a crisis of conscience and confesses to Louis, who says, "All I care about is my baby and you're going to go through with it." Rosa dresses in jeans, poses as her Native American maid Jenny (Dona Drake), and sneaks on a bus to go and get an abortion. Louis sees her getting on the bus and follows the bus route to find her. On the ride back, Rosa throws herself down a hillside to induce an abortion. Back in Loyalton, Rosa does not recover from her injuries. Rising from her deathbed, she crawls out of the house towards the railroad, hoping she can leave town. But Rosa dies before she reaches the locomotive.

Ranking among the most melodramatic of Vidor's films, it is also among his most complex—and polarizing. The story revisits one of Vidor's most frequent dramatic conflicts—the affair—but, for the first time, approaches it from the perspective of a woman. A counterpoint to *Cynara*, *The Wedding Night*, and *H.M. Pulham, Esq.*, in which the husband cheats on his wife and it is the woman who must learn to be more understanding of the man, in *Beyond the Forest* it is the wife who cheats and the husband who is not sympathetic to her needs and desires. The film is subversively sympathetic to Rosa, at once both perversely attracted to her infidelity and wickedness but also invested in her struggle and challenges. There is no moral counterweight to Rosa: Ruth, who might have been a symbol of virtue, is barely present in the film, and both Louis and Neil are portrayed as controlling and selfish. Rosa is the closest thing to a "hero" in the film.

Reviewers at the time were mostly quick to comment on Rosa's negative characteristics. However, Philip K. Scheuer in the *Los Angeles Times* made an apt comparison between Rosa and Cody Jarrett (James Cagney) in *White Heat* because she will "stop at nothing to gain her ends."[33] While Scheuer never calls her a hero, the comparison to the male gangster emphasizes *Beyond the Forest*'s upheaval of gender binaries in Hollywood at the time. Since the rise of the gangster film in the early 1930s with films like *Little Caesar* and *The Public Enemy* (both 1931), men who attempted to climb the social ladder through nefarious means were admired (even if they received their comeuppance at the hands of the law). Rosa's motivations were not so different from, and arguably more sympathetic than, those of male gangsters. She wanted to rise in social class, she did not want to be tied to a small town,

TWENTY. *On Our Merry Way*, *The Fountainhead*, and *Beyond the Forest*   245

Bette Davis as the rebellious Rosa Moline in King Vidor's *Beyond the Forest* (1949, Warner Brothers). This is one of Vidor's typically expressionistic shots where Rosa's erotic passion is symbolized by an erupting factory furnace in the background. The screenplay by Lenore Coffee is based on the 1948 novel of the same title by Stuart Engstrand. The film also stars Joseph Cotten as Rosa's husband, Dr. Lewis Moline (Warner Bros./Photofest).

and she did not want to be forced into motherhood (particularly with a husband she did not like).

Nearly half a century later, film scholar Jeannine Basinger revisited gender-bending in the gangster genre and reconfigured Rosa Moline as both an American and feminist icon:

> From a woman's point of view I would say that females in the audience understand exactly why Rosa Moline is "this way." No construction of an explanation is necessary other than her being a female character played by a woman. Rosa Moline didn't want to make her husband's nice dinner. She didn't want to have her husband's little child. She didn't want to be nothing or nobody. She was Rosa Moline, and she insisted that meant something. She fought on to the end, gallant but misguided, unwilling to accept repression and restriction. She's like Michael Corleone or Frankenstein's monster or Cody Jarrett. She may kill. She may look ugly. She may be something for the birds. But she never quits. Rosa Moline is an American hero.[34]

There is also an unspoken racial component in Rosa's character. Though the film does not explicitly say so, Rosa's first name and her dark hair can be read as code for Hispanic, which would make her one of two non-white people in the film, the other being Rosa's Native American maid, Jenny—ironically played by Dona Drake, a partly African American actress who passed as Hispanic for her career as a musician/actress.[35] Rosa's "difference" from others in town is also hinted at in a conversation with her husband: "I don't want people to like me. Nothing pleases me more than when they don't like me. It means I don't belong." Seen in this light, *Beyond the Forest* offers an even more pointed critique of American society, making Rosa's fight for independence all the more symbolic.

Hovering in the background through *Beyond the Forest* is the presence of the mill's incinerator and the railroad train. Unlike in Vidor's other films that glorify such American symbols (such as *An American Romance*), there is something foreboding and desolate about them in *Beyond the Forest*. The incinerator is visible from Rosa's bedroom window and her porch, fire raging like a volcano, black smoke obscuring the clouds and casting an infernal gloom over the horizon. And the train—an image of the west's conquest, and a metaphor for American class and geographic mobility—here is seen as a false prophet. The opening narrator speaks of how the train beckoned Rosa to Chicago; in the end, she dies reaching out for it, convinced it would still fulfill all of her wishes.

The Production Code office was not pleased with *Beyond the Forest*'s transgressions. Jack Vizzard, an administrator of the Code, recalled that "[w]e first had the editor cut the shots that implied that the woman was seeking an abortion. They replaced the shot of the doctor's office with a shot of the door in a legal office, to show that she was seeking a divorce, not an abortion. Then we made them reshoot a closeup of Bette Davis where she says 'I hope I die.' We made them add: 'And burn.' So that the character admits that she's doing wrong and will pay for it." The opening, with its overt condemnation of Rosa Moline, was also dictated by the Production Code and not created by screenwriter Lenore Coffee. Vizzard: "Finally we got a small commercial outfit to shoot a preface—which as I recall, Geoff Shurlock wrote. This was to tell them that the woman was immoral, since there was no voice for morality in the film as it stood."[36]

If *Beyond the Forest* is famous for anything today, it is for Rosa's assessment of her home in Loyalton—"What a dump!"—a line immortalized in Edward Albee's play *Who's Afraid of Virginia Woolf?* and spoken by Elizabeth Taylor in the 1966 film. The film is also notorious for the role it played in Bette Davis's career. "Bette Davis didn't want to do *Beyond the Forest*," reported gossip columnist Hedda Hopper, "but was talked into it against her will—and that's a strong will to talk against. She realizes now she should have kept refusing. Bette Davis has been the fall guy for *Beyond the Forest*."[37] Davis was so unimpressed with the film that she made it her last for the studio that she had called home since 1932's *The Man Who Played God*. Davis biographer Charlotte Chandler wrote, "*Beyond the Forest* was Bette's last film for Warner Brothers. It wasn't supposed to be that way. She still had ten years left on her contract. This film, however, had made up her mind. If *Beyond the Forest* was the kind of movie the studio had in mind for her during the next decade, then she had no future with Warner Brothers and she asked to be let out of her contract."[38]

Variety liked the film: "King Vidor seldom falters in his direction of the Lenore Coffee script.... The shades of the Rosa character, and of the others, are brought to the fore by his handling with the proper amount of emphasis."[39] Others were not so kind. Richard L. Coe commented in the *Washington Post*, "Unfortunately, her writer, Leonore Coffee, and her director, King Vidor, have clearly gone out of their minds and the result is a caricature of every wicked role Bette's ever played.... 'Rosa Moline' is a hot lass indeed, but you never once believe she exists."[40] Jose Yglesias in the *Daily Worker* remarked, "Never gets out of the psychiatric woods.... [Bette Davis] has been allowed to go berserk."[41] And in the *New York Times*, Bosley Crowther was particularly nasty: "[Davis] is so monstrous—so ghoulishly picturesque—that her representation often slips off into laughable caricature. We cannot imagine that King Vidor, her director, desired this last to be, but we strongly suspect that he was working to make her look just as vicious as he could. For not only has he accepted a thoroughly denigrating script, but he has harshened and uglified Miss Davis so that she's as repulsive as a witch in a cartoon."[42]

Beyond the Forest stands as one of the most misunderstood and underappreciated of Vidor's films. Unabashedly excessive in its melodrama and symbolism, it is also distinctive for being arguably Vidor's most biting commentary on America and for featuring arguably the most sympathetic, heroic, and American female protagonist of any of his films. Visually and dramatically, it is one of Vidor's most expressionistic works. Film scholar Richard Schickel has even suggested that Rosa Moline (not unlike such other Vidor characters as Howard Roark and Ruby Gentry) may well symbolize the director's own individualistic and rebellious impulses in the face of the conventions and constraints of the Hollywood studio system: "Rosa Moline and Ruby Gentry, for instance, are women of pride, energy and intelligence, trapped by dismal circumstances (and their own distaste for subtle maneuver) and desperate to escape them. Perhaps King felt the same way about a Hollywood that obliged him to suppress his natural imagistic gifts in favor of the mere professionalism that came awkwardly to him."[43]

Twenty-One

1951–1955

Lightning Strikes Twice, Japanese War Bride, Ruby Gentry, and *Man Without a Star*

Lightning Strikes Twice (1951)

A contemporary-set "Gothic" western noir, stylized with the visual flairs of a horror film, *Lightning Strikes Twice* is among the more personal of Vidor's later works. Based on the novel *A Man Without Friends* by Margaret Echard, the film reunites Vidor with screenwriter Lenore J. Coffee, who previously adapted *Beyond the Forest*. Vidor uses the soap operatic narrative to address thematic, stylistic, and philosophical issues that had preoccupied him since his first films. The film represents a confrontation between two contrasting tendencies in Vidor's cinema: the sacred and the profane.

The story begins with Richard "Trev" Trevelyan (Richard Todd) in prison for allegedly murdering his wife, Lorraine. After the jury is split on their verdict, the D.A. releases him. Meanwhile, theatrical actress Shelley Carnes (Ruth Roman) takes a respite from a touring production of *Othello* and travels for a rest at the Tumble Moon Ranch in Texas. Stopping at a hotel along the way, Shelley unknowingly steps into the middle of a murder mystery. Hotel owner Myra Nolan (Kathryn Givney) and her husband were Trev's guardians after his own parents died. However, they have been unable to reach him since the trial. Myra loans Shelley her car with instructions to leave it at the Tumble Moon, where she suspects Trev is staying. Waylaid by a storm, Shelley takes refuge at a different nearby ranch where, coincidentally, Trev is hiding. Arriving at the Tumble Moon the next day, Shelley discovers that it has been closed for the season. The brother and sister who run it, Liza (Mercedes McCambridge) and String (Darryl Hickman), take a liking to Shelley and allow her to stay. Shelley soon learns that Liza has long been in love with Trev and was the juror who split the vote that saved him from the gallows. Convinced he is innocent, Shelley tracks down Trev, who refuses her help. Rejected, Shelley intends to leave town when she meets flirtatious neighbor Harvey Turner (Zachary Scott). After a party, Turner drives Shelley to a secret destination where Trev is waiting for her. Trev proposes and the two are married. On their wedding night, Liza reveals

Twenty-One. *Lightning Strikes, Japanese War, Ruby Gentry, Man Without* 249

that she was at Trev's place on the night of the murder but rushes off before revealing what happened. After Trev tries to lock his wife in the bedroom, Shelley drives off to find Liza. Liza admits that she murdered Trev's wife out of jealousy. As Trev arrives at Liza's, she and String speed off into the night but are killed when Liza is blinded by headlights and goes off the road.

Among the most striking elements of *Lightning Strikes Twice* is not the central, heterosexual romance between Shelley and Trev, but the unspoken—and clearly evident—attraction between Shelley and Liza. From the moment that Shelley appears at the back door of the Tumble Moon, Liza's eyes are glued to Shelley. Later, as they walk down Main Street together, they appear almost like husband and wife, with Liza strutting in dungarees while Shelley carries a bag of groceries. Their conversation is noticeably charged with innuendo. Film historian Charles Silver states that "Vidor is at his best in suggesting unstated and understated perversities, especially through the performances of Miss McCambridge and Miss Givney."[1] In *Uninvited: Classical Hollywood Cinema and Lesbian Representability*, Patricia White describes how Shelley and Liza "share several moments of odd affect and butch-femme fashion

Mercedes McCambridge (as Liza McStringer) and Darryl Hickman (as her younger brother "String") in King Vidor's film noir melodrama *Lightning Strikes Twice* (1951, Warner Brothers). The screenplay by Lenore Coffee is based on the 1940 novel *A Man Without Friends* by Margaret Echard. The movie also stars Ruth Roman and Richard Todd (Warner Bros./Photofest).

coordination." White also takes note of how "Vidor leaves an auteurist mark with this transgressive woman in pants, akin to the heroines of *Duel in the Sun*, *Beyond the Forest*, and *Ruby Gentry*."[2]

While the narrative bears resemblance to *Duel in the Sun*, stylistically *Lightning Strikes Twice* is closer to *Beyond the Forest* and *Ruby Gentry*, rural morality plays dressed up as "Gothic" melodramas whose dark themes are manifested through the expressionistic style of film noir. A foreboding tone permeates *Lightning Strikes Twice*, beginning with its title sequence: credits superimposed against a prison lit by two titular lightning bolts. The image of the prison itself becomes a metaphor for much of the drama, with the ranches acting as prisons for the characters. Despite taking place in the desert, *Lightning Strikes Twice* is arguably Vidor's most claustrophobic work: Shelley is first introduced on a crowded bus; on her first night in the hotel, she awakens to discover that Myra has let herself in with a key; later, on her wedding night, Trev tries to lock Shelley in the bedroom; and all of the characters seem bound to their ranches, unable to escape the physical limits or the psychic binds that tie them to the land. To reinforce the feeling of imprisonment, Vidor frequently foregrounds different manifestations of jail bars (first introduced in the opening dramatic scene of Trev in jail) such as Venetian blinds, iron window grills, and slatted bannisters.

In spite of its plot, *Lightning Strikes Twice* is less interested in whodunnit mystery than in the moral themes of guilt, innocence, and sin. "There is much that is good in Trev, but there is also much that is violent and undisciplined," Father Paul (Rhys Williams) tells Shelley. "My child, some people like to believe there is no such thing as inherent evil, that man is naturally good, but every man has dark moments, and in the conquest of those dark moments lies his salvation." This speech harkens back not only to *Cynara* and *The Crowd*, but even to the morality shorts with which Vidor began his career. "Then you believe that souls are lost?" Shelley says to the priest. Father Paul's reply could be the epithet to Vidor's entire body of work: "I also believe that souls are saved."

* * * *

Japanese War Bride (1952)

Japanese War Bride is an anomaly in Vidor's later career, which was largely filled with epics and psycho-sexual melodramas. In contrast with those explosive works, *Japanese War Bride* is an intimate, modest, humanistic drama that more closely resembles Vidor's early silent work. Producer Joseph Bernhard at Eagle Lion Classics originally announced the film in June 1950 under the title *East Is East* with Ella Raines and John Dall in the leads.[3] A year and a half later, the film was still under development, but by November 1951 the title had been changed to *Japanese War Bride*; Vidor had been hired as director; Dall was replaced by Don Taylor;

Twenty-One. *Lightning Strikes, Japanese War, Ruby Gentry, Man Without*

Shirley Yamaguchi had been attached as the titular character; and Bernhard was now releasing the film through Bernhard Productions with distribution from Fox.[4] This would be the American debut of Yamaguchi, who began as a child actress in Japan in 1930, and she had recently been featured in leading roles in Akira Kurosawa's *Scandal* (1950), as well as two early features by Kon Ichikawa, *Human Patterns* (1949) and *Passion Without End* (1949). Later, she would star in Samuel Fuller's *House of Bamboo* (1955) alongside Robert Ryan and Robert Stack. Before production began, Raines was dropped from the cast and Marie Windsor was added.

Scripted by Catherine Turney and based on a story by Anson Bond, the film begins on the Korean battlefield, where Captain Jim Sterling (Taylor) is wounded. In a Japanese hospital, he is cared for by nurse Tae Shimizu (Yamaguchi). After Jim proposes to Tae, the couple encounter their first resistance: Tae's father is, at first, reluctant to accept their decision and tries to scare off Jim through a fictional ritual involving a monkey sacrifice. But eventually he consents. In America, Jim and Tae move in with Jim's family in Salinas, California. Some of Jim's family, too, are uncomfortable with the couple, such as Jim's mother Harriet (Louise Lorimer) and Jim's sister-in-law Fran (Windsor). Fran was once romantically involved with Jim before he went to war and she married his brother, Art (Cameron Mitchell). Now that Jim is back, her feelings for him have returned, too.

Tensions continue to rise when a longtime family friend, Mrs. Shafer (Kathleen Mulqueen), breaks off her ties to the Sterlings because her son was killed in Bataan. Soon thereafter, Tae goes mushroom picking with Jim's younger brother, Ted (Orley Lindgren), and their Japanese-American neighbor, Shiro Hasagawa (Lane Nakano). Born in America, Shiro was in Japan on business when the war broke out and was imprisoned by the Japanese. Back in America, Shiro's parents were sent to a Japanese internment camp (Shiro's father still refuses to set foot on the Shafers' property out of resentment for his treatment during World War II). While Ted sneaks off for a swim, Fran sees Tae and Shiro together and believes they are having an affair. She sends an anonymous poison pen letter to Jim's father, alleging that Shiro is the real father of Jim and Tae's son. Tae runs away with the child and, with the help of the Hasagawas, tries to book passage back to Japan. Jim tracks down Tae, who runs to the end of a cliff overlooking the Pacific; but the two reconcile and reunite as a couple.

Japanese War Bride is filled with many characteristically Vidorian locations and moments: the grim battlefield in the opening shot; the family home with the white picket fence; the pastoral American small town; the factory (here a produce packing plant); and communal dances. Such images evoke moments from *Hallelujah*, *The Stranger's Return*, *Our Daily Bread*, and *Stella Dallas*. In many ways, the film feels like a rural counterpoint to *Street Scene*, with the family home and neighborhood taking the place of the apartment building and city block.

The film is most notable for frankly addressing not only interracial marriage (which Vidor had previously addressed in *Bird of Paradise* and *Duel in the Sun*),

Marie Windsor (left, as Fran Sterling), Shirley Yamaguchi (as Tae Shimizu), and Don Taylor (as Tae's husband and Fran's brother-in-law) in King Vidor's *Japanese War Bride* (1952, 20th Century–Fox). This love story centers around racism as a reaction to an interracial marriage (20th Century–Fox/Photofest).

but also the history of Japanese internment camps as well as larger issues of anti–Japanese racism. "Vidor uses a familiar strategy of dramatizing social conflicts within the domestic sphere to address racism in postwar America," notes Gina Marchetti in her study *Romance and the "Yellow Peril": Race, Sex, and Discursive Strategies in Hollywood Fiction*.[5] Vidor offers no easy solutions in *Japanese War Bride*, though he does remain optimistic, and the final shot of Tae and Jim embracing is a strong and powerful image. "Time will heal the wounds of memory," Tae says to Shiro during their conversation about his and his family's experiences during World War II. The line not only embodies the film's hope for the future but could also be applied to many of Vidor's films and the triumphant spirit of his characters.

Despite its daring and progressive political viewpoint, the film was not embraced upon first release. *Photoplay* called it "indecisive" and rated it as only "fair."[6] And Mandel Herbstman, in *Motion Picture Daily*, remarked, "Miss Turner's screenplay could stand greater mobility in the earlier phases. Direction by King

Vidor is adequate."[7] The film remains one of Vidor's most overlooked movies, never having received an official home video release. It is a shame, because it is arguably the last glimpse of Vidor at his most humanistic.

* * * *

Ruby Gentry (1952)

Ruby Gentry is a "Southern Gothic" film noir that could have easily been scripted by Tennessee Williams. The movie recalls earlier Vidor melodramas going all the way back to his *Wild Oranges* in the silent era. Certainly there are clear echoes of *Hallelujah*, *Duel in the Sun*, and *Beyond the Forest*. The film was produced by Joseph Bernhard and King Vidor, with a screenplay by Sylvia Richards that was based on a story by Arthur-Fitz Richard. Russell Harlan directed the photography and he had previously served as cinematographer for Howard Hawks' *Red River* (1948) and *The Big Sky* (also released in 1952). Harlan would then go on to supervise the cinematography for such classics as *The Blackboard Jungle* (1955), *Lust for Life* (1956), *Witness for the Prosecution* (1957), *Rio Bravo* (1959), and *To Kill a Mockingbird* (1962). The film had been edited by Terry Morse, who had also edited Vidor's *Japanese War Bride* (released earlier in 1952).

Ruby Gentry suffers from the exaggerated melodrama and overly theatrical dialogue and acting that had weakened (or, to some viewers, enlivened) earlier Vidor sound era films, perhaps most famously the soap-opera–like *Stella Dallas*. But there are some film scholars who rate the film highly within the director's oeuvre. Film historian Charles Silver, in his program notes for the 1972 film retrospective of Vidor's work at the Museum of Modern Art, wrote, "*Ruby Gentry* ... can now be seen to be one of Vidor's finest sound films and the culmination of those films which immediately preceded it: *Duel in the Sun*, *The Fountainhead*, *Beyond the Forest*, *Lightning Strikes Twice*, and *Japanese War Bride*.... *Ruby Gentry* is a more controlled and coherent film, much of it typically fifties in its look and feel, but pure Vidor in its sympathy for and redemption of the 'girl from the wrong side of the tracks.'"[8] And as Raymond Durgnat and Scott Simmon declare in their book *King Vidor, American*: "[W]e would argue for Ruby Gentry's status as a truly great American movie, the *film noir* imbued with new fervor, at once understanding and radically critical, 'Hollywood' and personal."[9]

It is surprising that Vidor had agreed to do the film if only because he would be working once again with Jennifer Jones and that entailed the probable interference by her husband David Selznick, for whom he had worked on *Bird of Paradise* and *Duel in the Sun*. Vidor walked off the set toward the very end of the latter film production because he had become fed up with Selznick's near-constant intervention. But with *Ruby Gentry*, Selznick was not an official producer and so, as Vidor later reported, he did not meddle significantly in the production as he had in the making of *Duel*. On the other hand, Vidor was happy to work with Jones again as his lead actress. The director later said of her, "When I first saw Jennifer, I was impressed by the fact that her emotional reactions registered so clearly on her face. It is difficult to exactly define this quality. Perhaps plasticity does it. Does one classify her as a great actress or a great instrument? ... Whatever gentleness and patience the director expended on Jennifer, he was rewarded a hundred-fold with a sensitive and intriguing performance.... There was no excuse for a director who couldn't keep her in the proper mood and get a wonderful performance from her."[10]

The film opens with a brief prologue before flashing back to the main story. We are in the small waterfront town of Braddock, North Carolina. A narrator (who we soon learn is Dr. Saul Manfred, played by Barney Phillips) points us to a boat and its female skipper, Ruby Gentry (Jennifer Jones), a "strange and gaunt" woman, as he calls her. He tells us that she was once "beautiful and alive," "born on the wrong side of the tracks," and that the "class-conscious" townspeople will not let her forget it. The doctor tells us that he had been in Braddock for a year now but felt like an outsider, until he met the friendly Jim Gentry (Karl Malden), a successful

Love and death in the swamp: Ruby Gentry (played by Jennifer Jones) embraces a dying Boake Tackman (played by Charlton Heston) in King Vidor's romantic melodrama *Ruby Gentry* (1952, Bernhard-Vidor Productions with distribution by 20th Century–Fox). There are many aspects of the film that echo characters, themes, and situations in Vidor's earlier movie *Duel in the Sun* (1946), including the love-hate relationship between the two lead characters (20th Century–Fox/Photofest).

Twenty-One. *Lightning Strikes, Japanese War, Ruby Gentry, Man Without* 255

local businessman. Jim brings the physician along to the hunting lodge of Ruby's father Jud Corey (Tom Tully) for some socializing and some bird hunting. Ruby's old lover Boake Tackman (Charlton Heston), the son of parents who were once wealthy, has just returned to town that day and visits the lodge. Ruby's brother Jewel (James Anderson), a religious fanatic, warns his sister against pursuing Boake again. Jim Gentry, speaking with Dr. Manfred at the lodge, relates Ruby's past story: "Ruby doesn't belong. She's from the wrong side of the tracks." It becomes obvious that Jim, whose wife Letitia (Josephine Hutchinson) is dying at home and had befriended Ruby some time ago, is in love with their frequent house guest.

The group plans to go out on a bird hunt and Ruby is assigned to escort the doctor. Boake visits Ruby to ask her to bring the new doctor up to "their place" and then "get rid of him." Boake and Ruby meet along the hunt at their planned liaison spot and embrace passionately after the doctor has gone off to the ridge. The lovers then combine forces to kill a deer and Boake makes sexual advances on Ruby near the dead animal. Ruby then pulls her gun on him and tells him to leave. Soon, back at the lodge, Tracy McAuliffe (Phyllis Avery), the daughter of one of the hunters, arrives and it becomes clear that she is Boake's girlfriend. She invites the newly arrived doctor to a "welcome home" party for Boake. Ruby is visibly angry when Tracy leaves with Boake, and she runs to the kitchen to find her brother Jewel there singing to her about "sowing seeds" and "eternal shame." She throws his guitar to the floor, and we get a sense that Ruby is a highly instinctual person who acts more from emotion than reason. Jewel fuels her jealousy by telling her that Boake will most certainly marry Tracy and she responds, "Boake's mine."

We then see Ruby on a fishing boat with her father and brother. Her dad talks about hooking and reeling in a "big one" and she obviously thinks of Boake. In the next scene, she kisses Boake after they have presumably made love at his father's lodge. They listen to the "new pump" at the salt marsh. All that Boake has left from his inheritance is the swampland that he now tries to drain with the water pumps, creating fertile farmland so that he can sell the crops for quick cash. On the ride back along the shore, she tries to get him to say that he loves her, but he resists. The car crashes into the surf and, with the vehicle half-submerged in the ocean, Boake carries Ruby to shore in his arms, seemingly unconcerned about the car. He then tells Ruby that he will marry Tracy. She accuses him of marrying Tracy for her father's money. Boake tells her that his family had fallen economically and that his father had turned to alcohol and that he does not want to wind up as he did. He suggests that he will marry Tracy but that he will continue to romance Ruby on the side. Once again, he expresses his lust for Ruby, but she fights him off. She is not willing to share Boake.

Dr. Manfred visits Jim's wife "Lettie" to check on her health and the doctor informs Jim that his wife is dying and that she only has two weeks or less left. The doctor then tells Jim to bring Ruby to the house to give Mrs. Gentry some companionship, which is what Lettie had requested. We then see Ruby trying to cheer up

Mrs. Gentry, but the older woman is too ill. In a private moment, the doctor tells Ruby not to worry about the snobs in town, knowing that she is a scorned woman due to her class as well as her relationship with Boake. He tells her that someday someone will take her away from it all, and we know that the doctor refers implicitly to himself here. He tells Ruby that she is "wonderful." If it was not obvious to the viewer by now, Dr. Manfred is also in love with the wild, passionate Ruby. She later tells Jim that the doctor had almost proposed to her, as if to make him jealous.

The doctor, continuing his voice-over narration, talks of Jim's love for Ruby. Jim tells Ruby that he has been coping with his sick wife for over eight years and he asks Ruby to marry him once his wife dies. She likes the idea but tells him that the townspeople will simply say that she married him for the money. But Jim tells her that he does not care what anyone says. We soon see Jim and Ruby visiting New York City, and so we can assume that Letitia has by now passed on. Jim tells his friends that he will throw a party to announce his engagement, but come time for the celebration, almost everyone stays away.

A highly dramatic scene soon unfolds at a country club party when Jim finds Ruby happily dancing with Boake and then watches as the two long-time lovers walk off into the bushes. Jim returns to the bar to get drunk and Dr. Manfred, sitting at the bar, sees his face and asks jokingly, "What happened, Jim, did someone snatch her away?" He then sees that this must, in fact, be true. Jim goes to find them and Ruby soon returns to the bar to get ice in a towel. Dr. Manfred goes with Ruby to minister to a bruised Jim who swears revenge against Boake. Jim calls Ruby "a tramp" and then the doctor drives Jim back home to an empty house. Jim soon hears a car and peers through an upstairs window to see Boake dropping off Ruby. She enters the house and climbs the stairs and they meet at the top of the stairs. We expect an enraged Jim, but surprisingly, he now apologizes for insulting her and tells her that "tomorrow's another day." He loves her too much to lose her, Boake or no Boake. She cries and escapes to the bedroom where Jim is obviously not welcome.

The next day they are out on the ocean on Jim's sailboat, seemingly ready to make a fresh start. Ruby wants to talk about the previous night, but Jim does not want to talk. Jim replies that he knew long before about Ruby and Boake and he tells her that he "doesn't mind being second best." She responds that she loves Jim. The wind picks up and the sailboat speeds up. Jim goes below deck and Ruby soon calls for him to help her gain control of the boat. But when Jim emerges from the cabin, he is hit in the head by the swinging boom and falls overboard. The boat goes in circles and he is drowned.

We subsequently see Ruby back in the library of the house, telling Dr. Manfred and her father what happened to Jim. There are many car horns blaring outside. The phone rings and, when she picks it up, the caller shouts, "Murderer! Murderer!" The phone rings again and the same thing happens but it is a different caller. Then she goes to find the newspaper in the foyer. An article insinuates that the death of Jim Gentry may not have been an accident. She calls the newspaper writer to set

Twenty-One. Lightning Strikes, Japanese War, Ruby Gentry, Man Without

the record straight and the reporter scoffs at her. Cars keep honking and someone throws a rock through a window. Ruby swears vengeance against the townspeople and we then cut to Jim's office, where Ruby begins collecting all of the debts that others owe Jim since he had been kind enough in the past to give out loans to help his neighbors in need. She uses Jim's money to take over the newspaper since its editor owes Jim money as well. She does everything to call in loans vengefully, ruining local businesses and the waterfront commerce.

Meanwhile, her brother Jewel shows up to scold her for shutting down the town: "Evil, the spawn of the devil. You'll reap the whirlwind." Boake then appears and surprises her. He tells her, "I thought you might have blood dripping off your clothes."

Ruby Gentry (played by Jennifer Jones) holds a rifle as her lover Boake Tackman (played by Charlton Heston) lies dead in the swamp in King Vidor's "Southern Gothic" romantic melodrama *Ruby Gentry* (1952, Bernhard-Vidor Productions with distribution by 20th Century–Fox). The film also stars Karl Malden as Jim Gentry (20th Century–Fox/Photofest).

She tells him she has not hurt him but could. She shows him the $150,000 promissory note that Boake had signed when he took a large loan from Jim. He asks how much he needs to pay her so that she will not call in the whole loan, and she replies that she will forgive the debt, wildly expressing her love for him. They kiss but then he rejects her, telling her that she cannot buy her "way out of the swamp" and that she cannot buy *him*.

Dr. Manfred narrates again, telling us that hundreds of Boake's acres have been drained and plowed and that his ambition is growing. Ruby visits Boake's land in her expensive car and orders a man to turn off the drainage pumps, though he resists. A police officer arrives and confirms that Ruby owns the land. The workers are ordered to turn off the pumps and to dig through the dyke, at Ruby's behest, and Boake's prized, reclaimed land is soon flooded again. Ruby is so hell-bent on retribution that she almost seems to take revenge against the land itself, the voice-over narration tells us. Boake arrives to see the flooding and then gets into the car with Ruby, asking her to take them away from the ugly sight of the destruction of his land. They drive to the hunting lodge. He soon declares that when "swamp-trotters" (i.e., Ruby) take over, they turn everything into a "big stinking swamp." He goes to her room and they presumably make love, since the scene ends with Boake turning off the ceiling lamp.

The next day they go off hunting together in the misty swamp. He suddenly turns on her: "I didn't mind you taking the land but why did you have to scuttle it?" He almost strangles her and she retorts, "Kill me…. I didn't want this." Recalling the exaggerated and frenzied scene at the end of *Duel in the Sun* where Pearl and Lewt carry out their love-hate relationship to the bitter end, Ruby and Boake kiss passionately on the swampy ground. Suddenly, someone shoots and the bullet lands next to their heads and they flee. A man calls out Biblical phrases from the mist and we realize that it is Ruby's brother Jewel who is shooting at them. In a suspenseful scene with rapid montage, Ruby and Boake flee and crawl in the swamp water under fallen tree branches. They climb up a nearby bank and kiss again, covered with mud. We have reached the height of Vidor-ian melodrama. We hear Jewel proclaiming that "the wage of sin is death" and then we see him cocking his gun nearby as he becomes visible to us through the passing mist. He sits in a tree and shoots Boake while Ruby, in return, shoots her brother. She returns to Boake's body lying in the swamp and embraces and kisses him, rocking his corpse in her arms. Dr. Manfred narrates once again, but now we return to the prologue at the start of the movie and the flashback ends with Ruby on her fishing boat, sporting her captain's hat: "Yes, Ruby Gentry was born on the wrong side of the tracks and the people of Braddock never let her forget it."[11]

What makes *Ruby Gentry* especially interesting for the film fan interested in Vidor's career is the way in which the story echoes (whether intentionally or coincidentally or a bit of both) many of the director's earlier works. Charles Silver has pointed out that the female "swamp-trotter," as Boake refers to her, had appeared in Vidor's films since *The Jack-Knife Man* and then *Hallelujah*: "She first became a fully-fleshed character in *Hallelujah* in which Chick (Nina Mae McKinney) displayed the same kind of vulnerability and humanity which Ruby evinces even at her most whorish and 'evil' moments…." Silver also notes the clear parallel in the friendship between the two Mrs. Gentrys (Letitia and Ruby) and the relationship between Laura Belle McCanles and Pearl in *Duel*. He compares the climactic scene in the swamp with a similar scene in *Hallelujah*. And furthermore, Silver notes that James Anderson's role as a religious yet almost demonic "moral chorus" harkens back to the grandmother in *Wine of Youth* and Walter Huston's "Sinkiller" in *Duel*.[12]

Durgnat and Simmon, in their book *King Vidor, American*, summarize nicely the remarkable parallels between the two Vidor movies that featured Jones:

> Vidor could treat this film as *his* revision of *Duel in the Sun*. Which must have been satisfying. Again Jennifer Jones is a passionate savage brought into a rich family and "trained for a life she can't have" (as it's put here). Again she finds a spiritually beautiful "foster-mother"

who dies. Again she loves the scion of an unattainably superior family, who plays with her feelings and even repeats a few of Lewt's most annoying lines ("You're pretty when you lose your temper"). Again she's harassed by a demonic Bible-puncher. Again she falls back on betrothal to an older man who dies in ugly circumstances. Again love-hate escalates via rape to a brutal shootout. No less important is the physical atmosphere that links Jennifer Jones's two characters, and the recalcitrant egoism that Charlton Heston's Boake shares with Lewt. If the cards are extensively reshuffled, and new ones played, *Ruby Gentry* is recognizably a variation on the theme, an alternative answer. In *Duel*, rugged individualism is tied to negative excesses that doom it to defeat. Here there's still hope.

Whether praised or criticized or a little of both, *Ruby Gentry* is a movie whose story allows the currents of Vidor's many past melodramas to converge. And, given that Selznick reportedly refrained from his typical interference, the production allowed the director a fair degree of creative freedom in realizing his vision. It is an intriguing update of the film noir genre and one in which the protagonist and the femme fatale are one and the same. And Ruby joins the ranks of fascinating Vidor female characters such as Louise Starr (*The Stranger's Return*), Stella Dallas (*Stella Dallas*), Dominique Francon (*The Fountainhead*), Pearl Chavez (*Duel in the Sun*), Laura Belle McCanles (*Duel in the Sun*), Rosa Moline (*Beyond the Forest*), and Natasha (*War and Peace*).

* * * *

Man Without a Star (1955)

Man Without a Star (1955) marked Vidor's return to cinema after a three-year absence following *Ruby Gentry*. In the interim, Vidor participated in David O. Selznick's television debut, *Light's Diamond Jubilee*, a "tribute to the electrical industry and to the invention, 75 years ago, of the incandescent lamp by Thomas Alva Edison." This reunion with the producer of Vidor's earlier *Bird of Paradise* and *Duel in the Sun* was intended to be "an interpretation of the spirit and meaning of American life, both of the past 75 years and the future, with emphasis on the part which electricity has played in the development of our civilization."[13] It is easy to see why Vidor was interested in the project as it echoed *An American Romance*, his own patriotic ode to industry and progress.

In keeping with his reputation for mammoth productions, Selznick set out to create a grandiose television program. Called "the most ambitious" show of the season, it ran two hours, cost "approximately $965,000," and was broadcast "on about 329 interconnected stations, live."[14] Such a presentation was unprecedented, as it was "carried over all four of the then existing networks to an estimated 70,000,000 viewers."[15] In addition to Vidor, Selznick hired six additional directors to contribute content, including Alan Handley, Christian Nyby, Roy Rowland, Norman Taurog, William A. Wellman, and Bud Yorkin. Vidor ultimately contributed two segments: "A Kiss for the Lieutenant," from a story by Arthur Gordon that was adapted by

Ben Hecht, and "Leader of the People," from a story by John Steinbeck that was also adapted by Hecht. A third segment was planned, an adaptation of Ray Bradbury's "Powerhouse," but it was never filmed.[16] Vidor's only foray into television was not a positive experience and it was marred by a frantic and disorganized shooting schedule. Filming "without the [production] sketches," explains Christopher Anderson in his book *Hollywood TV*, "Vidor and company made many mistakes, including using extreme long shots that wouldn't register on the small TV screen, filming shots that wouldn't cut together well, and failing to provide the proper shots for editing the scenes effectively."[17]

With television behind him, Vidor embarked on the Western *Man Without a Star*. This would not be a personal project for the director, who considered it "a straight salary job."[18] The script was announced in *Variety* on February 24, 1954, with screenwriter D.D. Beauchamp attached to adapt Dee Linford's novel.[19] On June 16, Vidor was announced as director, with Jeanne Crain and Kirk Douglas in the leads.[20] *Man Without a Star* is decidedly a work of nostalgia. It represents not only Vidor's first western in nine years, since *Duel in the Sun*, but also his farewell to the genre, being his final film about the American frontier. Its jocular tone recalls *The Texas Rangers*, particularly the antics and jovial camaraderie between the protagonists, and it is also Vidor's last comedic work (though it cannot wholly be categorized as a comedy proper). Seen in this light, *Man Without a Star* takes on an elegiac quality—after all, it is about a man who heads westward, looking for a way of life that he cannot find and, in the end, leaves in perpetual search for a life that he will not find.

The film begins on a train heading from Kansas City to Wyoming. Stowed away on-board is drifter Dempsey Rae (Kirk Douglas). Riding beneath the train is Jeff Jimson (William Campbell), who is caught and attacked by a brakeman at a train stop. Dempsey rescues Jeff from the tracks before the train takes off and hides him in an empty car. That night, they witness another hobo (Jack Elam) stabbing a train guard. In the morning, the duo jump off the train but are stopped by a sheriff and his deputy who are looking for the brakeman's killer. Seeing Jeff's wounds, they suspect him, and he is reluctant to finger the real killer. Dempsey speaks up, however, and identifies the murderer, saving Jeff's life.

In town, Jeff reunites with his old flame, saloon girl Idonee (Claire Trevor). In the saloon, the sheriff tries to run the two men out of town for vagrancy, but ranch foreman Strap Davis (Jay C. Flippen) offers the pair a job herding cattle for his boss, Reed Bowman (Jeanne Crain). Bowman has the biggest herd in Wyoming, and plans to bring in more cattle from Texas, led by Steve Miles (Richard Boone). Bowman's ambitions frighten the other ranchers, who put up barbed wire on government land to preserve grass for themselves for the coming winter. Dempsey has always hated wire, since his younger brother died on barbed wire in a range war started by Steve Miles. Bowman wants to go to war with her neighbors and tries to hire Dempsey as her new foreman. He decides to leave town but stops at the saloon to say farewell

TWENTY-ONE. *Lightning Strikes, Japanese War, Ruby Gentry, Man Without* 261

Gunfighter Dempsey Rae (played by Kirk Douglas, left) fights Latigo (played by Shelby "Sheb" Wooley) in King Vidor's final Western, *Man Without a Star* (1955, Universal Pictures). The screenplay is based on the 1952 novel of the same title by Dee Lindford (Universal International Pictures/Photofest).

to Idonee. Reed also goes to the saloon, and Jeff shoots a man who harasses Reed. Dempsey strikes Jeff, who leaves with Reed. After Steve and his men beat him, Dempsey sides with the neighbors in their war with Reed, while Jeff rides with Steve. After Jeff refuses to kill Dempsey, Steve shoots him but the wound is not fatal. Steve plans to attack Dempsey using a cattle stampede, but Dempsey gains control of the herd and beats Steve in a fistfight. The neighboring ranchers offer Dempsey stock and land, but he declines, stating that he still does not like barbed wire. Dempsey encourages Jeff to stay behind with Tess (Myrna Hansen), daughter of neighboring rancher Tom Cassidy (Eddy Waller), while he rides westward in search of a dying world that is fast changing, leaving him and his way of life behind.

Much of the film is focused on the worldly, experienced, older Dempsey and the naive, inexperienced, younger Jeff. Their poignant rapport is arguably the most nurturing male-male bond in any Vidor film since *The Champ* (1931). Dempsey and Jeff's relationship also recalls woodcarver Peter Lane and the young boy Buddy from *The Jack-Knife Man*. From the opening scene, when Dempsey rescues Jeff from the tracks, a pattern is introduced that is repeated throughout the film: Dempsey allows

Jeff to make a mistake and then steps in to educate and, when necessary, to nurse the younger man. But even in his lessons, Dempsey does not try to mold Jeff in his image. Instead, he tries to lead Jeff to be a smarter, better man than he is, such as when he insists Jeff drink sarsaparilla while he drinks whiskey, or when he teaches Jeff how to shoot in self-defense rather than as a spectacle. In this way, Dempsey shows that he knows that his way of life is already part of the past, that he is a relic from a fabled, historical era whose days are numbered. Elegiac touches such as this remind us that *Man Without a Star* is the work of a director who has been making movies for four decades and who has lived to see much change in the industry and world around him.

Reed Bowman fits Clive Denton's characterization that "Vidor's ladies are not, or seldom are, 'Everywoman.' They are more forceful and individual than that and, compared to 'Mr. Anyman,' they are inclined to behave selfishly or at least oddly."[21] Reed's ambition certainly recalls Barbara Stanwyck in *Stella Dallas* and her ruthless cunning reminds us of Bette Davis in *Beyond the Forest*. But both of those women are from lower classes and strive for social improvement. Instead, Bowman's personality is most reminiscent of Howard Roark in *The Fountainhead*.

An on-the-set photograph taken during the production of King Vidor's final Western, *Man Without a Star* (1955, Universal Pictures). From left: Jeanne Crain (who plays Reed Bowman), director Vidor, and Kirk Douglas (who stars as Dempsey Rae). The film also stars Claire Trevor as Idonee and Richard Boone as Steve Miles (Universal International Pictures/Photofest).

Twenty-One. *Lightning Strikes, Japanese War, Ruby Gentry, Man Without*

Man Without a Star is structured around arrivals and departures, from its opening shot of a train crossing the length of the widescreen Cinemascope frame to its closing, an iconic image of Dempsey riding off into the horizon. Like Dempsey, Vidor returned to the frontier looking for the way life used to be; and like his protagonist, Vidor was, by 1954 (when it was filmed) and 1955 (when it was released), slowly nearing the time to ride on out of Hollywood. A parting gesture to the western, *Man Without a Star* is a fond farewell, indeed.

Twenty-Two

1956–1959

War and Peace and *Solomon and Sheba*

"All my films have to have some theme that sticks."[1]—King Vidor, 1959

War and Peace (1956)

Vidor's final two feature films, *War and Peace* (1956) and *Solomon and Sheba* (1959), are epic in terms of the scope of their stories as well as the complexity of their large-scale production. The former film is far superior to the latter, though not without major flaws of its own. And yet both works demonstrate that, even in the twilight of his professional Hollywood career, Vidor was able to marshal a cast of thousands and to coordinate a crew of hundreds in a manner that would rival a military general. And throughout his direction of these vast-ranging and highly intricate projects, Vidor maintained a steadfast vision that saw him through to the conclusion of making each film, despite the labyrinthine, convoluted scripts from which he had to work and the short preparation time permitted before the start of each production.

Vidor's *War and Peace* was produced by Dino De Laurentiis and hit the theaters in 1956, the same year as the releases of Cecil B. DeMille's *The Ten Commandments* and Robert Rossen's *Alexander the Great*. Vidor's *Solomon and Sheba* was released in 1959, the same year as William Wyler's *Ben-Hur*, which had been originally offered to Vidor. The 1950s had already seen several major historical and Biblical epics on the silver screen, including Henry King's *David and Bathsheba* (1951), Mervyn LeRoy's *Quo Vadis* (1951), and Henry Koster's *The Robe* (1953). These movies, along with Vidor's two contributions in this period, led the way for a parade of historical and Biblical epics that were soon to follow, including Stanley Kubrick's *Spartacus* (1960), Otto Preminger's *Exodus* (1960), Richard Fleischer's *Barabbas* (1961), Anthony Mann's *El Cid* (1961), David Lean's *Lawrence of Arabia* (1962), Joseph Mankiewicz's *Cleopatra* (1963), Peter Glenville's *Becket* (1964), Mann's *The Fall of the Roman Empire* (1964), Lean's *Doctor Zhivago* (1965), and George Stevens's *The Greatest Story Ever Told* (1965). In the Cold War era of Presidents Truman, Eisenhower, Kennedy, and Johnson—a period in which the conflict between good and evil on a global scale became more clear-cut for many—American audiences seemed to have an increasing affinity for movies with vast historical sweep, archetypal heroes and villains, and near-mythical drama.

Today, given that Vidor's adaptation of Tolstoy's great novel is often compared unfavorably to the seven-hour 1967 Russian version starring and directed by Sergei Bondarchuk, many easily forget the merits of Vidor's effort, even if they are admittedly mixed with massive flaws. In many ways, *War and Peace* is a type of prism that reflects the diversity, complexity, and variations of quality within Vidor's broad-ranging oeuvre. There are some scenes and sequences in this multifaceted film that evoke the very best of Vidor's earlier work. There are also aspects of *War and Peace* that remind us of places in his long career where Vidor fell flat. The very act of making a movie version of Tolstoy's sprawling, nearly unfilmable novel expresses the best qualities about Vidor: his bold, adventurous spirit, his technical and strategic mastery, and his fortitude and persistence in getting the job done. But it is ultimately a dramatically uneven film, mesmerizing and engaging in some spots but too convoluted or melodramatic or lumbering in others. And in this sense, such unevenness also mirrors Vidor's body of work taken as a whole.

In *The American Cinema*, Andrew Sarris places King Vidor in the section of his book titled "The Far Side of Paradise." This section includes those "directors who fall short of the Pantheon [of the greatest filmmakers] either because of a fragmentation of their personal vision or because of disruptive career problems." Sarris summarizes Vidor as follows: "King Vidor is a director for anthologies. He has created more great moments and fewer great films than any director of his rank …The classics of his humanistic museum period—*The Big Parade*, *The Crowd*, *Hallelujah*—are no less uneven or more impressive than the classics of his delirious modern period—*Duel in the Sun*, *The Fountainhead*, *Ruby Gentry*."[2] *War and Peace* encapsulates that Vidor-ian tension of being both uneven and impressive. It includes many astonishing moments and scenes, especially in visual terms, that are greater than the sum of the parts.

The movie failed to become nominated for a Best Picture Oscar (*Around the World in 80 Days* won that year, and the other nominees included *Friendly Persuasion*, *Giant*, *The King and I*, and *The Ten Commandments*). Nineteen fifty-six was certainly a year for films with large-scale productions. Vidor was nominated for the Best Director Oscar, but he lost to George Stevens for *Giant*. Jack Cardiff was nominated for Best Color Cinematography but lost to Lionel Lindon (*Around the World in 80 Days*). The film was also nominated for an Academy Award for Best Costume Design in a Color Film but lost to *The King and I*. However, *War and Peace* did win a Golden Globe as Best Foreign Language Foreign Film, bestowed by the Hollywood Foreign Press Association, and Vidor was awarded the D.W. Griffith Award from the Screen Directors Guild in 1956. He was also honored by the San Sebastian (Spain) and Karoli-Vevey (Czechoslovakia) film festivals after the release of *War and Peace*.[3] And Cardiff won the Best Cinematography Award by the British Society of Cinematographers.

Meanwhile, *War and Peace*, while being praised and nominated and awarded in certain quarters, did fairly dismally at the box office and met generally mixed reviews from the critics. Abel Green of *Variety* described the film as a "rich contribution to the art of form of the picture business in the best tradition."[4] Bosley Crowther of *The New York Times* lauded the movie as being as "massive, colorful and exciting as anything of this sort we've ever seen," and yet he judged the characters to be "second-rate people, hackneyed and without much depth." Crowther went on to say about the characters: "You view them with an objective interest as they do their parade across the screen, giving off little more personal vibrance than the nameless soldiers in the massive scenes of war."[5] Hollis Alpert of the *Saturday Review* declared Vidor's movie to be "only intermittently interesting and that aside from making a sort of pictorial sour-mash of the original work, it is not particularly good movie-making."[6]

Sometimes the flaws or unevenness of certain Vidor films were due to choices that Vidor had made, such as allowing for too much overly theatrical acting. But they were also sometimes due to weaknesses in the script or to bad casting decisions and to the inevitable limitations of certain actors and actresses. Furthermore, the innately collaborative nature of filmmaking always involves artistic risks as wells

Audrey Hepburn (as Natasha Rostova) and Henry Fonda (as Count Pierre Bezukhov) in King Vidor's *War and Peace* (1956, Paramount Pictures), based on Leo Tolstoy's epic 1869 novel of the same title. At the time, Hepburn was one of the most popular actresses in the world. Before Fonda was cast as Pierre, Vidor had considered actors Peter Ustinov and Paul Scofield for the role (Paramount Pictures/Photofest).

as triumphs, including the risks associated with the occasional need (due to budget and time constraints) to assign assistant directors and cameramen to film certain scenes (such as battle sequences or landscape shots) while the director is busy supervising others. Vidor was not afraid to delegate authority, especially when making these epics. His adaptation of the Tolstoy novel suffered from all of these defects, including a hopelessly convoluted script at the hands of several writers who worked on it (along with Vidor). The writers included Bridget Boland, Robert Westerby, Mario Camerini, Ennio DeConcini, and Ivo Perilli. The movie was also undermined by poor casting decisions (especially Henry Fonda as Pierre) and included weaker scenes that were not shot under the immediate supervision of the director. And then there is always the problem that occurs when the director does not have control over the final editing process, a problem that Vidor had experienced after filming *An American Romance* and *Duel in the Sun*. As Vidor told an interviewer: "I worked on *War and Peace* for a year and a half, supervised all the cutting, music, and everything. Then Paramount made some cuts without consulting me about it."[7] He later explained the editing problems to interviewer Nancy Dowd:

> The first running time of the picture was around six or eight hours. The first release print was three hours and forty minutes. It is such a production that there should be one show of it per night. There was no reason to cut it down just so you could show it three or four times per night so that the theatres could make more money.... The approach they took was to cut away whatever they could without making any noticeable jumps in the soundtrack, which was already complete. They didn't even have the courtesy to call me up and tell me that they were going to do some cutting on it. They didn't want to spend any more money in making a new score for the picture so that the editing could be done more judiciously. It was another painful thing to have to go through, especially after having the same thing happen to my other films as well.[8]

While some film critics and scholars have given high praise to the overall film, most agree that it is a mixed bag of a movie, one with many magical moments that shine more brightly because they are far superior to the entire mosaic into which they have been placed.[9] At the end of the day, the sprawling narrative and gargantuan production challenges did not allow Vidor the opportunity to express his sense of individuality. *War and Peace* and his following film, *Solomon and Sheba*, were ultimately viewed by Vidor as job assignments rather than passions, and it shows, except in certain moments. As Vidor told a gathering of American Film Institute fellows: "I think the basic interest in any work of art is that you're seeing that fellow's individuality.... But the strength of filmmaking has got to be the viewpoint of one person.... I'm a firm believer in the fact that you put your individual stamp on your work. I think the whole job is to show one's individual viewpoint.... I made *War and Peace* based on a book that's out of Tolstoy's guts, I guess. I agree with the leading character, the search for truth and meaning. But for me, it was just a job. The producer called me up and asked if I wanted to direct it. But that film isn't out of *my* guts."[10]

It is perhaps odd that Vidor did not feel more personal passion for the project, given that he has remarked more than once that one of the reasons why he loved the story, and why he thought Tolstoy's novel was "one of the greatest novels of all time," is that he identified so much with the character of Pierre. Vidor spoke of Pierre as a character "searching for truth," which the director described as his favorite theme and one that he had focused on in many films, including his 1919 *The Turn in the Road*.[11] But, of course, it was the scope of the story, the scale of the production, and the casting of Henry Fonda as Pierre that no doubt diminished Vidor's personal interest when adapting it.

It is interesting, however, than on certain occasions Vidor later reflected on his film with a very different and far more positive evaluation. One can see his changing opinions about his accomplishment almost as a reflection of the disjointed nature of the movie itself. And, of course, his responses when assessing his movie may well have been shaped by his audience or interviewer at the time, by what he was selectively remembering about the production, and by others' responses that he had most recently heard or read about. As he stated to interviewer Joel Greenberg: "I loved *War and Peace*. I thought we got great results. I wish I'd had Peter Ustinov playing Henry Fonda's part.... The art director on *War and Peace* is probably the best I've ever worked with, the assistant director ... was as good as any I've had any place, and the rest of the crew, mostly Italian ... was better than I've ever experienced here, and I really was inspired. Of course it's a great book; it's easy to be inspired by the book. I thought we got its atmosphere."[12]

So given that even Vidor, let alone the film-going public, has offered such mixed assessments of his adaptation of *War and Peace*, we might ask: what works and what does not work when it comes to this epic film? And how does such an evaluation allow us to look back with a critical eye on the director's rather uneven but highly prolific career, one filled with countless "moments" that rank alongside the greatest scenes and sequences in the history of cinema? Charles Silver, in his program notes about *War and Peace* for the Museum of Modern Art's comprehensive Vidor retrospective in the fall of 1972, clearly summarizes the mixed results in a way that clearly gives the director the benefit of the doubt:

> In terms of production values—color, lighting, costumes, sets, makeup, spectacle—*War and Peace* is probably Vidor's best-made film. That its luster is not quite the cinematic equivalent of Tolstoy's genius is beside the point. The adaptation of any huge novel to the screen is madness of a sort, and to attempt *War and Peace* or *Moby Dick* is to guarantee disappointment. The very necessity of including so many incidents and strands of narrative works against the vital flow of filmic expression. Vidor's film is too episodic and fragmented, but some of the fragments are among the most beautiful pieces of filmmaking in history. In his book (*King Vidor on Filmmaking*) the director describes at length what a massive operation it was to film the marvelous Battle of Borodino. Equal or better is Napoleon's retreat from Moscow.... Vidor had not been called upon to film on this grand a scale since *The Big Parade* thirty years before, and he obviously was fully up to the challenge. His use of VistaVision (ably abetted by the expert Jack Cardiff) is an important early lesson in the use of wider screen. Although one can always quibble over casting, all of the principal actors prove to be at least adequate; Audrey Hepburn, as always, is inspired and rapturous. After a decade of disputes with producers coinciding with the breakup of the studio system, Vidor had emerged with something of a triumph in the new age of international co-productions. As Natasha says to Pierre at the end of *War and Peace*, "You suffer; you show your wounds; but you stand."[13]

TWENTY-TWO. *War and Peace* and *Solomon and Sheba* 269

Herbert Lom as Napoleon on horseback in King Vidor's *War and Peace* (1956, Paramount Pictures). The battlefield sequences are highlights of the film. Eight writers worked on the script, including Vidor. Jack Cardiff served as cinematographer and Nino Rota composed the music. Dino De Laurentiis produced the film for Ponti-De Laurentiis Cinematografica and the film was distributed in the United States by Paramount Pictures (Paramount Pictures/Photofest).

In terms of its virtues, *War and Peace* is of course even more of a visual (one might say "cinematic") experience than other large-scale Vidor productions such as *The Big Parade* (especially with its battle scenes), *Northwest Passage* (especially with its river-crossing scene), and *Duel in the Sun* (especially with its scene of Senator McCanles' army of ranch hands amassing to confront the railway workers). Its battle scenes are as effective and well-crafted as those in such other war films as *Paths of Glory*, *Barry Lyndon*, and *1917*. A good deal of the visual merits of the movie must be credited to its expert cinematographer, Jack Cardiff, who had supervised the photography on such prior classics as John Huston's *The African Queen* (1951), John Boulting's *The Magic Box* (1951), and Joseph Mankiewicz's *The Barefoot Contessa* (1954), along with three masterworks by Michael Powell and Emeric Pressburger: *Matter of Life and Death* (1946), *Black Narcissus* (1947), and *The Red Shoes* (1948). And the film does a satisfactory job of weaving together scenes of personal drama and scenes of grandiose spectacle. The movie includes many remarkable scenes and sequences, especially in visual terms:

    1. The duel scene between Pierre (Fonda) and Dolokhov (Helmut Dantine) against a stark winter landscape that looks as if it had been painted by Caspar David Friedrich.

2. The sequence of the Battle of Austerlitz in which Napoleon (Herbert Lom) passes through the field of the dead and dying soldiers and happens upon a fallen Andrei (Mel Ferrer).

3. The Battle of Borodino sequence.

4. The retreat of the French army and its final sublime shot of a despondent Napoleon passing by in his horse-drawn coach.

5. The wonderfully photographed and edited sequence at the grand ball, which almost rivals the ball scene in Luchino Visconti's *The Leopard* [*Il Gattopardo*, 1963].

In terms of more personally dramatic moments, the romantic scenes between Natasha (Audrey Hepburn) and Andrei (Mel Ferrer), especially after he has been wounded in battle, are engaging. And the scenes between Pierre and Platon Karataev (John Mills) are effectively acted. One heart-rending scene occurs when Platon is fatally shot while on the long march with the retreating French soldiers and his beloved, loyal dog stays by him protectively until Pierre arrives to take the dog. And one of the movie's great virtues is lead actress Audrey Hepburn, who plays Natasha as very different from the character in Tolstoy's novel and yet who graces the film

Mel Ferrer (as Prince Andrei Balkonsky) and Audrey Hepburn (as Natasha Rostova) as doomed lovers in King Vidor's *War and Peace* (1956, Paramount Pictures), based on Leo Tolstoy's epic 1869 novel of the same title. In this scene, Natasha comforts Andrei after he has been seriously wounded in battle. Ferrer and Hepburn had been married shortly before they made the film (Paramount Pictures/Photofest).

with a charismatic performance in which she wavers between girlish vulnerability and persistent strength. The movie is most engaging in the middle part when the primary focus switches away from Pierre to Natasha, and that is due to the story as well as to Hepburn. Vidor typically had nothing but superlative things to say about his work with Hepburn and, when later reflecting on his long career, he chose her as perhaps his favorite actress of those with whom he had worked.[14]

Vidor had almost the opposite view of Fonda and later regarded the casting of Fonda as one of the detriments of the movie. He later said that he and the producers should have chosen Peter Ustinov, one of two actors (the other being Paul Scofield) who had been originally considered. As far as Vidor was concerned, Fonda did not express authenticity as a man who was searching for the truth, which is how Vidor conceived of Pierre's fundamental motivation throughout the story. And Fonda also proved combative on more than a few occasions during the production. One of the chief problems with Fonda's performance is that we do not get a real sense of his inner evolution when he changes from being drunkenly buffoonish (at a party earlier in the film) to a man who travels all the way to witness the Battle at Austerlitz so that he can really see what war is like. Above all, it is not simply that Fonda's Pierre is emotionally inconsistent, which he is at times, but that the viewer finds it difficult, if not impossible, to become emotionally aligned with him over the course of such an epic narrative. He is ultimately wooden and aloof, even as romance and war and despair swirl about him. And, ultimately, that reflects a major defect of the entire movie: it is emotionally uneven in some places and occasions a sense of icy detachment over the course of most of the story.

Despite all the spectacle and moments of melodrama, the viewer never really gains any sense of the deep torment and loss caused by the war's destruction and chaos, even as we see dead soldiers on battlefields or watch the Rostov family packing up its belongings and leaving its beloved mansion behind. And we often feel not only removed emotionally from Pierre, but also from most of the characters. Too much voice-over narration in places only amplifies that sense of detachment, as does a sudden and rather surreal musical scene that erupts out of nowhere when the Rostov family is heading to their country home on horse-drawn coaches in the middle of a wintry night. In addition, the first hour of the movie is too stilted, with overly stagy acting and dialogue, and the story does not really switch dramatically from "neutral" to "drive" until the memorable duel scene. And, on a minor note, the actor Wilfrid Lawson is oddly out of place and ineffective in playing Andrei's imperious father, Prince Bolkonsky.

Another reason for the viewer's difficulty in becoming emotionally involved in the lives of the characters is simply due to the fact that there are too many characters and their stories are woven together in too fragmented of a manner. *War and Peace* may be a greater visual experience than Vidor's earlier war classic, *The Big Parade*, in terms of sheer spectacle, but what makes that silent film a far better movie is the unifying and evolving viewpoint of John Gilbert's character James Apperson. In Vidor's later epic, the characters and viewpoints change so often that, when we do get to all of the glorious motion on the battlefield, we no longer quite know whom to cheer for, if anyone. And due to the disjointed, multi-perspectival nature of the film, we arrive at the most significant flaw in the story. After Andrei has left Natasha behind to go away to England for a year at the instructions of his father, and after Natasha falls victim to the wily, sinister, and lustful advances of Anatole Kuragin (Vittorio Gassman), we suddenly find Natasha ready and willing to pack her bags and ride off with Kuragin, a move that will later cause Andrei to alienate himself from her once he finds out. There is absolutely no justification provided as to this capricious change of heart on the part of Natasha. As far as the viewer can tell from the scenes provided, Kuragin has presented himself as a creepy, oppressive womanizer. Without more context provided, Natasha's choice to surrender to Kuragin and to leave with him makes no sense. At best, she appears as a fickle schoolgirl who is too impatient to wait for her beloved Andrei to return, as promised, from his trip to England. This is but one example of where the fragmentary nature of the movie detracts substantially from the audience's capacity to align itself with the feelings of a lead character.

* * * *

Solomon and Sheba (1959)

> "The historical facts are sketchy, so I used a lot of imagination in directing the film [*Solomon and Sheba*]."[15]—King Vidor, 1959

Just after finishing *War and Peace* and returning home at long last, Vidor received a phone call from MGM and was offered the directing job for *Ben-Hur*, which he turned down, just as he had long ago turned down the offer of making the 1925 silent film version of the same. One of the reasons that Vidor cited for turning down *Ben-Hur* but opting instead for *Solomon and Sheba* is that, with the latter film, he would be able to collaborate on the script while he was at home in the United States (though the director said that the studio "kept deferring" his "participation in the script").[16] Vidor was offered both films because he had by now clearly earned the reputation of being a reliable director of epic movies, capable of helming large-scale productions that included much visual spectacle. The job of *Ben-Hur* went to William Wyler and the movie went on to win eleven Academy Awards, including Best Picture, Best Director, and Best Actor (Charlton Heston). Vidor turned to the making of his final feature film, *Solomon and Sheba*. The movie was supposed to be made in Italy but, as Vidor later reported, most of the studio stages in Rome had by then been taken over by the crews involved with the production of *Ben-Hur*. So the director had to fly to Spain to begin finding locations so as to begin construction of the elaborate sets.[17]

Vidor was interested in the basic theme of the film: "What I remember about it was the issue of God against the pagans, and I felt that I could give some feeling

Twenty-Two. *War and Peace* and *Solomon and Sheba*

against pagan worship.... This again is the story of basically flesh and spirit. This is a basic theme for me, too."[18] But this Biblical epic would wind up suffering from most of the defects that plagued his prior movie, but without its merits or abundance of magical cinematic moments. Most of all, the film suffered because of the death of Tyrone Power, who originally played Solomon, after many of his scenes had been shot. His replacement, Yul Brynner, turned out to be adequate but little more. It was also another film in which Vidor seemed to try to do his best with a lackluster story and an incomplete and fragmented script. Vidor would later say: "The problem went back to not having a finished script before the production started. I finished up this picture saying that I would never do another picture unless the script was completely worked out. On this film I was writing scenes between shooting other scenes."[19]

Power, who had finished at least half of his scenes for the film, died suddenly of a massive heart attack midway through production. He was only 44 years old and collapsed just after finishing a rigorous sword fight scene. He was rushed by ambulance to a hospital in Madrid and died in transit, still wearing the robes of Solomon. (Power's actor father Tyrone Power, Sr., also died of a heart attack in 1931 after collapsing while making the movie *The Miracle Man*.) Power's replacement Yul Brynner was a very different type of actor. The scenes that Power had filmed needed to be re-done and this no doubt took a great deal of wind out of Vidor's sails. But as he usually did, he persisted until his assigned job was complete.

Vidor believed that *Solomon and Sheba* would have been far different and far better if Power had not died. He said that Power "was giving his best performance" and "that the completed picture would have been his best."[20] The director thought that Power expressed Solomon's uncertainty and vulnerability as well as the basic tension within him between flesh and spirit, a tension that was central to the story. Footage of several of the scenes in which Power acted show this to be true.[21] Brynner, on the other hand, portrayed Solomon as a more dominant, forceful ruler with little sense of inner conflict. Vidor compared the two men and their performances:

> Brynner likes to play strong, aristocratic, unwavering characters who are not troubled with indecision—in short—kings.... Many of the leading characters in my films must wrestle with the two sides of their psyche. In *Solomon and Sheba*, the core of the story was Solomon's inner struggle to choose between his responsibilities as head of state and church and his yearning to satisfy his sensual desires with the pagan queen. Tyrone Power had understood the dualistic problem of the anguished king. When Brynner took over after his death, he fought the idea of a troubled monarch and wanted to dominate each situation without conflict. It was an attitude that affected the depth of his performance and probably the integrity of the film.[22]

And as Vidor told interviewer Joel Greenberg in connecting the loss of Power to the decline of the film: "When Brynner came in he was cautious and diffident following Power, and because of the fact that Power had died on it, it turned into an unimportant, nothing sort of picture. It's strange. I guess the unreality, the phoniness—whatever it is—comes out unless you have a very sincere performance by the leading character."[23]

Yul Brynner as King Solomon and Marisa Pavan as Abishag, Solomon's loving servant, in King Vidor's *Solomon and Sheba* (1959, Edward Small Productions and distributed by United Artists). The screenplay is based on stories from the Books of Kings and Chronicles in the Holy Bible. The film also stars Gina Lollobrigida as the Queen of Sheba and George Sanders as Adonijah, Solomon's scheming brother and his ambitious, jealous rival. This would be Vidor's final feature film (United Artists Corp./Photofest).

Apart from major problems with the story and script, the acting was mediocre at best. All three of the lead actors—Yul Brynner, Gina Lollobrigida, and George Sanders—gave mostly hollow, wooden, stilted performances with no chance of engaging the viewer emotionally (a similar problem that diminished *War and Peace*, but to a lesser degree). Of course, Vidor had been praised before for his work with actors, and yet some of his melodramas (*Stella Dallas*, *Duel in the Sun*, *The Fountainhead*, *Beyond the Forest*, *Lightning Strikes Twice*, *Ruby Gentry*) include a fair degree of overly stagy melodrama. And the artificial acting witnessed throughout *Solomon and Sheba* (not to mention in certain scenes of *War and Peace*) is rather surprising, even if Vidor had not felt all that inspired in making the film—and even given that we are dealing with a Biblical epic where high-flung theatrics often reign supreme. After all, Vidor once told an interviewer, not long before his death: "When I arrived in Hollywood, there was a sort of unreality about films, a falseness. The acting was overdone. The make-ups were overdone. The acting had no connection with reality. I don't know what influenced my part of it … but I had the very definite idea to make my films look real. Not necessarily to *be* real, but to seem real. I wanted people to believe what was happening.… I don't know that I wanted to be different, but I wanted to be honest."[24]

With all of that said, there is one scene in the film that truly belongs to the pantheon of "special Vidor moments" in his long career. It is the scene toward the end in which the Egyptians, now allied with Solomon's ever-scheming brother Adonijah (George Sanders), confront Solomon and his army of Israelites. The Israelites have formed their lines on a hillside and stare across a deep chasm directly below them and, beyond that, to a vast plain where the Egyptians have assembled in the distance. The Israelites face east toward the rising sun and hold highly polished shields at their sides. The Egyptian army charges in unison and, not knowing that the chasm lies in wait at the other end of the plain, are suddenly blinded when Solomon's men, at his command, turn their shields toward their enemy as well as toward the sun. The Egyptians, some thundering ahead on horses and in chariots and some marching on foot, are instantly unable to see where they are going when the reflected light from the shields explodes into their view. Soldiers, horses, and chariots fall chaotically over the edge of the chasm like a human waterfall, one group after another. The Israelites have outsmarted their opponents and they return to Jerusalem in triumph so that Solomon can vanquish his brother Adonijah and reunite with his beloved Queen Sheba (Gina Lollobrigida).

This battle scene, both ludicrous on the one hand and mesmerizing on the other, clearly shows Vidor at his best when it comes to visual spectacle, just as we saw in such films as *The Big Parade*, *Northwest Passage*, *Duel in the Sun*, and *War and Peace*. He was a master strategist and expert coordinator of technical and human resources. When asked by an interviewer whether he enjoyed taking charge of complex, large-scale military scenes that require highly intricate supervision, Vidor replied: "Well, I'm of the nature that I like it and I'm technically minded enough so that I enjoy it and handle it.… It's like being the captain of a ship or a general in the army."[25]

Despite disappointing many critics, *Solomon and Sheba* did return a profit at the box office. Film historian Charles Silver has given a good summary statement of Vidor's final feature film: "Although it is probably not that much worse than any other Biblical film made for the commercial cinema ... [t]oo much of the film is just plain silly, and the Sheban religious rites are a regrettable throwback to Delores Del Rio's volcano worship in *Bird of Paradise*. Actually, the Sheban idolatry looks like a great deal more fun than Mr. Brynner's Judaism, and it is only through the most puerile of cinematic devices (such as God talking on the soundtrack and tossing around lightning bolts) that virtue ultimately triumphs. *Solomon and Sheba* takes itself too seriously and talks too much to get away with such nonsense. It is a film which cannot decide whether it wants to preach or entertain, and it winds up doing neither very well."[26]

Twenty-Three

1964 and 1980
Truth and Illusion and *The Metaphor*

Truth and Illusion (1964)

> "I have a 16mm Beaulieu camera and some zoom lenses and I wanted to make something, so I wrote a narration on metaphysics. I just figured it'd be something I'd like to do.... The young fellow working with me knew nothing about cameras or anything. It was just like a home movie, just the two of us."[1]—King Vidor, 1968

> "For an artist the thing to remember is, Know thyself. I think it's true of everybody in the art of living, whether you're doing an artistic thing or not, it's the art of being a person. We're all very distinctive individuals, and that's what it's all about.... Today we're getting at the immortal self, and to my way of thinking, that's God. He's not in an altar, not in a sunset, not in a sermon, he's inside. It all comes from inside, and that is the place of art."[2]—King Vidor (late 1970s)

In the later part of his life, after the completion of his last major feature film, *Solomon and Sheba*, Vidor failed to realize several projects that he had in mind, chiefly due to lack of studio funding. These projects included updated sound era re-makes of his silent movies *The Crowd* and *The Turn in the Road* (the former had the working title *Brother Jon* and the latter the working titles *The Milly Story* and *Conquest*), a filmed biography of Christian Science founder Mary Baker Eddy, an adaptation of Hawthorne's *The Marble Faun*, a film biography of the troubled actor James Murray (lead actor of *The Crowd*), and a movie about the legendary Spanish writer Miguel de Cervantes (portrayed as a young man).[3] Vidor also expressed a desire to film an adaptation of Bruce Catton's Civil War book *A Stillness at Appomattox*. None of these projects came to fruition, though Vidor came close in a few instances: he said that he had gained the interest of Francis Ford Coppola in the James Murray story and the interest of producer Arthur Jacobs in a re-make of *The Crowd*.[4]

After *Solomon and Sheba*, and relying on his own resources, he lowered his expectations for doing another major feature and turned to making more personal, low-cost films including a short documentary about the California town where his ranch was located (Paso Robles) as well as *Truth and Illusion: An Introduction to Metaphysics*, a highly personal and speculative experiment in filmmaking. This 25-minute-long documentary, made initially under the pseudonym Nicholas Rodiv (the surname is "Vidor" spelled backwards), is an effort to demonstrate the capacity of cinematic art to raise philosophical questions and to evoke philosophical ideas. In the end, it fails in the attempt to rise to the level of a great documentary (or even a good one, for that matter), and yet the very attempt shows that Vidor retained a bold interest in exploring the potential of his own art form to express a sense of individuality. While the result is on the amateurish side, both intellectually and cinematically, the idea behind the effort and the will to execute it are certainly not.

Later in his life, Vidor had often referred to philosophy—and "ontology," more specifically—as one of his passionate interests.[5] *Truth and Illusion*, initially based on a four- to five-page "narrative" that the director had written, makes clear that the director was interested in exploring the intersections between broader philosophical interests—the nature of truth, reality, and perception—and the philosophical aspects of cinema itself. As he told an interviewer, "[I]t was always said that you can't photograph thoughts. Producers always liked to say that, if the writer put in something that a person was thinking. That stuck with me, and I wanted to see if I could reproduce thoughts on film." He then said that he was also interested in seeing "what the limits were to an individual filmmaker without having to pay actors."[6]

Vidor is certainly not the only filmmaker to make explicitly philosophical movies or to philosophize about his own art form. Names such as Eisenstein, Pudovkin, Godard, Truffaut, Bresson, Antonioni, and Tarkovksy come to mind. But he is certainly the first major Hollywood director to do so, and one who began his career in the silent era. This is especially significant when contrasted with a contemporary such as John Ford who remained famously tight-lipped when asked in interviews about the more intellectual or psychological aspects of his own movies and who typically referred to his vocation as a simple "job of work," even resisting the label of "artist." Vidor, on the other hand, wrote an autobiography about his life as a film artist (*A Tree Is a Tree*, 1953) as well as a book on the art of filmmaking (*King Vidor on Film Making*, 1972). Both books conclude with more general philosophical reflections on the ways in which cinematic art reflects life and reality. And throughout his entire career, he did not shy away from interviews about his films and about cinema in general.

In *Truth and Illusion*, Vidor not only connects cinema and philosophy, but he also suggests a parallel between the optical phenomenon that is necessary for the very experience of movie-watching ("persistence of vision") and the nature of our relation to "reality." Vidor's interest in such philosophical topics is rooted in his oft-mentioned conviction in the fundamental primacy of individuality, a conviction that echoes such philosophers as Descartes, Locke, Kant, Emerson, Thoreau, and Nietzsche. Vidor's film makes clear that, for him, there can be no meaning or truth without the relation to a conscious subject. This is true not only for the perceiving, thinking mind of the movie viewer, one who provides for the integrated unity and orientation of the entire experience of a film. It is also, given what Vidor suggests, true for the integrated unity and meaning of "reality itself."

A viewing of this short documentary will show that his philosophizing here, not to mention his documentary filmmaking, remains at a fairly pedestrian level. He certainly raises interesting questions and he points to thought-provoking ideas, but they are all delivered in a rather fragmented manner. The tone of his narration of the film tends toward the didactic. His "theory" amounts to a rudimentary version of Bishop George Berkeley's idealistic denial of materialism. Vidor briefly mentions Berkeley in the film, but he also mentions such a diverse array of thinkers and writers as Plato, Aristotle, Lao-tze, Jonathan Edwards, Arthur Schopenhauer, William Blake, William Makepeace Thackery, and Mary Baker Eddy. They are all thrown into Vidor's mixing bowl of speculations.

Vidor began to ponder the ethical-spiritual implications of his filmmaking at the very start of his career, chiefly through his interest in expressing his Christian Science background. *The Turn in the Road* (1919) was the first clear result of that interest. His belief in the irreducibility of individuality and primacy of consciousness was represented indirectly in his adaptation of Ayn Rand's *The Fountainhead*, though one major difference between Vidor's and Rand's perspectives is that Vidor begins from a religious or spiritual basis that Rand rejects outright. (See Chapter Twenty for a discussion of Vidor and Rand in connection with *The Fountainhead*). And in *Truth and Illusion*, his interests in ethics and moral psychology become secondary to his interests in epistemology (the nature of perception and knowledge) and ontology (the nature of reality, which Vidor sometimes seems to equate with metaphysics). At times Vidor appears to equivocate between epistemology and ontology, particularly in terms of conflating the meaning of something and its existence in reality. For Vidor, meaning and existence are ultimately the same—or any difference between them does not seem to matter.

What makes *Truth and Illusion* significant is two-fold. First, the film can tell us much about Vidor's own intellectual and spiritual worldview, one that certainly helped to inform his movie-making over the years. Secondly, *Truth and Illusion* is relevant in terms of Vidor's very attempt to use film to "do philosophy." This effort connects with contemporary debates among "film-philosophers" about the capacity of movies to present, in cinematic terms, unified philosophical theories and arguments.[7] Can movies in and of themselves "do" philosophy? More than a few film scholars and film-philosophers have attempted to uncover a filmmaker's moral worldview and philosophical vision by weaving together various threads (chiefly interviews, biographers, memoirs, and the films themselves) into an explanation of why that director made certain choices. A pattern of such choices may reveal a broader, deeper approach to fundamental questions about human nature and even reality per se. Such an explanation proves helpful in an auteurist appreciation of a filmmaker's body of work when certain patterns appear that connect with these fundamental questions.

What complicates these efforts in identifying the moral-philosophical vision of certain great directors are the following: resistance on the part of the artist in answering questions about his works or intellectual interests (e.g., John Ford); a filmmaker's strategy in creating puzzling or highly ambiguous works (e.g., Luis Buñuel or Michelangelo Antonioni or David Lynch); and the simple fact that the film depends on a collaboration of decision-makers including, of course, the screenwriter(s). So with this in mind, *Truth and Illusion* is a rather remarkable "confession" of a director's philosophical interests and worldview, fragmented and cursory as it is. And since this documentary shows no signs of irony, we can assume that it can be taken seriously as an intellectual document of Vidor's ideas and interests. It helps, of course, that Vidor is responsible for the entire film, including the script. (See the last section of this chapter for the authors' transcription of the film's narration.)

Now a person's philosophical worldview can change over time, certainly, but in Vidor's case, there is indeed some consistency and continuity, particularly when one looks back to the influence of Christian Science in his youth. As he learned more about the history of philosophy over the course of his life and as he became more exposed to various forms of philosophical literature, Vidor built on his original beliefs rather than rejecting and replacing them. *Truth and Illusion* makes this clear. It is not surprising that David O. Selznick had Vidor in mind for undertaking a film adaptation of selected stories by Hermann Hesse.[8] The idea of basing a movie around Hesse's recurring themes, which range from the ultimacy of individuality and personal experience to the idea of communing mystically with the spiritual unity of the universe, must have been highly attractive to Vidor in terms of his own personal philosophy. The project did not take place, alas.[9]

Above all, *Truth and Illusion* reveals Vidor's roots in Christian Science. According to this religious perspective, and as outlined in Mary Baker Eddy's 1875 book *Science and Health with Key to the Scriptures*, one can overcome (at least to some degree) the suffering of the material world through a better understanding of the nature of the Divine Being. A proper insight into one's relationship with God can improve and enhance one's moral well-being as well as one's physical and mental health. The founder of this religion, Mary Baker Eddy (1821–1910), declared that everything is ultimately mind and not matter. And this is the main theme of *Truth and Illusion*. For Vidor as well as the philosophy of Christian Science, God is the universal Mind, eternal and infinite and spiritual, and the material world is essentially "nothingness" in terms of its transience, finitude, and perishability. For Christian Science, God is also Love and purely good. An intuition of this truth through prayer and through the guidance of the Bible has redemptive and restorative power, as exemplified by Jesus who transcended sinfulness and who healed those who were ill. Evil, like matter, is unreal. Sacred Love is evidenced most clearly by the figure of Christ as the unity of the human and the divine and as the teacher of the Golden Rule ("do unto others as you would have done unto you"). And the power of prayer relies not merely on faith, but on greater knowledge of the divine laws that help to define human nature.[10]

Twenty-Three. *Truth and Illusion* and *The Metaphor*

Vidor wrote a clear summary statement of his sweeping philosophical worldview in the final chapter ("What Is a Film?") of his book *King Vidor on Film Making*, connecting his philosophy of cinema with his personal ontological and spiritual theory. It serves as a very useful departure point in understanding what he was trying to express intellectually in *Truth and Illusion*:

> Film is life. We can learn about film from many angles. But anything with a touch of the infinite is impossible to circumscribe. Film, like life, can move in new directions without warning; we must be flexible, prepared at any moment for any eventuality. My growing awareness in recent years that God lives within each of us has come to determine the entire future of my professional and spiritual life. Life is like Everest. It is there, waiting to be conquered.... All my life I have been interested in the science of being: ontology. And this fascination has kept pace with my professional dedication: film making. En route to participate in a program celebrating the fiftieth anniversary of a community church, I thought over this dichotomy [between interests in ontology and cinema] which exists within me. The basis of my philosophy is a belief in Oneness: Unity.... Must I, as a director, continue to see films and life as an antinomy? Why must I painfully shuttle back and forth between the real and the unreal? Life is one. I must try to meld the science of being and the aesthetics of cinema. Only by doing this can I hope to evolve a comprehensive and viable philosophy of film making. In previous chapters I have often spoken about the mark of the individual on the integrity of the film he makes. Is this individual integrity the answer to the integrity of living? How else are we to express our humanness? How else are we to express God?[11]

One is certainly reminded here of the Tolstoy quote that concludes Vidor's *War and Peace*: "The most difficult thing—but an essential one—is to love Life, to love it even while one suffers, because Life is all, Life is God, and to love Life means to love God."

While many films evoke philosophical questions, illustrate philosophical ideas, and include intellectual dialogue (Vidor's *The Fountainhead* exemplifies this well), *Truth and Illusion* is one of the first efforts (given the director's stated intentions) to explore whether film can "philosophize" apart from the mere utterances of a specific character or narrator within a given narrative. The movie comes up short in this regard, especially since it relies so heavily on Vidor's narration. But he does use visual images that connect metaphorically and conceptually with the more abstract ideas that he tries to convey through his narration, even if much of this is done in a rather clumsy manner. Vidor tries to use the images to evoke a form of speculative thinking that (hopefully) goes beyond the narrator's mere words. The meanings of the images and their interconnections are abstract because they are metaphorical. They are shaped by the viewer's intellect while first suggested by the narration. They are not determined fully by a particular character within a dramatic situation—as with, say, Howard Roark's court speech about the dignity and value of the human individual toward the end of *The Fountainhead*.

Truth and Illusion may not make the most compelling viewing, but it is entirely refreshing as a testament to a filmmaker who not only entertained such fundamental philosophical questions, but who did not shy away from sharing that interest with the public. Vidor remains very much in the tradition of the public intellectual, not because of any special educational training but because of his bold openness to sharing ideas as well as discussing his cinematic expertise. *Truth and Illusion* has not been widely seen due its general lack of accessibility for so long. And so it has rarely been discussed.

The opening is a medium wide shot of rippling lake water. We immediately hear the Narrator (Vidor) in a matter-of-fact voice: "The oceans roll. The stars shine. The wind blows. And children play. The flower blooms. A dog sleeps. And birds fly. We take them all for granted when they move harmoniously. Yet, we are confounded when malfunction occurs. We feel the universe is governed by an infinite cause, that God is omnipotent, all-powerful. The Bible tells us: 'And God saw everything that he had made, and behold, it was very good.' Yet, we sometimes wonder if there could be another cause, an opposing cause to the primal one. We ask if one is fact and the other fiction. One truth; the other illusion."[12] We are introduced to the idea of a possible fundamental duality, one that Vidor does not ultimately accept.

According to Vidor, we believe conventionally that we live within a material world. Vidor's choices of activities for the opening of the scene (birds flying, a dog sleeping, the wind blowing) are actions which we only question when they do not function harmoniously. With this introductory scene, Vidor evokes the view of reality that he opposes, which is that of an illusory materialism. Vidor also introduces the concept of God here. Vidor remarks that most people believe that God is inherently good; however, he counters this with newspapers telling of bad news. At least as an initial hypothesis, the idea of some universal harmony is considered as merely that: an idea. So in this introductory sequence, Vidor raises questions about the nature of reality and asks whether reality can even be defined according to conventional ethical concepts.

Vidor goes on to suggest that without consciousness and the active role of one's mind, no physical reality would exist *for us*. This seems rather tautologous and certainly not earth-shattering. Perception and knowledge are required if we are to perceive and know the world. Vidor gives examples of how our perceptions of material reality can create illusions or errors. We often accept such illusions or errors without questioning them, chiefly because our minds (reason or thought) become habituated in correcting these perceptual "mistakes." Our senses would lead us to believe that two parallel train tracks running into the distance would eventually converge, particularly since they appear to do so as they near a vanishing point on the horizon in our perceptual field. But we know better: otherwise, all trains would arrive at disaster on each trip. Likewise, we can all "see" the sun descending past the horizon at the end of each day, and yet we know that the sun does not sink into the sea. The perceived motion of the sun led our ancestors to believe that the sun is in motion around the earth (geo-centrism) and it took many centuries until those like Galileo and Copernicus corrected this habituated perception through better astronomical knowledge (leading to the newer theory of helio-centrism). Error and illusion occur in consciousness, via our perceptions of the world, and yet they can also be corrected in consciousness, via our intelligence and knowledge.

As we will see, Vidor leads the viewer to the idea that perceptions (which can be mistaken) are really all that we have when we know the world. The mind must eventually come to terms with the fact that, while we have our countless perceptions of objects, including perceptions of our own bodies, we really do not perceive material reality per se. That is simply an abstract idea and one that we must acknowledge as a mere idea. Just as our mind must occasionally correct for mistaken perceptions (the sun does not really sink into the sea), so must our mind correct for more abstract mistakes like the habituated belief that we can know material reality directly. Vidor is in many ways circling around Immanuel Kant's famous distinction between a mind-dependent perception (a "phenomenon") and a mind-independent object (a "noumenon" or "thing-in-itself"). He mentions Kant, along with more than several other thinkers, later in the film.

Vidor then discusses the optical phenomenon known as the "persistence" or "subsistence" of vision, the very phenomenon that makes movie-watching (and therefore movie-making) possible. We see the movement of many consecutive still images which, when this movement is sped up enough, can fool the eye and brain into thinking that it is the same image moving. Here, Vidor uses his own art form to demonstrate how the senses can deceive us while our intelligence can lead us to knowledge about the truth of what is happening. Watching a film is a sensory but illusory experience because what is happening on the screen is not really happening *and*, furthermore, the images that appear to be moving are not really the same image moving. We are "tricked" by the perceptual side of our conscious mental activity while the conceptual side can correct this deception. We attain the truth (via our intelligence) when we become aware that the deception (via our senses) occurs only within our consciousness and not within any reality beyond our conscious mind.

Vidor then emphasizes the "Platonic" claim that happiness results from knowing the truth. On the reverse side of that principle, the more that we suffer from error or illusion, the unhappier we become. Such a claim runs counter to the dictum that "ignorance is bliss." Vidor assumes that the ability of our thinking mind to correct for a perceptual mistake or for conceptual confusion leads to a more rational, and hence happier, condition for the individual. Furthermore, there are general illusions or mistakes that result not from perceptual errors but from our wrong abstract ideas about truth and reality. The director believes that the belief in materialism, in basing our worldview on the idea that the physical world is all there is and that our perceptions give us direct access to physical reality, must be corrected if true happiness is to be attained.

Vidor mentions the perennial thought-experiment of a tree falling in a forest (or in his example, on a deserted island). Does the tree make a sound if there is no one around to hear it fall? He stresses here the centrality of the conscious mind. His clear answer to this famous question: the falling tree does not make a noise unless there is an ear (connected to a nervous system) to receive the sound vibration and, beyond that, unless there is a mind to identify and register this perception *as a* sound. Here we are in Kantian territory. The mind is the point of self-consciousness that unifies perceptions (built on the raw data of the senses) by an act of judgment: this perception is the perception of a given object *for me*. The raw sensory data without a corresponding act of judgment would be undifferentiated, non-unified, and thereby unintelligible. Vidor's perspective clearly echoes Kant's revolutionary idea that we only know the world through our perceptions, that genuine knowledge requires both a perception and a concept, and that it is the mind that "shapes" reality (rather than vice-versa). Reality beyond our perceptions and concepts remains as a sheerly unknowable "thing-in-itself." It is clear that the director views matter as this unknowable, mind-independent reality that is ultimately *nothing* (no *thing*) to us from the perspective of consciousness.

Vidor claims that we make our own reality and that this entails responsibility. His ontological-metaphysical view implies a general sense of ethics. As he admits in the film, this view also entails that we are responsible in many ways for our own suffering, a burden that not everyone is willing to accept and that drives some to repress the challenge of our existential freedom. As philosophers such as Nietzsche and Sartre have pointed out, those who resist the challenge of their own self-creation often escape into mere conformism or inauthenticity.

Vidor takes the extra leap of making metaphysical claims that Kant deemed impossible due to the very limits of human reason. Kant drew strict limits around the capacity of the mind to *know* that which is not given to us through our perceptions. And since God is by definition absolute, infinite, and unconditional, God cannot be given to us as an object of knowledge. For Kant, God is an idea that remains as empty and unknowable: we can believe in this idea, but we can have no claim to knowing God. Vidor, like Mary Baker Eddy as well as the idealist Bishop Berkeley before her, tries to account for the reality of that which exists but which is not perceived or known. And he does so by saying that the universe (the reality beyond our minds) can only exist if, like the objects that become real for humans by entering into our consciousness, there is some Universal Mind or Self in relation to which all realities become perceived and known. And this Universal Mind or Self, according to Vidor and Eddy, is God as the Supreme Being.

The Narrator concludes the film: "It would appear therefore that mind is substance and matter illusion. As you watch this film, or watch anything else, know that it is mind which is accepting or rejecting or interpreting or, for that matter, forming it. If you like, matter can be considered, but only as a concept, but in that case it becomes mind and not material substance. So in reality, we must conclude that all is mind, from the rolling of the waves to a potato patch. Probably nothing is more important to the progress of humanity from its still primitive limitations than the understanding that consciousness is fundamental to experience. Whether experience is subjective in mind or is an external phenomenon is something humanity must decide. The world may well be at a crossroads, where a decision must be made."

Unfortunately, the final narration above confusedly conflates experience (an experienced object) and existence (the object itself). The narrator's concluding words are accompanied by a shot of a professor drawing a circle on a blackboard and this is followed by a glimpse of a man chipping away at marble. We then see a garden (potato patch), a busy city street with a large crowd, a montage of different people performing different actions, and then a literal crossroads. We can either accept Vidor's (and Eddy's and Berkeley's) view that "all is mind" (Universal Mind) or we can reject such a leap into a sheerly subjective idealism. Why such a decision "must be made" is not immediately clear once we conclude that the earth keeps turning and people keep perceiving and knowing, regardless of whether we choose this idealism or reject it. Vidor seems to imply here that the prioritization of materialism as a worldview can lead to the type of dangers that we already see in the modern world, ranging from the oppression of human freedom to the potential vast destruction of the atomic bomb. Just as such post–World War II films as *Duel in the Sun* and *Beyond the Forest* and *Ruby Gentry* point to the moral and psychological dangers that can result from an individual's lack of spirituality and personal unity, so does Vidor's *Truth and Illusion* leave us with the question of where humanity may be headed when it clings only to a purely materialistic philosophy of life and reality.

* * * *

The Metaphor (1980)

Legendary painter N.C. Wyeth wrote to his equally talented artist son Andrew Wyeth in a letter dated 1944: "The great men Thoreau, Goethe, Emerson, Tolstoy forever radiate a sharp sense of that profound requirement of an artist, to fully understand that *consequences* of what he creates are unimportant. Let the motive for action be in the action itself and not in the event. I know from my own experience that when I create with any degree of strength and beauty, I have no thought of consequences. Anyone who creates for *effect*—to score a hit—does not know what he is missing!"[13]

Earlier in his career, Vidor certainly fulfilled N.C. Wyeth's idea of the "profound requirement of an artist" when he took large financial risks and completed three of his most personal films: *The Crowd, Our Daily Bread,* and *An American Romance*. Later in life, after making *Solomon and Sheba*, and failing to find major studio financing for his dream projects, he turned his attention once again to more personal projects which were the furthest thing from big-budget profit-makers or prestige-enhancers.

It seems fitting that Vidor, toward the end of his life, wanted to make a short documentary film about his town of Paso Robles, California, given his recurring emphasis on sense of place and his strong memories of his boyhood in Galveston (see Introduction). But his project on Paso Robles went unfinished because the director turned his attention to a new project: a short documentary that would center on his dialogue with painter Andrew Wyeth, who wrote to Vidor and told him that he was a life-long fan of the director's silent film classic *The Big Parade*, first released in 1925. *The Metaphor: King Vidor Meets with Andrew Wyeth* (sometimes listed as *Metaphor*) is also in many ways about sense of place, especially in Vidor's discussion with Wyeth about parallel landscapes— the hillside in the final scene of *The Big Parade*, where Jim and Melisande finally reunite, and the hillside in more than several of Wyeth's paintings. That latter hillside is part of the landscape of Chadds Ford, Pennsylvania, near Wyeth's home, the area where George Washington and his army lost the Battle of Brandywine to the British. And it was at the Wyeth home in Chadds Ford where these two elder artists, Wyeth and Vidor, held their in-person conversation as a movie camera recorded it all.

Publicity photograph of King Vidor in 1959, the year that his final feature film *Solomon and Sheba* was released. After this, Vidor worked on developing feature film projects, all of which were ultimately unrealized due to lack of studio funding. However, he did complete the 25-minute philosophical documentary short (*Truth and Illusion: An Introduction to Metaphysics*, 1964) as well as the 36-minute documentary short *The Metaphor* (1980). The latter is centered on a recorded conversation between Vidor and one of his most admiring fans, the painter Andrew Wyeth (Photofest).

While *The Metaphor* might seem at first glance to be little more than a self-congratulatory home movie, it winds up being the record of a profound and poignant meeting between two great artists who have much to say about life, memory, symbolism, landscape, and art. In some ways it may be one of the most meaningful 35 minutes of film ever devoted to demonstrating the power and passion of art, a film that resonates with deep nostalgia, with a shared passion for the creative process, and with an appreciation for the importance of one's sense of objects and their settings. Vidor's documentary and its central topic, the lasting influence of *The Big Parade* on Wyeth and his paintings, is also discussed in Glenn Holsten's illuminating documentary *Wyeth* (2018).

Later in life, Wyeth wrote a heartfelt letter to the director, telling him of the lasting personal impact of *The Big Parade*: "For years I have wanted to write and tell you that I consider your war film *The Big Parade* the only truly great film ever produced. Over the years I have viewed the film many, many times and [with] each showing the certainty of its greatness deepens.... I have always viewed it with awe and must tell you that in many abstract ways it has influenced my paintings."[14] In Vidor's documentary, Wyeth tells the director that he first saw the movie as a boy of about eight years old with his father. He then informs Vidor that he has seen it "over 180 times," to the director's astonishment.

Wyeth had absorbed imagery from the film and these memories had played a role in the creative visions that led to such masterly paintings as *Christina's World*, *Afternoon Flight of a Boy up a Tree*, *Winter 1946*, *Snow Flurries*, and *The Patriot* (Wyeth's portrait of the old ex-soldier Ralph Cline, a work that is one of the focal points of *The Metaphor*). After receiving the letter, Vidor contacted Wyeth and they arranged to meet and have a conversation (along with the painter's wife Betsy) at the Wyeth home in Chadds Ford. Vidor brought along a camera and a camera operator and, with the Wyeths' blessing, filmed their warm-hearted chat. Topics of their dialogue included *The Big Parade*, the intersections between painting and cinema, and the importance of landscape, symbolism, and the subconscious in the life of the artist. That recorded conversation became the basis of Vidor's final film in his career. As Vidor later said about his trip to visit the painter:

> I knew he felt about America the way I did.... Often I had heard filmmakers talk of the influence that famous artists have had on their films. To my knowledge, this was the first time that a great artist had agreed to talk of the influence that a movie had had upon his work.... We were calling each other by our first names in about half a minute. Having seen the picture so many times, I guess he felt he knew me, and I was familiar with his work, so I felt I sort of knew him. There is a language of understanding, a bond between two people who are working in an artistic medium whose styles are somewhat similar.[15]

The viewer recognizes an instant rapport between Vidor and Wyeth, and it is a dialogue between equals who have long admired each other's work. They praise one another frequently during the conversation and Wyeth says that the director is simply being polite when Vidor tells the painter that he has had an equally profound effect on the filmmaker's works. But we do know that Vidor had long been interested in studying the art of painting since the time that he focused on the use of color just before making *Northwest Passage* in Technicolor in 1940. And he also took up painting as his own personal hobby around that time. For him, it was not merely a subject of intellectual study. Certainly *Northwest Passage*, *An American Romance*, and *Duel in the Sun* are three of the most "painterly" films ever made, particularly in their symbolic and emotional uses of color (as well as, one might add, certain scenes and sequences in his later *War and Peace* and *Solomon and Sheba*).

Wyeth was interested in almost every aspect of *The Big Parade*, but he eventually gets to the heart of what is, for him, the most essential aspect of the movie. He refers to it as a quality in almost every shot and scene that the painter finds to be "undefinable" (and thus, he says, "metaphorical"). In discussing this, Wyeth focuses on a scene in the movie where a soldier pins a "sharpshooter medal" on another soldier as they read a letter. Wyeth then points out that he used precisely such a medal in his famous work *The Patriot*, whose model was an older man named Ralph Cline, a veteran of World War I and a neighbor of Wyeth in Spruce Head, Maine (the painting sessions took place in 1964 in the attic of the sawmill where Cline worked). Wyeth once said of that painting, "It's actually a world—it's the thunder of the [Battle of] Meuse-Argonne—it's the tobacco he chews, the smell of the wood in his sawmill. I love to dream [and] to think about this thing that is going to be in the background."[16] And in their conversation about the painting, Wyeth gains enthusiastic agreement from Vidor when he tries to pinpoint that unanalyzable, metaphorical, and almost mystical quality of experience that can be garnered from an artist's unexplainable focus on one small object in a work of art, an object that initially seems to play a very minor role in the overall work:

> But let me state here seriously: If you look at my painting, I'm not too certain whether that medal of the sharpshooter hanging on the chest of Ralph Kline isn't probably to me the most important—probably the most important thing in the whole picture in that there was something when I looked at that on his chest that seemed to express many things to me. And I remember looking at the thing and rough—very quickly painting it in and then he had to leave, he had to go down and work in the sawmill. I took his tunic, stuffed it full of some pillows, put it on the chair, hung the sharpshooter medal on, and very carefully painted that in. [Vidor: Wonderful. Yeah, yeah.] Because to me it was symbolic of something that I, at the time, didn't realize. And all of a sudden, it dawned on me. Of course. It was part of my own life as a child. It epitomized my whole feeling and *that is the reason for painting*. Rembrandt would spend a lot of time on a piece of jewelry and make a man's face under a broad Dutch hat disappear and a broach would gleam. See what I mean? [Vidor: That's wonderful.] You *have* to bring out something that interests you....[17]

Vidor then responds:

> Yes, yes.... It reminds me of what I've heard sometimes. They use the word "metaphor" [Wyeth: That's right] which means that you use one image to express some other idea [Wyeth: Absolutely]. What else? If you took the ideas and expressed them right on the nose, as it were, then people might reject them and they might turn away [Wyeth: That's right]. But you take one image that is pleasing to someone or that they'll accept—to hell with whether it's pleasing or not, but they'll accept it—but you're saying something else with it. I heard that talked of a few days ago with students who study films and I know that's what goes on with all of your paintings. You can't just look at it and say it's a girl in front of a house or something. It has another meaning but the way to tell the other meaning has come to you with these figures and these images that you're using. And that's what you're saying about the sharpshooter [medal] too.[18]

Wyeth's wife Betsy listens intently to their conversation and then engages briefly in the warm-hearted chat. She tells Vidor that she has been reading a student's dissertation on Wyeth, a student who calls her husband a "metaphoric realist." Betsy Wyeth tells her husband and Vidor that they are both "masters of metaphor" and the painter interrupts her to say, "And don't forget Robert Frost." She continues, adding Frost to the mix: "We have a poet, an artist, and a great director that are masters of American metaphor. Just possibly this is a unique *American* achievement." Vidor immediately replies, "That's interesting.... The only thing I thought of in the early days of my work: I thought that everything looked to be exaggerated. And I thought I want to make the pictures not look so exaggerated.... I want it to look real but not be real."

In relation to the topic of metaphor, Vidor then mentions the power and magic of silent film and the fact that silent cinema leaves much of the dialogue up to the viewer's imagination. Wyeth interrupts him at this point:

> I don't want to interrupt here but I want to make this statement: I think that's the great difference that makes *The Big Parade* a classic film. Now I've seen it many times. I know the story. There's nothing shocking about the story after seeing it 180 times. But this strange quality that you can't define—which is a metaphor—is in almost every shot in that film, even toward the beginning of the film, which today many people would say is stilted: the way Hobart Bosworth walks across the floor and all of a sudden comes to a stop and looks. The silence of that early part of that film brings out the power of the action of the later reels and it's the difference that makes all the difference [Vidor: Gee, that's interesting. That's interesting. You've seen it enough times to ... each time the meaning ...] ... That's it. It's symbolic. Now a lot of people say, Andy, why do you look at this film so many times? I don't understand it. And all I can think of is: Well, Christ, then they don't understand my painting.[19]

For a filmmaker who had always spoken openly of his works as well as his art form and who, in his later years, boldly connected his interests in cinematic art with his interests in philosophy, there could not be a final film that is more apt in providing closure to King Vidor's career. It is a warm, nostalgia-driven documentary that brings together two masterful artists, with the great painter paying profound tribute to one of the great director's most successful movies. But it is also a recorded demonstration of the ways in which a shared enthusiasm for the power of art can reach a certain spiritual level of discourse while remaining focused on people, places, paintings, objects, and films.

* * * *

Authors' Transcript of *Truth and Illusion*[20]

Narrator (Vidor): "The oceans roll. The stars shine. The wind blows. And children play. The flower blooms. A dog sleeps. And birds fly. We take them all for granted when they move harmoniously. Yet, we are confounded when malfunction occurs. We feel the universe is governed by an infinite cause, that God is omnipotent, all-powerful. The Bible tells us: 'And God saw everything that he had made, and behold, it was very good.' Yet, we sometimes wonder if there could be another cause, an opposing cause to the primal one. We ask if one is fact and the other fiction. One truth; the other illusion.

"This universe comes to us as consciousness. Otherwise, there would be no universe to us, we could not be aware of it. Truth and illusion, illusion and truth.

Aren't we all searching for truth in one way or another? Are any of us satisfied for very long with the lure of illusion? The search for truth can be misdirected or sublimated in many ways. Here is an example where intelligence and knowledge negate illusion: no one fears that if a railroad train travels along these converging rails, it will encounter serious trouble. We simply know the truth about the parallel rails and ignore what the senses tell us. Here is another illusion that bothers us not at all: every evidence of physical sight says the sun is setting into the ocean. But intelligence tells us differently.

"The illusion of motion pictures is deceiving you at this very moment. Generally, we want to be fooled by and accept the illusion of movement set forth by a moving picture film. It is only when we enter upon a search for reality concerning the operation of a motion picture that the facts of an illusion interest us. There is not the least bit of actual movement in the scene you just watched. The illusion of motion is dependent on a phenomenon of sight called 'subsistence of vision.' [We then hear a woman who asks:] 'Are you trying to tell me that the whole world of the motion picture—the busy studios, the stars' homes with their swimming pools, the large theaters, the tremendous cost of the big spectacles—are all based on an illusion?' [The Narrator answers:] Let me explain. In the mechanism of cinema projection, an absolutely still photograph is held rigidly in the aperture of the projection machine and is uncovered momentarily by a revolving curtain or shutter. Even the movement from one photograph to the next is obscured from the viewer by the revolving curtain. If we were not so easily fooled this is what we would see...."

[A man asks:] "But what are these exposés to do with our daily life?" [The Narrator responds:] "The basis for happiness is knowing what is true, thereby dispelling the illusion of what is untrue, as in the example of the railroad tracks. The conviction that truth, when found, necessarily results in definite, positive good was the cornerstone of the Platonic philosophy. Modern physics knows that the materialistic philosophy must be modified and has already discredited the concept of the materialistic 'truly real.' In the field of the atom, we cannot escape the conclusions that our earlier notions of reality are no longer applicable. Recently, Harold H. Heighton, a chemist with the Dupont Chemical Company, told a symposium on nuclear physics ..." [Words from Heighton:] "All matter, everything in the universe, could be broken down to a kind of energy akin to light." [The Narrator:] "What then can be considered real? What then can be considered substantial? Let us consider mind, not brain, but mind as distinct from brain."

[The Narrator:] "The problem of overcoming this world seems so overwhelming because we are not aware that the world is formed by each one of us in his own mind. Someone hurts us. Someone else gives us pleasure. And we react. Where is the hurt? Where is the pleasure? In our mind. It is like this with everything of which we are aware. From the standpoint of modern science, Professor [Alfred North] Whitehead, one of the great scientist-philosophers, points out the same fact. Says he ..." [Words from Whitehead:] "Nature gets credit which should in truth reserved for ourselves. The rose for its sight, the nightingale for its song, the sun for its radiance. The poets are entirely mistaken: they should address their lyrics to themselves and should turn them into odes of self-congratulation on the excellency of the human mind."

[The Narrator continues:] "Did matter precede thought? The pot cannot talk back to the potter. The tree cannot say: 'I am a tree, behold my beauty and majesty.' It is mind that identifies a tree and decides on its appearance. Perhaps you have heard the question: If a tree fell on a remote island, with no one around to hear its crash, would it make a noise? The answer is decidedly no. Sound or noise is made by waves or vibrations causing a movement in the diaphragm of the ear. What is more, even this action or reaction could not be transferred into sound unless there was a mind or mental process to interpret it. Are we beginning to discover that mind is necessary for experience? Well, perhaps as far as sound is concerned. What about the color of a wildflower on the remote island? Light and color vibrations are akin to sound vibrations. The answer is the same. We can readily admit that the retina of the eye is necessary to perceive color. But how much color could the eye interpret without mind? None. Without mind, an isolated, physical eye could not distinguish light from darkness. We might even consider the substance matter of the remote island itself and still come up with the same answer.

"In as much as we seem to be dealing with the subject of metaphysics, it might be well to give here a definition of metaphysics. According to Webster [*Webster's Dictionary*]: 'The primary meaning of metaphysics is derived from the discussions by Aristotle, which deal with the nature of being, with cause or genesis and with the existence of God.' Aquinas considered it [metaphysics] to be concerned with the cognition of God. Mary Baker Eddy wrote, 'Metaphysics is above physics and matter does not enter into metaphysical premises or conclusions. Metaphysics resolves things into thoughts and exchanges the objects of sense for the ideas of soul.' The alphabet and the multiplication table operate in the mental realm. We have all the letter A's that we will ever need. The supply is infinite. No one can manipulate a corner on [on the market for] the letter A's and run up the price whenever we need to use one. The same goes for numbers. Help yourself to all the 5's you need. So you see changing things into thoughts is not so bad as it first might appear." [A dejected car owner asks]: "You mean to tell me that that new car of mine is only an idea?" [Narrator:] "Don't be frightened pal! It will be just as useful to you in this new concept and you can be just as proud of it. A great number of shiny, new material cars end up in the junk heap in a few years. But the idea of a car as effortless, smooth transportation is something you don't even have to have insured. Like the letter A's. Help yourself to a new car." [The car owner observes:] "There went my brand new Lincoln."

[Narrator:] "Which do you think came first, the idea of an orange or the piece of perishable fruit? As regards the atom bomb, you certainly know what came first. The same is true of the orange and it remains an idea first and last. The idea of the dollar bill. If you have a well-fixed idea of infinite supply, you have something permanent and indestructible. And you can go anyplace in the world, as long as you have a well-founded, permanent idea of the true meaning of wealth. As a matter of fact, if the truth were known, you simply cannot have a dollar bill without having it in consciousness, in mind. Your dollars in the bank are a mental concept. Don't be frightened: they are more secure that way. Have you ever heard of the other multiplication table, the counterfeit one? This is the negation, the lie about the true one, the error. Sound ridiculous? Not so ridiculous as many other things the same evil thinking has conjured up to confuse us. But all experience being subject to mind or consciousness makes it possible for us to admit or reject those conditions which cause harmony or in-harmony, happiness or unhappiness.

"Shakespeare said, 'As a man thinketh in his heart, so is he.' Whatever a man accepts into his consciousness, so is he. There just isn't any other place for the condition to be. Do you want some other opinions? Confucius: 'When you see a good man, try to emulate him. When you see a bad man, examine your own heart.' What is heart, but consciousness? Plato: 'What thou see-est that thou be-est.' William Thackery: 'The world is a looking glass and gives back to every man the reflection of his own face.'"

[We then hear a doubtful woman:] "If we make our own world, our world of consciousness, it would mean that we could not blame anyone for any condition that we seem to be suffering under." [The Narrator:] "It takes courage to admit it, but that is true. Reality is right here and now, in our consciousness. There simply is no 'out there.'"

[We then hear from a skeptic:] "So now you're telling us that time and space have no reality?" [laughs] "Don't make me laugh. Even by the fastest jets, it takes hours to cross the Atlantic." [The Narrator:] "New York is a concept of mind. London is also a mental concept. And in reality, you even take the jet into consciousness. How often have we said, I will take the train or let us take a plane. The plane does not take us, but we take the plane. Did you ever try to think of the beginning of time or the end of space? These are impossible concepts. Consequently, time and space have no materialistic reality. Why, even to a present day astronaut, our concept of time goes askew. Albert Einstein explained the complete instability of time. Is there anything reliable about time as we know it? Someone traveling from Los Angeles to New York City in an afternoon finds his watch three hours off when he gets there. And from San Francisco to Tokyo, we find our time incorrect by a whole twenty-four hours. Our astronauts saw many sunrises and sunsets in a single day. Not very exact or reliable. Time should be considered as a concept, which we have formulated as an expediency. Useful, until it begins to dictate its terms to us. Consider as a concept, but only as a concept.

"Space. Space. Some stars are a million light years away. Some farther. But what is beyond that? And beyond that? And beyond that? As any young boy might justifiably ask. Dr. Alexis Carrel has said, 'Any man who doubts the existence of God should go outside some night and look up at the stars.' Actually, material space doesn't make very good sense. But as a mental concept, it is entirely reasonable. It would appear from these explanations that real being and the nature of reality are synonymous with God and that God is synonymous with truth. We can therefore find out more about God, if we find out more about truth. We can discover more about truth, if we can discover just what falls into the category of illusion. Schopenhauer has said, 'Man has to think to know matter, so he cannot be materialistic.' Plato esteemed matter nothing and mind everything. Berkeley came to the conclusion that 'apart from some mind to perceive it, matter would be nonexistent.' Jonathan Edwards could say that 'the material universe exists only in the mind. The laws of nature: creations of our own understanding, acting upon the data of our senses.' William Blake: 'Man has no body distinct from his soul.' Lao-tze avowed that 'matter is nothing but an appearance for our perception.' Mrs. [Mary Baker] Eddy said, 'All must be mind or else all must be matter. Neither can produce the other. Darkness and doubt encompass thought, so long as it bases creation on materiality.'"

[The Narrator concludes:] "It would appear therefore that mind is substance and matter illusion. As you watch this film, or watch anything else, know that it is mind which is accepting or rejecting or interpreting or, for that matter, forming it. If you like, matter can be considered, but only as a concept, but in that case it becomes mind and not material substance. So in reality, we must conclude that all is mind, from the rolling of the waves to a potato patch. Probably nothing is more important to the progress of humanity from its still primitive limitations than the understanding that consciousness is fundamental to experience. Whether experience is subjective in mind or is an external phenomenon is something humanity must decide. The world may well be at a crossroads, where a decision must be made."

Filmography:
King Vidor as Director

The Galveston Hurricane (1913). Photography: King Vidor and Ray Clough.

The Grand Military Parade (1914). Footage of army troop parade in Houston. Photography: King Vidor and John Boggs.

In Tow (1914). Produced by King Vidor and John Boggs. Directed and written by King Vidor. Photography: John Boggs. Two reels.

1915: Vidor shot newsreel footage for Ford weekly, filmed the simulated documentary of a car theft in Fort Worth, and co-wrote and co-directed (with John Boggs) a short documentary on sugar refining in Houston.

1916–1917: Vidor chiefly wrote scripts for one-reel and two-reel films directed by others and acted in a five-reel film directed by Frank Lloyd (*The Intrigue*).

1918: Vidor directed a series of two-reel films that formed the Judge Brown series. These were produced and written by Judge Willis Brown for the Boy City Film Corporation and released by the General Film Corporation. The films directed by Vidor were *Bud's Recruit* (1918), *The Chocolate of the Gang* (1918), *The Lost Lie* (1918), *Tad's Swimming Hole* (1918), *Marrying Off Dad* (1918), *The Preacher's Son* (1918), *Thief or Angel* (1918), *The Accusing Toe* (1918), *The Rebellion* (1918), and *I'm a Man* (1918).

The Turn in the Road (1919). Directed and written by King Vidor. Stars: George Nichols, Lloyd Hughes, Winter Hall, Helen Jerome Eddy, Pauline Curley, Ben Alexander. Production Company: Brentwood Film Corp. for Robertson-Cole Film Corporation. 5 reels.

Better Times (1919). Directed and written by King Vidor. Stars: ZaSu Pitts, David Butler, Jack McDonald, William De Vaull, Hugh Fay, George Hackathorne. Photography: William Thornley. Production Company: Brentwood Film Corp. for Robertson-Cole Film Corporation. 5 reels.

The Other Half (1919). Directed and written by King Vidor. Stars: Florence Vidor, Charles Meredith, ZaSu Pitts, David Butler, Alfred Allen. Photography: Ira H. Moran. Assistant Director: Roy Marshall. Production Company: Brentwood Film Corp. for Robertson-Cole Film Corporation. 5 reels.

Poor Relations (1919). Directed and written by King Vidor. Stars: Florence Vidor, Lillian Leighton, William De Vaull, Roscoe Karns, ZaSu Pitts, Charles Meredith. Photography: Ira H. Moran. Assistant Director: Roy Marshall. Production Company: Brentwood Film Corp. for Robertson-Cole Film Corporation. 5 reels.

The Family Honor (1920). Directed by King W. Vidor. Written by William Parker from a story by John Booth Harrower. Stars: Florence Vidor, Roscoe Karns, Ben Alexander, Charles Meredith, George Nichols, Harold Goodwin. Producer: King W. Vidor. Director of Photography: Ira H. Morgan. Production Company: King W. Vidor Productions and First National. 5 reels.

The Jack-Knife Man (1920). Directed by King Vidor. Written by King Vidor and William Parker from a novel by Ellis Parker Butler. Stars: F.A. Turner, Harry Todd, Lillian Leighton,

Claire McDowell, Charles Arling, Florence Vidor. Producer: King Vidor. Director of Photography: Ira H. Morgan. Production Company: King W. Vidor Productions. 5 reels.

The Sky-Pilot (1921). Directed by King Vidor. Written by John McDermott, Ralph Connor (novel), Faith Green (adaptation). Stars: John Bowers, Colleen Moore, David Butler, Harry Todd, Kathleen Kirkham. Producer: Cathrine Curtis. Directors of Photography: L. William O'Connell, Gus Peterson. Production Company: Cathrine Curtis Corporation and First National. 7 reels.

Love Never Dies (1921). Directed by King Vidor. Written by William Nathaniel Harban (story: "The Cottage Delight"), King Vidor (adaptation). Stars: Lloyd Hughes, Madge Bellamy, Joseph Bennett, Lillian Leighton, Frank Brownlee, Winifred Greenwood, Claire McDowell. Producer: King Vidor. Director of Photography: Max Dupont. Production Company: King W. Vidor and Thomas Ince Productions. 7 reels.

Real Adventure (1922). Directed by King Vidor. Written by Mildred Considine, Henry Kitchell Webster (novel). Stars: Florence Vidor, Clyde Fillmore, Nellie Peck Saunders. Producer: King Vidor. Director of Photography: George Barnes. Production Company: Florence Vidor Productions—Cameo Pictures. 5 reels.

Dusk to Dawn (1922). Directed by King Vidor. Written by Frank Howard Clark, Katherine Hill (Story: "The Shuttle Soul"). Stars: Florence Vidor, Jack Mulhall, Truman Van Dyke, James Neill, Lydia Knott, Herbert Fortier. Producer: King Vidor. Director of Photography: George Barnes. Production Company: Florence Vidor Productions. 6 reels.

Conquering the Woman (1922). Directed by King Vidor. Written by Frank Howard Clark, Henry C. Rowland (story: "Kidnapping Coline"). Stars: Florence Vidor, David Butler, Roscoe Karns, Harry Todd, Bert Sprotte. Producer: King Vidor. Director of Photography: George Barnes. Production Company: King W. Vidor Productions. 6 reels.

Peg o' My Heart (1922). Directed by King Vidor. Written by J. Hartley Manners (play), Mary O'Hara (script). Stars: Laurette Taylor, Mahlon Hamilton, Russell Simpson, Ethel Grey Terry, Nigel Barrie, Lionel Belmore. Producer: Not listed. Director of Photography: George Barnes. Production Company: Metro Pictures Corporation. 8 reels.

The Woman of Bronze (1923). Directed by King Vidor. Written by Henry Kistemaekers (play), Hope Loring & Louis D. Lighton (adaptation). Stars: Clara Kimball Young, John Bowers, Kathryn McGuire, Edwin Stevens, Lloyd Whitlock, Edward Kimball. Producer: Harry Garson. Director of Photography: L. William O'Connell. Production Company: Samuel Zierler Photoplay Corporation. 6 reels.

Three Wise Fools (1923). Directed by King Vidor. Written by June Mathis, John McDermott (adaptation), James O'Hanlon (adaptation), Winchell Smith (play), Austin Strong (play) & King Vidor. Stars: Claude Gillingwater, Eleanor Boardman, William H. Crane, Alec B. Francis, John St. Polis. Director of Photography: Charles Van Enger. Producer: Not listed. Production Company: Goldwyn Pictures Corporation. 7 reels.

Wild Oranges (1924). Directed by King Vidor. Written by Joseph Hergesheimer (novel) & King Vidor (adaptation). Starring: Frank Mayo, Virginia Valli, Ford Sterling, Nigel De Brulier, Charles A. Post. Music by: Vivek Maddala. Director of Photography: John W. Boyle. Producer: Not listed. Production Company: Goldwyn Pictures Corporation. 7 reels.

Happiness (1924). Directed by King Vidor. Written by J. Hartley Manners (play and screenplay). Starring: Laurette Taylor, Pat O'Malley, Hedda Hopper, Lawrence Grant, Charlotte Mineau. Director of Photography: Chester A. Lyons. Producer: Not listed. Production Company: Metro Pictures Corporation. 8 reels.

Wine of Youth (1924). Directed by King Vidor. Written by Rachel Crothers (play) and Carey Wilson. Starring: Eleanor Boardman, James Morrison, Johnnie Walker, Niles Welch, Creighton Hale, Ben Lyon, William Haines, William Collier, Jr., Pauline Garon, Eulalie Jensen. Director of Photography: John J. Mescall. Producers: King Vidor & Louis B. Mayer. Assistant Director: David Howard. Production Company: Metro-Goldwyn Pictures Corporation. 7 reels.

His Hour (1924). Directed by King Vidor. Written by Elinor Glyn. Starring: Aileen Pringle, John Gilbert, Emily Fritzroy, Lawrence Grant, Dale Fuller. Director of Photography: John J. Mescall. Producer: Irving Thalberg. Assistant Director: David Howard. Production Company: Louis B. Meyer Productions. 7 reels.

The Wife of the Centaur (1924). Directed by King Vidor. Written by Douglas Z. Doty (adaptation) and Cyril Hume (novel). Starring: Eleanor Boardman, John Gilbert, Aileen Pringle, Kate Lester, William Haines, Kate Price. Director of Photography: John Arnold. Editor: Hugh Wynn. Assistant Director: David Howard. Produced by: Metro-Goldwyn Pictures Corporation. 7 reels.

Proud Flesh (1925). Directed by King Vidor. Written by Harry Behn, Agnes Christine Johnson, Lawrence Irving Rising (novel). Starring: Eleanor Boardman, Pat O'Malley, Harrison Ford, Trixie Fringaza, William J. Kelly. Director of Photography: John Arnold. Assistant Director: David Howard. Produced by: Metro-Goldwyn-Mayer, Metro-Goldwyn Pictures Corporation. 7 reels.

The Big Parade (1925). Directed by King Vidor & George W. Hill (uncredited). Written by Laurence Stallings (story), Harry Behn (scenario) & King Vidor (screenplay). Starring: John Gilbert, Renée Adorée, Hobart Bosworth, Claire McDowell, Claire Adams, Robert Ober, Tom O'Brien, Karl Dane. Producers: Irving Thalberg & King Vidor. Music: William Axt & David Mendoza (uncredited). Directors of Photography: John Arnold & Charles Van Enger (uncredited). Assistant Director: David Howard (uncredited). Editor: Hugh Wynn. Produced by: Metro-Goldwyn-Mayer. Runtime: 141 minutes (12 reels).

La Bohème (1926). Directed by King Vidor. Written by Frédérique De Grésac (screenplay) and Henri Murger (source). Starring: Lillian Gish, John Gilbert, Renée Adorée, George Hassell, Roy D'Arcy, Edward Everett Horton, Karl Dane, Mathilde Comont, Gino Corrado. Producer: Irving Thalberg. Music: William Axt, David Medoza & Maurice Baron (orchestrator). Director of Photography: Hendrik Sartov. Editor: Hugh Wynn. Production Company: Metro-Goldwyn-Mayer. Runtime: 95 minutes (9 reels).

Bardelys the Magnificent (1926). Directed by King Vidor. Written by Rafael Sabatini (novel) & Dorothy Farnum (adaptation). Starring: John Gilbert, Eleanor Boardman, Roy D'Arcy, Lionel Belmore, Emily Fitzroy, George K. Arthur, Arthur Lubin, Theodore von Eltz, Karl Dane, Edward Connelly, Fred Malatesta, John T. Murray. Music: William Axt. Director of Photography: William H. Daniels. Producer: Not listed. Produced by: Metro-Goldwyn-Mayer. Runtime: 90 minutes (9 reels).

The Crowd (1928). Directed by King Vidor. Written by King Vidor, John V.A. Weaver and Harry Behn. Starring: Eleanor Boardman, James Murray, Bert Roach, Estelle Clark, Daniel G. Tomlinson, Dell Henderson, Lucy Beaumont. Producer: Irving Thalberg. Music: Carl Davis. Director of Photography: Henry Sharp. Editor: Hugh Wynn. Produced by: Metro-Goldwyn-Mayer. Runtime: 98 minutes (9 reels).

The Patsy (1928). Directed by King Vidor. Written by Barry Conners. Starring: Marion Davies, Orville Caldwell, Marie Dressler, Lawrence Gray, Dell Henderson, Jane Winton. Producers: Marion Davies, William Randolph Hearst, King Vidor. Music: Videk Maddala & Richard Bronskill. Director of Photography: John F. Seitz. Editor: Hugh Wynn. Produced by: Cosmopolitan Pictures & Metro-Goldwyn-Mayer. Runtime: 78 minutes (8 reels).

Show People (1928). Directed by King Vidor. Written by Agnes Christine Johnson & Laurence Stallings. Starring: Marion Davies, William Haines, Dell Henderson, Paul Ralli, Tenen Holtz, Harry Gribbon, Sidney Bracey, Polly Moran, Albert Conti. Cameos: Renée Adorée, George K. Arthur, Eleanor Boardman, Charlie Chaplin, Lew Cody, Karl Dane, Douglas Fairbanks, John Gilbert, Elinor Glyn, William S. Hart, Leatrice Joyce. Produced by: Marion Davies, Irving Thalberg, and King Vidor. Music: William Axt. Director of Photography: John Arnold. Editor: Hugh Wynn. Assistant Director: Will Sheldon. Produced by: Metro-Goldwyn-Mayer & Cosmopolitan Pictures. Runtime: 83 minutes (9 reels)

Hallelujah (1929). Directed by King Vidor. Written by Wanda Tuchock (scenario), Richard

Schayer (treatment), Ransom Rideout (dialogue) & King Vidor (story). Starring: Daniel L. Haynes, Nina Mae McKinney, William Fountaine, Harry Gray, Fanny Belle McKnight, Everett McGarrity, Victoria Spivey. Producers: King Vidor & Irving Thalberg. Director of Photography: Gordon Avil. Editors: Hugh Wynn & Anton Stevenson (uncredited). Assistant Directors: Robert A. Golden & Harold Garrison. Music: Eva Jessye. Produced by: Metro-Goldwyn-Mayer. Runtime: 108 minutes (silent version: 7 reels).

Not So Dumb (1930). Directed by King Vidor. Written by George S. Kaufman (play), Marc Connelly (play), & Edwin Justus Mayer (dialogue). Starring: Marion Davies, Elliot Nugent, Raymond Hackett, Franklin Pangborn, Julia Faye, William Holden, Donald Ogden Stewart, Sally Starr, George Davis. Producers: Marion Davies and King Vidor. Director of Photography: Oliver T. Marsh. Editor: Blanche Sewell. Assistant Director: Harold S. Bucquet. Produced by: Metro-Goldwyn-Mayer & Cosmopolitan Pictures. Runtime: 75 minutes.

Billy the Kid (1930). Directed by King Vidor. Written by Walter Noble Burns (book), Laurence Stallings (dialogue), Charles McArthur (dialogue), Harry Behn, Willard Mack, John T. Neville, W.L. River. Starring: Johnny Mack Brown, Wallace Beery, Kay Johnson, Karl Dane, Wyndham Standing, Russell Simpson, Blanche Friedrici, Roscoe Ates, Warner Richmond. Producers: King Vidor and Irving Thalberg. Music: Fritz Stahlberg. Director of Photography: Gordon Avil. Editor: Hugh Wynn. Produced by: Metro-Goldwyn-Mayer. Runtime: 95 minutes.

Street Scene (1931). Directed by King Vidor. Written by Elmer Rice. Starring: Sylvia Sydney, William Collier, Jr., Estelle Taylor, Beulah Bondi, David Landau, Matt McHugh, Russell Hopton, Greta Granstadt. Produced by: Samuel Goldwyn. Music: Alfred Newman & Ray Heindorg (orchestrator). Director of Photography: George Barnes & Gregg Toland (uncredited). Editor: Hugh Bennett. Assistant Director: H. Bruce Humberstone. Produced by: The Samuel Goldwyn Company & Feature Productions. Runtime: 80 minutes.

The Champ (1931). Directed by King Vidor. Written by Frances Marion. Starring: Wallace Beery, Jackie Cooper, Irene Rich, Roscoe Ates, Edward Brophy, Hale Hamilton, Jesse Scott, Marcia Mae Jones. Producers: King Vidor, Harry Rapf, Irving Thalberg, William M. Weiss. Director of Photography: Gordon Avil. Editor: Hugh Wynn. Assistant Director: Robert A. Golden. Produced by: Metro-Goldwyn-Mayer. Runtime: 86 minutes.

Bird of Paradise (1932). Directed by King Vidor. Written by Richard Walton Tully (play), Wells Root (screenplay), Wanda Tuchock (screenplay) & Leonard Praskins. Starring: Dolores del Rio, Joel McCrea, John Halliday, Richard "Skeets" Gallagher, Bert Roach, Lon Chaney, Jr., Wade Boteler, Arnold Gray. Produced by: David O. Selznick & King Vidor. Music: Max Steiner. Cinematography: Lucien N. Andriot, Edward Cronjager & Clyde De Vinna. Editor: Archie Marshek. Assistant Director: H. Bruce Humberstone. Produced by: RKO Radio Pictures. Runtime: 80 minutes.

Cynara (1932). Directed by King Vidor. Written by R. Gore Brown (novel), Frances Marion & Lynn Sterling. Starring: Ronald Colman, Kay Francis, Phyllis Barry, Henry Stephenson, Viva Tattersall, Florine McKinney, Clarissa Selwynne, Paul Porcasi. Producers: Samuel Goldwyn. Music: Alfred Newman. Director of Photography: Ray June. Editor: Hugh Bennett. Assistant Director: Sherry Shourds. Produced by: The Samuel Goldwyn Company. Runtime: 78 minutes.

The Stranger's Return (1933). Directed by King Vidor. Written by Brown Holmes, Philip Stong (screenplay & novel). Starring: Lionel Barrymore, Miriam Hopkins, Franchot Tone, Stuart Erwin, Irene Hervey, Beulah Bondi, Grant Mitchell, Tad Alexander. Produced by: Lucien Hubbard. Director of Photography: William H. Daniels. Editors: Richard Fantl & Ben Lewis. Produced by: Metro-Goldwyn-Mayer. Runtime: 88 minutes.

Our Daily Bread (1934). Directed by King Vidor. Written by King Vidor (story), Elizabeth Hill (scenario) & Joseph L. Mankiewicz (dialogue). Starring: Karen Morley, Tom Keene, John Qualen, Barbara Pepper, Addison Richards, Lloyd Ingraham, Henry Hall. Producer: King Vidor. Music: Alfred Newman. Director of Photography: Robert H. Planck. Editor: Lloyd

Nosler. Assistant Director: Ralph Slosser. Produced by: Viking Productions. Runtime: 74 minutes.

The Wedding Night (1935). Directed by King Vidor. Written by Edwin H. Knopf (story) & Edith Fitzgerald (screenplay). Starring: Gary Cooper, Anna Sten, Ralph Bellamy, Helen Vinson, Sig Ruman, Esther Dale, Leonard Snegoff, Eleanor Wesselhoeft, Mila Davenport, Agnes Anderson, Hilda Vaughn, Walter Brennan. Producer: Samuel Goldwyn. Music: Alfred Newman. Director of Photography: Gregg Toland. Editor: Stuart Heisler. Assistant Director: Walter Mayo. Produced by: Howard Productions & The Samuel Goldwyn Company. Runtime: 81 minutes.

So Red the Rose (1935). Directed by King Vidor. Written by Maxwell Anderson, Edwin Justus Mayer, Laurence Stallings & Stark Young (novel). Starring: Margaret Sullavan, Walter Connolly, Randolph Scott, Janet Beecher, Elizabeth Patterson, Robert Cummings, Harry Elerbe, Dickie Moore, Charles Starret. Producer: Douglas Maclean. Music: W. Franke Harling. Director of Photography: Victor Milner. Editor: Eda Warren. Produced by: Paramount Pictures. Runtime: 82 minutes.

The Texas Rangers (1936). Directed by King Vidor. Written by King Vidor (story), Elizabeth Hill (story), Louis Stevens (screenplay) and Walter Prescott Webb (book). Starring: Fred MacMurray, Jack Oakie, Jean Parker, Lloyd Nolan, Edward Ellis, Benny Bartlett, Frank Shannon, Frank Cordell, Richard Carle, Jed Prouty, Fred Kohler. Producer: King Vidor. Music: Gerard Carbonara. Director of Photography: Edward Cronjager. Editor: Doane Harrison. Assistant Director: Russell Matthews. Produced by: Paramount Pictures. Runtime: 95 minutes.

Stella Dallas (1937). Directed by King Vidor. Written by Sarah Y. Mason (screenplay), Victor Heerman (screenplay) and Olive Higgins Prouty (novel). Starring: Barbara Stanwyck, John Boles, Anne Shirley, Barbara O'Neil, Alan Hale, Marjorie Main, George Walcott, Ann Shoemaker, Tim Holt, Nella Walker. Producers: Samuel Goldwyn and Merritt Hulburd. Music: Alfred Newman. Director of Photography: Rudolph Maté. Editor: Sherman Todd. Assistant Director: Walter Mayo. Produced by: The Samuel Goldwyn Company (as Howard Pictures). Runtime: 106 minutes.

The Citadel (1938). Directed by King Vidor. Written by Ian Dalrymple (screenplay), Frank Wead (screenplay), Elizabeth Hill (screenplay), Emlyn Williams (additional dialogue) and A.J. Cronin (novel). Starring: Robert Donat, Rosalind Russell, Ralph Richardson, Rex Harrison, Emlyn Williams, Penelope Dudley-Ward, Francis L. Sullivan, Mary Clare, Cecil Parker. Producers: Victor Saville & Hayes Goetz. Music: Louis Levy & Charles Williams. Director of Photography: Harry Stradling, Sr. Editor: Charles Frend. Assistant Director: Pen Tennyson. Produced by: Metro-Goldwyn-Mayer British Studios. Runtime: 110 minutes.

The Wizard of Oz (1939). King Vidor: uncredited director of most of the Kansas scenes as well as the Technicolor "We're Off to See the Wizard" scene.

Northwest Passage (1940). Directed by King Vidor, Jack Conway (uncredited) & W.S. Van Dyke (uncredited). Written by Laurence Stallings (screenplay), Talbot Jennings (screenplay) & Kenneth Roberts (novel). Starring: Spencer Tracy, Robert Young, Walter Brennan, Ruth Hussey, Nat Pendleton, Louis Hector, Robert Barrat, Lumsden Hare, Donald McBride, Isabel Jewell. Producer: Hunt Stromberg. Music: Herbert Stothart. Director of Photography: William V. Skall & Sidney Wagner. Editor: Conrad A. Nervig. Produced by: Metro-Goldwyn-Mayer. Runtime: 125 minutes.

Comrade X (1940). Directed by King Vidor. Written by Ben Hecht (screenplay), Charles Lederer (screenplay) and Walter Reisch (original story). Starring: Clark Gable, Hedy Lamarr, Oskar Homolka, Felix Bressart, Eve Arden, Sig Ruman, Natasha Lytess, Vladimir Sokoloff, Edgar Barrier. Producers: Godfried Reinhardt and King Vidor. Music: Bronislau Kaper. Director of Photography: Joseph Ruttenberg. Editor: Harold F. Kreiss. Assistant Director: Tom Andre. Produced by: Metro-Goldwyn-Mayer. Runtime: 90 minutes.

H.M. Pullman, Esq. (1941). Directed by King Vidor. Written by John P. Marquand (novel), Elizabeth Hill (screenplay) and King Vidor (screenplay). Starring: Hedy Lamarr, Robert Young, Ruth Hussey, Charles Coburn, Van Heflin, Fay Holden, Bonita Granville, Douglas Wood, Charles Halton, Leif Erickson, Phil Brown. Producer: King Vidor. Music: Bronislau Kaper. Director of Photography: Ray June. Editors: Harold F. Kreiss & Frank Sullivan. Assistant Director: Walter Strohm. Produced by: Metro-Goldwyn-Mayer. Runtime: 120 minutes.

An American Romance (1944). Directed by King Vidor. Written by King Vidor (story), Herbert Dalmas (screenplay) and William Ludwig (screenplay). Starring: Brian Donlevy, Ann Richards, Walter Abel, John Qualen, Stephen McNally. Producer: King Vidor. Music: Louis Gruenberg. Director of Photography: Harold Rosson. Editor: Conrad A. Nervig. Produced by: Metro-Goldwyn-Mayer. Runtime: Released at 151 minutes and soon cut to 122 minutes.

Duel in the Sun (1946). Directed by King Vidor. Written by David O. Selznick (screenplay), Oliver H.P. Garrett (adaptation), Ben Hecht (uncredited). Starring: Jennifer Jones, Joseph Cotten, Gregory Peck, Lionel Barrymore, Herbert Marshall, Lillian Gish, Walter Huston, Charles Bickford, Harry Carey, Joan Tetzel. Producer: David O'Selznick. Music: Dimitri Tiomkin. Cinematography: Lee Garmes, Ray Rennahan, and Harold Rosson. Uncredited directorial contributions: Otto Brewer, William Dieterle, Sidney Franklin, William Cameron Menzies, David O. Selznick, Josef von Sternberg. Edited by John D. Faure, Charles L. Freeman, Hal Kern, William H. Ziegler. Produced by: Selznick International Pictures & Vanguard Films. Runtime: Released at 135 minutes and cut to 126 minutes.

On Our Merry Way (a.k.a. *A Miracle Can Happen*) (1948). Directed by Leslie Fenton & King Vidor. Written by Laurence Stallings (screenplay), Lou Breslow (screenplay) and Arch Oboler (original story). Starring: Paulette Goddard, Burgess Meredith, James Stewart, Henry Fonda, Harry James, Dorothy Lamour, Victor Moore, Fred MacMurray, William Demarest. Producers: Benedict Bogeaus and Burgess Meredith. Music: Heinz Roemheld. Cinematography: Gordon Avil, Joseph F. Biroc, Edward Cronjager & John F. Seitz. Produced by: Benedict Bogeaus Production (Miracle Productions). Runtime: 106 minutes.

The Fountainhead (1949). Directed by King Vidor. Written by Ayn Rand (screenplay and novel). Starring: Gary Cooper, Patricia Neal, Raymond Massey, Kent Smith, Robert Douglas, Henry Hull, Ray Collins, Moroni Olsen, Jerome Cowan. Producer: Henry Blanke. Music: Max Steiner. Director of Photography: Robert Burks. Editor: David Weisbart. Produced by: Warner Bros. Runtime: 114 minutes.

Beyond the Forest (1949). Directed by King Vidor. Written by Lenore J. Coffee & Stuart Engstrand (novel). Starring: Bette Davis, Joseph Cotten, David Brian, Ruth Roman, Minor Watson, Dona Drake, Regis Toomey, Sarah Selby. Producers: Henry Blanke & Jack L. Warner. Music: Max Steiner. Director of Photography: Robert Burks. Editor: Rudi Fehr. Assistant Director: Al Alleborn. Produced by: Warner Bros. Runtime: 96 minutes.

Lightning Strikes Twice (1951). Directed by King Vidor. Written by Lenore J. Coffee (screenplay) & Margaret Echard (novel). Starring: Ruth Roman, Richard Todd, Mercedes McCambridge, Zachary Scott, Frank Conroy, Kathryn Givney, Rhys Williams, Darryl Hickman, Nacho Galindo. Producer: Henry Blanke. Music: Max Steiner. Director of Photography: Sidney Hickox. Editor: Thomas Reilly. Assistant Director: Frank Mattison. Produced by: Warner Bros. Runtime: 91 minutes.

Japanese War Bride (1952). Directed by King Vidor. Written by Anson Bond (story) and Catherine Turney. Starring: Shirley Yamaguchi, Don Taylor, Cameron Mitchell, Marie Windsor, James Bell, Louise Lorimer, Philip Ahn. Producer: Joseph Bernhard. Music: Arthur Lange & Emil Newman. Director of Photography: Lionel London. Editor: Terry O. Morse. Assistant Director: Jack R. Berne. Produced by: Joseph Bernhard Productions Inc. Runtime: 91 minutes.

Ruby Gentry (1952). Directed by King Vidor. Written by Silvia Richards (screenplay) & Arthur

Fitz-Richard. Starring: Jennifer Jones, Charlton Heston, Karl Malden, Tom Tully, Barney Phillips, James Anderson, Josephine Hutchinson, Phyllis Avery, Herbert Heyes. Producers: Joseph Bernhard and King Vidor. Music: Heinz Roemheld. Director of Photography: Russell Harlan. Assistant Director: Milton Carter. Produced by: Bernhard-Vidor Productions Inc. Runtime: 82 minutes.

"Light's Diamond Jubilee." Television. (1954). Two segments directed by King Vidor: "A Kiss for the Lieutenant" and "Leader of the People." Producer: David O. Selznick.

Man Without a Star (1955). Directed by King Vidor. Written by Borden Chase (screenplay), D.D. Beauchamp (screenplay) and Dee Linford (novel). Starring: Kirk Douglas, Jeanne Crain, Claire Trevor, William Campbell, Richard Boone, Jay C. Flippen, Myrna Hansen, Mara Corday. Producer: Aaron Rosenberg. Music: Hans J. Salter & Herman Stein. Director of Photography: Russell Metty. Editor: Virgil W. Vogel. Produced by: Universal International Pictures (UI). Runtime: 89 minutes.

War and Peace (1956). Directed by King Vidor. Written by Leo Tolstoy (novel), Bridget Boland (adaptation), Robert Westerby (adaptation), King Vidor (adaptation), Mario Camerini (adaptation), Ennio De Concini (adaptation), Ivo Perilli (adaptation), Gian Gaspere Napolitano (screenplay) and Mario Soldati (screenplay). Starring: Audrey Hepburn, Henry Fonda, Mel Ferrer, Vittorio Gassman, Herbert Lom, Oskar Homolka, Anita Ekberg, Helmut Dantine, Tullio Carminati, Barry Jones, Milly Vitale. Producers: Dino De Laurentiis & Carlo Ponti. Music: Nina Rota. Director of Photography: Jack Cardiff. Editor: Leo Catozzo. Produced by: Ponti-De Laurentiis Cinematografica. Runtime: 208 minutes.

Solomon and Sheba (1959). Directed by King Vidor. Written by Crane Wilbur (story), Anthony Veiller (screenplay), Paul Dudley (screenplay), and George Bruce (screenplay). Starring: Yul Brynner, Gina Lollobrigida, George Sanders, Marisa Pavan, David Farrar, John Crawford, Finlay Currie, Harry Andrews, José Nieto, Maruchi Fresno, William Devlin. Producers: Ted Richmond (Copa Productions). Music: Mario Nascimbene & Malcolm Arnold. Director of Photography: Freddie Young. Editor: Otto Ludwig. Produced by: Edward Small Productions. Runtime: 139 minutes.

Truth and Illusion: An Introduction to Metaphysics (1964). Directed by King Vidor (as Nicholas Rodiv). Written by King Vidor (as Nicholas Rodiv). Narrator: King Vidor. Director of Photography: King Vidor. Editor: Fred Y. Smith. Assistant Director: Michael Neary. Runtime: 25 minutes.

A Personal Culture: Artist Tony Duquette (1973). Directed by King Vidor. Starring: King Vidor and artist-designer Tony Duquette. Producer: Bernard Kantor. Director of Photography: Douglas Knapp. Produced by the University of California's School of Cinematic Arts.

The Metaphor (1980). Directed by King Vidor. Starring: King Vidor, Andrew Wyeth, Betsy Wyeth. Producer: King Vidor. Photography: Deone Hanson & Brianne Murphy. Editors: Christopher Cooke and Rex McGee. Runtime: 36 minutes.

Chapter Notes

Preface

1. "King Vidor at N.Y.U.," *Cineaste* 1, no. 4, 1968, 3.
2. Peter Besas, "Today's Pix No Better Than in His Prime, Asserts Pioneer King Vidor," *Variety*, Aug. 11, 1971, 33.
3. Vidor dates this hurricane as 1909 in his interview with Nancy Dowd. Dowd and Shepard, 3. Histories of Texas hurricanes show that 1909 was the year of the famous Velasco hurricane along the eastern Texas coast. There is no record of a major hurricane in 1913.
4. On Vidor's references to some of these unrealized projects, see Dowd and Shepard, *King Vidor: A Directors Guild of American Oral History*, 278–90. For the reference to his hope to make a film adaptation of *A Stillness at Appomattox*, see Murray Schumach, "War Is a Game for King Vidor," *The New York Times*, Sept. 1959.

Introduction

1. See Raymond Durgnat and Scott Simmon, *King Vidor, American*, 31.
2. Nancy Dowd and David Shepard, *King Vidor: A Directors Guild of America Oral History*, 1.
3. Dowd and Shepard, 2.
4. King Vidor, *A Tree Is a Tree*, 15.
5. *Moving Picture World*, March 16, 1918.
6. *Exhibitor's Herald*, vol. 6, no. 12, March 16, 1918.
7. Vidor, *A Tree Is a Tree*, 16.
8. Vidor, *A Tree Is a Tree*, 16.
9. Vidor, *A Tree Is a Tree*, 17.
10. Vidor, *A Tree Is a Tree*, 18.
11. Vidor, *A Tree Is a Tree*, 19–20.
12. Vidor, *A Tree Is a Tree*, 19–20.
13. Vidor, *A Tree Is a Tree*, 21–22.
14. Dowd and Shepard, 54.
15. Dowd and Shepard, 54, 183, 273–74.
16. Dowd and Shepard, 54.
17. Vidor, *A Tree Is a Tree*, 22.
18. Vidor dates this hurricane as taking place in 1909 in his interview with Dowd and Shepard, 3.
19. Vidor, *A Tree Is a Tree*, 22–23.
20. Vidor, *A Tree Is a Tree*, 24.

Chapter One

1. Louise Williams, "A Hoosier from Texas," *Picture-Play Magazine*, 1920, 63.
2. Left out of Vidor's memoir is mention of Boggs' wife, who is listed in *Motography* as co-owner of the company. "The charter of the Hotex Motion Picture Company of Houston was filed in the state department, capitol stock, $13,000. Incorporators, King W. Vidor, John N. Boggs and Lula Boggs." *Motography*, Dec. 19, 1914.
3. King Vidor, *A Tree Is a Tree*, 28.
4. Vidor, *A Tree Is a Tree*, 33.
5. Raymond Durgnat and Scott Simmon, *King Vidor, American*, 334.
6. Vidor, *A Tree Is a Tree*, 47–48.
7. Vidor, *A Tree Is a Tree*, 50–51.
8. "Bravely she ventures forth in the dead of night, into the pouring rain, to rescue her favorite puppy from the storm. But horrors! She locks herself out and is forced to take refuge in a neighboring house, not knowing that the house is quarantined on account of smallpox. And not only that, but Bobbie, in whom she is particularly interested, is also under quarantine." *Moving Picture World*, July 8, 1916, 214.
9. Vidor, *A Tree Is a Tree*, 66.
10. Vidor, *A Tree Is a Tree*, 69.
11. Vidor, *A Tree Is a Tree*, 72–73.
12. "Henry, hungry, and disappointed in love, intends suicide, and sells his body for ten bucks. With that much coin life seems sweet. Then his uncle dies and leaves him a billion dollars and he proposes to the undertaker that he take uncle at seven-fifty." *Moving Picture Weekly*, Oct. 6, 1917, 32.
13. "'Texas Tommy' goes to Peaceful Gulch looking for rest. He enters the dance hall and finds things too lively for him. A large and lovely lady protects him from the 'terrors.' They are all cowed by her except 'Montana Joe,' who decides to kidnap her and hires two Mexicans to help him. 'Texas Tommy' escapes and takes refuge in a deserted cabin. To this same cabin 'Montana Joe' brings his kicking prize and then despatches [sic] the Mexicans for a minister. 'Texas Tommy' sees his chance. He gives 'Montana Joe' a swinging blow and the plump and lovely Ida falls into the arms of her rescuer as the minister arrives." *Motography*, Nov. 3, 1917.

14. Louise Williams, "A Hoosier from Texas," *Picture-Play Magazine*, April 1920, 62.
15. Durgnat and Simmon, 335.
16. *The Moving Picture Weekly*, Oct. 20, 1917, 34.
17. Vidor, *A Tree Is a Tree*, 75.
18. *Exhibitors Herald*, Sept. 8, 1917, 38.
19. "Dug is the leader of the Jesse James Honor Club… They made a raid on Mrs. Thompson's chicken coop, are caught and taken to jail. In the Juvenile Court the Judge says he will let the boys go if each will earn three dollars and a half to pay Mrs. Thompson for the chickens. Tommy, who had eluded the officers, goes back to the coop and steals eight more chickens. When the boys arrive with their earnings the eight chickens are not accounted for and the Judge, disappointed in the boys, is about to send them to jail when Tommy confesses his share in the raid." *Motography*, Nov. 3, 1917.
20. *Motion Picture News*, Oct. 20, 1917.
21. *Motion Picture News*, Sept. 8, 1917.
22. "[Brown's studio] was located across from where the Selznick Studio now is, in Culver City on Washington Boulevard," Vidor recalled. "[Brown] didn't have enough money to build it. The people who financed the films furnished the money. The studio was called Boy's City. That was his idea, to have a Boy's Town, and [the kids] worked on the films and lived there. These films were released by the biggest company then, General Film. They own all of the patents." Nancy Dowd and David Shepard, *King Vidor: A Directors Guild of America Oral History*, 18.

Chapter Two

1. Maude Cheatham, "Veni, Vidi Vidor!" *Motion Picture Classic*, Aug. 6, 1919, 66.
2. Cheatham, 67.
3. Scott Simmon, "National Film Preservation Foundation: Bud's Recruit (1918) Film Notes," https://www.filmpreservation.org/dvds-and-books/clips/bud-s-recruit-1918-clip.
4. *The Moving Picture World*, Jan. 5, 1918, 106.
5. *The Dramatic Mirror*, Jan. 5, 1918.
6. *Motion Picture News*, Jan. 19, 1918.
7. *Moving Picture World*, March 23, 1918.
8. "The Picture Oracle," *Picture-Play Magazine*, Aug. 1918.
9. "King Vidor," Internet Movie Database (IMDB) filmography, www.imdb.com.
10. *Motion Picture News*, March 9, 1918.
11. Dowd and Shepard, *King Vidor: A Directors Guild of America Oral History*, 18.
12. Dowd and Shepard, 19.
13. *Motion Picture News*, Dec. 28, 1918.
14. *Exhibitors Herald*, April 5, 1919, 36.
15. *Wid's Daily*, March 9, 1919, 9.
16. *Wid's Daily*, May 13, 1919, 4.
17. *Motion Picture News*, Oct. 18, 1919.
18. Dowd and Shepard, 20.
19. Dowd and Shepard, 21.
20. *Motion Picture News*, Nov. 30, 1918.

21. *Exhibitors Herald and Motography*, March 22, 1919, 24.
22. It is worth noting that after the film was picked up for distribution, it played at an additional theater in Los Angeles where an alternate version of the movie was exhibited. This would mean that *The Turn in the Road* is not one lost film but two. "Since the initial showing of the film at this theatre [the Rialto in Los Angeles] it has been re-edited and contains many changes." *Motion Picture News: The West Coast*, Jan. 25, 1919, 8.
23. King Vidor, *Better Times*, American Film Institute Catalog of Feature Films, http://www.afi.com/members/catalog.
24. *Wid's Daily*, June 15, 1919, 17.
25. *Photoplay*, Sept. 1919, 84.
26. *Motion Picture News*, June 21, 1919.
27. *Motion Picture News*, Aug. 23, 1919.
28. *Exhibitors Herald*, Sept. 13, 1919, 62.
29. King Vidor, *Poor Relations*, American Film Institute Catalog of Feature Films, http://www.afi.com/members/catalog.
30. Laurence Reid, *Motion Picture News*, Nov. 1, 1919.
31. *Wid's Daily*, Oct. 26, 1919, 19.
32. *Motion Picture News*, Oct. 4, 1919.

Chapter Three

1. Richard Schickel, "King Vidor: Romantic Idealist," *Matinee Idylls*, 23.
2. Nancy Dowd and David Shepard, *King Vidor: A Directors Guild of America Oral History*, 25–26.
3. Vidor, *A Tree Is a Tree*, 85.
4. Vidor, "Creed and Pledge," *Variety*, Jan. 1920.
5. Herbert Howe, "The Healing Drama," *Picture-Play Magazine*, May 1920, 72–73.
6. "I Don't Want To," *Photoplay*, Aug. 1920, 35.
7. Frederick James Smith, "The Celluloid Critic," *Motion Picture Classic*, Sept. 1920, 44.
8. *Wid's Daily*, Aug. 8, 1920, 3.
9. Burns Mantle, "The Shadow Stage," *Photoplay*, Nov. 1920, 110.
10. *Exhibitors Herald*, Aug. 21, 1920, 91.
11. Charles Silver, "The Jackknife Man," Program Notes for the Museum of Modern Art's Vidor film retrospective "King Vidor: September 1–November 13, 1972."
12. Dowd and Shepard, 25–26.
13. *Moving Picture World*, Dec. 18, 1920, 898.
14. *Moving Picture World*, Jan. 1, 1921, 93.
15. *Picture-Play Magazine*, March 1921, 69.
16. Doris Claire, "Catherine Curtis: Producer," *Exhibitors Herald*, Nov. 27, 1920, 36.
17. *Exhibitors Herald and Motography*, June 21, 1919, 22.
18. *Variety*, Aug. 27, 1919, 73.
19. *Variety*, Aug. 27, 1919, 73.
20. Claire, 36.
21. Catherine Curtis Corporation records, American Heritage Center, University of Wyoming, Rocky Mountain Online Archive, https://rmoa.

unm.edu/docviewer.php?docId=wyu-ah07656.xml#idm629408.
  22. *The Film Daily*, Feb. 10, 1924, 1.
  23. *Variety*, Nov. 12, 1924, 1.
  24. Kari Frederickson, "Cathrine Curtis and Conservative Isolationist Women, 1939–1941," *The Historian*, vol. 58, no. 4, 1996, 827. JSTOR, www.jstor.org/stable/24451913.
  25. Glen Jeansonne, *Women of the Far Right: The Mothers' Movement and World War II*, 57.
  26. Vidor, *A Tree Is a Tree*, 88.
  27. Vidor, *A Tree Is a Tree*, 88–89.
  28. Sergei Eisenstein, "A Dialectic Approach to Film Form," orig. published 1929, reprinted in *Film Form*, ed. and trans. Jay Leyda, 45.
  29. *Exhibitors Herald*, May 7, 1921, 73.
  30. Burns Mantle, "The Shadow Stage," *Photoplay*, July 1921, 60.
  31. *Wid's Daily*, April 24, 1921, 5.
  32. *Variety*, April 18, 1921.
  33. *Motion Picture News*, Feb. 26, 1921, 1651.
  34. *Moving Picture World*, Feb. 26, 1921, 1083.
  35. Charles Silver, Program Notes, MoMA Vidor retrospective, 1972.
  36. Laurence Reid, *Motion Picture News*, Dec. 3, 1921, 2984.
  37. *Exhibitors Trade Review*, March 25, 1922, 1215.
  38. Summer Smith, "Newest Reviews and Comments," *Moving Picture World*, Dec. 17, 1921, 854.

Chapter Four

  1. Adele Whitely Fletcher, "Across the Silversheet," *Motion Picture Magazine*, July 1921, 103.
  2. *Exhibitors Trade Review*, Jan. 14, 1922, 497.
  3. *Exhibitors Trade Review*, March 11, 1922, 1031.
  4. *Exhibitors Herald*, March 11, 1922, 62.
  5. *The Film Daily*, July 2, 1922, 6.
  6. *Exhibitors Trade Review*, June 10, 1922, 79.
  7. *Moving Picture World*, July 8, 1922, 172.
  8. *Exhibitors Trade Review*, Sept. 9, 1922, 1025.
  9. *The Film Daily*, Sept. 3, 1922, 13.
  10. *The Film Daily*, Dec. 17, 1922, 9.
  11. *The Film Daily*, Dec. 17, 1922, 9.
  12. King Vidor, "A Pledge and a Creed," *Variety*, Jan. 1920.
  13. Vidor, *A Tree Is a Tree*, 99.
  14. *Variety*, July 8, 1925, 9.
  15. Vidor, *A Tree Is a Tree*, 93.
  16. *The Film Daily*, Jan. 24, 1923, 6.
  17. *Camera!* vol. 5, no. 30, Nov. 4, 1922, 18.
  18. *Motion Picture News*, Dec. 16, 1922, 3076.
  19. *Exhibitors Trade Review*, vol. 11, no. 13, Feb. 25, 1922, 899; *Exhibitors Trade Review*, vol. 11, no. 16, March 18, 1922, 1112.
  20. *Exhibitors Trade Review*, vol. 13, no. 22, April 28, 1923, 1109; *Motion Picture News Booking Guide*, April 1923, 111–12.
  21. Mary Kelly, *Moving Picture World*, April 14, 1923, 757.
  22. *Exhibitors Trade Review*, vol. 13, no. 22, April 28, 1923, 1109.
  23. *Exhibitors Herald*, March 10, 1923, 49.
  24. *The Film Daily*, vol. XXII, no. 86, Dec. 28, 1922, 1.
  25. *Exhibitors Herald*, Jan. 27, 1923, 30.
  26. *Motion Picture News*, March 17, 1923, 1267.
  27. *Camera!* vol. V, no. 45, Feb. 17, 1923, 16.
  28. Vidor, *A Tree Is a Tree*, 101.
  29. *Screen Opinions*, vol. 12, no. 9, August 15–31, 1923, 133–34. *Motion Picture News Booking Guide*, vol. 5, Oct. 1923, 52–53. *Exhibitors Trade Review*, July 21, 1923, 339. *New York Times*, July 23, 1923.
  30. *Moving Picture World*, July 14, 1923, 157.
  31. Vidor, *A Tree Is a Tree*, 103.

Chapter Five

  1. "King Vidor Says Story Need Not Be Kinetic," *New York Tribune*, Nov. 11, 1923, E4.
  2. *Motion Picture News*, Sept. 15, 1923, 1307.
  3. Vidor, *A Tree Is a Tree*, 103.
  4. *Motion Picture News*, Sept. 29, 1923, 1527.
  5. Charles S. Sewell, "Newest Reviews and Comments," *Moving Picture World*, March 15, 1924, 213.
  6. Frank Elliott, *Motion Picture News*, Jan. 12, 1924, 170.
  7. George T. Pardy, *Exhibitors Trade Review*, Feb. 16, 1924, 29.
  8. *Motion Picture Magazine*, July 1924, 52.
  9. *The Film Daily*, vol. 25, no. 17, July 20, 1923, 1. *Camera's Weekly Wake-em-up*, Special News Section, July 28, 1923, 1.
  10. Agnes O'Malley, "With the Producers," *The Story World and Photodramatist*, Sept. 1923, 89. *Scenario Bulletin Digest*, vol. 9, no. 7, Sept. 1923, 23.
  11. *Camera's Weekly Wake-em-up*, Special News Section, July 28, 1923, 1.
  12. "Coming Attractions," *Motion Picture News*, July 10, 1926, 1975.
  13. *The Film Daily*, Oct. 15, 1923, 4.
  14. *Exhibitors Trade Review*, March 8, 1924, 26.
  15. *Screen Opinions*, vol. 14, no. 2, April 1924, 38.
  16. *The Film Daily*, March 2, 1924, 9.
  17. *Exhibitors Trade Review*, March 8, 1924, 26.
  18. Vidor, *A Tree Is a Tree*, 107.
  19. Charles S. Sewell, "Reviews and Comments," *Moving Picture World*, July 26, 1924, 301.
  20. Herbert K. Cruikshank, "Box Office Reviews," *Exhibitors Trade Review*, July 26, 1924, 29.
  21. Denise K. Cummings, "Her American Career," Women Film Pioneers Project, https://wfpp.cdrs.columbia.edu/pioneer/ccp-elinor-glyn/.
  22. Vidor, *A Tree Is a Tree*, 107.
  23. Vidor, *A Tree Is a Tree*, 108.
  24. Vidor, *A Tree Is a Tree*, 109–10.
  25. George T. Pardy, "Box Office Reviews," *Exhibitors Trade Review*, Oct. 11, 1924, 34.

26. Charles S. Sewell, *Moving Picture World*, Sept. 20, 1924, 246.
27. Stanley Wallis, "What the Fans Think," *Picture-Play Magazine*, vol. 22, no. 6, Aug. 6, 1925, 9.
28. Dowd and Shepard, *King Vidor: A Directors Guild of America Oral History*, 64.
29. George T. Pardy, *Exhibitors Trade Review*, Jan. 31, 1925, 47.
30. Agnes Smith, "The Screen in Review," *Picture-Play Magazine*, vol. 22, no. 2, April 1925, 56.

Chapter Six

1. "Changes in Screen Art Predicted," *Los Angeles Times*, Feb. 25, 1925, A9.
2. Charles Silver, "*Proud Flesh*," Program Notes, King Vidor Retrospective at the Museum of Modern Art, Sept. 1–Nov. 13, 1972.
3. *Moving Picture World*, Feb. 28, 1925, 921.
4. Nancy Dowd and David Shepard, *King Vidor: A Directors Guild of America Oral History*, 56.
5. Sally Benson, "The Screen in Review," *Picture-Play Magazine*, vol. 22, no. 5, July 1925, 54.
6. Frederick James Smith, "Making 'The Big Parade,'" *Motion Picture Classic*, vol. 23, May 1926, 26.
7. H. Mark Glancy, "MGM Film Grosses, 1924–28: The Eddie Mannix Ledger," *Historical Journal of Film, Radio, and Television*, vol. 12, no. 2, 1992, 127–44.
8. Patrick Robinson, *Guinness Book of Movie Facts and Feats* (4th ed.), 30. See also Richard P. May, "Restoring *the Big Parade*," *The Moving Image*, vol. 5, no. 2, Fall 2005, 140–46.
9. "Honors for Arnold," *American Cinematographer*, Dec. 1926, 5.
10. Vidor, *A Tree Is a Tree*, 111.
11. Vidor, *A Tree Is a Tree*, 112.
12. Dowd and Shepard, 60.
13. Vidor, *A Tree Is a Tree*, 119. For the gum chewing scene, see also Dowd and Shepard, 62.
14. Vidor, *A Tree Is a Tree*, 117.
15. Vidor, *A Tree Is a Tree*, 115–16.
16. Vidor, *A Tree Is a Tree*, 116.
17. Vidor, *A Tree Is a Tree*, 116–17.
18. Frederick James Smith, "Making 'The Big Parade,'" 26.
19. Dowd and Shepard, 68–69.
20. Dowd and Shepard, 70.
21. Vidor, *A Tree Is a Tree*, 125–126.
22. "King Vidor—*The Metaphor* (1980)," *Cinema of the World* website, Sept. 25, 2021, https://worldscinema.org/2021/09/the-metaphor-1980/.
23. These lines from *The Metaphor* have been faithfully transcribed by the authors directly from the documentary.

Chapter Seven

1. "Vidor Tells of Desire to Film 'Bohème,'" *The New York Herald Tribune*, Jan. 31, 1926, D3.
2. Louis B. Mayer, "Louis B. Mayer, on Trip East, Announces Great Production Program for M.-G.-M.," *Moving Picture World*, vol. 76, no. 6, Oct. 10, 1925, 464.
3. Margaret Reid, "Looking On with an Extra Girl," *Picture-Play Magazine*, vol. 23, no. 6, Feb. 1926, 52–55, 100.
4. Nancy Dowd and David Shepard, *King Vidor: A Directors Guild of America Oral History*, 93.
5. Edwin and Elza Schallert, "Hollywood High Lights," *Picture-Play Magazine*, vol. 23, no. 3, Nov. 1925, 55.
6. Agnes Smith, "Just Among Ourselves," *Motion Picture Magazine*, vol. 31, no. 4, May 1926, 57.
7. James R. Quirk, "Speaking of Pictures," *Photoplay*, vol. 29, no. 5, April 1926, 27.
8. *Variety*, Dec. 31, 1925.
9. Sally Benson, "The Screen in Review," *Picture-Play Magazine*, vol. 24, no. 4, June 1926, 54.
10. *Variety*, March 3, 1926, 34.
11. Vidor, *A Tree Is a Tree*, 132–33.
12. The other Garbo-Gilbert films are *Love* (1927), *A Woman of Affairs* (1928), and *Queen Christina* (1933).
13. *The Film Daily*, Oct. 17, 1926, 8.
14. "The Picture Parade," *Motion Picture Magazine*, vol. 32, no. 6, Jan. 1927, 61.
15. Mordaunt Hall, "Vidor-Sabatini Film," *The New York Times*, Nov. 7, 1926, 182.
16. Norbert Lusk, "The Screen in Review," *Picture-Play Magazine*, vol. 25, no. 5, Jan. 1927, 58.
17. David Bret, *Greta Garbo: A Divine Star*.
18. Vidor, *A Tree Is a Tree*, 171–72.

Chapter Eight

1. V.F. Perkins and Mark Shivas, "Interview with King Vidor," *Movie*, July/August 1963, 7.
2. "King Vidor Discusses Motion Pictures: His New Film Is Built Like a Play," *New York Times*, May 22, 1927, X5.
3. Nancy Dowd and David Shepard, *King Vidor: A Directors Guild of America Oral History*, 296.
4. *Motion Picture News*, vol. XXIV, no. 15, Oct. 9, 1926, 1382.
5. *Moving Picture World*, vol. 82, no. 6, Oct. 9, 1926, 4.
6. L.C. Moen, "Picking the Ten Best Films of 1927," *Motion Picture News*, Jan. 28, 1927, 293.
7. *The Film Daily*, vol. xl, no. 40, May 17, 1927, 4.
8. *The Film Daily*, vol. xl, no. 75, June 28, 1927, 4.
9. *Variety*, vol. LXXXVII, no. 12, July 6, 1927, 8.
10. *Motion Picture News*, vol. xxxvi, no. 2, July 15, 1927, 118.
11. *The Film Daily*, vol. XLII, no. 70, Dec. 22, 1927, 5.
12. B.G. Braver-Mann, "Vidor and Evasion," *Experimental Cinema*, vol. 1, no. 3, 1931, 26.
13. *The Film Daily*, vol. 38, no. 54, Dec. 3, 1926, 1.
14. Vidor, *A Tree Is a Tree*, 145.
15. *Motion Picture News*, March 25, 1927, 1043.

16. *Motion Picture News*. Dec. 28, 1918, 3912.
17. Vidor, *A Tree Is a Tree*, 145–46.
18. Jordan R. Young, *King Vidor's THE CROWD: The Making of a Silent Classic*, 16, 25, 29.
19. Jordan R. Young, 34–35.
20. "King Vidor: From Silents to 16mm," in *The Animator: Published Quarterly of the Northwest Film Study Center*, vol. III, no. 3, Summer 1975.
21. Jordan R. Young, 38.
22. Jordan R. Young, 35.
23. Our Film Correspondent, "King Vidor in England," *The Observer*, June 19, 1938, 11.
24. Jordan R. Young, 48–49.
25. Dowd and Shepard, 88.
26. Kevin Brownlow, "Foreword," in Jordan R. Young, 7.
27. Brownlow, "Foreword," 7.
28. Kevin Brownlow, *Behind the Mask of Innocence*, 299.
29. The above excerpts from reviews are given in Jordan R. Young's *King Vidor's THE CROWD: The Making of a Silent Classic*, 53–55.
30. Jordan R. Young, 57.
31. Charles Silver, "*The Crowd*," Program Notes for the King Vidor retrospective at the Museum of Modern Art, New York City, Sept. 1–Nov. 13, 1972.
32. Richard Schickel, "King Vidor: Romantic Idealist," *Matinee Idylls*, 21.
33. Schickel, 21–22.
34. Schickel, 27.
35. Jordan R. Young, 37.
36. Schickel, 29.
37. "King Vidor at N.Y.U.," *Cineaste* 1, no. 4, 1968, 7.
38. See Peter Bogdanovich's documentary *Directed by John Ford* that is included in the *Ford at Fox* DVD collection (which includes *Four Sons* and *Hangman's House*). And see especially John Cork's excellent documentary *Murnau, Borzage, and Fox* as part of the *Murnau, Borzage, and Fox* DVD collection (20th Century Fox).
39. Schickel, 23–24.
40. Schickel, 24.
41. Schickel, 24.
42. Raymond Durgnat and Scott Simmon, *King Vidor, American*, 78.
43. For Vidor's references to some of these unrealized projects, including Coppola's interest in his idea for the proposed movie *The Actor*, see Dowd and Shepard, 278–290.
44. King Vidor, "Screen Treatment for *The Actor*," *City* (S.F.), Sept. 9, 1975, 45.
45. Vidor, *A Tree Is a Tree*, 159.
46. Karina Longworth, "The Mistress, the Magnate, and the Genius," http://www.slate.com/articles/podcasts/you_must_remember_this/2015/09/marion_davies_actress_and_mistress_of_william_randolph_hearst_was_portrayed.html.
47. "'School Sessions' Held by Director King Vidor," from MGM "*Press Material: Eight Pages of Publicity, Ads and Exploitation*," no. 26, 1928.
48. "The Patsy," *Variety*, 1928, 28.
49. Mordaunt Hall, "The Screen," *New York Times*, April 23, 1928, 20. ProQuest.
50. "We Pay Our Respects to Miss Marion Davies," *The Film Spectator*, vol. 5, no. 8, June 9, 1928.
51. "Miss Davies Extols Vidor," *New York Times*, Jan. 29, 1928, 109. ProQuest.
52. "Miss Davies Extols Vidor."
53. Dowd and Shepard, 88.
54. "'Polly Preferred' Called Plagarism," *New York Times*, June 13, 1925, 10.
55. Dowd and Shepard, 91.
56. Dowd and Shepard. 90.
57. Dowd and Shepard, 99. And Vidor, *A Tree Is a Tree*, 170.
58. Dowd and Shepard, 91.
59. Durgnat and Simmon, 90.
60. Durgnat and Simmon, 92.
61. Angela Dalle Vacche, "Movies, Social Conformity, and Imminent Traumas," in *American Cinema of the 1920s: Themes and Variations*, ed. Lucy Fischer, 229.
62. Charles Silver, "American Film Comedy: May 13, 1976–January 4, 1977: *Show People*," Museum of Modern Art program notes, June 18, 1976.

Chapter Nine

1. "Another Negro Film," *New York Times*, June 2, 1929, X5.
2. "King Vidor's Fondest Dream Is Realized by Clever Work of Performers in *Hallelujah*," *The Chicago Defender*, June 8, 1929, 6.
3. Robert W. Dana, "King Vidor, Director of 'The Citadel,'" *New York Herald Tribune*, Nov. 13, 1938, E3.
4. Our Film Correspondent, "King Vidor in England," *The Observer*, June 19, 1938, 11.
5. King Vidor, "Director's Notebook," *Cinema Progress*, vol. 4, no. 2, July 1939, 2.
6. King Vidor, transcript of tape recording made by King Vidor and played at Cinema 16 on Feb. 1, 1955, when Vidor was unable to attend a screening of Hallelujah, as planned.
7. Nancy Dowd and David Shepard, *King Vidor: A Directors Guild of America Oral History*, 98.
8. King Vidor, "Scenes in 'Hallelujah' Stirred Players, Says Vidor," MGM Press Notes from NYPL.
9. Donald Bogle, *Toms, Coons, Mulattoes, Mammies, and Bucks: An Interpretive History of Blacks in American Films*, 30.
10. Judith Weisenfeld, *Hollywood Be Thy Name: African American Religion in American Film, 1929–1949*, 45.
11. Paul Robeson, *Film Weekly*, Sept. 1, 1933, quoted in Edward Mapp, *Blacks in American Films: Today and Yesterday*, 23–24.
12. Charles Silver, "King Vidor's Hallelujah," Inside/Out (A MoMA/MoMA PS1 Blog), June 15, 2010, https://www.moma.org/explore/inside_out/2010/06/15/king-vidors-hallelujah/.

13. Bogle, 30.
14. Vidor, *A Tree Is a Tree*, 176, 183.
15. Scott Eyman, *The Speed of Sound*, 291.
16. Vidor, *A Tree Is a Tree*, 182.
17. Vidor, *A Tree Is a Tree*, 183.
18. Bogle, 31.
19. Daniel L. Haynes, Internet Broadway Database, https://www.ibdb.com/broadway-cast-staff/daniel-l-haynes-48601.
20. Bogle, 31–34.
21. Vidor, "Scenes in 'Hallelujah' Stirred Players, Says Vidor," MGM Press Notes from the New York Public Library.
22. *Hallelujah*, Internet Movie Database, imdb.com.

Chapter Ten

1. Coincidentally, Davies's film right before *Not So Dumb* was a musical remake of *The Big Parade* called *Marianne* (1929), directed by Robert Z. Leonard.
2. Nancy Dowd and David Shepard, *King Vidor: A Directors Guild of America Oral History*, 110.
3. Vidor, *A Tree Is a Tree*, 183.
4. Dowd and Shepard, 111
5. David Nasaw, *The Chief: The Life of William Randolph Hearst*, 411.
6. Mordaunt Hall, "The Screen," *New York Times*, Feb. 8, 1930, 7.
7. "Not So Dumb," *Variety*, vol. 98, no. 5, Feb. 12, 1930, 19.
8. *Exhibitors Herald-World*, Feb. 15, 1930, 29.
9. "The Theatre: Dulcy Adapted," *Wall Street Journal*, Feb. 10, 1930, 4.
10. A.H. Frederick, "Picture Reviews, Previews, Shorts," *Inside Faces of Stage and Screen*, Feb. 8, 1930, 4.
11. Schallert, Edwin. "Billy the Kid Whitewashed," *Los Angeles Times*, Aug. 24, 1930, B15.
12. "New Wide-Screen Idea," *New York Times*, Oct. 19, 1930, 117.
13. Vidor, quoted in Elana Boland, "Honest or Hokum—Which does public want?" *Los Angeles Times*, Nov. 2, 1930, B9.
14. Dowd and Shepard, 113–114.
15. King Vidor, "King Vidor's New Film," *New York Times*, July 6, 1930, 90.
16. Vidor, *A Tree Is a Tree*, 189.
17. Vidor, *A Tree Is a Tree*, 192.
18. Edwin Schallert, "Billy the Kid White Washed: Western Epic Gives Outlaw Clean Bill of Health," *Los Angeles Times*, Aug. 24, 1930, B15.
19. Exterior shots were filmed in the Grand Canyon, Zion National Park, near Monument Valley, and in the Gallup, New Mexico, cave where Kit Carson had reportedly hid. The town set was "built from photos we found of the town," recalled Vidor. "It was built against the hills on the other side of [San Fernando Valley]." Dowd and Shepard, 114–15.
20. Raymond Durgnat and Scott Simmon, *King Vidor, American*, 185.
21. Vidor, quoted in Elana Boland, "Honest or Hokum—Which does public want?" *Los Angeles Times*, Nov. 2, 1930, B9.
22. Dowd and Shepard, 114.
23. H. David Strauss, "Billy, the Kid," *The Billboard*, vol. 42, no. 43, Oct. 25, 1930, 10.
24. Jay M. Shreck, "New Product," *Exhibitors Herald-World*, vol. 1010, no. 4, Oct. 25, 1930, 41.
25. H.A. Potamkin, "Reelife," *Close Up*, vol. 7, no. 6, Dec. 1930, 387–89.
26. "Billy the Kid," *Variety*, Oct. 22, 1930, 23.
27. Bill Crouch, *Motion Picture News*, vol. xlii, no. 11, Sept. 13, 1930, 55.

Chapter Eleven

1. "'Street Scene' Breaks Ancient Screen Mold," *Los Angeles Times*, July 26, 1931, B13.
2. Bosley Crowther, "Vidor's Individualist Manifesto," *New York Times*, Nov. 13, 1938, 181.
3. Elmer Rice also authored the book for Kurt Weill's 1946 opera *Street Scene*, based on Rice's original play. Weill provided the music, Rice provided the book, and Langston Hughes penned the lyrics.
4. Vidor, *A Tree Is a Tree*, 203.
5. Robert E. Sherwood, "Realistic Setting Contrived for Filming of Street," *The Sun*, Aug. 30, 1931, MR1.
6. *Motion Picture Herald*, vol. 104, no. 8, Aug. 22, 1931, 32.
7. "The Shadow Stage," *Photoplay*, vol. XL, no. 5, Oct. 1931.
8. Ralph Bond, "Street Scene," *Close Up*, vol. VIII, no. 4, Dec. 1931, 331.
9. Dalton Trumbo, "Trumbo Reviews," *Hollywood Spectator*, vol. 12, no. 8, Sept. 26, 1931, 22.
10. Mordaunt Hall, "When Murder Is Done," *New York Times*, Aug. 27, 1931, 25.
11. Jorge Luis Borges, "Street Scene," *Sur*, no. 5, Summer 1932, republished in *October*, vol. 15, Winter 1980, 6.
12. "Hollywood in Person," *The Atlanta Constitution*, March 1, 1935, 8.
13. Frances Marion, Internet Movie Database, https://www.imdb.com/name/nm0547966/.
14. Cari Beauchamp, *Without Lying Down: Frances Marion and the Powerful Women of Early Hollywood*, 273–74.
15. Jackie Cooper with Dick Kleiner, *Please Don't Shoot My Dog: The Autobiography of Jackie Cooper*, 50–52.
16. Alicoate, "The Champ," *Film Daily*, vol. LVII, no. 34, Nov. 10, 1931, 1.
17. Herman G. Weinberg, "Note from America: Part Two," *Close Up*, vol. IX, no. 1, March 1932, 52.
18. Mordaunt Hall, "Father and Son," *New York Times*, Nov. 10, 1931, 32.
19. King Vidor, quoted in Margaret Reid, "Intelligent Audiences Starved to Feed Morons," *Los Angeles Times*, Nov. 22, 1931, B11.

Chapter Twelve

1. "Doings Among the Writing Craft," *Hollywood Filmograph*, April 26, 1930, 20.
2. Christopher B. Balme, "Selling the Bird: Richard Walton Tully's 'The Bird of Paradise' and the Dynamics of Theatrical Commodification," *Theatre Journal*, vol. 57, no. 1, March 2005, 1–2.
3. "He Stole My Play, Says Woman Author," *New York Times*, Feb. 17, 1912, 11.
4. "Theatre Notes, Aug. 13, 1928," *Time*, Aug. 13, 1928.
5. "Doings Among the Writing Craft," 20.
6. Vidor, *A Tree Is a Tree*, 193.
7. Vidor, *A Tree Is a Tree*, 193.
8. Nancy Dowd and David Shepard, *King Vidor: A Directors Guild of America Oral History*, 130.
9. "In the Realm of Shadow Stories," *New York Times*, March 27, 1932, x4.
10. Rosalind Shaffer, "When the Movies Go Native," *The Washington Post*, May 1, 1932, TG10.
11. Richard Maltby, *Hollywood Cinema*, 593–97.
12. Joanne Hershfield, "Race and Romance in *Bird of Paradise*," *Cinema Journal*, vol. 37, no. 3, Spring 1998, 3.
13. "Bird of Paradise," *The Film Daily*, Aug. 12, 1932, 3.
14. Norbert Lusk, "The Screen in Review," *Picture-Play Magazine*, vol. xxxvii, no. 3, Nov. 1932, 51.
15. Harry Burns, "The Bird of Paradise," *Hollywood Filmograph*, July 30, 1932, 9.
16. Vidor, *A Tree Is a Tree*, 201.
17. Baxter, *King Vidor*, 49–50.
18. Dorothy Manners, "Looking Them Over," *Movie Classic*, vol. 3, no. 6, Feb. 1933, 25.
19. Mae Tince, "Cynara, in Film, Is Warning to Blithe Ladies," *Chicago Daily Tribune*, 1932, 23.
20. King Vidor, "Creed and Pledge," *Variety*, Jan. 1920.
21. "Cynara," *Variety*, Jan. 3, 1933, 19.
22. Mordaunt Hall, "Ronald Colman, Kay Francis and Henry Stephenson in the Pictorial Translation of 'Cynara,'" *New York Times*, Dec. 26, 1932, 26.
23. Hal Wiener, "Chit, Chat and Chatter," *Hollywood Filmograph*, Oct. 29, 1932, 11.
24. "Cynara," *Film Daily*, Nov. 12, 1932, 6.
25. Dowd and Shepard, 136.

Chapter Thirteen

1. Woejeong Joo, *The Cinema of Ozu Yasujiro*.
2. For a similar point about the film-going preferences of small-town audiences and former rural dwellers during the Great Depression, see Peter Stanfield's book *Horse Opera: The Strange History of the 1930s Singing Cowboy*.
3. Nancy Dowd and David Shepard, *King Vidor: A Directors Guild of America Oral History*, 138.
4. Dowd and Shepard, 140.
5. John Baxter, *King Vidor*. For example: "What sets Vidor apart from his contemporaries in this gentle field is, however, a dark, almost demonic view of the land. Where [John] Ford, even at his most engaged, remains relaxed and affectionate towards his subjects, Vidor sees America in another light, that of a treacherous and actively hostile environment in which one survives only by struggle and sacrifice" (Baxter, 2).
6. Dowd and Shepard, 139.
7. Raymond Durgnat and Scott Simmon, *King Vidor, American*, footnote, 139.
8. Leonard Maltin, *Leonard Maltin's 2012 Movie Guide*, 1332.
9. Woejeong Joo, *The Cinema of Ozu Yasujiro*.
10. Vidor: "The romance I had with Miriam Hopkins broke me up and left me with a terrible torch" (Dowd and Shepard, 143).
11. *New York Times*, July 28, 1933.
12. For example, John Mosher, "The Current Cinema," *The New Yorker*, Aug. 5, 1933, 40, or "Stranger's Return," *Harrison's Reports*, Aug. 5, 1933, 123.
13. Leonard Maltin, "Two Unsung Gems on TCM This Week," *Film Journal*, Oct. 13, 2014, www.leonardmaltin.com.
14. See "TCM Unearths Another Gem: *Stranger's Return* (1933) Returns to Television," Oct. 23, 2014, http://greenbriarpictureshows.blogspot.jp/2014/10/tcm-unearths-another-gem.html.
15. *Interview*, Oct. 1972.
16. Durgnat and Simmon, 140.
17. Dowd and Shepard, 143.
18. Jonathan Rosenbaum, Review of *The Stranger's Return*, Dec. 12, 2008, https://www.jonathanrosenbaum.net/2008/12/the-strangers-return-1933/.
19. Durgnat and Simmon, 146.
20. Dowd and Shepard, 143.

Chapter Fourteen

1. Vidor, *A Tree Is a Tree*, 220.
2. Vidor, *A Tree Is a Tree*, 222–223.
3. Vidor, *A Tree Is a Tree*, 149–150. This story is also detailed in Vidor's later "Screen Treatment for *The Actor*," which was his proposal for a later career movie based on Murray's life, career, decline, and demise.
4. Vidor, *A Tree Is a Tree*, 226–227.
5. Nancy Dowd, "*Our Daily Bread*," Program Notes, King Vidor Retrospective, Museum of Modern Art, Sept. 1–Nov. 13, 1972.
6. Nancy Dowd and David Shepard, *King Vidor: A Directors Guild of America Oral History*, 157.
7. King Vidor, "From a Vidor Notebook," *New York Times*, March 10, 1935, X3.
8. Raymond Durgnat and Scott Simmon, *King Vidor, American*, 168.
9. Dowd and Shepard, 151.
10. Vidor, *A Tree Is a Tree*, 207–208.
11. Andrew Sennwald, "'The Wedding Night,'

King Vidor's New Production, at the Rivoli—'High School Girl,'" *New York Times*, March 16, 1935, 19.
12. Norbert Lusk, "Critics Unite in Praise for New Sten Film," *Los Angeles Times*, March 24, 1935, A3.
13. Richard Watts, Jr., "Sight and Sound," *New York Herald Tribune*, March 24, 1935, D1.
14. Durgnat and Simmon, 172. See also Steve Pond's article "Before the Guild" (Winter 2011) and David Thomson's article "The Man Who Would Be King" (also Winter 2011) in the *Directors Guild of America Quarterly*, www.dga.org.
15. Durgnat and Simmon, 185.
16. Durgnat and Simmon, 183.
17. King Vidor, quoted in Hubbard Keavy, "Outdoor Film Is Real Measure of Cinema's Appeal," *The Washington Post*, July 12, 1936, AA1.
18. Dowd and Shepard, 160.
19. Watt, "Showmen's Reviews," *Motion Picture Herald*, Aug. 28, 1936, 44.
20. "Reviews of New Films," *The Film Daily*, Aug. 22, 1936, 4.
21. Leo Townsend, "Reviews," *Modern Screen*, Nov. 1936, 108.
22. "Texas Rangers (with Songs)," *Variety*, Sept. 30, 1936, 17.
23. Frank S. Nugent, "The Screen," *The New York Times*, Sept. 24, 1936, 29.

Chapter Fifteen

1. Vidor, *A Tree Is a Tree*, 261,
2. Lee Thomas Mason, "A private list of Akira Kurosawa's 100 favorite films of all time," *Far Out* magazine online, June 15, 2023.
3. Raymond Durgnat and Scott Simmon, *King Vidor, American*, 203–04.
4. Durgnat and Simmon, 204–05.
5. Vidor, *King Vidor on Filmmaking*, 130.
6. Nancy Dowd and David Shepard, *King Vidor: A Directors Guild of America Oral History*, 165.
7. Dowd and Shepard, 167.
8. Down and Shepard, 167–68.
9. Dowd and Shepard, 166.

Chapter Sixteen

1. King Vidor, "Director's Notebook," *Cinema Progress*, vol. 4, no. 1, July 1939, 2.
2. "An expectant public: 1948–2008–60 years of the NHS," *Birth of the NHS in Scotland*, Government of Scotland, 2008. See also S. O'Mahony, "AJ Cronin and *The Citadel*: did a work of fiction contribute to the foundation of the NHS?" National Library of Medicine online, National Institutes of Health (https://pubmed.ncbi.nlm.nih.gov), June 2012.
3. Charles Silver, "*The Citadel*," Program Notes for the 1972 King Vidor Retrospective, The Museum of Modern Art, New York City, Sept. 1–Nov. 13, 1972.

4. Vidor, *Vidor on Film Making*, 54.
5. Richard Schickel, *The Men Who Made the Movies*, 151–52.
6. Nancy Ellen Dowd, "*The Citadel*," Program Notes for the 1972 King Vidor Retrospective, Museum of Modern Art, New York City, Sept. 1–Nov. 13, 1972.
7. Richard Schickel, *The Men Who Made the Movies*, 153–54.

Chapter Seventeen

1. "Screen News Here and in Hollywood," *New York Times*, August 22, 1940, 23.
2. Philip K. Scheuer, "Town Called Hollywood," *Los Angeles Times*, Sept. 29, 1940, C3.
3. "Metro Sets Comrade as Next Gable Film," *Variety*, Aug. 28, 1940, 3.
4. Stanley Cavell, *Pursuits of Happiness: The Hollywood Comedy of Remarriage*, 1–2.
5. "The Strange Case of Comrade X," *New York Times*, Nov. 10, 1940, 152.
6. "Reviews of New Films," *The Film Daily*, Dec. 11, 1940, 5.
7. Lionel Collier, "Shop for Your Films," *Picturegoer and Film Weekly*, April 26, 1941, 14.
8. "Comrade X," *Variety*, Dec. 11, 1940, 16.
9. Bosley Crowther, "The Screen in Review," *New York Times*, Dec. 26, 1940, 23.
10. David Platt, "Lords of the Silver Screen," *Daily Worker*, Jan. 1, 1941, 7.
11. "Eugene Lyons Names Plenty of Film Notables as 'Pro-Red' in His New Book," *Variety*, Sept. 3, 1941, 3, 12.
12. Eugene Lyons, *The Red Decade: The Stalinist Penetration of America*, 287.
13. John Cogley, *Report on Blacklisting 1: Movies*, 1956, 11.
14. Nancy Dowd and David Shepard, *King Vidor: A Directors Guild of America Oral History*, 181.
15. Vidor, *A Tree Is a Tree*, 236.
16. Dowd and Shepard, 181–2.
17. In his essay "Country Music and the 1939 Western: From Hillbillies to Cowboys," Peter Stanfield begins by asking why so few A-Westerns were made between 1931 and 1939 and why so many A-Westerns were produced in and just after 1939. An important part of his answer has to do with the effects of the Great Depression as well as the growing specter of world war. During the Depression many laborers were driven from rural regions (particularly in the South) to the urban centers to find work and some of them were able to find jobs in the ever-growing defense industry. The migrants' "sense of dislocation," according to Stanfield, led to a need for "a nostalgic and sentimental reckoning with the recent past." Some of this need was satisfied by music and this led to a popularization of country and western music at the time, as an attempt to return for a moment to one's roots in the soil. Another part of the need was

satisfied by the major studios' committed investment in a cinematic renewal of the Western (Peter Stanfield, "Country Music and the 1939 Western," *The Book of Westerns*, eds. Ian Cameron and Douglas Pye, 33).

18. Andre Bazin, "The Evolution of the Western" (1955), in *The Western Reader*, eds. Jim Kitses and Gregg Rickman, 49.

19. Susan Paterson Glover, "East Goes West: The Technicolor Environment of *Northwest Passage* (1940)," in *The Landscape of Hollywood Westerns*, ed. Deborah Carmichael, 117–18.

20. Dowd and Shepard, 181.

21. "Roberts's novel *Northwest Passage* is not, of course, about the fictional artist Langdon Towne, but about the historical figure, Robert Rogers, a frontiersman who joined the New Hampshire Regiment in 1755. He became famous during the Seven Years' War (known in North America as the French and Indian War) as the founder and leader of the Rangers, a unit that adopted 'Indian' practices and pioneered what we now call guerila tactics… Following the war he traveled to London where he published in 1765 *The Journals of Major Robert Rogers* … [and] *A Concise Account of North America*… The publications were designed in part to help Rogers extricate himself from difficulties arising from his confused financial affairs (he argued that the British Army still owed him money for expenses incurred during the war and for this recruiting and provisioning of the Rangers) and also to promote his scheme of launching a search for a northwest passage to the West Coast of North America. In any event both ambitions were doomed to failure. Rogers died alone, forgotten, and in debt in the Fleet prison in London in 1795. The debts were never paid, others took up the search for a northwest passage, and Rogers seemed to disappear into obscurity" (Glover, "East Goes West," 114).

22. For an intriguing consideration of the influence of modern painting on King Vidor's aesthetic vision, with references to both Vidor's *The Metaphor* and *Truth and Illusion*, see Tag Gallagher's article "How to Share a Hill" in the archive of the online journal *Senses of Cinema* (http://archive.sensesofcinema.com/contents/07/43/king-vidor-andrew-wyeth.html). Included in Gallagher's online article are images from *Northwest Passage*, used as evidence to show that the style of Andrew Wyeth's father N.C. Wyeth in his illustrations had an influence on Vidor's imagery in this film.

23. Glover, "East Goes West," 117, 121.

24. Glover: "Eventually, Payette Lake in Idaho was chosen to represent the frontier 'west' of mid-eighteenth-century America. Crews were sent to begin filming in June 1938. In early July the crew moved to the Yellowstone River to shoot background film for a scene where the Rangers undertake a dangerous crossing through the rapids. Plans to continue filming in August were postponed, in part due to logistical and management problems, in part due to the advancing fall weather. With the script still incomplete, the crew returned the following spring to continue shooting. Because of advances in the technology of Technicolor in the interim, the film shot the previous summer under Van Dyke's direction was not used, and all the work for the film was done under the direction of Vidor" (Glover, "East Goes West," 117–18).

25. Glover: "Because of early frosts, the leaves began to change color; consequently none of the film could be used when production resumed the following summer. The risk of tick fever meant inoculating the entire crew, and costumes had to be checked nightly for ticks—clothes were laid out on white sheets at night so that the escaping insects could be seen and removed. And even 'the set' kept changing. The director, King Vidor, recalled a problem with scenes shot at the reproduction fort built on the lake; by midsummer natural fluctuations in the water table meant that the water's edge would 'recede so rapidly that in the space of a few days it would be impossible to get the lake and the fort in the same camera setup.' The physical environment posed formidable challenges to shooting the film, but the representation of that environment dominates the visual narrative in a way that subtly reshapes both the 'historical' and the 'novel'" (Glover, "East Goes West," 111).

26. Glover: "The scene where the Rangers form a human chain across the rapids was begun on location at the Payette River but given up when it proved too dangerous. Film was shot of the two riverbanks, and the balance of the scene was shot back at MGM's Lot 3, in an exterior water tank …" (Glover, "East Goes West," 121).

27. Glover, "East Goes West," 112–13.

28. Prats: "The Myth of Conquest is no less *appropriative* than is Conquest itself. What is Conquest if not omnivorously acquisitive—'just robbery with violence,' as Joseph Conrad might have put it, 'aggravated murder on a great scale'? And so Conquest's *mythology* presupposes the methodology of historical and cultural appropriation. I am referring to the notion, virtually enjoying the status of a first axiom, that the mythological alterations of historical events—*regardless, and often because, of the resulting distortions*—influence the national character, and that the selfsame alterations, taken as a system, structure, and pattern, become not only the major constituents of American culture but also the presumed methodology that articulates it" (Prats, *Invisible Natives*, 3).

29. See Prats' Introduction ("Representation and Absence in Northwest Passage") in his *Invisible Natives*, 1–20.

30. See Prats, *Invisible Natives*, 19.

31. Prats observes that Konkapot's "Otherness" is expressed most clearly, not by his drunkenness or simplicity, but by his complete dependence upon Rogers, even in terms of needing to be introduced to Langdon through Rogers's degrading description of him. See Prats, *Invisible Natives*, 16–17.

32. Fenin and Everson: "*Northwest Passage* has

a place in the general history of the Western for being one of the most viciously anti-Indian films ever made. Hatred for the Indian is apparently justified only by a sequence in which Indian tortures of a particularly revolting nature are described by a member of Rogers' Rangers, a man whose brother was put to death by the Indians. The motivating factor for the Rangers' raid is revenge, and the raid is actually a carefully planned massacre, in which Indian men, women, and children are wiped out ruthlessly. The Indian's side of the question is never presented..." (Fenin and Everson, *The Western: From Silents to the Seventies*, 245–46).

33. Glover: "In another reversal, while we are *told* about the savagery of 'the Indians' as Rogers prepares his men on the eve of the attack, we are *shown* the savagery of the Rangers as they silently enter the sleeping village and massacre the men, women, and children... In the cultural mapping of the film, the Indians are part of the landscape that must be overcome in order for the westward expansion of colonial settlement to continue. Yet the representations in the film show us only the retaliatory gesture of the Rangers, who are acting as part of the British Army" (Glover, "East Goes West," 123).

34. Vidor: "I was so enthused about the possibilities of the picture [*An American Romance*] that I thought at the time that it would not be dependent on stars to carry the story. I didn't realize until later that personalities can make or break a picture. They all had symbols that they stood for, and you had to have the right people playing the roles. I really learned a lesson on that film ... I think Brian Donlevy gave a wonderful performance in the part, but he symbolized something else entirely" (Dowd and Shepard, 200).

35. King Vidor, *King Vidor on Filmmaking*, 60–61.

Chapter Eighteen

1. Frank Daugherty, "Steel Comes to the Films," *The Christian Science Monitor*, May 8, 1943, B8 and 14.
2. Thornton Delechanty, "'Orson Welles Woke Us Up,' King Vidor," *New York Herald Tribune*, Nov. 16, 1941, E3.
3. Vidor, *A Tree Is a Tree*, 250.
4. Jean Francis Webb and Kay Hardy, "H.M. Pulham, Esq.," *Modern Screen*, Feb. 1942, 77.
5. Nancy Dowd and David Shepard, *King Vidor: A Directors Guild of America Oral History*, 187.
6. Dowd and Shepard, 192.
7. Vidor, *A Tree Is a Tree*, 251.
8. "H.M. Pulham, Esq.," *Variety*, Nov. 19, 1941, 9.
9. "Reviews of the New Films," *The Film Daily*, Nov. 13, 1941, 7.
10. Bosley Crowther, "The Screen in Review," *New York Times*, Dec. 19, 1941, 35.
11. Dee Lowrance, "An American Romance: King Vidor Films Saga of Steel," *New York Herald Tribune*, Oct. 29, 1944.
12. Frank Daugherty, "Steel Comes to the Films," *The Christian Science Monitor*, May 8, 1943, B8 and 14.
13. Author's transcription from the film.
14. Hollywood Renegades Archive, "The Motion Picture Alliance for the Preservation of American Ideals," The Society of Independent Motion Pictures Producers, http://www.cobbles.com/simpp_archive/huac_alliance.htm.
15. Raymond Durgnat and Scott Simmon, *King Vidor, American*, 319–320.

Chapter Nineteen

1. "Speaking Editorially," *Motion Picture News*, July 31, 1926, 388.
2. King Vidor, "Hollywood in Person," *The Atlanta Constitution*, March 1, 1935, 8.
3. Vidor, *A Tree Is a Tree*, 261.
4. Raymond Durgnat and Scott Simmon, *King Vidor, American*, 235.
5. *Duel in the Sun*, American Film Institute Catalog of Feature Films, online.
6. Vidor, *A Tree Is a Tree*, 265–66.
7. André Bazin, "The Evolution of the Western" (1955), in *The Western Reader*, eds. Kitses and Rickman, 49–56, 51.
8. While paying due attention to the psychological dynamics of *Duel in the Sun*, Patrick McGee concentrates on the class, race, and gender conflicts around which the movie often revolves. See McGee, *From Shane to Kill Bill: Re-Thinking the Western*, 59–68. He also refers substantially here (see McGee 61) to Laura Mulvey's emphasis on the film's gender and sexual dynamics in her book *Visual and Other Pleasures*.
9. The confrontation between the Senator's troop of ranch hands and the railway men (later joined by the cavalry) was filmed at Lasky Mesa in the West Hills of Los Angeles. The final scene between Lewt and Pearl was shot in Tucson Mountain Park in Arizona.
10. Vidor: "I think [Huston] stood absolutely alone in his excellence as a character actor. There was a man who knew how to act. I don't think there is anyone who can surpass his work, and I don't think anyone could ever take his place" (Nancy Dowd and David Shepard, *King Vidor: A Directors Guild of America Oral History*, 218).
11. Vidor, *A Tree Is a Tree*, 266–67.
12. Dowd and Shepard, *King Vidor: A Directors Guild of America Oral History*, 217–18.
13. *Duel in the Sun*, American Film Institute Catalog of Feature Films, online.
14. Dowd and Shepard, 222.
15. Dowd and Shepard, 210.
16. Dowd and Shepard, 222.
17. Dowd and Shepard, 226.
18. Durgnat and Simmon, 235–36.

Chapter Twenty

1. Nancy Dowd and David Shepard, *King Vidor: A Directors Guild of America Oral History*, 296.
2. Raymond Durgnat and Scott Simmon, *King Vidor, American*, 355.
3. Marc Eliot, *Jimmy Stewart: A Biography*, 216.
4. Durgnat and Simmon, 355.
5. "Bogeaus Revising Episodic Picture," *New York Times*, Aug. 9, 1947, 16.
6. Neil Sinyard, *George Stevens: The Films of a Hollywood Giant*, 93.
7. "Bank Claims Lien Also on Cutting Room Footage," *Variety*, July 14, 1948, 4.
8. "Miracle Title NG for B.O., Bogeaus Change Ups Biz," *Variety*, June 30, 1948, 7.
9. "Title Changes," *Boxoffice*, April 17, 1948, 53.
10. "Miracle Title NG for B.O., Bogeaus Change Ups Biz."
11. Durgnat and Simmon, 355.
12. John Baxter, *King Vidor*, 70.
13. Emanuel Levy, "*The Fountainhead* (1949): King Vidor's Powerfully Erotic Melodrama, Starring Gary Cooper and Patricia Neal," April 25, 2011, Emanuellevy.com.
14. David Thomson, "King Vidor," *The New Biographical Dictionary of Film*, 898.
15. David Kehr, "The Fountainhead," *The Chicago Reader* online, October 26, 1985, https://chicagoreader.com/film/the-fountainhead-2/.
16. "King Vidor at N.Y.U.," *Cineaste* 1, no. 4, 1968, 7.
17. *Ayn Rand: A Sense of Life*, written and directed by Michael Paxton, Strand Releasing Home Video, 2004.
18. *Ayn Rand: A Sense of Life*.
19. Christopher Beach, *A Hidden History of Film Style, Cinematographers, Directors, and the Collaborative Process*, 132–34.
20. Lead actress Patricia Neal mentioned Rand's frequent visits to the set. See J. Hoberman, *An Army of Phantoms: American Movies and the Making of the Cold War*, 96–98.
21. Durgnat and Simmon, *King Vidor, American*, 268.
22. *Ayn Rand: A Sense of Life*.
23. Hoberman, *An Army of Phantoms*, 96–98. See also "The Making of *The Fountainhead*" (DVD featurette), Warner Home Video, 2006.
24. "King Vidor at N.Y.U.," 7.
25. Dialogue excerpt transcribed by the authors.
26. Ayn Rand, "Screen Guide for Americans," 1947, published online by the Ayn Rand Institute, https://newideal.aynrand.org/ayn-rands-1947-screen-guide-for-americans-part-1/.
27. Merrill Schleier, "Masculine Heroes, Modernism, and Political Ideology in *The Fountainhead* and *The Big Clock*," in *Skyscraper Cinema: Architecture and Gender in American Film*, edited by Merrill Schleier, 119.
28. King Vidor episode, *The Men Who Made the Movies*, written and directed by Richard Schickel, television series, 1973, YouTube (https://www.youtube.com/watch?v=hHwTdPxJh8I). Excerpt transcribed by the authors.
29. *Ayn Rand: A Sense of Life*.
30. *Atlas Shrugged*, a sequel of sorts to *The Fountainhead*, was published in 1957. In one 1997 survey by the Library of Congress and *Reader's Digest Magazine* it was rated by readers as the second most influential book in America after the Holy Bible. It tells the story of a female railway tycoon, Dagny Taggart, who refuses to sell out her business and her dreams to a government that is becoming increasingly hostile to profit-making businesspeople. She falls in love with a man named Hank Reardon, who makes a fortune after inventing a new type of metal that is stronger than any other metal on earth and that Dagny uses in constructing new railways. Dagny and Hank stand up against an overly imposing government and against those "second-handers" who are conformists and who are resentful of creative individuals like Dagny and Hank. Hollywood and TV producers had tried unsuccessfully trying for years to make a movie or mini-series version of *Atlas Shrugged*, and Ayn Rand herself was working on a screenplay based on the novel in the early 1980s, but she died when it was only a third completed. A film trilogy based on the novel was made in the 2010s and earned generally abysmal reviews.
31. "Beyond the Forest," *Kirkus*, Sept. 24, 1948, https://www.kirkusreviews.com/book-reviews/stuart-engstrand/beyond-the-forest/.
32. Lenore Coffee, https://wfpp.cdrs.columbia.edu/pioneer/ccp-lenore-coffee/.
33. Philip K. Scheuer, "Beyond Forest Dissects Life of Vicious Woman," *Los Angeles Times*, Nov. 10, 1949, A12.
34. Jeannine Basinger, *A Woman's View: How Hollywood Spoke to Women, 1930–1960*, eBook.
35. Dona Drake, *Glamour Girls of the Silver Screen*, http://www.glamourgirlsofthesilverscreen.com/show/76/Dona+Drake/index.html.
36. Jack Vizzard, Production Code administrator, quoted in Mark A. Viera, *Into the Dark: The Hidden World of Film Noir, 1941–1950*, 282.
37. Hedda Hopper, "Think It Over," *Los Angeles Times*, Nov. 4, 1949, quoted in Mark A. Viera, *Into the Dark: The Hidden World of Film Noir, 1941–1950*, 282.
38. Charlotte Chandler, *The Girl Who Walked Home Alone: Bette Davis: A Personal Biography*, eBook.
39. "Beyond the Forest," *Variety*, Oct. 19, 1949, 8.
40. Richard L. Coe, "On the Aisle: Bette Parades Wickedest Roles," *Washington Post*, Oct. 29, 1949, 7.
41. Jose Yglesias, "*Beyond the Forest* Gets Lost in Psychiatric Woods," *Daily Worker*, Oct. 24, 1949, 11.
42. Bosley Crowther, "Beyond the Forest with Bette Davis and Joseph Cotten Is New Bill at Strand," *New York Times*, Oct. 22, 1949, 11.

43. Richard Schickel, "King Vidor: Romantic Idealist," *Matinee Idylls*, 27.

Chapter Twenty-One

1. Charles Silver, *"Lightning Strikes Twice,"* Program Notes for the 1972 King Vidor Retrospective, The Museum of Modern Art, New York City, Sept. 1–Nov. 13, 1972.
2. Patricia White, *Uninvited: Classical Hollywood Cinema and Lesbian Representability*, 178.
3. "Independents May Tie-In with New Releasing Combo," *Film Bulletin*, June 19, 1950, 29.
4. "Studio Size-Ups," *Film Bulletin*, Nov. 5, 1951, 17.
5. Gina Marchetti, *Romance and the "Yellow Peril": Race, Sex, and Discursive Strategies in Hollywood Fiction*, 161.
6. "Brief Reviews," *Photoplay*, April 1952, 13.
7. Mandel Herbstman, *"Japanese War Bride,"* *Motion Picture Daily*, Jan. 7, 1952, 7.
8. Charles Silver, *"Japanese War Bride,"* Program Notes for the 1972 King Vidor Retrospective, The Museum of Modern Art, New York City, Sept. 1–Nov. 13, 1972.
9. Raymond Durgnat and Scott Simmon, *King Vidor, American*, 295.
10. King Vidor, *King Vidor on Film Making*, 51–52.
11. The story of *Ruby Gentry* is loosely echoed by the 1989 Mexican telenovela *Teresa* starring Salma Hayek. A young ambitious woman struggles to escape poverty and uses her beauty and cunning to rise above her circumstances. She enters into a relationship with a wealthy, troubled man who is obsessed with her, even though he comes to realize that she has deceived him. Her scheming leads to a life of misery and solitude.
12. Charles Silver, *"Ruby Gentry,"* Program Notes for the 1972 Vidor retrospective at the Museum of Modern Art, New York City, Sept. 1–Nov. 13, 1972.
13. "Selznick to Produce Edison Tribute on TV," *Motion Picture Daily*, March 17, 1954, 1 and 4.
14. Florence Small, "TV Picks Up Its Costliest Check," *Broadcasting*, Sept. 20, 1954, 103.
15. "What TV and Radio Have Done to N.W. Ayer," *Sponsor*, Oct. 11, 1958, 39.
16. Christopher Anderson, *Hollywood TV: The Studio System in the Fifties*, 307.
17. Christopher Anderson, 118.
18. Nancy Dowd and David Shepard, *King Vidor: The Director's Guild of America Oral History*, 261.
19. "28 Scripts Pen 26 UI Pix In Record Prod'n Surge," *Variety*, Feb. 24, 1954, 13.
20. "Jeanne Crain Gets 'Star,'" *Variety*, June 16, 1954, 7.
21. Clive Denton, "King Vidor: A Texas Poet," in *The Hollywood Professionals*, Volume 5, 21.

Chapter Twenty-Two

1. Carolyn F. Hummel, "King Vidor's Strong Themes," *The Christian Science Monitor*, Nov. 25, 1959, 11.
2. Andrew Sarris, *The American Cinema*, 1968.
3. Herbert G. Luft, "King Vidor: A Career That Spans Half a Century," *The Film Journal*, Summer 1971, 44.
4. Abel Green, "Film Reviews: *War and Peace*," *Variety*, Aug. 22, 1956, 6.
5. Bosley Crowther, "Screen: *War and Peace*," *The New York Times*, Aug. 22, 1956, 26.
6. Hollis Alpert, "Tolstoy in VistaVision," *Saturday Review*, Sept. 8, 1956, 32–33.
7. V.F. Perkins and Mark Shivas, "Interview with King Vidor," *Movie*, July/Aug. 1963, 9.
8. Nancy Dowd and David Shepard, *King Vidor: A Directors Guild of America Oral History*, 272–73. Vidor told another interviewer: "I worked on *War and Peace* for a year and a half, supervised all the cutting, music and everything. Then Paramount made some cuts without consulting me about it. I never went to see the film after they cut it" (V.F. Perkins and Mark Shivas. "Interview with King Vidor," *Movie*, July/August 1963, 9).
9. Film scholar and Vidor afficionado Tag Gallagher chose *War and Peace* as one of the ten greatest films ever made in the British Film Institute's 2012 survey. https://www2.bfi.org.uk/films-tv-people/sightandsoundpoll2012/voter/68.
10. George Stevens, Jr., ed., *Conversations with the Great Moviemakers of Hollywood's Golden Age*, 50–53.
11. Dowd and Shepard, 265.
12. Joel Greenberg, "War, Wheat, & Steel: King Vidor interviewed by Joel Greenberg," 197.
13. Charles Silver, Program Notes, *War and Peace*, King Vidor Retrospective, Museum of Modern Art, New York City, Sept. 1–Nov. 13, 1972.
14. King Vidor, *King Vidor on Film Making*, 53.
15. Hummel, "King Vidor's Strong Themes," 11.
16. Dowd and Shepard, 273.
17. Dowd and Shepard, 274.
18. Dowd and Shepard, 274–75.
19. Dowd and Shepard, 276–77.
20. Vidor, *King Vidor on Filmmaking*, 55.
21. See the video embedded in the online article "The Tragic Death of Tyrone Power Before His Time," Classic Movie Favorites, www.classicmoviefavorites.com, Aug. 2015.
22. Vidor, *King Vidor on Film Making*, 58.
23. Joel Greenberg, "War, Wheat, & Steel," 197.
24. Kay Mills, "He helped mold early Hollywood," *Philadelphia Inquirer*, Sept. 18, 1981, D1 and D3.
25. Dowd and Shepard, 186.
26. Charles Silver, Program Notes for the 1972 King Vidor Retrospective, Museum of Modern Art, New York City, Sept. 1–Nov. 13, 1972.

Chapter Twenty-Three

1. "King Vidor at N.Y.U," *Cineaste* 1, no. 4, 1968, 8, 33.

2. Nancy Dowd and David Shepard, *King Vidor: Directors Guild of America Oral History*, 296–97.

3. For the working title *Brother Jon* for Vidor's unrealized re-make of *The Crowd*, see Raymond Durgnat and Scott Simmon, *King Vidor, American*, 86. For the working titles *The Milly Story* and *Conquest* for the director's unrealized re-make of *The Turn in the Road*, see Durgnat and Simmon, 315.

4. On Vidor's references to some of these unrealized projects, see Dowd and Shepard, 278–90. For the reference to his hope to make a film adaptation of *A Stillness at Appomattox*, see Murray Schumach, "War Is a Game for King Vidor: Director Who Has Ordered Many Film Troops Eyes 'Stillness at Appomattox,'" *The New York Times*, Sept. 17, 1959, 49.

5. Dowd and Shepard, 281.

6. Down and Shepard, 283–84.

7. For example, see Thomas Wartenberg's book *Thinking on Screen: Film as Philosophy*, the volume *Film as Philosophy*, ed. Bernd Herzogenrath, and *Film as Philosophy: Essays on Cinema after Wittgenstein and Cavell*, eds. Rupert Read and Jerry Goodenough.

8. Durgnat and Simmon, *King Vidor, American*, 236.

9. Though Hesse's cult classic novel *Siddhartha* (first published in German in 1922) was later filmed in the early 1970s by Conrad Rooks. Hesse's famous novel *Steppenwolf* (first published in German in 1927) was adapted to film in 1974 by Fred Haines and it starred Max von Sydow.

10. Mary Baker Eddy, *Science and Health with Key to the Scriptures*. See also "What Is Christian Science?" www.christianscience.com.

11. King Vidor, *King Vidor on Film Making*, 230–31.

12. All quotes here from *Truth and Illusion* are taken from the authors' faithful transcription of the film narration.

13. D. Lawson, *Posterity: Letters of Great Americans to Their Children*, 96–97.

14. "King Vidor—The Metaphor (1980)," *Cinema of the World* website, Sept. 25, 2021.

15. Carol A. Crotta, "Masters of Metaphor, Part One," *Los Angeles Herald Examiner*, Mar. 30, 1980, https://worldscinema.org/2021/09/the-metaphor-1980/.

16. "Andrew Wyeth's World War I," www.farnsworthmuseum.org.

17. The above excerpt from *The Metaphor* is taken from the authors' faithful transcription of the documentary.

18. The above excerpt from *The Metaphor* is taken from the authors' faithful transcription of the documentary.

19. The above excerpt from *The Metaphor* is taken from the authors' faithful transcription of the documentary.

20. All quotes here from *Truth and Illusion* are taken from the authors' faithful transcription of the film narration.

Bibliography

Alicoate, Jack. "The Champ." *Film Daily*, vol. LVII, no. 34, Nov. 10, 1931.

Alpert, Hollis. "Tolstoy in VistaVision." *Saturday Review*, Sept. 8, 1956.

Anderson, Christopher. *Hollywood TV: The Studio System in the Fifties*. Austin: University of Texas Press, 1994.

"Andrew Wyeth's World War I." Farnsworth Museum. www.farnsworthmuseum.org.

"Another Negro Film: King Vidor Realizes Ambition by Making 'Hallelujah,' An Audible Picture." *New York Times*, June 2, 1929.

Balme, Christopher B. "Selling the Bird: Richard Walton Tully's 'The Bird of Paradise' and the Dynamics of Theatrical Commodification." *Theatre Journal*, vol. 57, no. 1, March 2005.

"Bank Claims Lien Also on Cutting Room Footage." *Variety*, July 14, 1948.

Basinger, Jeannine. *A Woman's View: How Hollywood Spoke to Women, 1930–1960*. New York: Alfred A. Knopf, 1993, 2013. eBook.

Baxter, John. *King Vidor*. New York: Monarch Press, 1976.

Bazin, André. "The Evolution of the Western." 1955. In *The Western Reader*, eds. Kitses and Rickman. New York: Limelight Editions, 1998.

Beach, Christopher. *A Hidden History of Film Style, Cinematographers, Directors, and the Collaborative Process*. Oakland: University of California Press, 2015.

Beauchamp, Cari. *Without Lying Down: Frances Marion and the Powerful Women of Early Hollywood*. Berkeley: University of California Press, 1998.

Benson, Sally. "The Screen in Review." *Picture-Play Magazine*, vol. 22, no. 5, July 1925.

Benson, Sally. "The Screen in Review." *Picture-Play Magazine*, vol. 24, no. 4, June 1926.

Besas, Peter. "Today's Pix No Better Than in His Prime, Asserts Pioneer King Vidor." *Variety*, Aug. 11, 1971.

"Beyond the Forest." *Kirkus*. Sept. 24, 1948. https://www.kirkusreviews.com/book-reviews/a/-stuart-engstrand/beyond-the-forest/.

"Beyond the Forest." *Variety*, Oct. 19, 1949.

"Big Film Theory Runs Afoul of Producer." *Courier-Journal*, May 14, 1922.

"Billy the Kid." *Variety*, Oct. 22, 1930.

"Bird of Paradise." *The Film Daily*, Aug. 12, 1932.

Bloch-Morphanage, Lise, and David Alper. "Né avec." *Le Monde*, Oct. 1, 1981.

Bogdanovich, Peter, writer and director. *Directed by John Ford* (documentary). Revised version (2006). Turner Classic Movies. Also included in the *John Ford/John Wayne* DVD collection (Warner Brothers, 2009).

"Bogeaus Revising Episodic Picture." *New York Times*, Aug. 9, 1947.

Bogle, Donald. *Toms, Coons, Mulattoes, Mammies, and Bucks: An Interpretive History of Blacks in American Films*, Fourth Edition. London: Continuum International/Bloomsbury Academic, 2001.

Boland, Elana. "Honest or Hokum—Which Does Public Want?" *Los Angeles Times*, Nov. 2, 1930.

Bond, Ralph. "Street Scene." *CloseUp*, vol. VIII, no. 4, Dec. 1931.

Borges, Jorge Luis Borges. "Street Scene." *Sur*, no. 5, Summer 1932, and republished in *October*, vol. 15, Winter 1980.

Brandes, Naomi. "Shocking, Lurid, and True! The Case of the Dead Director." *Biography Magazine*, July 1998.

Braver-Mann, B.G. "Vidor and Evasion." *Experimental Cinema*, vol. 1, no. 3, 1931.

Bret, David. *Greta Garbo: A Divine Star*. The Robson Press, 2012. eBook.

"Brief Reviews." *Photoplay*, April 1952.

Brooks, Richard, and King Vidor. "Two Story Conferences." *Sight and Sound*, vol. 22, no. 2, Oct. 1952.

Brownlow, Kevin. *Behind the Mask of Innocence*. London: Jonathan Cape, 1990.

Brownlow, Kevin. "ForewOrd." In Jordan R. Young, *King Vidor's THE CROWD: The Making of a Silent Classic*. Film Close-Up Series, vol. 8. Past Times Publishing Co., 2014, 2016.

Burns, Harry. "The Bird of Paradise." *Hollywood Filmograph*, July 30, 1932.

Camera! Vol. 5, no. 30, Nov. 4, 1922. Vol. 5, no. 45, Feb. 17, 1923.

Camera's Weekly Wake-em-up. Special News Section, July 28, 1923.

Cameron, Ian, and Douglas Pye, eds. *The Book of Westerns*. New York: Continuum, 1996.

Carmichael, Deborah, ed. *The Landscape of*

Hollywood Westerns: Ecocriticism in an American Film Genre. Salt Lake City: University of Utah Press, 2006.

Cathrine Curtis Corporation records. American Heritage Center, University of Wyoming. Rocky Mountain Online Archive.

Cavell, Stanley. *Pursuits of Happiness: The Hollywood Comedy of Remarriage.* Cambridge: Harvard University Press, 1981.

Chandler, Charlotte. *The Girl Who Walked Home Alone: Bette Davis: A Personal Biography.* New York: Simon & Schuster, 2007. eBook.

"Changes in Screen Art Predicted: Vidor Says Intelligence of Audience Underrated by Producers." *Los Angeles Times,* Feb. 25, 1925.

Cheatham, Maude. "The Human Photoplay: The Vidor Idea." *Motion Picture Classic,* vol. X, no. 4, June 1920.

Cheatham, Maude. "Veni, Vidi, Vidor!" *Motion Picture Classic,* no. 6, Aug. 1919. (From the New York Public Library's PA Robinson Locke Collection, Ser. 2, 87–89.)

Claire, Doris. "Catherine Curtis: Producer." *Exhibitors Herald,* Nov. 27, 1920.

Coe, Richard L. "On the Aisle: Bette Parades Wickedest Roles." *Washington Post,* Oct. 19, 1949.

Cogley, John. *Report on Blacklisting 1: Movies.* The Fund for the Republic, Inc., 1956.

Cohn, Bernard. "Entretien avec King Vidor." *Positif—Revue mensuelle de cinema,* Sept. 1974.

Collier, Lionel. "Shop for Your Films." *Picturegoer and Film Weekly,* April 26, 1941.

"Coming Attractions." *Motion Picture News,* July 10, 1926.

"Comrade X." *Variety,* Dec. 11, 1940.

Cooke, Alistair. "Some Memorable American Films: *The Big Parade.*" The Museum of Modern Art Film Library, 1941.

Cooper, Jackie, with Dick Kleiner. *Please Don't Shoot My Dog: The Autobiography of Jackie Cooper.* New York: Berkley Books, 1982.

Cork, John. *Murnau, Borzage, and Fox* (documentary). 2008. Included in the *Murnau, Borzage, and Fox* DVD collection (20th Century Fox).

Crotta, Carol A. "Masters of Metaphor, Part One." *Los Angeles Herald Examiner,* March 30, 1980. https://worldscinema.org/2021/09/the-metaphor-1980/.

Crouch, Bill. *Motion Picture News.* vol. xlii, no. 11, Sept. 13, 1930.

Crowther, Bosley. "Beyond the Forest with Bette Davis and Joseph Cotten Is New Bill at Strand." *New York Times,* Oct. 22, 1949.

Crowther, Bosley. "The Screen in Review." *New York Times,* Dec. 19, 1941.

Crowther, Bosley. "The Screen in Review." *New York Times,* Dec. 26, 1940.

Crowther, Bosley. "Screen: *War and Peace.*" *New York Times,* Aug. 22, 1956.

Crowther, Bosley. "Vidor's Individualist Manifesto." *New York Times,* Nov. 13, 1938.

Cruikshank, Herbert K. "Box Office Reviews." *Exhibitors Trade Review,* July 26, 1924.

Cummings, Denise K. "Her American Career." Women Film Pioneers Project. https://wfpp.cdrs.columbia.edu/pioneer/ccp-elinor-glyn/.

Curtiss, Thomas Quinn. "Honored in Paris: King Vidor Recalls Making 'Hallelujah!'" *The New York Herald Tribune* (Paris), July 10, 1962.

"Cynara." *Film Daily,* Nov. 12, 1932.

"Cynara." *Variety,* Jan. 3, 1933.

Dahl, Arlene. "Director King Vidor Likes Women to Be Individuals." *Chicago Daily Tribune,* Nov. 12, 1956. Note: this interview with Arlene Dahl was also re-published: see Dahl, Arlene. "You Can't Be Too Feminine," *Picturegoer,* Feb. 2, 1957.

Dalle Vacche, Angela. "Movies, Social Conformity, and Imminent Traumas." In *American Cinema of the 1920s: Themes and Variations,* ed. Lucy Fischer. New Brunswick: Rutgers University Press, 2009.

Dana, Robert W. "King Vidor, Director of 'The Citadel.'" *New York Herald Tribune,* Nov. 13, 1938.

Daugherty, Frank. "Steel Comes to the Films." *The Christian Science Monitor,* May 8, 1943.

Delchanty, Thornton. "'Orson Welles Woke Us Up,' King Vidor." *New York Herald Tribune,* Nov. 16, 1941.

Denton, Clive. "King Vidor: A Texas Poet." In *The Hollywood Professionals, Volume 5: King Vidor, John Cromwell, Mervyn LeRoy.* London: The Tantivy Press and A.S. Barnes & Co., 1976.

Dinoff, Lester. "Big Pictures Are Salvation, Vidor Says." *Motion Picture Daily,* vol. 80, no. 24, Aug. 3, 1956.

"Doings Among the Writing Craft." *Hollywood Filmograph,* April 26, 1930.

Dowd, Nancy, and David Shepard. *King Vidor: A Directors Guild of America Oral History.* Metuchen, NJ: Rowman & Littlefield, 1988. (Date of interviews with Vidor: late 1970s.)

Dowd, Nancy. Program Notes for the 1971 King Vidor retrospective. Los Angeles County Museum of Art, May 7–June 12, 1971.

Dowd, Nancy. Program Notes for the 1972 King Vidor retrospective. Museum of Modern Art, New York City, Sept. 1–Nov. 13, 1972.

The Dramatic Mirror, Jan. 5, 1918.

Durgnat, Raymond. "King Vidor: A Retrospective, Part 2." *Film Comment,* Sept.–Oct. 1973. https://www.filmcomment.com, Issue Archive.

Durgnat, Raymond. "King Vidor: A Retrospective, Part I." *Film Comment,* July–Aug. 1973. https://www.filmcomment.com, Issue Archive.

Durgnat, Raymond, and Scott Simmon. *King Vidor, American.* Berkeley: University of California Press, 1988.

Eddy, Mary Baker. *Science and Health with Key to the Scriptures.* Christian Science Publishing Co., 1875.

Eisenstein, Sergei. "A Dialectic Approach to Film Form." Originally published 1929, reprinted in *Film Form,* ed. and trans. Jay Leyda. New York: Harvest/HBJ, 1949/1977.

Eliot, Marc. *Jimmy Stewart: A Biography.* New York: Three Rivers Press, 2006.

Bibliography

Elliott, Frank. *Motion Picture News*, Jan. 12, 1924.

"Eugene Lyons Names Plenty of Film Notables as 'Pro-Red' in His New Book." *Variety*, Sept. 3, 1941.

Exhibitors Herald. Issues cited: Sept. 8, 1917. March 16, 1918. April 5, 1919. Sept. 13, 1919. August 21, 1920. May 7, 1921. March 11, 1922. Jan. 27, 1923. March 10, 1923.

Exhibitors Herald and Motography. March 22, 1919, and June 21, 1919.

Exhibitors Herald-World. Feb. 15, 1930.

Exhibitors Trade Review. Issues cited: Jan. 14, 1922. Feb. 25, 1922. March 11, 1922. March 18, 1922. March 25, 1922. June 10, 1922. Sept. 9, 1922. April 28, 1923. July 21, 1923. March 8, 1924.

"An expectant public: 1948–2008—60 years of the NHS." *Birth of the NHS in Scotland*. Government of Scotland, 2008.

Eyman, Scott. *The Speed of Sound: Hollywood and the Talkie Revolution: 1926–1930*. New York: Simon & Schuster, 2015.

Fenin, George, and William K. Everson. *The Western: From Silents to the Seventies*. New York: Penguin, 1973.

The Film Daily. Issues cited: July 2, 1922. Sept. 3, 1922. Dec. 17, 1922. Dec. 28, 1922. Jan. 24, 1923. July 20, 1923. Oct. 15, 1923. Feb. 10, 1924. March 2, 1924. Oct. 17, 1926. Dec. 3, 1926. May 17, 1927. June 28, 1927. Dec. 22, 1927.

Fischer, Lucy, ed. *American Cinema of the 1920s: Themes and Variations*. New Brunswick: Rutgers University Press, 2009.

Flatley, Guy. "King Vidor and the Search for Maturity in Today's Films." *The New York Times*, Jan. 14, 1977.

Fletcher, Adele Whitely. "Across the Silversheet." *Motion Picture Magazine*, July 1921.

Frederick, A.H. "Picture Reviews, Previews, Shorts." *Inside Faces of Stage and Screen*, Feb. 8, 1930.

Frederickson, Kari. "Cathrine Curtis and Conservative Isolationist Women, 1939–1941." *The Historian*, vol. 58, no. 4, 1996, 827. JSTOR.

Friedrich, Otto. "Hollywood Gothic: (1922–1986)." Review of Sidney Kirkpatrick's book *A Cast of Killers*. *Time*, May 19, 1986.

Gallagher, Tag. "How to Share a Hill." *Senses of Cinema*. http://archive.sensesofcinema.com/contents/07/43/king-vidor-andrew-wyeth.html.

Gallagher, Tag. "Ten greatest films ever made." British Film Institute's 2012 survey. https://www2.bfi.org.uk/films-tv-people/sightandsoundpoll2012/voter/68.

Garnett, Tay. *Directing: Learn from the Masters*. Ed. Anthony Slide. Filmmakers series No. 48. Lanham, MD: Scarecrow Press, Inc., 1996, 268–277. (Date of Vidor's responses to Tay Garnett's interview questionnaire: mid–1970s.)

Gebhard, Myrtle. "Star? Director? Author?" *Silver Screen*, Feb. 1934.

Glancy, H. Mark. "MGM Film Grosses, 1924–28: The Eddie Mannix Ledger." *Historical Journal of Film, Radio, and Television*, vol. 12, no. 2, 1992.

Glover, Susan Paterson. "East Goes West: The Technicolor Environment of *Northwest Passage* (1940)." In *The Landscape of Hollywood Westerns*, ed. Deborah Carmichael, 111–126.

Graf, Victor. "King Vidor: From Silents to 16mm." *The Animator*, published quarterly by the Northwest Film Study Center, vol. III, No. 3, Summer 1975.

Green, Abel. "Film Reviews: *War and Peace*." *Variety*, Aug. 22, 1956.

Greenberg, Joel. "War, Wheat, and Steel." *Sight and Sound*, vol. 37, Aug. 1968.

"H.M. Pulham, Esq." *Variety*, Nov. 19, 1941.

Hall, Mordaunt. "Father and Son." *New York Times*, Nov. 10, 1931.

Hall, Mordaunt. "Ronald Colman, Kay Francis and Henry Stephenson in the Pictorial Translation of 'Cynara.'" *New York Times*, Dec. 26, 1932.

Hall, Mordaunt. "The Screen." *New York Times*, Feb. 8, 1930.

Hall, Mordaunt. "Vidor-Sabatini Film." *The New York Times*, Nov. 7, 1926.

Hall, Mordaunt. "When Murder Is Done." *New York Times*, Aug. 27, 1931.

Hall, Mordaunt. "The Screen." *New York Times*, April 23, 1928.

Harrington, Curtis. "The Later Years: King Vidor's Hollywood Progress." *Sight and Sound*, vol. 22, no. 4, April/June 1953.

"He Stole My Play, Says Woman Author." *New York Times*, Feb. 17, 1912.

Herbstman, Mandel. "*Japanese War Bride*." *Motion Picture Daily*, Jan. 7, 1952.

Hershfield, Joanne. "Race and Romance in Bird of Paradise." *Cinema Journal*, vol. 37, no. 3, Spring 1998.

Herzogenrath, Bernd, ed. *Film as Philosophy*. Minneapolis: University of Minnesota Press, 2017.

Higham, Charles, and Joel Greenberg. "King Vidor." In *The Celluloid Muse: Hollywood Directors Speak*. Chicago: Henry Regnery, 1969, 223–43.

Hoberman, J. *An Army of Phantoms: American Movies and the Making of the Cold War*. New York: The New Press, 2012.

"Hollywood in Person." *The Atlanta Constitution*, Mar. 1, 1935.

Hollywood Renegades Archive. http://www.cobbles.com/simpp_archive/huac_alliance.htm.

"Honors for Arnold." *American Cinematographer*, Dec. 1926.

Hopper, Hedda. "King Vidor Speaks Out! Detests Movie Violence." *Chicago Daily Tribune*, Feb. 7, 1961.

Hopper, Hedda. "Think It Over." *Los Angeles Times*, Nov. 4, 1949. Quoted in Mark A. Viera, *Into the Dark: The Hidden World of Film Noir, 1941–1950*, 2016.

Howe, Herbert. "The Healing Drama." *Picture-Play Magazine*, May 1920.

Hummel, Carolyn F. "King Vidor's Strong Themes." *The Christian Science Monitor*, Nov. 25, 1959.

Hyams, Joe. "Road Back to 'Truth' for Vidor." *New York Herald Tribune*, July 9, 1961.

"I Don't Want To." *Photoplay*, Aug. 1920.

"The Patsy." *Variety*, 1928.

"In the Realm of Shadow Stories." *New York Times*, March 27, 1932.

"The Independence of Mr. Vidor." *New York Times*, July 29, 1934.

"Independents May Tie-In with New Releasing Combo." *Film Bulletin*, June 19, 1950.

James, Frederick. "The Celluloid Critic." *Motion Picture Classic*, Sept. 1920.

"Jeanne Crain Gets 'Star.'" *Variety*, June 16, 1954.

Jeansonne, Glen. *Women of the Far Right: The Mothers' Movement and World War II*. Chicago: University of Chicago Press, 1997.

Joo, Woejeong. *The Cinema of Ozu Yasujiro*. Edinburgh: Edinburgh University Press, 2017.

"'Judge Picture in General': King Vidor Believes Opinion Should Not Be on Star, Story and Director." *General Motion Picture News*, Aug. 30, 1919.

Keavy, Hubbard. "Outdoor Film Is Real Measure of Cinema's Appeal." *The Washington Post*, July 12, 1936.

Kehr, David. "The Fountainhead." *The Chicago Reader*, Oct. 26, 1985. https://chicagoreader.com/film/the-fountainhead-2.

Kelly, Mary. *Moving Picture World*, April 14, 1923.

"King Vidor Airs His Opinions on Race Psychology." *The Chicago Defender (National edition) (1921-1967)*, Dec. 14, 1929.

"King Vidor at NYU." *Cinéaste*, vol. 1, no. 4, Spring 1968.

"King Vidor Believes in Clean Production: Claims Them Just as Effective When Free from Sex Appeal." *The Atlanta Constitution*, Oct. 10, 1920.

"King Vidor Discusses Motion Pictures: His New Film Is Built Like a Play." *New York Times*, May 22, 1927.

"King Vidor Flays Censorship Advocated by Humane Society." *The Washington Herald*, Jan. 16, 1921.

"King Vidor: From Silents to 16mm." *The Animator*, published Quarterly by the Northwest Film Study Center, vol. III, no. 3, Summer, 1975.

"King Vidor in England: His Favorite Picture Tricks in the Silent Days." *The Observer*, June 19, 1938.

"King Vidor on European Films." *CloseUp*, Oct. 1928.

"King Vidor on His Screen Work." *The Christian Science Monitor*, March 15, 1921.

"King Vidor Says Screen Themes Will Not Be Dependent on Plays and Books." *Motion Picture World*, Nov. 6, 1920.

"King Vidor Says Story Need Not Be Kinetic: May Still Be Full of Screen Possibilities, This Director Contends." *New York Tribune*, Nov. 11, 1923.

"King Vidor Speaks of Sound." *New York Times*, July 8, 1928.

"King Vidor Tells of Work in Filming 'Big Parade.'" *New York Times*, Feb. 21, 1926.

"King Vidor's Fondest Dream Is Realized by Clever Work of Performers in *Hallelujah*." *The Chicago Defender (National edition)*, June 8, 1929.

"King Vidor's New Film: The Director of 'Billy the Kid' Describes the Pioneer Days of the Wild West." *New York Times*, July 6, 1930.

Kitses, Jim, and Gregg Rickman, eds. *The Western Reader*. New York: Limelight Editions, 1998.

Lawson, Dorie McCullough. *Posterity: Letters of Great Americans to Their Children*. New York: Broadway Books/Doubleday, 2004.

Leguebe, Eric. "King Vidor." In *Le Cinema Americain Par Ses Auteurs*. Paris, 1977.

Lehman-Haupt, Christopher. Review of Sidney D. Kirkpatrick's book *A Cast of Killers*. *New York Times*, June 30, 1986.

Levy, Emanuel. "*The Fountainhead* (1949): King Vidor's Powerfully Erotic Melodrama, Starring Gary Cooper and Patricia Neal." April 25, 2011, www.emanuellevy.com.

Levy, N. Notes for screening of *The Big Parade*. Roosevelt University Film Society, Oct. 5, 1966.

Leyda, Jay, ed. and trans. *Film Form*. New York: Harvest/HBJ, 1949/1977.

Longworth, Karina. "The Mistress, the Magnate, and the Genius." *Slate*. http://www.slate.com/articles/podcasts/you_must_remember_this/2015/09/marion_davies_actress_and_mistress_of_william_randolph_hearst_was_portrayed.html.

Lowrance, Dee. "An American Romance—King Vidor Films Saga of Steel." *New York Herald Tribune*, Oct. 29, 1944.

Luft, Herbert G. "King Vidor: A Career That Spans Half a Century." *The Film Journal*, Summer 1971, 27–44.

Lusk, Norbert. "Critics Unite in Praise for New Sten Film." *Los Angeles Times*, March 24, 1935.

Lusk, Norbert. "The Screen in Review." *Picture-Play Magazine*, vol. 37, no. 3, Nov. 1932.

Lusk, Norbert. "The Screen in Review." *Picture-Play Magazine*, vol. 25, no. 5, Jan. 1927.

Lyons, Donald, and Glenn O'Brien. "King Vidor." *Andy Warhol's Inter/View*, Oct. 1972.

Lyons, Eugene. *The Red Decade: The Stalinist Penetration of America*. Indianapolis: Bobbs-Merrill, 1941.

"The Making of *The Fountainhead*" (DVD featurette). Warner Home Video, 2006.

Maltby, Richard. *Hollywood Cinema*, Second Edition. Oxford: Blackwell, 2003.

Maltin, Leonard. *Leonard Maltin's 2012 Movie Guide*. New York: Signet, 2011.

Maltin, Leonard. "Two Unsung Gems on TCM This Week." *Film Journal*, Oct. 13, 2014. www.leonardmaltin.com.

Manners, Dorothy. "Looking Them Over." *Movie Classic*, vol. 3, no. 6, Feb. 1933.

Mantle, Burns. "The Shadow Stage." *Photoplay*, July 1921.

Mantle, Burns. "The Shadow Stage." *Photoplay*, Nov. 1920.

Mapp, Edwin. *Blacks in American Films: Today and Yesterday*. Metuchen, NJ: Scarecrow Press, 1971.

Marchetti, Gina. *Romance and the "Yellow Peril": Race, Sex, and Discursive Strategies in Hollywood Fiction*. Berkeley: University of California Press, 1993.

Mason, Lee Thomas. "A private list of Akira Kurosawa's 100 favorite films of all time." *Far Out* magazine online, June 15, 2023. faroutmagazine.co.uk.

May, Richard P. "Restoring *The Big Parade*." *The Moving Image*, vol. 5, no. 2, Fall 2005.

Mayer, Louis B. "Louis B. Mayer, on Trip East, Announces Great Production Program for M.-G.-M." *Moving Picture World*, vol. 76, no. 6, Oct. 10, 1925.

McGee, Patrick. *From Shane to Kill Bill: Re-Thinking the Western*. Malden, MA: Wiley-Blackwell, 2006.

"Metro Sets Comrade as Next Gable Film." *Variety*, Aug. 28, 1940.

Mills, Kay. "He Helped Mold Early Hollywood." *The Philadelphia Inquirer* (Los Angeles Times Service), Sept. 18, 1981.

"Miracle Title NG for B.O., Bogeaus Change Ups Biz." *Variety*, June 30, 1948.

"Miss Davies Extols Vidor." *New York Times*, Jan. 29, 1928, 109.

Moen, L.C. "Picking the Ten Best Films of 1927." *Motion Picture News*, Jan. 28, 1927.

Mosher, John. "The Current Cinema." *The New Yorker*, August 5, 1933.

Motion Picture Herald, vol. 104, no. 8, Aug. 22, 1931.

Motion Picture Magazine, July 1924.

Motion Picture News. Issues cited: Sept. 8, 1917. Oct. 20, 1917. Jan. 19, 1918. March 9, 1918. Nov. 30, 1918. Dec. 28, 1918. June 21, 1919. Aug. 23, 1919. Oct. 4, 1919. Oct. 18, 1919. Feb. 26, 1921. Dec. 16, 1922. March 17, 1923. Sept. 15, 1923. Sept. 29, 1923. Oct. 9, 1926. Jan. 28, 1927. March 25, 1927. July 15, 1927.

Motion Picture News Booking Guide, April 1923 and Oct. 1923.

Motion Picture News: The West Coast, Jan. 25, 1919.

Motography. Issues cited: Dec. 19, 1914. Nov. 3, 1917.

Moving Picture Weekly, Oct. 6 and Oct. 20, 1917.

Moving Picture World. Issues cited: July 8, 1916. Jan. 5, 1918. March 16, 1918. March 23, 1918. Dec. 18, 1920. Jan. 1, 1921. Feb. 26, 1921. July 8, 1922. April 14, 1923. July 14, 1923. Feb. 28, 1925. Oct. 9, 1926.

"Must Vitalize Screen Art, Vidor Tells N.Y. Critics." *The Moving Picture World*, March 28, 1925.

Nasaw, David. *The Chief: The Life of William Randolph Hearst*. Boston: Houghton Mifflin, 2000.

Nash, Alanna. "King Vidor on D.W. Griffith's Influence." *Films in Review*, vol. XXVI, no. 9, Nov. 1975.

"New Wide-Screen Idea." *New York Times*, Oct. 19, 1930.

"Not So Dumb." *Variety*, vol. 98, no. 5, Feb. 12, 1930.

Nugent, Frank S. "The Screen." *The New York Times*, Sept. 24, 1936.

O'Mahony, S. "AJ Cronin and *The Citadel*: did a work of fiction contribute to the foundation of the NHS?." National Library of Medicine online, National Institutes of Health, June 2012, https://pubmed.ncbi.nlm.nih.gov.

O'Malley, Agnes. "With the Producers." *The Story World and Photodramatist*, Sept. 1923.

Ones, Kristin. "'King Vidor' Review: The Film Director's Wide Realm." *Wall Street Journal*, Opinion/Commentary/Cultural Commentary section, July 30, 2022. Online.

Our Film Correspondent. "King Vidor in England." *The Observer*, June 19, 1938.

Pardy, George T. "Box Office Reviews." *Exhibitors Trade Review*, Feb. 16, 1924.

Pardy, George T. "Box Office Reviews." *Exhibitors Trade Review*, Jan. 31, 1925.

Pardy, George T. "Box Office Reviews." *Exhibitors Trade Review*, Oct. 11, 1924.

Paxton, Michael, writer and director. *Ayn Rand: A Sense of Life*. Strand Releasing Home Video, 2004.

Perkins, V.F., and Mark Shivas. "Interview with King Vidor." *Movie*, no. 11, July/Aug. 1963.

Photoplay, Sept. 1919.

"The Picture Oracle." *Picture-Play Magazine*, Aug. 1918.

"The Picture Parade." *Motion Picture Magazine*, vol. 32, no. 6, Jan. 1927.

Picture-Play Magazine, March 1921.

Platt, David. "Lords of the Silver Screen." *Daily Worker*, Jan. 1, 1941.

"'Polly Preferred' Called Plagarism." *New York Times*, June 13, 1925.

Pond, Steve. "Before the Guild." *Directors Guild of America Quarterly*, Winter 2011. www.dga.org.

Potamkin, H.A. "Reelife." *Close Up*, vol. 7, no. 6, Dec. 1930.

Pratt, Armando José. *Invisible Natives: Myth & Identity in the American Western*. Ithaca: Cornell University Press, 2002.

Quirk, James R. "Speaking of Pictures." *Photoplay*, vol. 29, no. 5, April 1926.

Quirk, Lawrence J. "King Vidor Looks Back on a Great Career." *Quirk's Reviews*, vol. 1, no. 6, Sept. 25, 1972.

Rand, Ayn. *Atlas Shrugged*. New York: Plume/Penguin, 1957, 1992.

Rand, Ayn. *The Fountainhead*. New York: Signet, 1996.

Rand, Ayn. "Screen Guide for Americans." Published by the Ayn Rand Institute, 1947. https://newideal.aynrand.org/ayn-rands-1947-screen-guide-for-americans-part-1/.

Read, Rupert, and Jerry Goodenough, eds. *Film as Philosophy: Essays on Cinema After Wittgenstein and Cavell*. London: Palgrave Macmillan, 2005.

Reid, Laurence. *Motion Picture News*, Nov. 1, 1919.

Reid, Laurence. *Motion Picture News*, Dec. 3, 1921.

Reid, Margaret. "Intelligent Audiences Starved to Feed Morons." *Los Angeles Times*, Nov. 22, 1931.

Reid, Margaret. "Looking on with an Extra Girl." *Picture-Play Magazine*, vol. 23, no. 6, Feb. 1926.

"Reviews of New Films." *The Film Daily*. Aug. 22, 1936. Dec. 11, 1940. Nov. 13, 1941.

Robinson, Patrick. *Guinness Book of Movie Facts and Feats* (4th ed.). Abbeville Publishing Group, 1991.

Rosenbaum, Jonathan. Review of Vidor's *The Stranger's Return*. Dec. 20, 2008. https://www.jonathanrosenbaum.net/2008/12/the-strangers-return-1933/.

St. Johns, Adela Rogers. "A Young Crusader." *Photoplay*, vol. XVII, no. 1, Dec. 1919. From the New York Public Library PA Robinson Locke Collection, Ser. 2.

Sarris, Andrew. *The American Cinema: Directors and Directions 1929–1968*. Boston: DaCapo Press, 1996.

Sarris, Andrew. "The Remembered Vitality of King Vidor." *Voice*, Dec. 7, 1982.

Scenario Bulletin Digest, vol. 9, no. 7, Sept. 1923.

"Scenes in 'Hallelujah' Stirred Players, Says Vidor." MGM Press Notes from the New York Public Library.

Schallert, Edwin. "Billy the Kid White-Washed: Western Epic Gives Outlaw Clean Bill of Health." *Los Angeles Times*, Aug. 24, 1930.

Schallert, Edwin. "King Vidor Likes Ruling Own Roost." *Los Angeles Times*, Aug. 5, 1951.

Schallert, Edwin, and Elza. "Hollywood High Lights." *Picture-Play Magazine*, vol. 23, no. 3, Nov. 1925.

Scheuer, Philip K. "'Beyond Forest' Dissects Life of Vicious Woman." *Los Angeles Times*, Nov. 10, 1949.

Scheuer, Philip K. "King Vidor in Fresh Venture: Director of 'Big Parade' Experiments Again." *Los Angeles Times*, Oct. 13, 1929.

Scheuer, Philip K. "Shooting, Dubbing of Spectacle Told." *Los Angeles Times*, July 17, 1959.

Scheuer, Philip K. "Town Called Hollywood." *Los Angeles Times*, Sept. 29, 1940.

Schickel, Richard, "King Vidor: Romantic Idealist." 1993. In Richard Schickel, *Matinee Idylls: Reflections on the Movies*. Chicago: Ivan R. Dee, 1999, 21–30.

Schickel, Richard. "King Vidor." In Richard Schickel, *The Men Who Made the Movies*. New York: Atheneum, 1975, 131–60.

Schickel, Richard. *Matinee Idylls: Reflections on the Movies*. Chicago: Ivan R. Dee, 1999.

Schickel, Richard. *The Men Who Made the Movies*. New York: Atheneum, 1975.

Schickel, Richard, writer and director, King Vidor episode. *The Men Who Made the Movies*. Television series, 1973. YouTube. https://www.youtube.com/watch?v=hHwTdPxJh8I.

Schleier, Merrill. "Masculine Heroes, Modernism, and Political Ideology in *The Fountainhead* and *The Big Clock*." In *Skyscraper Cinema: Architecture and Gender in American Film*, ed. Merrill Schleier. Minneapolis: University of Minnesota Press, 2009.

"'School Sessions' Held by Director King Vidor." *MGM Press Material: Eight Pages of Publicity, Ads and Exploitation*. No. 26, 1928.

Schumach, Murray. "War Is a Game for King Vidor: Director Who Has Ordered Many Film Troops Eyes 'Stillness at Appomattox.'" *The New York Times*, Sept. 17, 1959.

"Screen News Here and in Hollywood." *New York Times*, Aug. 22, 1940.

Screen Opinions. Vol. 12, no. 9, Aug. 15–31, 1923. Vol. 14, no. 2, April 1924.

"Selznick to Produce Edison Tribute on TV." *Motion Picture Daily*, March 17, 1954.

Sennwald, Andrew. "'The Wedding Night,' King Vidor's New Production, at the Rivoli—'High School Girl.'" *New York Times*, March 16, 1935.

Sewell, Charles S. *Moving Picture World*, Sept. 20, 1924.

Sewell, Charles S. "Newest Reviews and Comments." *Moving Picture World*, March 15, 1924.

Sewell, Charles S. "Reviews and Comments." *Moving Picture World*, July 26, 1924.

"The Shadow Stage." *Photoplay*, vol. XL, no. 5, Oct. 1931.

Shaffer, Rosalind. "When the Movies Go Native." *The Washington Post*, May 1, 1932.

Sherwood, Robert E. "Realistic Setting Contrived for Filming of *Street Scene*." *The Sun*, Aug. 30, 1931.

Shivas, Mark, and V.F. Perkins. "Interview with King Vidor." *Movie*, vol. 11, July/Aug. 1963.

Shreck, Jay M. "New Product." *Exhibitors Herald-World*, vol. 1010, no. 4, Oct. 25, 1930.

Silver, Charles. "King Vidor's Hallelujah." *Inside/Out* (A MoMA/MoMA PS1 Blog), June 15, 2010. https://www.moma.org/explore/inside_out/2010/06/15/king-vidors-hallelujah/.

Silver, Charles. Program notes, "American Film Comedy: May 13, 1976–January 4, 1977: *Show People*." June 18, 1976.

Silver, Charles. Program Notes for the 1972 King Vidor retrospective. Museum of Modern Art, New York, Sept. 1–Nov. 13, 1972.

Simmon, Scott. "National Film Preservation Foundation: *Bud's Recruit* (1918) Film Notes." https://www.filmpreservation.org/dvds-and-books/clips/bud-s-recruit-1918-clip.

Sinyard, Neil. *George Stevens: The Films of a Hollywood Giant*. Jefferson, NC: McFarland, 2019.

Small, Florence. "TV Picks Up Its Costliest Check." *Broadcasting*, Sept. 20, 1954.

Smith, Agnes. "Just Among Ourselves." *Motion Picture Magazine*, vol. 31, no. 4, May 1926.

Smith, Agnes. "The Screen in Review." *Picture-Play Magazine*, vol. 22, no. 2, April 1925.

Smith, Frederick James. "The Celluloid Critic." *Motion Picture Classic*, Sept. 1920.

Smith, Frederick James. "Making The Big Parade." *Motion Picture Classic*, vol. XXIII, no. 3, May 1926.

Smith, Summer. "Newest Reviews and Comments." *Moving Picture World*, Dec. 17, 1921.

"Speaking Editorially." *Motion Picture News*, July 31, 1926.

Stanfield, Peter. "Country Music and the 1939 Western." In *The Book of Westerns*, eds. Ian Cameron and Douglas Pye. New York: Continuum, 1996.

Stanfield, Peter. *Horse Opera: The Strange History of the 1930s Singing Cowboy*. Champaign: University of Illinois Press, 2002.

Stevens, George, Jr., ed. *Conversations with the Great Moviemakers of Hollywood's Golden Age at the American Film Institute*. New York: Vintage, 2006, "King Vidor" chapter, 33–57. (Date of Vidor interview: Nov. 2, 1977.)

"Stranger's Return." *Harrison's Reports*, Aug. 5, 1933.

"The Strange Case of Comrade X." *New York Times*, Nov. 10, 1940.

Strauss, H. David. "Billy, the Kid." *The Billboard*, vol. 42, no. 43, Oct. 25, 1930.

"'Street Scene' Breaks Ancient Screen Mold." *Los Angeles Times*, July 26, 1931.

"Studio Size-Ups." *Film Bulletin*, Nov. 5, 1951.

Taylor, Charles. "Conscience of the King." Review of Sidney D. Kirkpatrick's book *A Cast of Killers*. *Boston Phoenix*, June 27, 1986, Sect. 3, 4.

Terkel, Studs. "King Vidor." In Studs Terkel, *The Spectator: Talk About Movies and Plays with Those Who Made Them*. New York: The New Press, 2001. (Date of Vidor interview: 1975.)

Terkel, Studs. *The Spectator: Talk About Movies and Plays with Those Who Made Them*. New York: The New Press, 2001. (Date of Vidor interview: 1975.)

"Texas Rangers (with Songs)." *Variety*, Sept. 30, 1936.

"The Theatre: *Dulcy* Adapted." *Wall Street Journal*, Feb. 10, 1930.

"Theatre Notes, Aug. 13, 1928." *Time*, Aug. 13, 1928.

Thomson, David. "King Vidor." In David Thomson, *The New Biographical Dictionary of Film*. New York: Alfred A. Knopf, 2002, 897–98.

Thomson, David. "The Man Who Would Be King." *The Directors Guild of America Quarterly*, Winter 2011. www.dga.org.

Thomson, David. *The New Biographical Dictionary of Film*. New York: Alfred A. Knopf, 2002.

Tince, Mae. "Cynara, in Film, Is Warning to Blithe Ladies." *Chicago Daily Tribune*, 1932.

"Title Changes." *Boxoffice*, April 17, 1948.

Townsend, Leo. "Reviews." *Modern Screen*, Nov. 1936.

"Traditional Negro Songs Myths, King Vidor Says." *Los Angeles Times*, Dec. 2, 1928.

"The Tragic Death of Tyrone Power Before His Time." *Classic Movie Favorites*, August 2015. www.classicmoviefavorites.com.

Trumbo, Dalton. "Trumbo Reviews." *Hollywood Spectator*, vol. 12, no. 8, Sept. 26, 1931.

"28 Scripts Pen 26 UI Pix in Record Prod'n Surge." *Variety*, Feb. 24, 1954.

Valentine, Sydney. "Stars Temperament? Smoke Screen! Says Vidor." *Screenland*, vol. 31, no. 2, June 1935.

Van Gelder, Lawrence. "Did Vidor Discover the Killer?" ("At the Movies" column). *New York Times*, March 21, 1986.

Variety. Issues cited: Aug. 27, 1919. April 18, 1921. Nov. 12, 1924. July 8, 1925. Dec. 31, 1925. March 3, 1926. July 6, 1927.

Vernon, Scott. "Movie 'Spectaculars' Urged by King Vidor." *The Austin Statesman*, Nov. 13, 1959.

Vidor, King. "An Art or a Business?" *Journal of the Screen Producers Guild*, March 1964.

Vidor, King. "Director's Notebook." *Cinema Progress*, vol. 4, no. 1 and no. 2, July 1939.

Vidor, King. "From a Vidor Notebook." *New York Times*, March 10, 1935.

Vidor, King. "How to Make a Sophisticated Movie: As told by King Vidor" ("Collector's Item" column). *Action*, vol. 5, no. 6, Nov.–Dec. 1970. (Originally written by Vidor in 1924 for *The Director*, official publication of The Motion Picture Directors Association.)

Vidor, King. *King Vidor on Filmmaking*. New York: David McKay Company, 1972.

Vidor, King. *Metaphor: King Vidor Meets with Andrew Wyeth*. 1980. https://worldscinema.org/2021/09/the-metaphor-1980/ and https://www.youtube.com/watch?v=NQCgr4Y2Pd0.

Vidor, King. "Movies Are Not All Harmony." *Music Journal*, vol. 18, no. 5, July/Aug. 1960.

Vidor, King. "A Pledge and a Creed." *Variety*, Jan. 1920.

Vidor, King. "Rubber Stamp Movies." *Film Comment*, vol. 12, no. 4, July/Aug. 1976.

Vidor, King. "Screen Treatment for *The Actor*." *City* (S.F.), Sept. 9, 1975.

Vidor, King. "The Strain in Spain Was Mainly on the Brain." *Photo Bargains*, July/Aug.1961.

Vidor, King. *A Tree Is a Tree*. New York: Harcourt, Brace, and Company, 1953.

Vidor, King. *Truth and Illusion: An Introduction to Metaphysics*. 1964. https://www.youtube.com/watch?v=rpEr7DoSUC8.

"Vidor on Stars" ("Events on the March" page). *Independent Exhibitors Film Bulletin*, April 3, 1935.

"Vidor Tells of Desire to Film 'Bohème.'" *The New York Herald*, The New York Tribune, January 31, 1926.

Viera, Mark A. *Into the Dark: The Hidden World of Film Noir, 1941–1950*. Philadelphia: Running Press, 2016.

Wallis, Stanley. "What the Fans Think." *Picture-Play Magazine*, vol. 22, no. 6, Aug. 1925.

Wartenberg, Thomas, *Thinking on Screen: Film as Philosophy*. London: Routledge, 2007.

Watt. "Showmen's Reviews." *Motion Picture Herald*, Aug. 28, 1936.

Watts, Richard, Jr. "Sight and Sound." *New York Herald Tribune*, March 24, 1935.

"We Pay Our Respects to Miss Marion Davies." *The Film Spectator*, vol. 5, no. 8, June 9, 1928.

Webb, Jean Francis, and Kay Hardy. "H.M. Pulham, Esq." *Modern Screen*, Feb. 1942.

Weinberg, Herman G. "Note from America: Part Two." *Close Up*, vol. 9, no. 1, March 1932.

Weisenfeld, Judith. *Hollywood Be Thy Name: African American Religion in American Film, 1929–1949*. Berkeley: University of California Press, 2007.

Weller, S.M. "Without Benefit of Scripts: Scenarists are Excess Baggage, says King Vidor to S.M. Weller." *Motion Picture Classic*, Sept. 1927.

"What Is Christian Science?" www.christianscience.com.

"What TV and Radio Have Done to N.W. Ayer." *Sponsor*, Oct. 11, 1958.

White, Patricia. *Uninvited: Classical Hollywood Cinema and Lesbian Representability*. Bloomington: Indiana University Press, 1999.

Whitely, Fletcher, and Adele. "Across the Silversheet." *Motion Picture Magazine*, July 1921.

Wid's Daily. Issues cited: March 9, 1919. May 13, 1919. June 15, 1919. Oct. 26, 1919. Aug. 8, 1920. April 24, 1921.

Wiener, Hal. "Chit, Chat and Chatter." *Hollywood Filmograph*, Oct. 29, 1932.

Williams, Louise. "A Hoosier from Texas." *Picture-Play Magazine*, April 1920.

"World War Pictured Through Veterans' Eyes." *New York Times*, Nov. 8, 1925.

Yglesias, Jose. "*Beyond the Forest* Gets Lost in Psychiatric Woods." *Daily Worker*, Oct. 24, 1949.

"You Ought to Be in Pictures? Maybe! Replies King Vidor." *Picturegoer*, Aug. 24, 1935.

Young, Jordan R. *King Vidor's THE CROWD: The Making of a Silent Classic*. Film Close-Up Series, vol. 8. Past Times Publishing Co., 2014, 2016.

Index

The Accusing Toe (1918) 17, 295
Adorée, Renée 61, 64, 68, 297
The Adventures of Tom Sawyer 165, 213
An American Romance (1944) 2, 5, 62, 63, 87, 91, 105, 108, 137, 194, 202, 208–212, 214, 225, 240, 241, 246, 259, 267, 285, 287, 300
Anderson, Maxwell 62, 152, 299
Aristotle 237, 279, 291
Atlas Shrugged 231

Bardelys the Magnificent (1926) 71, 76–80, 81
Barrymore, Lionel 138, 140, 143, 153, 216, 217, 298, 300
Baum, L. Frank 13, 182
Beery, Wallace 116, 123–127, 298
Behn, Harry 72, 83, 297, 298
Bellamy, Ralph 157, 299
Berkeley, Busby 129
Berkeley, Bishop George 279, 284, 285, 293
Bernhard, Joseph 250, 251, 253, 254, 257, 300, 301
Better Times (1919) 17, 18, 20–21, 24, 31, 295
Beyond the Forest (1949) 48, 73, 87, 107, 109, 140, 166, 207, 227, 233, 242–247, 248, 250, 253, 259, 262, 275, 285, 300
The Big Parade (1925) 2, 11, 16, 22, 30, 45, 48, 57, 59, 61–70, 71, 72, 73, 74, 75, 78, 80, 81, 82, 83, 84, 85, 87, 89, 91, 93, 94, 95, 98, 106, 121, 122, 129, 148, 151, 152, 154, 155, 173, 182, 183, 184, 194, 205, 206, 210, 220, 240, 265, 268, 269, 271, 275, 286, 287, 289, 297
bigotry *see* race/racism)
Billy the Kid (1930) 5, 82, 83, 113–118, 119, 121, 125, 152, 161, 163, 164, 190, 191, 214, 298
Bird of Paradise (1932) 39, 48, 109, 123, 128–132, 134, 135, 158, 159, 163, 165, 207, 213, 242, 251, 253, 259, 276, 298
Blake, William 279, 293
Blanke, Henry 233, 300
Boardman, Eleanor 43, 44, 45, 53, 57, 59, 60, 76, 79, 80, 84, 86, 91, 132, 134, 140, 235, 296, 297

Bogeaus, Benedict 227, 229, 230, 300
Boggs, John 11, 12, 295
La Bohème (1926) 61, 69, 70, 71–76, 77, 78, 80, 82, 83, 93, 94, 297
Boles, John 166, 299
Bonaparte, Napoleon *see* Napoleon
Bondi, Beulah 121, 138, 141, 143, 298
Borzage, Frank 34, 86, 88, 89, 91, 123, 159, 160
Brennan, Walter 195, 197, 200, 203, 211, 235, 299
Brentwood Film Corporation 18, 20, 25, 295
Brown, Johnny Mack 115, 298
Brown, Judge Willis 12, 13, 14, 16, 17, 18, 19, 21, 24, 295
Brown, R. Gore 133, 134, 298
Brynner, Yul 273, 274, 276, 301
Bud's Recruit (1918) 15–18, 21, 22, 295

Capra, Frank 158
Cardiff, Jack 265, 268, 269, 301
The Champ (1931) 2, 48, 73, 83, 91, 109, 122–127, 133, 139, 165, 173, 174, 182, 183, 202, 261, 298
Chaplin, Charlie 2, 29, 50, 64, 85, 101, 147, 188, 297
Chase, Borden 301
The Chocolate of the Gang (1918) 295
Christian Science 1, 3, 19–22, 25, 26, 28, 32, 33, 35, 39, 48, 241, 277, 279, 280
The Citadel (1938) 2, 4, 48, 73, 91, 102, 109, 132, 155, 173–182, 183, 213, 299
Civil War 3, 47, 118, 142, 144, 153, 156, 183, 191, 193, 277
Clough, Ray 8, 295
Coffee, Lenore J. 243, 245, 246, 247, 249
Colman, Ronald 133, 298
Communism 2, 185, 186, 187, 189, 236, 237, 240, 241
Comrade X (1940) 4, 55, 185–190, 299
Confucius 292
Connolly, Walter 153, 299

Conquering the Woman (1922) 37, 39, 296
Cooper, Gary 87, 157, 206, 211, 230, 232, 234, 236, 299, 300
Cooper, Jackie 123, 125, 126, 183, 298
Cotten, Joseph 216, 217, 243, 245, 300
Crain, Jeanne 108, 260, 262, 301
Cronin, A.J. 173, 175, 176, 182, 299
The Crowd (1928) 2, 3, 5, 19, 23, 27, 28, 30, 48, 61, 73, 76, 81–93, 94, 101, 115, 120, 122, 141, 147, 148, 149, 173, 182, 189, 205, 209, 230, 231, 238, 240, 241, 250, 265, 277, 285, 297
Curtis, Cathrine 30, 31, 34, 296
Cynara (1932) 132–135, 140, 158, 159, 206, 207, 208, 242, 244, 250, 298

Dalrymple, Ian 174, 179, 299
Davies, Marion 60, 79, 93, 96, 97, 99, 100, 110, 112, 113, 123, 139, 144, 172, 185, 297, 298
Davis, Bette 87, 165, 207, 233, 242, 243, 245, 246, 247, 262, 300
De Laurentiis, Dino 264, 269, 301
Del Rio, Dolores 39, 48, 128, 129, 130, 131, 132, 276, 298
DeMille, Cecil B. 37, 54, 55, 153, 191, 211, 235, 238, 264
Donat, Robert 173, 174, 175, 176, 179, 181, 182, 183, 203, 299
Donlevy, Brian 202, 209, 210, 300
Douglas, Kirk 260, 261, 262, 301
Drake, Dona 244, 245, 300
Dressler, Marie 94, 96, 297
Duel in the Sun (1946) 2, 4, 5, 59, 73, 87, 109, 137, 138, 145, 164, 165, 166, 173, 174, 189, 191, 194, 202, 207, 210, 211, 213–226, 231, 235, 242, 243, 250, 251, 253, 254, 258, 259, 260, 265, 267, 269, 275, 285, 287, 300
Dusk to Dawn (1922) 37, 38, 39, 296

Eddy, Mary Baker 3, 277, 279, 280, 284, 291, 293
Einstein, Albert 292
Engstrand, Stuart 243, 245, 300

Index

ethics and morality 1, 4, 7, 12, 18, 19, 25, 33, 35, 37, 46, 48, 54, 55, 56, 73, 109, 114, 117, 133, 134, 135, 141, 146, 148, 154, 155, 156, 173, 176, 178, 179, 180, 181, 182, 207, 211, 213, 215, 216, 218, 222, 224, 226, 236, 242, 243, 244, 246, 250, 258, 279, 280, 282, 284, 285

The Family Honor (1920) 25–27, 29, 37, 295
Fascism 2, 240
Ferrer, Mel 270, 301
Fitzgerald, F. Scott 80
Fitzgerald, Zelda 80
Fleming, Victor 2, 174, 182, 183, 204, 211, 235
Fonda, Henry 87, 197, 209, 222, 228, 266, 267, 268, 269, 271, 300, 301
Ford, John 5, 11, 34, 62, 81, 88, 91, 114, 123, 132, 137, 152, 153, 154, 160, 169, 172, 173, 174, 191, 194, 211, 215, 228, 235, 278, 280
Fountaine, William 106, 298
The Fountainhead (1949) 2, 4, 5, 63, 73, 87, 149, 152, 166, 189, 207, 212, 230–242, 243, 253, 259, 262, 265, 275, 279, 281, 300

Gable, Clark 174, 186, 187, 188, 211, 235, 299
Galveston, Texas 1, 5–8, 11, 12, 60, 183, 285, 295
The Galveston Hurricane (aka *The Hurricane in Galveston*, 1913) 1, 8, 11, 183, 295
Garland, Judy 183
Gassman, Vittorio 272, 301
Gilbert, John 55, 56, 57, 61, 62, 63, 65, 68, 71–80, 91, 100, 184, 203, 206, 271, 297
Gish, Lillian 35, 71–76, 78, 95, 123, 217, 218, 221, 223, 224 297, 300
Goddard, Paulette 227, 228, 300
Goldwyn, Samuel 119, 121, 123, 133, 134, 165, 167, 170, 172, 298, 299
Goldwyn Company 298, 299
Goldwyn Pictures Corporation 44, 49, 134, 29, 297
The Grand Military Parade (1914) 295
Grandeur (widescreen process) 113, 160
The Great Depression 136, 137, 147, 150, 160, 192, 209, 241
Griffith, David Wark (D.W.) 2, 11, 27, 29, 35, 45, 61, 72, 75, 77, 83, 85, 86, 104, 217, 223, 224, 265

Haines, William 53, 98, 99, 100, 296, 297
Hallelujah (1929) 2, 6, 12, 22, 80, 83, 102–109, 110, 111, 115, 119, 121, 125, 136, 152, 153, 174, 184, 202, 206, 229, 242, 251, 253, 258, 265, 297
Happiness (1924) 42, 52, 296
Harrison, Rex 175, 176, 180, 299
Hawks, Howard 42, 160, 215, 228, 253
Haynes, Daniel L. 103, 104, 105, 107, 108, 298
Hearst, William Randolph 93, 96–98, 100, 110–112, 297
Hecht, Ben 114, 185, 187, 260, 299
Hepburn, Audrey 266, 268, 270, 301
Hergesheimer, Joseph 46, 47, 51, 296
Hesse, Hermann 226, 280
Heston, Charlton 8, 254, 255, 257, 259, 272, 301
Hickman, Darryl 248, 249, 300
Hill, Elizabeth 134, 140, 147, 158, 161, 162, 173, 174, 179, 205, 207, 298, 299, 300
His Hour (1924) 55–57, 58, 59, 61, 100, 185, 242, 297
H.M. Pullman, Esq. (1941) 2, 48, 132, 140, 204–208, 229, 242, 244, 300
Holden, William 110, 298
Hopkins, Miriam 138, 139, 140, 143, 172, 235, 298
Hussey, Ruth 197, 205, 299, 300
Huston, Walter 217, 220, 258, 300

I'm a Man (1918) 17, 295
In Tow (1914) 12, 295
It Happened One Night 158, 187

The Jack-Knife Man (1920) 16, 20, 22, 26–29, 32, 33, 34, 35, 37, 41, 45, 46, 48, 50, 60, 73, 94, 123, 157, 258, 261, 295
Japanese War Bride (1952) 4, 6, 16, 22, 48, 108, 207, 250–253, 300
Jennings, Talbot 152, 190, 192, 195, 299
Jones, Jennifer 207, 213, 217, 218, 219, 221, 225, 253, 254, 257, 258, 259, 300, 301

Kant, Immanuel 278, 283, 284
King, Henry 123, 160, 165, 191, 264
Knopf, Edwin 80, 157, 159

Lamarr, Hedy 186, 187, 188, 205, 207, 213, 299, 300
Lamour, Dorothy 228, 300
Lao Tze (a.k.a. Lao Tzu) 279, 293
Lightning Strikes Twice (1951) 48, 73, 107, 109, 207, 242, 248–250, 253, 275, 300
Lloyd, Frank 13, 76, 295
Lollobrigida, Gina 274, 275, 301
Lom, Herbert 269, 270, 301
The Lost Lie (1918) 17, 295
Love Never Dies (1921) 20, 22, 32–36, 37, 41, 45, 48, 73, 157, 207, 296
Lubitsch, Ernst 159, 160, 185, 233

MacMurray, Fred 161, 162, 163, 228, 299, 300
Malden, Karl 254, 257, 301
Mankiewicz, Joseph L. 264, 269, 298
Man Without a Star (1955) 5, 118, 164, 191, 202, 259–263, 301
Manners, J. Hartley 40, 296
Marion, Frances 122, 123, 124, 126, 133, 159, 298
Marquand, John P. 194, 205, 207, 300
Marrying Off Dad (1918) 17, 295
Marshall, Herbert 217, 218, 300
Maté, Rudolph 171, 299
Mayer, Louis B. 71, 296
McCambridge, Mercedes 248, 249, 300
McCrea, Joel 128, 130, 132, 298
McDaniel, Hattie 153
McKinney, Nina Mae 103, 105, 107, 108, 258, 298
Meredith, Burgess 227, 228, 300
The Metaphor (1980) 1, 3, 70, 194, 240, 285–289, 301
Metro-Goldwyn-Mayer (studio) 56, 61, 62, 65, 68, 74, 78, 79, 81, 84, 88, 96, 99, 100, 105, 107, 112, 116, 124, 126, 139, 143, 176, 179, 181, 188, 189, 192, 195, 200, 207, 296, 297, 298, 299, 300
Milestone, Lewis 130, 137, 160, 227
A Miracle Can Happen see *On Our Merry Way*
Mitchell, Cameron 251, 300
Moore, Colleen 31, 34, 99, 140, 296
morality see ethics
Murnau, Friedrich Wilhelm (F. W.) 86–89, 130
Murray, James 3, 19, 82, 84, 86, 88, 90, 91, 92, 148, 277, 297

Napoleon Bonaparte 67, 94, 268, 269, 270
Neal, Patricia 87, 230, 232, 236, 300
The New Deal 31, 241
Northwest Passage (1940) 2, 4, 5, 16, 82, 87, 132, 137, 152, 155, 164, 173, 190–203, 204, 205, 210, 214, 220, 269, 275, 287, 299
Not So Dumb (1930) 110–113, 298

Index

Oakie, Jack 161, 162, 299
O'Brien, Tom 63, 65, 184
On Our Merry Way (aka *A Miracle Can Happen*, 1948) 82, 227–230, 300
The Other Half (1919) 17, 20, 21, 22, 24, 25, 26, 31, 37, 73, 295
Our Daily Bread (1934) 2, 5, 62, 73, 87, 89, 91, 92, 96, 108, 132, 136, 138, 147–152, 155, 174, 183, 190, 206, 209, 210, 212, 240, 241, 251, 285, 298

Pangborn, Franklin 110, 112, 298
Paramount Pictures (studio) 13, 152, 153, 156, 162, 238, 266, 267, 269, 270, 299
Paso Robles, California 137, 140, 278, 285
The Patsy (1928) 16, 22, 60, 83, 93–97, 98, 106, 112, 113, 139, 297
Pavan, Marisa 274, 301
Peck, Gregory 204, 213, 217, 219, 221, 225, 300
Peg o' My Heart (1922) 37, 40, 41, 42, 47, 49, 52, 94, 296
Pitts, Zasu 22, 295
Plato 279, 283, 290, 292, 293
politics: fascism 2, 240; politics and *Our Daily Bread* 148–151; politics and *The Fountainhead* 235–242; socialism 240; Vidor's political views 189, 211–212, 235–236, 240–242; *see also* Communism.
Poor Relations (1919) 17, 22–23, 24, 25, 37, 295
Power, Tyrone 273
The Preacher's Son (1918) 17, 295
Proud Flesh (1925) 16, 22, 59–61, 83, 91, 297
Prouty, Olive Higgins Prouty 165, 167, 299

Qualen, John 121, 148, 149, 298, 300

racism : and *Hallelujah* 103–109; in *Northwest Passage* 198–200; in *So Red the Rose* 152–153
Rand, Ayn 4, 63, 149, 189, 211, 212, 230, 23, 232, 237, 279, 300
The Real Adventure (1922) 37, 38, 39, 296
Realife (Widescreen process) 113, 116, 118
The Rebellion (1918) 17, 295
religion: in *An American Romance* 210; in *Northwest Passage* 201; and *The Turn in the Road* 19–22; Vidor's interest in the religious story in *Solomon and Sheba* 272–273; Vidor's spiritual views expressed in *Truth and Illusion* 279–285, 289–293; *see also* Christian Science
Rice, Elmer 119, 298
Richards, Ann 210, 300
Richardson, Ralph 175, 176, 181, 299
RKO Radio Pictures (aka RKO) 129, 130, 213, 214, 298
Roberts, Kenneth 190, 192, 195, 299
Rogers, Will 137, 152
Roman, Ruth 207, 244, 248, 249, 300
Roosevelt, Franklin D. (aka FDR) 136, 193, 205, 212, 241
Rosson, Harold 210, 300
Ruby Gentry (1952) 2, 5, 22, 48, 59, 73, 107, 109, 140, 166, 207, 219, 225, 242, 243, 247, 250, 253–259, 265, 275, 285, 300
Russell, Rosalind 175, 176, 177, 299

Sabatini, Rafael 76, 77, 297
Samuel Goldwyn Company *see* Goldwyn Company and Goldwyn Pictures)
Sanders, George 274, 275, 301
Schopenhauer, Arthur 279, 293
Scott, Randolph 154, 156, 299
Scott, Zachary 248, 300

The Searchers 154–155, 201, 215, 233
Selznick, David O. 2, 129, 130, 165, 183, 189, 211, 213–214, 216, 217, 219, 221, 222, 224–226, 229, 235, 253, 259, 280, 298, 300, 301
Shakespeare, William 139, 187, 292
Shirley, Anne 168, 170, 183, 299
Show People (1928) 2, 30, 60, 61, 82, 83, 87, 91, 92, 97–113, 139, 152, 187, 297
The Sky Pilot (1921) 20, 30, 30–33, 34, 36, 39, 48, 114, 140, 157, 229, 296
So Red the Rose (1935) 16, 22, 63, 69, 73, 82, 90, 104, 108, 110, 118, 147, 152–157, 183, 184, 299
socialism 240
Solomon and Sheba (1959) 2, 3, 8, 12, 87, 166, 194, 202, 214, 220, 229, 264, 267, 272–276, 277, 285, 286, 287, 301
spirituality *see* Christian Science; religion
Stallings, Laurence 62, 63, 82, 98, 114, 152, 190, 192, 195, 228, 297, 298, 299, 300
Stanwyck, Barbara 165, 166, 167, 169, 170, 171, 172, 211, 233, 235, 262, 299
Sten, Anna 157, 159, 299
Steiner, Max 230, 233, 298, 300
Stella Dallas (1937) 2, 22, 73, 87, 109, 123, 140, 165–172, 183, 207, 213, 215, 231, 233, 251, 253, 259, 262, 275, 299
Stewart, James 174, 228, 300
Stong, Philip 136, 138, 139, 143, 298
The Stranger's Return (1933) 2, 4, 5, 16, 22, 73, 91, 136–146, 147, 153, 173, 182, 183, 231, 251, 259, 298
Street Scene (1931) 2, 4, 12, 41, 73, 91, 119–122, 123, 129, 138, 139, 140, 151, 182, 190, 202, 206, 207, 242, 251, 298
Sullavan, Margaret 154, 156, 299
Sydney, Sylvia 298

Tad's Swimming Hole (1918) 7, 17, 295
Taylor, Don 250, 252, 300
Taylor, Laurette 40, 41, 42, 52, 296
Technicolor 4, 191, 195, 196, 202, 203, 210, 214, 217, 287, 299
The Texas Rangers (1936) 5, 132, 160–164, 191, 214, 260, 299
Thalberg, Irving 52, 55, 61, 62, 78, 80, 81, 83, 85, 86, 111, 112, 114, 123, 297, 298
Thief or Angel (1918) 17, 295
Three Wise Fools (1923) 43–45, 47, 91, 98, 296
Todd, Richard 248, 249, 300
Toland, Gregg 157–158, 298, 299
Tolstoy, Leo 209, 265, 266, 267, 268, 270, 281, 285, 301
Tone, Franchot 141, 143, 298
Tracy, Spencer 16, 174, 186, 191, 192, 195, 200, 202, 204, 299
Trevor, Claire 260, 262, 301
Truth and Illusion: An Introduction to Metaphysics (1964) 1, 4, 209, 229, 240, 241, 242, 277–285, 286, 289–293, 301
Tuchock, Wanda 98, 110, 114, 123, 129, 297, 298
Tully, Richard Walton 128, 129, 130, 298
Tully, Tom 255, 301
The Turn in the Road (1919) 1, 3, 17, 18–20, 24, 26, 27, 29, 34, 82, 91, 205, 206, 268, 277, 279, 295
Twain, Mark 165, 213

United Artists (studio) 121, 147, 149, 150, 167, 170, 274

Van Dyke, W. S. 130, 196, 299
Vidor, Florence 12, 15, 29, 38, 40, 73, 140, 295, 296
Vidor Village (studio) 25, 32, 39, 40, 43

Index

War and Peace (1956) 2, 3, 4, 16, 55, 66, 67, 87, 152, 155, 166, 184, 185, 194, 202, 209, 210, 214, 220, 259, 264–272, 274, 275, 281, 287, 301

Warner Brothers (aka Warner Bros.) (studio) 138, 189, 230, 231, 232, 233, 234, 236, 243, 245, 246, 249, 300

Wayne, John 113, 154, 160, 174, 191, 211, 213, 235

Wead, Frank ("Spig") 174, 179, 299

Weaver, John V.A. 83, 297

The Wedding Night (1935) 5, 80, 91, 136–137, 140, 147, 157–160, 183, 206, 207, 208, 242, 244, 299

Wellman, William 42, 86, 160, 228

Whitehead, Alfred North 290

Widescreen *see* Realife and Grandeur

The Wife of the Centaur (1924) 57, 59, 83, 91, 98, 297

Wild Oranges (1924) 8, 45, 46–51, 52, 60, 213, 242, 253, 296

Williams, Emlyn 175, 176, 179, 299

Windsor, Marie 251, 252, 300

Wine of Youth (1924) 16, 22, 53–54, 58, 59, 94, 98, 258, 296

The Wizard of Oz (1939) 2, 4, 12, 73, 95, 106, 182–184, 195, 196, 210, 299

The Woman of Bronze (1923) 42–43, 296

Wood, Natalie 154, 243

World War I 15, 21, 61, 62, 66, 82, 98, 152, 205, 206, 288

World War II 109, 191, 209, 215, 216, 251, 252, 285

Wright, Frank Lloyd 231, 234, 235

Wyeth, Andrew 1, 70, 194, 285–289, 301

Yamaguchi, Shirley 207, 250–252, 300

Young, Robert 197, 200, 204, 205, 207, 208, 299, 300

Young, Stark 152, 156, 299